The State of Economics in Canada

FESTSCHRIFT IN HONOUR OF DAVID SLATER

Patrick Grady and
Andrew Sharpe, Editors

**Centre for the Study of
Living Standards**

JOHN DEUTSCH INSTITUTE
FOR THE STUDY OF
ECONOMIC POLICY
QUEEN'S UNIVERSITY

Published for the School of Policy Studies, Queen's University
by McGill-Queen's University Press
Montreal & Kingston • London • Ithaca

ISBN: 0-88911-940-6 (bound)   ISBN: 0-88911-942-2 (pbk.)
© 2001   John Deutsch Institute for the Study of Economic Policy
Queen's University, Kingston, Ontario K7L 3N6
Telephone: (613) 533-2294   FAX: (613) 533-6025
and Centre for the Study of Living Standards, 111 Sparks Street,
Suite 500, Ottawa, Ontario K1P 5B5
Telephone: (613) 233-8891   FAX: (613) 233-8250
Printed and bound in Canada

Canadian Cataloguing in Publication Data

Main entry under title:

    The state of economics in Canada : festschrift in honour of David
Slater

Includes bibliographical references.
ISBN   0-88911-940-6 (bound)   ISBN   0-88911-942-2 (pbk.)

    1. Canada--Economic conditions--1991- 2. International
economic relations. I. Slater, David W., 1921- II. Sharpe, Andrew
III. Grady, Patrick, 1947- IV. John Deutsch Institute for the Study of
Economic Policy.

HC115.S733 2001   338.971   C2001-903216-1

Acknowledgements

We would like to thank everyone who was so eager to join with us to honour David Slater. First and foremost, we would like to thank the institutions that provided the financial support that made this volume possible. These include: the Bank of Canada; the Department of Finance; Environment Canada; Industry Canada; Health Canada; Human Resources Development Canada; and Statistics Canada. We would also like to thank the individuals who championed the Festschrift in their institutions: David Dodge; Kevin Lynch; Alan Nymark; Someshwar Rao; Denis Gauthier; Jim Lahey; and Stewart Wells.

We are also grateful to the staff of the John Deutsch Institute for the Study of Economic Policy at Queen's University for their participation in this project. In particular, we would like to thank: former JDI Director Tom Courchene for initially agreeing to undertake the project; current JDI Director Charles Beach for his continued support of the project; Sharon Sullivan who did an excellent job providing editorial support and managing the production process for the volume within a very tight time frame; Marilyn Banting who helped with the copy editing; and Mark Howes who was responsible for cover design and print coordination.

Next, we would like to thank the many old friends of David Slater who came to his 80th birthday dinner to join in the Festschrift's celebration. In particular, we would like to thank Bill Hood, Ed Neufeld, Steve Handfield-Jones, Simon Reisman, and Alan Green for sharing some of their reminiscences of David's career.

Finally, it goes without saying that this volume could not have become a reality without the excellent papers provided by the contributors, all of whom had some connection with David Slater over the years and who embraced wholeheartedly the objective of the volume.

**David W. Slater
on the Bluenose II in Halifax Harbour**

Contents

v

Pensions

International Economics

Globalization

Regional Issues

Environmental Economics

Labour Economics

Contributors

Introduction

Overview of the Festschrift

Patrick Grady and Andrew Sharpe

What is a Festschrift?

Festschrift literally means "celebration-writing" in German. And that is what this volume is. It celebrates the remarkable career of David Slater, which in the best Queen's University tradition of John Deutsch and Clifford Clark spanned academia and public service, on the occasion of his 80th birthday. It follows an old academic tradition that at an appropriate stage in the career of an eminent scholar a volume be put together in their honour containing the writings of colleagues. Usually, the writings must have something to do with the scholar's life work. In David Slater's case, this was an easy task as his research and interests have been omnivorous. Finding contributors was also easy as over David's long career he had many colleagues, friends and students who jumped at the chance to honour him and to participate in this endeavour.

The title of this volume, *The State of Canadian Economics*, indicates that the contributions are all from prominent Canadian economists and deal with Canadian economic issues. While we encouraged the invited contributors to pick more general topics, we did not exclude papers with a specific focus. The key criteria for inclusion in the volume were that the papers had to be readable and had to deal with important Canadian economic policy issues. The one exception to this latter rule is the article by **Patrick Grady** on David Slater's career. A Festschrift would hardly be a Festschrift without an appearance by the main character — Shakespeare's play would not be Hamlet without the Prince of Denmark.

The topics covered by the papers in this volume include: fiscal federalism, taxation, pensions, international economics, globalization, regional issues, environmental economics, and labour economics. These are all fields that are dear to David Slater's heart and that he contributed to in one way or another.

Fiscal Federalism

Fiscal federalism is a quintessentially Canadian topic that all Canadian economists eventually must grapple with. When David Slater was Chair, the Economic Council launched and completed its landmark study entitled *Financing Confederation*. This study, which was published in 1981, the year before the constitution was patriated, provided the economic justification for the far-reaching set of principles governing the relative roles and responsibilities of the federal and provincial governments in delivering social policies set out in the new constitution.

Against the backdrop of *Financing Confederation*, **Robin Boadway** examines the development of fiscal arrangements and considers the substantial fiscal decentralization that has occurred over the past 20 years. Boadway makes the case that the fiscal arrangements have played an important role in improving the performance of the Canadian economy with respect to both equity and efficiency. But he also observes that over this period our federation has become the most decentralized federation in the world. Looking forward, he sees major challenges facing the fiscal arrangements. The equalization system and the political will to maintain it are in peril at the same time as disparities are likely to increase. The federal government has effectively lost control of the spending power, which has historically been one of the most powerful instruments at the hands of the federal government for managing the federation. This has left the federal government with no effective mechanism for managing the economic union. The income tax system is becoming disharmonized as provinces are engaged in competitive reductions in income tax progressivity. Attempts to arrive at cooperative solutions by federal-provincial negotiation have not been successful.

Boadway believes that the decentralized Canadian federation could evolve into one in which the provinces behave "cooperatively" with respect to the national objectives of equity and efficiency. However, he sees little evidence that this is happening. He argues that an overall vision is needed such as one that could be provided by an updated version of *Financing Confederation*. Unfortunately, Canada does not have an institution like the former Economic Council, the Commonwealth Grants Commission in Australia, or the Financial and Fiscal Commission in South Africa capable of doing the job. This is an institutional gap that David Slater has also lamented since the Economic Council was abolished.

Taxation

Taxation is an area in which David Slater has always taken an interest. When he was Chair, the Economic Council of Canada initiated its study of taxation entitled *Road Map for Tax Reform*. It is thus fitting that this volume contain three papers on taxation.

In a survey of tax reform in recent years, **Richard Bird and Michael Smart** explore the relationship between tax policy and tax research. They conclude that there have been important examples of apparent influences of research on policy. For instance, they are encouraged that the downward pressure on personal and corporate taxes has certainly been supported, if not initiated, by the increasing evidence of distortions caused by high marginal tax rates. In their view, the adoption of the GST can be explained by the acceptance of the federal government of the economic argument that Canada had to switch to a value-added tax to reduce economic distortions. On the other hand, they are disappointed that the equally convincing economic studies of the damage done by poorly-designed excise, property and payroll taxes do not seem to have had any effect. Consequently, they believe that political economy factors were probably the more dominant explanation of the tax reforms than the simple acceptance of advice from economists. Their conclusion is that if economists want to have a greater influence on policy, they need to pay more attention to the issues that motivate policymakers, including, most notably, distributional issues, and they need to write in a way, and in a forum, that will most likely come to the notice of the policy-makers.

The Economic Council's *Road Map for Tax Reform* laid the groundwork for a greater discussion of the consumption tax principle as a basis for taxation in Canada. In his paper, **Jack M. Mintz** continues this discussion by setting out the case for and against a consumption tax. He argues that the tax treatment of savings is likely to become a more central policy focus for the medium term. More practically, he cites three possible evolutionary changes that could lead to a greater reliance on consumption taxes: a sharp increase in sales tax revenues (sales and excise) to reduce reliance on income taxes; a major expansion of RRSP and pension limits to allow for greater accumulation of wealth to meet future contingencies of various sorts; the introduction of an exempt-yield tax savings plan (with restrictions on contributed amounts) that would encourage saving by individuals expecting increases in future tax rates.

More fundamentally, Mintz observes that the income tax could even be replaced with an expenditure tax system with continuing reliance on the other indirect forms of consumption taxation (sales taxes). Even though Mintz believes that the adoption of a consumption tax would certainly set Canada apart from other countries, including the United States, he holds that the technical issues, including implementation and transition issues, are not insurmountable if promoting future consumption is the key to Canada's overall development.

In the third paper on taxation, **Jack M. Mintz and Thomas A. Wilson** consider the best way to allocate the "fiscal dividend". This is the amount available to the government that can be used for tax cuts or expenditure increases within the framework of a balanced budget. In their view, although the current growth recession will reduce the potential surplus somewhat, the medium-term outlook is still for increasing surpluses. Concerned about lagging economic growth and emphasizing the importance of efficiency and productivity growth, they argue that priority should be given to debt reduction and tax cuts designed to stimulate investment and potential growth.

Mintz and Wilson make the case that a large part of the remaining fiscal dividend should be allocated towards reducing the relatively large personal income tax burden faced by many Canadian families and individuals. But they also stress that it is important to steadily reduce payroll and business taxes as well. This case is supported by extensive international comparisons of taxes in Canada with other countries that show that the burden of taxation is higher in Canada than in many other industrialized countries. It is also bolstered by the results of simulations, using the FOCUS macroeconometric model, of a fiscal package containing significant debt reduction, modest spending increases and cuts in personal, business and payroll taxes. These simulations show such a fiscal package should have favourable supply-side effects on output, employment and productivity over the medium term. In addition, since their analysis reveals that there are still important issues of tax structure that need to be addressed, they recommend that the government establish a task force to review personal income taxes and to consider the need for additional tax cuts.

Finally, Mintz and Wilson also remind us that while planned debt reduction is an important component of a growth-oriented fiscal policy, in the short run the size of the surplus should be allowed to vary with the level of economic activity. Otherwise fiscal policy will exacerbate the slowdown that is currently underway. This was a message that David Slater also preached when he was Chair of the Economic Council and that is particularly relevant in the current economic juncture.

Pensions

In recent years, David Slater's research interests have turned to pension issues both private and public. In the first of four papers in this section, **James E. Pesando** looks at the 1998 package of reforms to the Canada Pension Plan (CPP) that the federal government and the provinces implemented after extensive consultation. Most significantly, these reforms included: a sharp increase in the combined employer-employee contribution rate, from 5.85 per cent in 1997 to the steady-state rate of 9.9 per cent in the year 2003 and beyond, which will result in a much larger reserve fund — estimated to rise to about five years' worth of benefits; and the establishment of an independent, trusteed CPP Investment Board with a mandate to invest in marketable securities, including equities, in order to obtain a higher rate of return on the enlarged CPP reserve fund. The benefit reductions in the 1998 package were relatively modest.

Pesando argues that the case for the 1998 CPP reform was made entirely in terms of intergenerational equity. Surprisingly, efficiency arguments played virtually no role in the debate. Pesando questions whether the actuarial assumptions with respect to inflation and rates of return that underlie the reforms are overly optimistic and whether additional increases in premiums or reductions in benefits will be required. In his view, the next round of debate on the reform of public pension programs is already underway in other countries like the United States. He expects that the issue will soon resurface in Canada and that policy options like benefit reductions, raising the retirement age, and partial privatization of benefits, which were dismissed in the last round, will once again be on the table.

David Slater's strong interest in the pension issue is directly related to his concern over the economic well-being of the elderly. **Lars Osberg**, a student of David's at Queen's University in the 1960s, makes the case in his paper that the major success story of Canadian social policy in the twentieth century has in fact been the reduction of poverty among senior citizens.

According to Osberg, the poverty rate, defined with the poverty line measured as one-half median equivalent income after taxes and transfers, for households headed by a person 65 or over fell from 28.4 per cent in 1973 to 5.4 per cent in 1997, while the poverty gap or income shortfall below the poverty line fell from 26.2 per cent to 15.8 per cent over the same period. In contrast, the elderly poverty rate and gap before tax and transfer income are much higher and show no downward trend. Osberg attributes the difference between the before and after transfers and taxes poverty rate and gap to the introduction of the Old Age Security in 1952 and Guaranteed Income Supplement in 1968 and the reduction in poverty after 1973 to the maturing of the Canada/Quebec Pension Plan regimes established in 1966.

Osberg notes that income trends capture only part of the improvement in well-being enjoyed by seniors over the past several decades. Many of the current elderly population received significant capital gains from a large run up in housing prices in the 1970s and 1980s. In addition, the elderly have not been hit by the labour market insecurity that has affected the non-elderly, particularly youth, in the 1980s and 1990s. They have also greatly benefited from the introduction of universal medicare.

Osberg also finds that relative to the United States, Sweden and the United Kingdom, Canada has done the best job in boosting the income levels of seniors above the poverty line. In his view, Canada has done a remarkable job in ensuring that senior citizens receive an income sufficient to prevent poverty.

William B.P. Robson, a co-author with David Slater of a series of papers on pension issues, has written an ambitious survey of the state of Canadian economic policy in the areas of pensions and health care. He argues that it is appropriate to tackle both issues in the same paper because they are both major spending programs strongly related to the life cycle of Canadians, and face challenges arising from the aging of the population.

Robson notes that the pension debate uses the metaphor of three pillars to describe a comprehensive pension system: a safety net to guard against destitution in old age; a mandatory employment-related system to provide basic replacement income; and a voluntary system supported by provisions that reduce the double-taxation of saving. The main elements of public policy related to pensions in Canada cover these pillars. He recognizes that all three of the pillars cannot be directly applied to health care, but he argues that the three-pillar metaphor is still a fruitful perspective because it facilitates constructive responses to the pressures confronting Canada's health system and illuminates interactions between the pension and health systems. Hence his title "six pillars of social policy".

Based on his examination of Canada's pension and health-care systems, Robson makes a number of recommendations. First, he advocates more pre-funding in both the pension and health areas to cover the future cost of the aging baby-boom cohort. Second, he recommends a gradual increase in the normal age of eligibility for pension benefits. Third, he recommends the creation of a second pillar, a mandatory contribution scheme in the health area as a way to avoid the development of a means-tested system that would exacerbate the disincentives to work and save. Fourth, he puts forward the idea of a new type of saving vehicle that provides tax-relief on distributions rather than on contributions so that Canadians can avoid the high marginal effective tax rates associated with means-tested programs.

It is well recognized that the incomes of the elderly are on average much lower than those of the non-elderly reflecting their limited participation in the labour market. But do the elderly have lower levels of economic well-being? Indeed, the financial circumstances of the elderly differ significantly from those of the non-elderly and these differences may compensate for lower income, increasing consumption potential relative to the non-elderly. In his paper, **Malcolm Hamilton** uses hitherto unexploited data from Statistics Canada's Survey of Consumer Spending to examine the financial circum-stances of the elderly and discusses the implications for the design of Canada's retirement income system.

Hamilton notes that there are five reasons why the unadjusted incomes of senior households should not be compared to those of younger households. Younger households often support children; devote a significant portion of their income to acquiring and financing consumer durables (cars, appliances, furniture) that seniors already possess; incur employment-related expenses (union dues, day-care, commuting costs, insurance); save part of their income for retirement; and pay higher taxes, including CPP and Employment Insurance (EI) premiums.

Hamilton presents fascinating data for different types of households on uses of income by age group. He shows that the amount of income available for consumption, that is income after taxes, mortgage payments, savings, union dues, day-care and provision for children, is actually greater for fully retired senior couples than for prime age couples ($30,400 versus $28,600) even though average before-tax income of prime age couples is double that of senior couples.

According to Hamilton, the data suggest that seniors need only around 50 per cent of their employment income to maintain their standard of living, not the 70 per cent that is commonly assumed in pension discussions. The implications of this finding for the design of the retirement system are many. Since government transfers replace 40 per cent of the income of the typical retiring Canadian, average Canadians will need little in the way of occupational pensions or retirement saving to live comfortably after 65. Most Canadians can retire in comfort if they eliminate debt and save a modest amount to supplement government pensions.

International Economics

Ever since he was in graduate school and chose imports as the topic for his PhD thesis, David Slater has been keenly interested in international economics. Over his long career, he watched with much interest the evolution of the international trading system as it expanded to cover a larger and larger share of the global economy. The next big step will be the accession of China into the World Trade Organization (WTO), which will bring a fifth of the world's population into the system. This will obviously have widespread implications for the overall system, which will be of overarching importance for Canada.

In her paper, **Sylvia Ostry**, who was Chair of the Economic Council when David was a Director, argues that if China had joined the GATT, the negotiations would have been far easier since market access under GATT was mainly about border barriers. But since the Uruguay Round the concept of market access has been extended to include not only domestic regulatory policies but also both substantive and procedural legal issues. The issue is no longer what governments must not do, but what governments must do. And it extends the Western or American administrative procedures to cover many more areas such as telecommunications, and intellectual property. Over it all is a supranational juridical system housed in the WTO, which is becoming increasingly litigious. It will be extremely difficult to integrate the non-transparent way the Chinese economy functions without "rule of law" into the WTO's highly legalized system. The Chinese will also make it more difficult to achieve the "consensus" required for the WTO to function. In addition, Chinese accession will not help to break the North-South gridlock that has tied up the WTO. Ostry proposes that China's entry into the WTO would be smoother if there were a new transition mechanism that allowed varying time deadlines for different parts of liberalization commitments and was subject to review by the WTO's Trade Policy Review Committee. In her view, the same mechanism could also be applied to Russia.

The North-South gridlock touched on by Sylvia Ostry is explored in more depth in the paper by **Kathleen Macmillan** whose first job was working for the Economic Council when David was a Director. She notes that statements from Western political leaders, under pressure from increasingly vocal protestors, emphasizing the potential of trade liberalization to alleviate poverty in the developing world, have been greeted with much scepticism by the leaders of developing countries. In spite of its pious preaching in favour of trade liberalization, the North has left in place high protectionist barriers in the textiles, clothing and agricultural sectors that discriminate against imports from the South. And at the same time, the South is still being held to WTO commitments to introduce Western-style regimes such as intellectual property measures. Nevertheless, she notes that the over 100 developing country members of the WTO and the dozens of other developing countries seeking to accede to the WTO shows that poorer countries are not yet ready to give up on the WTO.

In her paper, Macmillan takes a hard look at how effectively the multilateral trading system has really addressed developing country concerns. She also presents some concrete proposals for achieving a fairer balance in the world trading system. These include: the removal of tariff and non-tariff barriers to exports from the developing world; the reform of domestic agricultural programs; the provision of generous financial assistance and assistance in kind to developing nations to help them with implementation and trade adjustment; a substantial weakening of anti-dumping regimes; and the refusal to include environmental and labour standards in WTO Agreements.

In an empirical analysis of the migration patterns of University of British Columbia (UBC) graduates, **John F. and David F. Helliwell** show in their paper how much the situation has changed between the 1960s and the 1990s. Canadian research and graduate education have expanded dramatically, leading many more undergraduates to stay in Canada for their graduate work. According to the Helliwells, this is perhaps the single most important reason why the south-bound flows of bachelor's graduates has fallen so much from the early 1960s to the 1990s. Consequently, they argue that the resurgence of discussion of a brain drain in the 1990s has much less basis in the data, and probably represents factors specific to certain sectors, such as health spending, research and university financing, where funding support has risen much less rapidly than in the United States. It has also been fuelled to some extent by sharp increases in the numbers in temporary NAFTA visas to Canadians working in the United States, and in part to increasing gaps in salaries and tax rates in the 1990s that favoured high-income earners in the United States, relative to their Canadian counterparts.

The UBC graduate data show that over the past five decades there have been continuing reductions in the shares of UBC graduates living in the United States. For all of the large-scale bachelor's programs the proportion of graduates living in the United States has continued to fall during the 1990s. For the graduate programs, the proportion living outside Canada is and has always been high, reflecting a very international mix of both the student intake and the available career positions. For all degrees, the proportion of 1990s UBC graduates living in the rest of the world is higher than that in the United States. For graduate degrees, the proportion of the graduates subsequently living and working in Canada, and especially in British Columbia, is much higher than the share of Canadian citizens among the incoming students. With respect to the international distribution of those with the highest level of educational aptitude and attainments, as represented by the master's and PhD graduates of UBC, Canada and British Columbia stand in the middle ground between the United States and the rest of the world. Comparing the citizenship of UBC's graduate intake with the country of residence of the graduates, the United States is the largest proportionate net recipient (7 per cent U.S. citizen intake, 14 per cent U.S.-resident 1990s PhDs), Canada is the largest recipient in terms of numbers of PhDs (46 per cent Canadian citizen intake, 70 per cent Canadian-resident 1990s PhDs), with students from 100 other countries providing a net flow into Canada and the United States.

Globalization

David Slater was most closely involved in monetary and financial issues during the five years he served as Editor of *The Canadian Banker* during the mid-1960s. Those were the good old days for Canadian bankers before the Canadian banking system was opened up to foreign competition. Now it is a whole new competitive ball game as **Edward P. Neufeld** points out in his paper on the challenges that globalization poses for the Canadian banking system. He argues that the ability of Canadian institutions to withstand increasing foreign competition will depend on their economic efficiency relative to that of the encroaching competitors. In his view, the forces that have facilitated globalization of financial services have also made obsolete past measures of economies of scale and of the "optimum" size of financial institutions, and past guidelines concerning excessive domestic market concentration are no longer reliable. For Canadian financial institutions to experience solid growth in the future will require them to be internationally competitive at home and abroad. But unfortunately they have been slipping down the list of important international financial institutions as measured by the size of their assets and of their capital bases, and as a result their non-interest costs are 10 to 20 per cent higher than they would be if mergers were permitted. Otherwise, the forces of globalization will generate a persistent tendency towards increased foreign ownership of Canadian financial institutions, as has already begun to happen, and towards an increase in non-Canadian executives running them.

Neufeld is very concerned that Bill C-8, which is the new legislation reforming the financial service sector passed this year, contains discriminatory measures that will undermine the international competitiveness of the Canadian banking system. These include: a restrictive and politicized bank merger policy, which risks preventing Canadian banks from achieving the economies of scale that their much larger international competitors are achieving; the continued prohibition against the distribution of life insurance through bank branches, which directly restricts competition in the Canadian market; the continued exclusion of the banks from the car leasing business, a business almost completely dominated by foreign institutions; and the threat in the bill directed at the large Canadian banks, and not at smaller competing institutions or foreign institutions located in Canada or entering the Canadian market through the Internet, that if they do not provide certain low-cost services they will be forced to do so.

In Neufeld's view, the most glaring weakness of the new policy as concerns competition is its failure to recognize clearly that by far the most important source of future competition will be large international institutions operating directly in Canada and through the Internet from outside Canada. He regards the merger process as flawed in that it is tortuous, and therefore inevitably subject to long delays, and risks being hostage to short-term political considerations. Neufeld believes that the key question that needs to be addressed is not whether Canadians will get the world-class financial services they require, because international competition will ensure that, but whether the services will be provided by Canadian banks or foreign financial institutions.

In the second paper in this section, **Morley Gunderson** presents an overview of issues related to North American economic integration and globalization. He provides a particularly balanced perspective, a rarity in this area of highly charged, ideology-driven and emotional debate. He first notes that economic integration has both a deepening and widening dimension and enumerates the various aspects of these two dimensions in the context of North American integration, noting that in practice the different dimensions complement one another in a self-reinforcing fashion. He also points out that deeper and wider economic integration can foster internal consolidation since this integration is generally regarded as a precondition for external competitiveness.

Gunderson pays particular attention to the issue of policy integration. He argues that the emerging competitive pressures on the North from low-cost, less regulated jurisdictions in the South is the most important consequence of trade liberalization and globalization, although there is still insufficient evidence of harmonization leading to the lowest common denominator. The policy-making process is now subject to the forces of competition that apply to business and labour. He argues that the laws and regulations that will be under the most pressure will be those that are the most inefficient, that is those that protect interest group rents and impose costs without commensurate benefits.

Gunderson notes that integration represents a threat to distributional or equity-oriented policies that do not have positive feedback effects on efficiency even when the population considers such policies highly desirable. Raising taxes to finance these policies may not be the solution if mobile factors of production consequently flee to lower-tax jurisdictions. He documents the wide range of policy responses to the potential policy vacuum created by globalization and integration, including the NAFTA labour side agreement, the inclusion of social clauses in trade agreements, corporate codes of conduct, social labelling, and consumer boycotts, transnational efforts amongst unions, social groups and NGOs and union-to-union co-operation. But he finds that effectiveness of these responses to date is moot.

Gunderson raises the issue of whether the more circumscribed role of governments and greater role of market forces will in fact benefit the most disadvantaged. He notes that so far this has not been the case, although whether this negative trend will continue is an open question. He concludes by cautioning that the long-run sustainability of integration depends on the equitable sharing of the efficiency gains arising from this process.

Regional Issues

Quebec's relative growth performance with Ontario has always been an issue of concern for economic historians. In his paper **Pierre Fortin** discusses trends in Quebec's real domestic income relative to that in Ontario over the last half-century. He finds that per capita real domestic income in Quebec, as a percentage of that in Ontario, fell from 78 per cent in 1926 to 74 per cent at the end of the 1950s, with a particularly steep decline during World War II. After WWII, it then started an upward climb, reaching 86 per cent in 1999, and exhibited a particularly strong performance in the 1975–85 period. Fortin sees the WWII slump related to the proportionally smaller number of men in Quebec enrolled in the armed forces, which reduced the share of overall military pay going to Quebec. He attributes what he calls the big bubble of the 1975–85 period to the strong cyclical expansion associated with a large number of major projects accompanied by a wage explosion.

The key development Fortin seeks to explain is the 12 percentage point increase in Quebec's per capita real domestic income from 74 per cent of that in Ontario in 1960 to 86 per cent in 1999. He decomposes this change into three sources: productivity, employment and the demographic structure, and finds that faster growth in output per worker in Quebec was the most important factor, accounting for 55 per cent of the decline in the gap. In 1999, output per worker in Quebec was 93 per cent of that in Ontario, up from 83 per cent in 1954. Faster growth in the working age population accounted for 35 per cent of the decline in the income gap, and more rapid rate of increase in the employment rate for 10 per cent.

Fortin points out that the massive investment Quebec has made in education has greatly reduced that gap in average years of schooling between persons in Quebec and Ontario. Indeed, in 1991 the average 25-year-old man had received more years of schooling in Quebec than in Ontario. This development bodes well for future income growth. Equally, Quebec has also done well in investment in infrastructure and equipment and in research and development. Fortin explains the continued income gap with Ontario by the long gestation period required before the education revolution filters up to all age groups.

Environmental Economics

With global warming, Canadians are becoming increasingly aware of the importance of effective environmental policies. In his paper **Anthony Scott**, a pioneer in the areas of resource and environmental economics in this country, provides a comprehensive discussion of the role economists can and should play in the development of more effective environmental policies. A key theme of his paper is that environmental policy, particularly in crucial areas like global air pollution, is still in its infancy and effective national institutions to respond to policy challenges are still in the developmental stage.

Scott first reviews the history of environmental policy in England, the United States and Canada. He then examines the approaches of economists to environmental issues, including the market failure and ideal output approach, benefit-cost analysis of pollution, and environmental impact assessment, and identifies topics that environmental economists teach and research. The paper then compares what economists do in Canada in the environmental area compared to that in the United States, finding that academic environmental economists in Canada specialize more in theory and show little knowledge or interest in issues directly related to the environmental policy debate in their country of residence.

Scott argues that the nature of Canadian federalism has put an imprint on our environmental policy issues and on how economists relate to them. In the United States, Washington is the headquarters of environmental policy research. In Canada, Ottawa does not play a comparable role because of the shared jurisdiction with the provinces, leaving this country without a national centre having economies of scale in environmental law-making and enlightenment. Scott calls for closer relations between academic economists working in the environmental area and policymakers at both the federal and provincial level, seeing it as a win-win situation for both groups.

Labour Economics

The first paper in this section by **Charles M. Beach and Ross Finnie** represents the first attempt to quantify short-term or cyclical changes in earnings mobility in Canada. Mobility analysis can be seen as a complement to the analysis of income distribution. For a given degree of earnings inequality, more earnings mobility corresponds to securing greater labour market opportunity.

Using longitudinal income-tax-based data, the authors divide the employed population into eight age/sex groups: entry workers (20–24), younger workers (25–34), prime-age workers (35–54), and older workers (55–64) for both sexes; and divide the earnings distribution into lower, middle and upper regions or earnings intervals based on median earnings levels for the distribution as a whole, and calculate the proportion of workers in each group for all years over the 1982–96 period. They also develop transition matrices that show the probability of moving from one earnings interval to another over a one-year period.

They find that there have been major cyclical changes in earnings polarization and that these changes have been concentrated in recessions, notably in the 1990–92 downturn. They also find that men in particular experienced a marked decrease in their net probability of upward mobility in the earnings distribution during recessions, as the probability of moving up fell sharply as did the probability of moving down. The results of the paper are particularly relevant for an understanding of how earnings mobility may be affected by the current economic slowdown.

The skills issue is currently at or near the top of the federal government's policy agenda, given its importance for harnessing the benefits of technological advances. Policy initiatives in the area should be premised on an accurate assessment of Canada's recent experience in education and skill formation. In his paper, **W. Craig Riddell** attempts such an assessment. He provides a careful examination of trends in education expenditures and outcomes in Canada compared to other countries, looks at trends in the incidence of education, and analyzes the link between education and labour market success.

Riddell's overall assessment of Canada's record in education and skills is quite positive. He finds that relative to other OECD countries, Canada ranks near the top in terms of expenditure per student and share of GDP devoted to elementary, secondary and post-secondary education; that Canada's population is well educated by international standards, with the highest proportion of the population with non-university, post-secondary education in the OECD; and that the country's literacy skills, particularly for the young and well educated, are above average among the G7 countries that participated in the International Adult Literacy Survey. One possible weakness he identifies is the relatively low student achievement in mathematics among the G7 countries that participated in the standardized tests. This suggests Canada may not be obtaining good "value for money" from its relatively high expenditure on education.

Riddell notes that the conventional estimates of the return to education appear downward biased so that the causal effect of education on earnings may be higher than previously believed. Evidence suggests that the marginal return to incremental investment in education exceeds the average from previous investments and that there is no evidence that investments in schooling are running into diminishing returns. Riddell concludes that investments in human capital remain an important potential source of economic growth and equality of opportunity.

David W. Slater: An Economist for All Seasons

Patrick Grady

Introduction

As David Slater begins his eighth decade, it is a fitting time to look back over his remarkable career of public service, which has spanned the worlds of academe and government. In the over half a century that he has been active as an economist, there is scarcely an area of economics and public policy that he has not been involved in as a researcher and/or policy advisor. His interests are catholic. Just name a topic and David will have something important and useful to say. And the way he says it in his characteristic *basso profundo* voice commands attention in even the largest of rooms filled with the sleepiest of audiences. David's great strength as an economist has always been his integrity. In all his work, he has consistently been guided by a philosophy that balances a deep commitment to markets and the key role of the private sector with an equally deep commitment to social policies

---

I personally had the great pleasure to work with David Slater at the Department of Finance, the Economic Council and *Canadian Business Economics*. This account draws on detailed notes provided by David W. Slater and an interview with him as well as personal impressions.

19

designed to create equality of opportunity and provide support for those who were disadvantaged. And the same human touch David brings to economics, he brings to all his personal relationships, creating friends and admirers wherever his long career took him.

The Early Years

Even as a boy, David was concerned about those less fortunate. He lived in a municipality on the outskirts of Winnipeg where he had been born in 1921. His father was a grain merchant and his mother was actively involved in volunteer social work. David remembers how he helped his mother bring Christmas baskets to the less fortunate in his community and how awkward it was when they delivered a basket to a girl in his grade school class whose father was out of work. Even though the girl sat right next to him in class, she could never look him in the eye again after that. This taught David the limitations of private charity and the need for a social safety net.

Even though David's family was relatively well-off, things were not handed to him "on a platter". Living at home to save on lodging, he worked his way through the University of Manitoba with summer jobs repairing and renovating country grain elevators. This was hard gruelling work 12 hours a day, seven days a week as a member of a work crew. It taught David respect for those who work with their hands. While the pay was only 35 or 45 cents per hour, David always went back to school in the fall with plenty of money in his pockets. And as an added benefit he learned carpentry from the superb carpenters he worked with.

At the University of Manitoba, David worked on a Bachelor of Commerce degree, concentrating on actuarial science. It was there that David's interest in economics was kindled by Pete McQueen, the head of the Economics Department (whose life was tragically cut short in a plane crash on his way back from a Bank of Canada Board of Directors meeting in the winter of 1941). Once David became convinced that economics was one of the ways to solve all the world's problems, actuarial science lost its limited and more practical appeal.

Wartime Service

As a student, David was very active in the Canadian Officers Training Program as a 2nd lieutenant. With the war raging in Europe and the Far East, it was hard for young David to stay focused on his studies and as a result his marks dropped. Finally, in the spring of 1942, he could stand on the sidelines no longer and he joined the army, leaving economics behind.

As a lieutenant in the Royal Canadian Army Service Corps, David served overseas from the spring of 1943 to the summer of 1945. His job was in supply and service, a field in which economists, not to speak of actuaries, are often expected to excel. To put it simply, David was responsible for providing the supplies needed by the Allied Forces. This included ammunition and shells for the artillery and infantry and the gasoline and diesel that powered all the military's vehicles. The main supply depot was on the beaches of Normandy where David was deposited once the landing zones were secure. According to David, there was not much danger as long as they had air cover, but every once and awhile a few German planes would get through. In the army, David mastered many subsequently useless skills such as mine-laying, anti-gas warfare protection and shooting 20mm cannons.

David followed the invading Allied Forces all the way into Germany. When the war was over in Europe, he volunteered for the Pacific Forces and was sent back home to Winnipeg. The war in Japan ended before he could be shipped out again. His final assignment in the army was to take some troops who were being demobilized from Winnipeg to Toronto by train. Once his task was completed, he continued on to Kingston, free from the army and back to economics.

Life in the Groves of Academe

After the war was over, it was only natural that David should go to Queen's University in economics. His old professor Peter McQueen had been good friends with W.A. Mackintosh, Frank Knox and C.A. Curtis of Queen's. And one of his classmates had spent a visiting student year at Queen's and talked it up to David as a "real university" on his return.

David took to Queen's like a duck to water. Its best professors were returning from wartime service in Ottawa and had a practical orientation that appealed to a young returning officer such as David. He quickly earned a First Class Honours Degree in economics in the spring of 1947. His performance was so good that he was asked to be a sessional lecturer for the 1946–47 and 1947–48 academic years to help out with all the returning veterans.

Not all was business at Queen's. In the spring of 1946, David met his future and present wife, Lillian Bell, who was a student in the Industrial Relations certificate course. By the next spring, they were married.

David's most memorable experiences at Queen's were: learning about the national accounts and the General Theory from Mac Urquhart; learning to teach under Frank Knox; learning economic history from Knox and Bill Mackintosh; learning about welfare economics and the theory of socialism from C.A. Curtis; and studying Canadian political science under Alex Corry. Even though David was just a junior lecturer, he felt that he was a full participant in the meetings of the Department of Political and Economic Science. David was also excited to learn about the foundation of the postwar world's main institutions in a graduate course offered by Mackintosh who was present at their creation.

Recognizing David's promise as an economist, his senior colleagues at Queen's counseled him to go to the University of Chicago for doctoral studies. While David was also accepted at Harvard and the London School of Economics, he took their advice and went off to Chicago. There he found himself in a much larger pond. In class, he was no longer one of the few good students, but only one of many. It took him the first term to get settled in, but by the end he had managed to get a complete set of firsts in the graduate program.

David still remembers with fondness and awe many of the Chicago faculty who instructed and befriended him: Theodore Schultz, the department head, Milton Friedman, Lloyd Metzler, Tjalling Koopmans, Kenneth Arrow, Jacob Marshak, Gale Johnson, Bert Hoselitz, and Allan Wallis. The names read like a Who's Who of postwar economics. Milton Friedman captured the spirit of this incredibly lively and friendly department in his memoirs, with his wife Rose, *Two Lucky People* (Friedman and Friedman, 1999).

Lloyd Metzler became David's supervisor for his thesis on the terms of trade. Like many graduate students, David did not wait to finish his, but instead took a junior appointment in the Department of Economics at Stanford University, where he thought he could quickly finish up. Fortune did not smile on him, however. During his first year at Stanford, Lloyd Metzler became ill, with what was subsequently diagnosed in September 1951 as a brain tumour. During that year before anyone knew what was wrong, David had a number of puzzling exchanges with his supervisor over his evolving draft. When Metzler had to step down, David was given Bert Hoselitz as a new supervisor, and continued to struggle with his thesis.

David was offered a regular appointment at Queen's as an Assistant Professor, beginning in the autumn of 1952. As such appointments were scarce, he jumped at the opportunity to return to Canada and finish off his thesis. But the fates were not kind. When he and his wife Lillian were driving from Palo Alto to Kingston with all their belongings, including the only draft of his thesis, in a trailer behind them. David looked in the rear view mirror, only to see, to his horror, the trailer in flames. In those days before computers, an empirical thesis was built on paper worksheets, and four by six cards, all of which made very good kindling. They lost everything, and David was back at square one with his thesis.

The Gordon Commission

After an understandably troubled and fallow period, David started to work on his thesis again, but before it was finished he was offered a year-long post on the Gordon Royal Commission on Canada's Economic Prospects. There he worked under Bill Hood's leadership, and made many new friends including Anthony Scott, Doug LePan and Doug Fullerton. It was also a very productive period of research for him and he wrote two books — *Consumption Expenditures in Canada* (Slater, 1957a) and *Canada's Imports* (Slater, 1957b), which are still found in all Canadian and most major foreign research libraries. The first book on consumer expenditures challenged some of the analysis and forecasting that had been done based on cross-section data; the second on imports provided some insights into the changing import structure of the Canadian economy. In addition, after he returned to Queen's, he continued to go to Ottawa weekly by train to spend a couple of days working with Bill Hood to pull together most of the chapters of the commission's final report.

The debates that took place inside of the Gordon Commission were very stimulating for David. He found himself swept up in the heated discussions that raged between the supporters of the nationalistic economic policy championed by Walter Gordon, and the hard-nosed realism promoted by Simon Reisman, Jack Young and Ed Safarian. Like most economists, David found himself sympathizing with the latter group.

Back to Academe

After completing his tasks for the Gordon Commission, David extended his work on imports, and submitted it as his doctoral dissertation to the University of Chicago. His long-sought-after Ph.D. was finally awarded in 1957.

At Queen's, David was responsible for teaching a course in money, banking and international finance and another in international trade and finance. David was a natural teacher. Perhaps his greatest contribution to Canadian economics is the large number of students he inspired both through his teaching and as a role model. Some of his most outstanding students at Queen's were Ian and Gail Stewart, Alan and Ann Green, David Dodge, Lars Osberg, Scott Clark and Alison Morgan (née Mackintosh).

When the Department of Economics, under the leadership of Knox and Mackintosh, decided to develop a graduate program, David enthusiastically joined the team building a Masters' and Ph.D. program. Initially, the team was comprised of Mac Urquhart, Gideon Rosenbluth and David, but it was strengthened with the addition of David Smith and L. A. Skeoch. Being only a small group and needing to cover the core subjects in depth, they each abandoned their secondary interests and concentrated on their specialties to provide a satisfactory graduate program. David led the work in international economics, and helped out with model-building and dynamic analysis. The group worked very hard and succeeded in obtaining more resources, recruiting good faculty and gradually attracting good students.

Beginning about 1962, David's interests started to go beyond the university. He was appointed editor of *The Canadian Banker,* succeeding Frank Knox. In that capacity, he served for five years and worked closely with Harvey Perry. He also became one of the few academic members of the Ontario Committee on University Affairs, engaged alongside Douglas Wright, the chairman, and Ed Stewart, the deputy minister, in building and monitoring the whole Ontario university system. And he was active in the Canadian Association of University Teachers, becoming National Treasurer under Bora Laskin, then of the University of Toronto Law School. David was also called to serve on the Canada Council and the Board of Directors of the Bank of Canada, and the (then) Industrial Development Bank. While on the board of the Bank, he became close friends with Louis Rasminsky, Bill Lawson and Gerry Bouey.

As a member of the Canada Council, David was involved in the establishment of the first art bank. The premise behind the bank was that the best way to promote visual arts was to buy it. Given his great interest in art, David is particularly proud of this contribution which combines art and economics.

David's involvement in the bigger world outside did not prevent him from climbing the ladder of administration at Queen's University. He rose to be the Dean of Graduate Studies and Research, first under Principal Alex Corry and then under John Deutsch. But an unfortunate side effect was that his steadily increasing administrative responsibilities cut substantially into the time available for his research. During this time, which should have been his most productive, his main research outputs were limited to a few pamphlets on international trade and finance for the Private Planning Association and the Economic Council (Slater, 1964, 1965, 1968 and 1969) and some survey pieces for the Canadian Banker.

David welcomed the opportunity presented by a sabbatical leave in 1964–65 to get back to economics and replenish his intellectual capital. Going to England, he divided his time between the London School of Economics and Cambridge. Harry Johnson had arranged for him to give a course of lectures in LSE's new M.Sc. in Economics program. David was also asked to take a few students in each year of the Tripos program at Cambridge. During his stay in England, David gave seminar papers at Cambridge, LSE, Strathclyde and Edinborough.

As a diversion in the early 1960s, David became the president of a small semi-cooperative urban land development project in Kingston, called Alwington Place. It owned the best available land at that time on the shores of Lake Ontario. There he was able to put to practical use all his knowledge of urban development, town planning and land development. He and Lillian built a house there, which to this day, in its delightful garden near the lake, remains one of the loveliest houses in Kingston.

The Lion's Den

In early 1970 David was approached by Bora Laskin, on behalf of the Board of Governors, to be the president of York University. This was an offer David could not refuse and he served from the summer of 1970 until the spring of 1973. The search for the presidency had been a very divisive affair, both at the level of the board and of the faculty. As an outsider, David was, of course, not aware of all the ins and outs of the situation. However, he knew that somehow he had to get the warring factions to work together. Unfortunately, given the need for sharp budget cuts, this challenge proved too much for even David's strong interpersonal and conciliatory skills and he resigned his post.

Refuge in, of all Places, the Department of Finance

As always though, David soon landed on his feet. He was invited by Simon Reisman, the deputy minister of finance and old friend from Gordon Commission days, to join the department in the spring of 1973, as the director of the Economic Analysis Division, under another old friend Bill Hood, who was the assistant deputy minister. That experience proved to be a wonderful restorative for David. He welcomed the opportunity to actually do economics again after several years of being absorbed in increasingly heavy administrative responsibilities. And the Department of Finance turned out to be remarkably harmonious and collegial without the interpersonal conflicts that had plagued his term at York.

When David first came to Finance, Reisman told him that, of course, the job came first, but he also had to learn "a little French" with the help of a tutor. In his inimitable style, Reisman growled that if David could not pass the tests in two years, they would have to send him away to language school, implying that this was somehow a fate worse than death for a self-respecting economist. While he had to work day and night for two years, David managed both to do the demanding job and to pass the language test.

David had many rewarding experiences in Finance. He was a member of the small team that put together the budget each year. He also joined with representatives of the Bank of Canada to go on semi-annual visits to New

York and Washington to meet with key business and government economists to take the pulse of the U.S. economy. David also represented Canada on OECD working parties, and was even chosen chairman of the key macroeconomic working party. These trips to Paris gave David an opportunity to pursue his interest in art. Anyone who ever went to Paris with David on OECD business always knew they would end up at some special art exhibit that only he knew about, such as a Michael Snow exhibit he took me to one time. When Steve Handfield-Jones became ADM, David was promoted to become the general director in the Fiscal Policy and Economic Analysis Branch. While at Finance, David served three ministers: John Turner, Donald MacDonald and Jean Chrétien.

The Economic Council of Canada

When Sylvia Ostry was appointed chair of the Economic Council of Canada, she recruited David as vice-chairman in 1978. After she left for the OECD in Paris, David became chairman of the Council in 1980. The Council was then a research, advisory, consensus-seeking body. In addition to the *Annual Review* which was required under its statute, it undertook four to six special studies a year. David was given responsibility for the Newfoundland reference, and picked up the responsibility for the Regulation reference after Sylvia left. Under David's leadership, the Council built up a strong econometric team for the CANDIDE model, and a strong labour market team, and it did some good work on taxation, federal-provincial finance, and reforming Canada's financial system. David attributes the quality of the work to the strong project directors the Council had, such as Neil Swan, Ross Preston, Bob Jenness, Keith Newton, Bert Waslander and Ron Hirshhorn.

The Council had a good record for tackling medium- to long-term economic problems and policies, and doing empirical and policy analysis work in depth. This enabled it to play a key role in developing a national consensus on important policy issues. During his tenure at the Council, David managed to escape the usual hostility of the Bank of Canada and the Department of Finance because of his close ties with these organizations. Previous and subsequent chairs were not so fortunate.

At the Economic Council of Canada, David was in his element, discussing, debating and encouraging others to do research across a wide range of important Canadian economic issues. He served as an inspiration to the many bright young economists who went through the Council.

David was also a master at bringing the Council to a consensus or almost-consensus. At one particularly contentious Council meeting over the annual report, which I attended, at the end it seemed that everybody had disagreed about almost everything. But David just thanked everyone for expressing their views and summarized what he viewed as the consensus, which bore a remarkable similarity to his own position. Since no one objected, the deemed consensus stood.

When David retired as chairman of the Council late in 1984, it was with a sense of a job well done. Despite some disappointment over the slowness with which the Council's recommendations were implemented, he had a belief that the venture was worth the time and money. It was consequently with much regret that David watched the Council being disbanded by the government in 1992.

An Active "Retirement"

Shortly after David retired from the Council, he was asked by the Government of Ontario to chair a task force on the reform of the teachers and public service pensions. The main task was to develop a workable model of Trustee Partnerships, which would solve the unfunded liability problems and put the new programs on a self-reliant basis, and then to sell it to the provincial government and employee stakeholders. After the required analytical work was done, the model of a sound fully-funded pension program based on market investments was presented to the employees at a two-day meeting at Niagara-on-the-Lake and was accepted even though it required increased contributions at the outset. This was the model that was subsequently approved by the government (Slater, 1988b).

Based on his success in Ontario, David was asked about two years later to help reach an agreement between the Government of Nova Scotia and the Nova Scotia Teachers' Union on their pension program. That program faced such a large and accelerating unfunded liability that it was in danger of collapsing. It differed from the situation in Ontario in that the government was only partly responsible for the unfunded liability and the provincial finances were not strong enough for it to accept the full responsibility for financing the unfunded liability. The solution worked out by David between the stakeholders was a new Trustee Partnership agreement, in which the province picked up part of the unfunded liabilities, and the teachers in return gave up a part of the indexation of their pensions (past and prospective), and increased their contributions into the new partnership agreement. The new program was also allowed to invest its assets in a wide range of market investments.

In addition to his role in reforming the financing of the Ontario and Nova Scotia public sector pensions, David was also the chair of a small task force for the Ontario government on the problems of the property and casualty insurance sectors. The property and casualty insurance industry has a long history of cyclical crises, in which insurance coverage was reduced, made more expensive, or even became unavailable in certain phases of the cycle. The central issue was to determine whether the then existing crisis in Ontario was just another such cyclical crisis or whether there were more fundamental structural problems at work. The question as it was alarmingly put to David was: "For property and casualty insurance, had Ontario become the California of the North?" By this was meant, was the development and application of tort law in medical services, property services, export services, product distribution, and motor vehicle accidents, which had given rise to indiscriminate litigation and to huge increases in insurance costs in California, also at work in Ontario?

To answer these difficult questions, David was assisted by Deborah Coyne, who served as the task force's executive director, in commissioning the required research. The powerful research team they assembled included Michael Trebilcock, Frank Mathewson, Marsha Chandler, and Carolyn Tuohy, all of the University of Toronto. This was always one of David's greatest strengths, pulling together the right people to do the required research.

Based on this research, the task force determined that the tort-based explosion of claims and settlements had not and were not likely to affect insurance in Ontario to the same degree (Ontario Task Force on Insurance, 1986). But it did find that the data and analysis base of insurance and reinsurance in Ontario was weak and that therefore reinsurers were charging higher rates than necessary to protect themselves against possible risks, particularly in the area of automobile insurance.

The task force investigated the competitive and industrial organization aspects of the property and casualty insurance industry operating in Ontario, and concluded that deficiencies in the structure and regulatory systems were factors in exacerbating the industry cycles.

The task force also studied non-fault auto insurance, including partially shared fault risks, and concluded that the fault system for the application of tort law in Ontario was unsound and unfair, and recommended a change to a no-fault system of automobile insurance. While this recommendation was not fully accepted by the Ontario government, it eventually led to the development of a partially-limited fault system in Ontario.

In the early 1990s, David prepared a literature survey and commentary on transportation and economic development for the Royal Commission on National Passenger Transportation. It was discussed in a colloquium held by the Commission and subsequently published in one of the Commission's research volumes.

But most of David's scholarly work in the early 1990s was focused on the preparation of the book: *War Finance and Reconstruction: The Role of Canada's Department of Finance, 1939-1946* (Slater, 1995a). This was the second volume of a history of the Department of Finance begun earlier by Robert Bryce (1986). In this volume, David was asked by Robert Bryce to cover the domestic side of the experience, with Bryce contributing material on international aspects. The book tells the story of J.L. Ilsley and the handful of public officials who carried most of the burden of the financial and economic management of the war and the planning and implementation of postwar reconstruction.

In 1992, David became one of the founding editors of *Canadian Business Economics* along with Andrew Sharpe and myself. The three-person team edited the journal for the first three years with Gordon Betcherman replacing me during the next three years. In our view, the journal filled a niche as an applied economics and policy journal, and was highly regarded both for its economic content and the non-technical writing style.

The policy research topic that most concerned David in the mid-to-late 1990s was Canada's retirement income system. At an age when most people are only concerned about their own personal retirement, he published a review and analysis paper on reforming the retirement income system in *Canadian Business Economics* (Slater, 1995b), as well as several papers in the C.D. Howe Institute's Commentary Series (Slater, 1997a,b, 1998; and Slater and Robson, 1999). As a result of his extensive work and expertise, he was called on to participate in many discussions on pension issues and served as the reader and commentator on the draft pension proposals prepared for the Association of Canadian Pension Managers. He also testified before the House of Commons Finance Committee on the Canada Pension Fund Investment Board.

David, always the teacher with a great fondness for and deep interest in students, also continued to teach. In the spring of 1996 and 1997, he led the economic policy seminar in the Masters' of Public Administration program for Queen's University. In recognition of his long service to Queen's University, David was granted a honourary LL.D. from the university in 1989.

David Now

Even at 80, David remains very active. He continues to do work on pension issues and has a couple of papers in progress and circulating privately for comment. He has been secretary-treasurer for the Centre for the Study of Living Standards since 1995. In addition, he is the treasurer of the condominium in which he lives, and he is the chair of the Board of Trustees of the Dominion-Chalmers United Church.

David and Lillian travel widely, pursuing their interest in art, gradually visiting all of the world's greatest art museums. Art has long been their shared passion.

In the year of David and Lillian's 54th wedding anniversary, they take great comfort in the lives and works of their four daughters and five grandchildren. Barbara is the Assistant Deputy Minister for Government On-Line and Business Transformation in Human Resources Development Canada. Gail and her husband own and run a computer training and advisory firm in England. Carolyn is a free lancer in Ottawa. Leslie is a partner in a strategic planning operation in Toronto.

Over his long career, David has made a great contribution to Canadian economics in the proud Queen's tradition of public service best exemplified by Clifford Clark, W.A. Mackintosh and John Deutsch. It has taken the form of building institutions both university and government, teaching and mentoring younger economists in both academe and the public service, participating in the analysis and development of policy, and contributing to the national policy debate.

Selective Bibliography

Bryce, R.B. (1986), *Maturing in Hard Times: Canada's Department of Finance through the Great Depression* (Kingston and Montreal: McGill-Queen's University Press).

Friedman, M. and R.D. Friedman (1999), *Two Lucky People: Memoirs* (Chicago: University of Chicago Press).

Glorieux, G. and D.W. Slater (1990), *Building on Success in the Dynamic Asian Economies: The Recent Experience of Canadian Financial Institutions* (Ottawa: The Conference Board of Canada).

Knox, F.A., C.L. Barber and D.W. Slater (1955), *The Canadian Electrical Manufacturing Industry: An Economic Analysis* (Toronto: Canadian Electrical Manufacturers Association).

Ontario Task Force on Insurance (1986), *Final Report of the Ontario Task Force on Insurance* (Toronto: Ministry of Financial Institutions).

Slater, D.W. (1957a), *Consumption Expenditures in Canada* (Ottawa: Royal Commission on Canada's Economic Prospects).

_____ (1957b), *Canada's Imports* (Ottawa: Royal Commission on Canada's Economic Prospects).

_____ (1963), "Some Problems of Taxation in Canada: A Preliminary Brief to the Royal Commission on Taxation" (Kingston, Ontario).

_____ (1964), *Canada's Balance of International Payments: When is a Deficit a Problem?* (Montreal: Canadian Trade Committee, Private Planning Association of Canada).

_____ (1965), *Perspective on Canada's International Payments: A Background Sketch and Survey,* prepared for the Economic Council of Canada (Ottawa: Queen's Printer).

_____ (1968), *Trade and Economic Growth: Trends and Prospects with Applications to Canada* (Toronto: Published for the Private Planning Association by University of Toronto Press).

_____ (1969), *Perspective on Canada's International Payments: A Background Sketch and Survey,* prepared for the Economic Council of Canada (Ottawa: Queen's Printer).

_____ (1982a), *Economics of the University* (Cambridge, ON: Collier-Macmillan Canada).

_____ (1982b), *Federal-Provincial Finances* (Guelph: School of Agricultural Economics and Extension Education, Ontario Agricultural College, University of Guelph).

_____ (1982c), *Regulations and Agriculture* (Guelph: School of Agricultural Economics and Extension Education, Ontario Agricultural College, University of Guelph).

_____ (1988a), *Fresh Start: Report to the Treasurer of Ontario, the Chairman of Management Board of Cabinet and the Minister of Education on Teachers' and Public Servants' Pensions* (Toronto: Queen's Printer for Ontario).

_____ (1988b), *Equity and Efficiency: The Theory and Realities Relating to Employment, Unemployment and Income Security: A Report to the Commission of Inquiry on Unemployment Insurance,* Research study no. 5 (Ottawa: Commission of Inquiry on Unemployment Insurance).

_____ (1992), *The Contribution of Investment and Savings to Productivity and Economic Growth in Canada,* by D. Slater and Investment Canada staff including John Knubley ... [et al.] (Ottawa: Investment Canada).

_____ (1995a), *War Finance and Reconstruction: The Role of Canada's Department of Finance, 1939-1946,* with two chapters by R.B. Bryce (Ottawa: D.W. Slater).

_____ (1995b), "Reforming Canada's Retirement Income System", *Canadian Business Economics,* Fall.

_____ (1997a), *The Pension Squeeze: The Impact of the March 1996 Federal Budget,* Commentary No. 87 (Toronto: C.D. Howe Institute).

_____ (1997b), *Prudence and Performance: Managing the Proposed CPP,* Commentary No. 98 (Toronto: C.D. Howe Institute).

_____ (1998), *Fixing the Seniors Benefit* (Toronto: C.D. Howe Institute).

Slater, D.W. and W.B.P. Robson (1999), *Building a Stronger Pillar: The Changing Shape of the Canada Pension Plan,* Commentary No. 123 (Toronto: C.D. Howe Institute).

Fiscal Federalism

Financing Confederation Revisited: The Economic State of the Federation

Robin Boadway

Introduction

This festschrift for David Slater coincides with the twentieth Anniversary of two important events in Canadian fiscal federalism: the completion of the Economic Council of Canada's landmark study entitled *Financing Confederation* and the passage by Parliament of what would become the *Constitution Act, 1982*. David was the Chair of the Economic Council at the time, and as such was responsible for what is arguably the most influential and lasting of the Council's projects. By apparent coincidence, the publication of *Financing Confederation* coincided with the coming into force of the *Constitution Act*. While the *Constitution Act* is perhaps better known for repatriation of the constitution and the implementation of the Charter of Rights and Freedoms, it also included a rather far-reaching set of principles governing the relative roles and responsibilities of the federal and provincial governments in delivering social policies. Although these principles are no more than that, their elevation to constitutional status gives them a special standing as ideals against which our federal fiscal arrangements should be judged. Remarkably, *Financing Confederation* provided the economic justification for at least some of these principles, and explored their implications for the design of the fiscal arrangements.

This paper takes a brief retrospective view of the development of the fiscal arrangements in light of the principles enunciated in both these documents. In particular, we consider the consequences of the substantial fiscal decentralization that has occurred in the past 20 years for the achievement of the objectives set out in these principles. We use as our benchmark not only the principles enunciated in *Financing Confederation,* which have stood the test of time, but also the relevant principles of the *Constitution Act.* In particular, we might remind ourselves of the content of Section 36, entitled Equalization and Regional Disparities, which states:

(1) Without altering the legislative authority of Parliament or of the provincial legislatures, or the rights of any of them with respect to the exercise of their legislative authority, Parliament and the legislatures, together with the government of Canada and the provincial governments, are committed to
   (a) promoting equal opportunities for the well being of Canadians;
   (b) furthering economic development to reduce disparity in opportunities; and
   (c) providing essential public services of reasonable quality to all Canadians.
(2) Parliament and the Government of Canada are committed to the principle of making equalization payments to ensure that provincial governments have sufficient revenues to provide reasonably comparable levels of public services at reasonably comparable levels of taxation.

This section not only commits the federal government to the principle of a strong form of equalization, but also essentially makes the federal government jointly responsible for the delivery of important social policies. Other relevant aspects or interpretations of the constitution for the fiscal arrangements include the assignment of powers, in particular, the exclusive provincial legislative responsibility in the areas of education, health and social services; the spending power, which includes the right to make conditional transfers to the provinces as well as targeted transfers to individuals and institutions; and the surprising absence of the assignment of responsibility for maintaining and promoting efficiency in the internal economic union, which is generally regarded as a prerequisite of a smoothly functioning federation.

Principles and Values

This is an exercise in policy evaluation, and as such, the perspective that we take is unabashedly a normative or prescriptive one. Policy evaluation and advice necessarily involves value judgements. This issue is the extent to which one's policy stances ought to be conditioned by positive considerations, in particular by political feasibility. This is especially important in fiscal federalism, given that many of the conflicts that constrain policy implementation are political in nature. Nonetheless, we take the view, as did the authors of *Financing Confederation*, that economic policy analysis should not be unduly constrained by considerations of political feasibility. To do so would be to eschew that which economists are best prepared to contribute. At the same time, it should be recognized that the design of the fiscal arrangements cannot be based solely on economic considerations. There are obviously other issues involved that non-economists are in a better position to judge, and that may in the end be more telling.

The normative approach involves adopting some normative principles or objectives and investigating their implications for policy. This means we must make clear what one's societal value criteria are. We take as our basic economic objectives the following three: economic efficiency, redistributive equity and horizontal equity or fairness.

Efficiency

The criterion of efficiency is taken for granted by economists. It refers broadly to the exploitation of all gains from trade, both those that can be obtained best through markets and those that require collective action. From the point of view of fiscal federalism, one can identify three relevant ways in which economic efficiency is relevant.

The first involves *efficiency in the internal economic union*. This requires that there be free and non-distorted flows of goods, services, labour and capital across the borders within the federation. This can only be achieved if lower level governments do not engage in actions that, intentionally or otherwise, impede cross-border flows. This is a very difficult principle to fulfill, and almost certainly will be violated to some extent. The essence of federalism is that lower level jurisdictions be able to enact policies within their spheres without restraint. These policies will almost certainly impinge upon cross-border flows. The challenge is to devise a system whereby distortions are the result of legitimate policy objectives, such as social policies or the protection of language and culture, and not the result of protectionism at the expense of other provinces.

The second involves the efficient provision of public goods and services. Some of these will be national in nature and others of a regional or local level. Moreover, some will be public in nature, some will involve infrastructure, and others will take the form of services to individuals or firms. Their efficient provision is a challenge because their allocation is outside the market. The quest for efficient provision of public goods and services is one of the main arguments for the decentralization of expenditures in a federation.

The third efficiency issue in federal systems is one that was emphasized in *Financing Confederation*, and is referred to as fiscal efficiency. The issue arises as a direct consequence of the decentralization of fiscal responsibilities. This brings with it differences in the need for public services and the fiscal capacity to finance them across jurisdictions. These differences can imply that otherwise identical persons receive different benefits per tax dollar in different jurisdictions, referred to as net fiscal benefits (NFBs). These NFB differences provide incentives for households and firms to relocate based on fiscal considerations rather than productivity. Such fiscally-induced migration will cause economic activity to be allocated inefficiently across provinces.[1]

Given the importance of NFBs for the design of the fiscal arrangements, it is worth dwelling briefly on their relevance and some caveats for policy purposes. First, it should be noted that NFB differences arise across jurisdictions only to the extent that public services are not financed by benefit taxation. The latter would imply that benefits are reflected in individual taxes so there can be no systematic differences in NFBs across provinces. The evidence is fairly convincing that services provided by provincial and local governments are, in fact, redistributive, in which case regions with higher resources are able to provide services at lower tax rates. Given that, NFB differences will arise from differences in the ability to raise revenues at given tax rates, as well as differences in the need for public services because of

---

[1]This source of inefficiency in a federation was first identified by Buchanan (1952). Its application in a Canadian context was due to Graham (1964), and formalized in Boadway and Flatters (1982a).

Robin Boadway

demographic differences. Differences in the cost of providing public services are not, however, sources of NFB differential that lead to fiscal inefficiency.

Second, there is an issue with respect to the empirical relevance of migration induced by differences in tax rates or spending programs across jurisdictions, which is mixed. Watson (1986) had argued, based on the empirical estimates of Winer and Gauthier (1982), that the efficiency cost was very low. However, that has been challenged in a recent paper by Wilson (2000) who argues that when one takes a stock rather than a flow perspective with respect to migration, the efficiency cost of fiscally induced migration is much higher. Others argue that the impact of NFB differentials on migration will be muted to some extent by capitalization into land prices. In short, the empirical evidence is not convincing one way or the other, especially when one considers that only labour migration is studied and not the movement of business activity more generally. However, it turns out that the case for equalizing NFB differentials does not rely solely on fiscally induced migration. A key part of the *Financing Confederation* argument was that fiscal equity arguments also call for equalization.

Finally, it should be noted that most arguments for equalization are based on static modes of analysis. There is growing realization that the development of regions in an economy may be influenced by agglomeration effects and other externalities, and these could have important implications for equalization and other transfers. This is yet unexplored terrain, and it is not at all obvious what the implications for equalization might be. On the one hand, to the extent that equalization causes economic activity to be spread more thinly across the country, the benefits of agglomeration are not being exploited. On the other, equalization might induce regions to develop more quickly precisely by reinforcing local agglomeration effects where they might not otherwise exist.

Redistributive Equity

Redistributive equity encompasses what public finance economists traditionally refer to as vertical equity. However, it has come to be interpreted more widely in recent years. One can think of there being three dimensions of redistributive equity, all of which are objectives of government policy.

The first of these is equality of opportunity, to which Section 36(1) draws attention. This can be thought of as an *ex ante* objective. The aim is for the public sector to offer redress for the different opportunities that households face to participate in the economy. Thus, youth are educated and trained to upgrade their skills and talents. Given that different persons are born with different abilities, equality of opportunity can be interpreted as requiring that society compensate to some extent for differences in abilities. But, of course, there are efficiency costs involved so equality of opportunity is bound to be less than perfect.

This leads to the second dimension of equity, equality of outcomes. This takes the form of *ex post* redistribution, such as through progressive taxation, income-tested or targeted transfers, and in-kind transfers.

The final form of redistribution is social insurance, which as the name implies is insurance offered by the public sector. This encompasses not just insurance in the usual meaning of the word, but also compensation for bad luck that is otherwise uninsurable privately, such as that resulting from bad demographic luck, ill health, unemployment and other misfortunes that are deemed not to be the responsibility of the person. Major social programs like unemployment insurance, disability benefits, workers' compensation, and health care fall into this category.

The relevance of redistributive equity for fiscal federalism should be evident. Virtually everything governments do at all levels have redistributive consequences. Moreover, some of the most important policy instruments used to achieve redistributive equity are in the hands of lower-level governments.

Horizontal Equity

The criterion of horizontal equity is widely accepted as an objective of government policy. However, its logical extension to a federal setting is contentious. Horizontal equity requires that persons who are equally well off in the absence of government ought to remain so after government policy. In other words, persons in comparable circumstances ought to be treated comparably by the government. Of course, there will be conceptual difficulties in determining who are equally well off, especially given differences in preferences and need among households, as well as differences in family size. For our purposes, we need not enter that debate; much income tax policy debate revolves around such issues. We can presume that there is some measure of real income or ability to pay that suitably reflects one's economic well-being.

Robin Boadway

In a federalism context, horizontal equity takes on special, and somewhat demanding, importance: persons of a given real income ought to be treated comparably no matter where they reside in the federation. This can be viewed as a form of equal treatment or fairness — everyone counts with the same weight in society's social welfare function — and can be interpreted as a natural consequence of citizenship. Two things should be emphasized. The first is that horizontal equity is compatible with any degree of vertical redistribution, and in that sense there is no conflict between the two objectives. Indeed, as noted below, there is no conflict between horizontal equity and efficiency either: in fact, the two are complementary.

Second, in a federation, it will not be literally possible, or desirable, to achieve horizontal equity to the fullest. That would require provinces and municipalities to apply exactly the same tax and expenditure policies, which is obviously inconsistent with the idea of federalism. Instead, horizontal equity must be compromised to a federal setting. One way of doing so, which is compatible with the views of *Financing Confederation*, is to ensure that all provinces have the potential to satisfy horizontal equity. This means that they must have the fiscal capacity to provide comparable levels of public services at comparable levels of tax rates, so they could, if they so choose, satisfy the requirements of horizontal equity. At the same time, they should not be compelled to provide exactly the same public service levels and have the same tax/transfer structures. (Of course, there may be reasons based on efficiency and redistributive equity why some harmonization of policies is desirable.) The objective of horizontal equity in potential terms has come to be referred to as fiscal equity.[2] Like fiscal efficiency, it is achieved by equalizing NFBs across provinces, precisely the prescription found in Section 36(2).

Not all economists will agree with the above objectives. And, even if they do, they will not agree with the prescriptions. There are three main sources of disagreement. The first is that different economists will make different judgements about the relative weight to be given to equity versus efficiency. Moreover, they may not accept the values embodied in the principle of fiscal equity, that is, equal treatment of comparable citizens no matter where they reside. Unfortunately, alternative principles are not readily found in the

---

[2]The concept of fiscal equity is due to Buchanan (1950). *Financing Confederation* and Boadway and Flatters (1982b) proposed a restricted version of fiscal equity referred to as narrow-based fiscal equity as an attempt to take account of the presumed property rights of provincial residents in their own jurisdictions.

literature, though presumably they have to do with some notion of differences in property rights depending on where one resides. The second source of disagreement concerns one's views of the benevolence of government. The less benevolent the government is thought to be, the less willing might one be to have the government involved in the economy, including in its redistributive functions. Roughly speaking, those who put low weight on equity and low weight on benevolence tend to prefer government to be smaller and less redistributive. They will also tend to favour decentralization as a brake on both intervention and redistribution. Finally, economists may disagree with the way the markets work, especially the severity of the trade-off between equity and efficiency. This too can lead to different views of the role of government, but differences that are less ideologically charged.

Whatever one's views of the role of government, the incontrovertible fact is that much of what governments do through their budgets — especially that which is controversial — is redistributive in nature and intent. This is reflected in the most important policy instruments used. These include the progressive tax system, including transfers administered through the tax system; targeted transfers to the needy; social insurance programs (unemployment insurance, workers' compensation, pensions, disability); health-care expenditures; education and training. These comprise a substantial proportion of what governments do, and are of critical importance to the fiscal arrangements, given the shared responsibility between the federal government and the provinces for social policy.

Federalism and Decentralization

The essence of federalism is decentralized decision-making, although this is by no means restricted to federations. The arguments for decentralization of fiscal responsibilities are well known and widely accepted among economists. The big issue is how to manage the consequences of decentralization.

The alleged benefits of decentralization can be briefly summarized. They amount largely to improving the efficiency of delivering public services. Lower jurisdictions can cater to local needs and preferences. They are better informed about these needs and preferences as well as about local cost conditions, which they are better able to control. So-called agency costs arising from the imperfect ability to monitor service deliverers are less, and

Robin Boadway

layers of bureaucracy are reduced. Innovation is enhanced by decentralized provision by independent units of government. And, efficiency and accountability improvements are induced by decentralization and the competitive federalism that accompanies it. These arguments apply especially to the delivery of local public goods, the delivery of services to households and firms, and the delivery of targeted transfers. These include many policy instruments that are of importance from a redistributive point of view.

It is important to note that the benefits of decentralization apply largely to the expenditure side of the budget. There are no particular benefits to decentralizing taxation, except perhaps those based on accountability. Indeed, while many multi-level governments decentralize the provision of public services in the key areas of health, education and welfare, the decentralization of revenue-raising varies widely across countries (and even within them with respect to provincial-local fiscal arrangements). In other words, countries have a wide variety of discretion in the extent of the so-called vertical fiscal imbalance (VFI). The decentralization of revenue-raising responsibility in Canada — and the effective VFI — is probably the greatest in the Organisation for Economic Co-operation and Development (OECD) countries.[3]

This leads us to the potential costs of fiscal decentralization, including the decentralization of both spending and taxing decisions. These can be grouped under the usual headings of efficiency and equity.

Efficiency

Three sorts of efficiency effects of decentralization of fiscal responsibility can be identified. The first are distortions in the internal economic union simply because of uncoordinated or different policies that affect cross-border trade in labour, capital, goods and services. These reflect *fiscal externalities* arising from tax or expenditure competition: policies implemented in one province will affect the well-being of households in other provinces either

---

[3]One must be cautious in interpreting statistics on the VFI. Some countries, like Germany, might appear to have a low VFI because of revenue-sharing agreements that direct a proportion of federal revenues to the states. However, revenue-sharing is really a form of transfer because the states have no individual discretion over their amount or structure.

directly or indirectly through its effect on provincial budgets.[4] Such externalities can be positive, such as when one province provides public services that benefit residents of neighbouring provinces. These fiscal externalities often provide a basis for policy harmonization and/or federal intervention. Negative externalities are more pervasive, and include such things as tax distortions on interprovincial trade, beggar-thy-neighbour policies, residency restrictions for the use of public services, and policies of discrimination or local protection. Some of these reflect legitimate policies of a social, linguistic, cultural, environmental, or labour standards nature and must be simply taken as a cost of federalism. They may also represent legitimate differences in provincial preferences over tax-transfer policies. In fact, as in the international sphere, it is hard to distinguish protection from legitimate social policy, which is why it has been very difficult to implement effective free trade within the internal economic union, or to achieve an understanding of the role of the federal government in fostering efficiency in the internal economic union.

The second source of inefficiency is a relatively newly discovered phenomenon referred to as vertical fiscal externalities.[5] This refers to the fact that provincial level fiscal decisions have effects that spill over onto the federal government, and thereby to residents of other provinces. For example, an income tax increase in one province reduces the tax base and thereby causes federal tax revenues to shrink. This is a cost of revenue-raising that is neglected by the province and leads to an incentive to over-expand. The overall consequences of this are not obvious. Vertical fiscal externalities work in a direction that offsets horizontal tax competition, so it is not obvious that on balance it is a bad thing. Nor is it clear how the fiscal arrangements can overcome them, except perhaps by either limiting the extent of decentralization of revenue-raising responsibilities to the provinces or implementing effective tax harmonization agreements.

The third source of inefficiency is what we have referred to as fiscal inefficiency. Recall from above that decentralization in itself entails that

---

[4]A taxonomy of fiscal externalities and how they affect the efficiency of resource allocation may be found in Dahlby (1996).

[5]Canadian economists especially have been involved in their study, including Boadway and Keen (1996); Dahlby (1996); Boadway, Marchand and Vigneault (1998); and Dahlby and Wilson (2000). For a general survey of vertical fiscal externalities and their relevance, see Keen (1998).

different provinces will have different capacities to provide public services to their citizens because of differences in tax capacity and need. Given that the activities of provincial governments are redistributive in nature (rather than being based on the benefit principle), differences in NFBs will arise that provide a purely fiscal incentive to economic activity to gravitate towards more advantaged provinces. This is a critical efficiency effect for the fiscal arrangements, since it is one that can readily be corrected without compromising the integrity of the federation. A system of unconditional equalizing transfers can effectively undo NFB differences and thus facilitate the very process of decentralization. The more decentralization there is, the greater is the need for fiscal equalization (but also the more difficult it may be to achieve politically).

Equity

Decentralization can have parallel effects on the extent and structure of redistribution policies implemented by the various levels of government in a federation. Evaluating these effects is much more tenuous than in the case of efficiency since additional value judgements are involved. As in the case of horizontal fiscal externalities, interprovincial competition for business activity and for tax bases can result in a competing down of redistribution policies. Provinces have an incentive to attract higher income persons and firms at the expense of lower income ones or those who are likely to be heavier users of public services. The extent to which this competing down of redistribution (the co-called race to the bottom) occurs in practice is more a matter of anecdotal evidence than substantiated analysis.[6] As well, the influence of vertical fiscal externalities tempers horizontal competition effects. To the extent that the costs of redistribution can be shifted to the federal budget, provinces will be induced to over-redistribute, and this latter effect can dominate if transfer-recipients are relatively immobile.

Whether or not these fiscal externalities induce too much or too little redistribution, different provinces are almost certainly likely to adopt different standards of redistribution with respect to various groups. As we

---

[6]There is, however, some strong evidence that provincial welfare policies respond to incentives introduced by federal shared-cost versus block-funding. See the recent study by Baker, Payne and Smart (1999).

have argued, redistribution policy is multi-faceted, and relies on a variety of policy instruments. It would be surprising if different provinces adopted similar structures. The consequence is that from a national point of view, needy persons of a given type in different provinces may face very different standards of redistribution, potentially violating the notions of equal opportunity, reduction in economic disparity and the availability of public services of reasonable quality set out in Section 36(1).

Whether one should be concerned with differences in standards of redistribution across provinces is a matter of judgement. It could certainly be argued that the essence of federalism is that different provinces should be able to choose their own standards of redistribution. At the same time, this might be tempered by the fact that these differences may simply reflect the consequences of fiscal competition. It might also be argued that citizenship in a nation implies some minimal expectation of reasonably comparable treatment in different jurisdictions, as set out in Section 36(1). This is obviously a debate that is well beyond economics.

One remaining equity consequence of decentralization is less susceptible to concerns about the nature of federalism and the desire for autonomy by provincial governments in their own spheres of legislative authority. As we have stressed, decentralization inevitably results in differences in fiscal capacity and need across provinces. If these are not addressed citizens in different provinces will receive different levels of service for given tax rates. In addition to providing incentives for inefficient fiscally induced migration, these also result in fiscal inequity. This, along with the complementary principle found in Section 36(2), provides a strong case for full equalization of fiscal capacities across jurisdictions. Equalization is in a sense the quintessential instrument of federalism. It equips the provinces with the ability to provide comparable levels of public services to their citizens at comparable tax rates, without at the same time compelling them to do so. It thus represents a healthy compromise between achieving horizontal equity and fiscal efficiency on the one hand, and maintaining effective decentralization on the other.[7]

---

[7]Another role of equalization is sometimes stressed, and that is its role as a risk-sharing device. It effectively acts as a form of insurance against adverse shocks to provinces' tax bases. This was not stressed in *Financing Confederation*, but is in no way inconsistent with equalization as a device for addressing fiscal efficiency and equity.

The Fiscal Arrangements: Can They Deliver?

Standard fiscal federalism theory holds that the fiscal arrangements represent the means by which decentralization can be facilitated, while at the same time the costs of decentralization are contained, the principles of the constitution are fulfilled, and the responsibilities of the federal government in achieving national objectives are accomplished. The greater the amount of decentralization, the more important are the fiscal arrangements, but at the same time the more difficult and challenging their task.

The extent of decentralization in Canada has evolved dramatically over the past four decades, especially since the years of fiscal restraint in the early 1990s. For example, the proportion of public spending (excluding inter-governmental transfers) attributable to the provinces and their municipalities went from 47 per cent in 1961 to 61 per cent in 1999. Over the same period, the provincial share of total revenues went from 40 per cent to 53 per cent, and federal transfers as a share of provincial revenues declined from 22 per cent to 13 per cent. This change has been accompanied by a change in the structure of federal-provincial transfers. Equalization payments doubled in the 1980s from about $3.6 billion to $7.3 billion, while block grants for health, education and welfare rose by about 70 per cent from about $8 billion to $13.5 billion. In the 1990s, equalization rose by much less, from $7.3 billion to $8.5 billion, partly reflecting the fiscal retrenchment at the provincial level. At the same time, block transfers for health, education and welfare actually declined from $13.5 billion to $12.5 billion.

As mentioned, provinces in Canada now have much more fiscal autonomy than in virtually any other federation in the world. It can be presumed that this decentralization is virtually irreversible; indeed, it seems to breed further decentralization. The issue is whether the fiscal arrange-ments can cope with this degree of fiscal decentralization. To me this is an open question.

Much depends upon the view one takes of the role of the federal government. The constitution provides some limited guidance here. The legislative powers of the federal government are not controversial. What is controversial is how these powers — especially taxation, regulation and the spending power — are used in areas that overlap with provincial legislative responsibilities. Some guidance is found in section 36, which as we have seen gives the federal government some responsibility for ensuring that equality of opportunity and the provision of basic public services apply across the country. However, this does not clearly specify the role of the federal government in achieving either efficiency in the internal economic union or national equity. And, it is not just a matter of agreeing to these objectives as goals of government. One can vigorously argue for national efficiency and equity as legitimate objectives of government, but at the same time take the position that the federal government is not primarily responsible for achieving them.[8] Our position, which is consistent with that taken by *Financing Confederation*, is that the federal government has a legitimate interest in national efficiency and equity objectives, and that without federal initiative it is unlikely that these objectives can be suitably addressed.

The components of the fiscal arrangements can be summarized as follows.

Vertical Fiscal Imbalance

In virtually every multi-level system of government, including federations, higher level governments collect more in revenue than they need for their own program expenditures. This is true with respect to the federal government and the provinces in Canada, as well as with respect to the provinces and their municipalities. Interjurisdictional transfers, of course, balance this VFI. In itself, the existence of a VFI between the federal government and the provinces reduces the incidence of fiscal externalities, contributes to harmonization of tax and transfer policies, avoids excessive fiscal imbalance, without at the same time necessarily reducing provincial responsibility in the areas of provincial legislative responsibility. But it does so largely by making the federal government preponderant, allegedly at the expense of provincial autonomy and accountability. Moreover, this preponderance lends itself to the possibility that the transfers used to close the VFI are used in ways that expose the provinces to the uncertainly associated with unannounced changes.

---

[8]Indeed, some might argue that they are objectives that could be achieved by collaborative provincial action, with minimal participation by the federal government. The position taken by Courchene (1996) is close to that.

Equalization

Equalization is the *sine qua non* of fiscal decentralization, and is also present in virtually every multi-level system of government. Its purpose in the Canadian federation is twofold. First, from a constitutional point of view, it is meant to fulfill the principles of both parts of Section 36 of the *Constitution Act*. That is, it redresses the differences in fiscal capacity that come about simply from fiscal decentralization (the equalization principle of Section 36(2)), and it facilitates the ability of provinces to achieve the objectives set out in Section 36(1). Second, by redressing fiscal capacity differences, equalization avoids the fiscal inefficiencies and fiscal inequities that would otherwise arise, a position well documented in *Financing Confederation*.

There has been much debate about the relevance of these problems, and a large literature has developed.[9] Some allege that fiscal inefficiency is empirically unimportant. More important, others do not accept the value judgement on which the notion of fiscal inequity is based, essentially a notion of equal treatment of citizens regardless of where they reside. Suffice it to say that it is the principle that underlies Section 36(2), and, it seems to be a natural extension of the notion of citizenship and equal treatment. It is a principle that does not detract from the responsibilities meant to be enjoyed by the provinces. And, it applies whatever one's views about the redistributive role of government. In short, it is a very powerful principle, and one that is widely accepted.

The Spending Power

The spending power represents the only realistic policy instrument available to the federal government to achieve its presumed responsibilities for efficiency and equity in the economic union, and its joint constitutional responsibility with respect to redistributive equity (Section 36(1)).[10] In much

---

[9]See the recent overview in Boadway and Hobson (1998).

[10]In principle, the federal government could use its power of disallowance to cajole the provinces into conformity. But that is clearly an unrealistic alternative to the spending power. Other alternatives that involve collective federal-provincial decision-making are discussed below.

of the economic literature, its use is taken for granted. As with equalization, the spending power is also a widely used instrument in all federations around the world, and usually with less controversy (Watts, 1999). It has been found by the courts to be a constitutionally valid federal policy instrument (Hogg, 1996), and it underlies some of the most important federal social policy initiatives, including refundable tax credits, grants to various institutions including universities, the Canada Health and Social Transfer, shared cost transfers, and even equalization.

Its use is not without difficulty, quite apart from concerns of a political nature. It can be viewed as intrusive and unpredictable, especially if it is used in intrusive and unpredictable ways! While there is nothing inherent in the spending power that requires that it be used unilaterally, unpredictably and without adequate consultation, detractors argue that since the instrument is ultimately a federal legislative power involving budgetary spending, it is prone to such problems. Not surprisingly, there is a constant search for alternatives that might avoid these difficulties. The main alternative is negotiation and joint decision-making, the final element of the fiscal arrangements.

Policy Harmonization

Interjurisdictional agreement over the structure of tax or expenditure policies is an alternative to the spending power, with or without the connivance of the federal government. It is not the only alternative, but others would be even less palatable than the spending power. These include the use of federal mandates, the power of disallowance, or resort to the courts. Examples of these occur in other federations around the world, but it seems clear that they would be unacceptable in our decentralized federation (and they were not seriously considered in *Financing Confederation*).

We have had some mixed experience in Canada with policy harmonization. There have been various tax collection agreements that have served to harmonize various taxes between the federal government and several provinces. These include the highly successful income tax collection agreements, which have been widely regarded as model forms of tax harmonization. Harmonization of sales taxes has been much less widespread, but has enjoyed some success with the Quebec Sales tax and the Harmonized Sales Tax in three of the Atlantic provinces. The federal-provincial agreement on child tax credits can be regarded as successful, as can the Canada Pension

Plan. On the other hand, the Agreement on Internal Trade (AIT), intended to bring some order to interprovincial trade, is notable for its lack of bite. And, the Social Union Framework Agreement (SUFA) changes the status quo relatively little. It is notable that the main successes among these agreements occur when the federal government uses it spending or taxing power as a carrot or stick.

Canada has been a bit of an innovator in the use of federal-provincial agreements, perhaps being driven by the imperatives of decentralization. The extent of success remains to be seen. There are two grounds for being sceptical about the efficacy of federal-provincial agreements as means of achieving national policy objectives. First, negotiating a successful agreement can only be done with unanimous consent. Not only is that difficult to do with ten to fourteen governments involved, by its nature it implies that such agreements cannot involve any redistribution among provinces. That rules out effective agreements involving national equity considerations. Second, to be effective, such agreements must have a means of enforcement — a so-called dispute settlement mechanism — and that must be binding. The most successful agreements have been the tax collection agreements, and that has been because the federal government was effectively able to induce the provinces into participation because of the disparity in tax room that existed when the agreements were negotiated. It is instructive that these agreements are undergoing a considerable transformation as the balance of tax room shifts gradually in favour of the provinces.

Tensions Resolved versus Tensions Created

The past four decades have witnessed a gradual decentralization in fiscal responsibilities to the provinces, a trend that was abruptly accelerated in the early 1990s. Our federation is now the most decentralized federation in the world. The proportion of subnational government revenues that come from own sources is the highest among all federations. The subnational share of total government expenditures is also among the highest. And, provinces in Canada exercise more actual discretion over their own spending than in other federations, where mandates, conditionality and federal oversight are often the norm. Some of this decentralization has been a result of conscious policy. But, most of it has occurred piecemeal as the cumulative result of a series of decisions taken as part of the budgetary process, and in response to fiscal pressures that have had little to do with fiscal federalism. Indeed, it could be held that the process of decentralization itself fed centrifugal tendencies rather than the reverse. In other words, decentralization has done more to create tensions than to resolve them.

There are many signs of strain in virtually all aspects of the federal system. The following list is intended to indicate the strains that now exist in the system.

Equalization. Most seriously, the equalization system and the will to maintain it are in peril, at the same time that fiscal disparities are more likely to rise than to fall. The latter is an inevitable consequence of the gradual decentralization of revenue-raising responsibility to the provinces: for a given pattern of per capita tax bases across provinces, fiscal capacity differences are greater the larger is the amount of revenues raised by the provinces. The equalization system is no longer comprehensive, and is unable to cope with the huge disparities arising from oil and gas revenues. The current system does not even accomplish what *Financing Confederation* referred to as the narrow-based approach to dealing with resource revenues. It suffers from a number of structural defects that are likely to be more serious as the federation becomes more decentralized. For example, equalization is based solely on revenue-raising capacity, whereas disparities in the ability to provide reasonably comparable levels of public services at reasonably comparable levels of taxation can arise because of different demographic compositions of provincial populations. These differences in the need for public services are components of equalization in many other countries (e.g., Australia, South Africa, Japan, Scandinavia). Proposals that are now on the table, such as moving to an apparently simpler macro formula, are unlikely to resolve the underlying problems.

The Spending Power. As the VFI has fallen, the federal government has effectively lost control of the spending power. This means that there is no effective mechanism by which they can exercise their responsibility for pursuing equality of opportunity and for maintaining reasonable standards of quality in public services. There are many who would argue that this is a good thing, but so far there is no effective alternative in place for achieving national equity objectives.

The Economic Union. Nor is there a mechanism for maintaining the integrity of the internal economic union. There are signs that both national equity standards and the efficiency of the economic union are beginning to erode. Examples can be found in provincial tax policies (tax holidays, preferential treatment for provincial residents), education policies (differential fees, local preferences in university admissions, preferential tax treatment of provincial scholars) and welfare policies (waiting periods and rate reductions). International free trade has itself enhanced the incentives for provinces to engage in tax competition, expenditure competition and beggar-thy-neighbour policies with respect to one another.

Tax Harmonization. The income tax system is becoming disharmonized, and provinces seem to be engaged in competitive reductions in income tax progressivity. Attempts at harmonizing the sales tax system have been stalled, and are unlikely to make any headway in the near future.

Cooperative Solutions. Attempts at arriving at cooperative solutions by federal-provincial negotiation have not been very successful. We have discussed above the fact that the most successful negotiated arrangements seem to be in circumstances in which enforcement is implicitly achieved by the federal power of the purse.

It may well be that the decentralized Canadian federation will evolve into one in which provinces behave "cooperatively" with respect to national objectives of efficiency and equity. After all, provinces do not take their decisions in isolation. However, there is little evidence that we are evolving to such a cooperative outcome. Perhaps the time has come for an updated version of *Financing Confederation*. Unfortunately, we now lack the Economic Council of Canada from which the original wisdom emanated. As well, we lack institutions such as the Commonwealth Grants Commission in Australia or the Financial and Fiscal Commission in South Africa that could do the job. These bodies have the mandate to take a longer run view of the evolution of their respective federations, one that is at arm's length from the year-to-year budgetary problems of the central government. In both cases, the force and logic of their recommendations have been very influential in formulating policy.

References

Baker, M., A. Payne and M. Smart (1999), "An Empirical Study of Matching Grants: The 'Cap on CAP'", *Journal of Public Economics* 72, 269-288.

Boadway, R.W. and F.R. Flatters (1982a), "Efficiency and Equalization Payments in a Federal System of Government: A Synthesis and Extension of Recent Results", *Canadian Journal of Economics* 15, 613-633.

_____ (1982b), *Equalization in a Federal State: An Economic Analysis* (Ottawa: Economic Council of Canada).

Boadway, R.W. and P.A.R. Hobson, eds. (1998), *Equalization, Its Contribution to Canada's Economic and Fiscal Progress* (Kingston: John Deutsch Institute, Queen's University).

Boadway, R.W. and M. Keen (1996), "Efficiency and the Optimal Direction of Federal-State Transfers", *International Tax and Public Finance* 3, 137-155.

Boadway, R.W., M. Marchand and M. Vigneault (1998), "The Consequences of Overlapping Tax Bases for Redistribution and Public Spending in a Federation", *Journal of Public Economics* 68, 453-478.

Buchanan, J.M. (1950), "Federalism and Fiscal Equity", *American Economic Review* 40, 583-599.

_____ (1952), "Federal Grants and Resource Allocation", *Journal of Political Economy* 60, 208-217.

Courchene, T. (1996), *ACCESS: A Convention on the Canadian Economic and Social Systems*, a working paper prepared for the Ministry of Intergovernmental Affairs (Toronto: Government of Ontario).

Dahlby, B. (1996), "Fiscal Externalities and the Design of Intergovernmental Grants", *International Tax and Public Finance* 3, 397-411.

Dahlby, B. and L.S. Wilson (2000), "Vertical Fiscal Externalities and the Provision of Productivity-Enhancing Activities by Sub-National Governments", unpublished manuscript (Edmonton: University of Alberta).

Graham, J.F. (1964), *Intergovernmental Fiscal Relationships* (Toronto: Canadian Tax Foundation).

Hogg, P. (1996), *Constitutional Law of Canada*, 4th ed. (Toronto: Carswell).

Keen, M.J. (1998), "Vertical Fiscal Externalities in the Theory of Fiscal Federalism", *International Monetary Fund Staff Papers* 45, 454-484.

Watson, W.G. (1986), "An Estimate of the Welfare Gain from Fiscal Equalization", *Canadian Journal of Economics* 19, 298-308.

Watts, R.C. (1999), *The Spending Power in Federal Systems: A Comparative Study* (Kingston: Institute of Intergovernmental Relations, Queen's University).

Wilson, L.S. (2000), "Efficiency and Migration: Watson Revisited", unpublished manuscript (Edmonton: University of Alberta).

Winer, S.L. and D. Gauthier (1982), *Internal Migration and Fiscal Structure: An Econometric Study of the Determinants of Interregional Migration in Canada* (Ottawa: Economic Council of Canada).

Taxation

Tax Policy and Tax Research in Canada

Richard Bird and Michael Smart

Introduction

Many people seem to think that taxation is like the weather. Everyone talks about it but no one does anything about it. This common impression is quite wrong for Canada. Even excluding such major upheavals as the 1971 income tax revision that followed the report of the Carter Commission, almost every year the federal government does something about the tax system: it introduces new levies or alters existing taxes by changing their rates or bases. Sometimes such changes amount to little more than tinkering. Sometimes they indicate major changes in direction. In recent years, provincial governments too have made more and more tax policy changes — introducing an incentive here, adjusting a rate or base there, or, occasionally, making major changes such as "provincializing" all or some of the property tax or changing from a "tax-on-tax" to a "tax-on-base" approach to personal income taxation.

To what extent are such tax policy changes based upon, or supported by, economic research? This is the question that we consider in this paper. It is an important question, not least because one of the main results emerging from much recent research in public economics is that taxes affect economic incentives in many complex, sometimes unexpected, and often significant ways. One effect of the Carter Commission in the 1960s was that a group of serious and well-informed academic analysts of tax policy became established in Canadian universities. Did the subsequent output of serious research papers on tax matters affect tax policy?[1] Why do some research results seem to have been largely ignored, while others appear to have had much more impact? Are there academically respectable ways in which the work of researchers might be rendered more productive in terms of public policy impact? These are some of the questions raised, if not always answered very satisfactorily, in this brief paper.

Personal Income Taxes

An outstanding feature of Canadian tax policy in the last decade of the twentieth century was the extent to which Canada, almost alone among the Organisation for Economic Co-operation and Development (OECD) countries, attacked its deficit problem by increasing the share of personal income taxes in gross domestic product (GDP). Despite the importance economists typically assign to the incentive effects of income taxes, this trend received surprisingly little attention in academic or policy circles through much of the period. Although the effects of taxes on out-migration from Canada seem small (Helliwell, 1999) relative to their impact on purely domestic decision-making, it was more perceptions of a "brain drain" than concern for the effects of taxes on the domestic economy that led to tax rates becoming a focus of recent political debate.

High marginal tax rates (MTRs) induce a variety of changes in the behaviour of taxpayers, with resulting economic costs. Changes in hours worked and in labour force participation — the standard preoccupations of the theory of income taxation — are, of course, especially important, but tax-induced changes may also include a variety of tax avoidance devices, such as substitution from taxable to non-taxable consumption, changes in the timing of income realizations, changes in the form of compensation (including incorporation), use of deferred compensation and other tax shelters, and increases in tax evasion. Understanding the magnitude of such behavioural responses to tax rate changes is critical to forecasting the effects

---

[1]An earlier paper touching on this question is Bird and Wilson (1999).

Richard Bird and Michael Smart

of tax reforms on government revenues. It is also essential to measuring the *excess burden* of taxation — the loss in welfare due to the tax system in excess of the revenue raised for government.

As marginal tax rates rose through the 1990s, economists increasingly measured their levels and debated their effects on economic activity. Davies and Zhang (1996), for instance, analyzed the changes in MTR schedules over the post-war period. They stressed the long upward trend in the average of marginal tax rates faced by all taxpayers since 1949, but particularly in the 1960s and 1970s. Davies (1998) extended the analysis to address recent tax reforms. He provides a useful review of the economic principles that might guide the design of an income tax system and the evaluation of existing MTR schedules. High MTRs are unambiguously undesirable in efficiency terms, as they create disincentives to work and pay taxes. On the other hand, although high MTRs do not per se increase the progressivity in the tax system, high MTRs for *some* taxpayers are a necessary condition for a progressive income tax. If the tax system is to apply low or negative *average* tax rates to low-income families and higher average tax rates to those with higher incomes, it follows that some taxpayers with intermediate incomes must face high *marginal* tax rates.

These statements may be uncontroversial. Unfortunately, they are also not particularly useful. The difficult practical question concerns where in the income distribution those high MTRs should be levied. Economists argue there are three basic principles that should govern this choice. First, the economic cost of a high MTR is proportionally larger the more people there are in the relevant tax bracket. Second, the cost of a high MTR is also worse the higher the wage rate received by taxpayers in the relevant bracket. Although this simply reflects the fact that work disincentives are more costly to the economy the more valuable is the labour that is lost, the notion that we should spend more time worrying about tax disincentives faced by stock-brokers than by high school dropouts is not one that goes over well in public discussion. Third, a high MTR is more costly when applied to a tax base that is more responsive to tax rates — when, for example, affected taxpayers may easily substitute from paid work to unpaid family care, or from conventional employment to activities in the less-taxed informal sector, or they may even move to another country.

A convenient summary statistic of behavioural responses to taxation is the "elasticity of taxable income" proposed by Feldstein (1995) — the average percentage decrease in a taxpayer's taxable income due to all behavioural responses when the taxpayer's marginal share (one minus the marginal tax rate) is decreased by 1 per cent. Examining the effects of the 1986 U.S. tax reform on a sample of taxpayers, Feldstein estimated the elasticity of taxable income to be quite large, with preferred estimates ranging from 1.0 to 1.5. To put these estimates in perspective, note that an elasticity of one implies that government revenues would reach their maximum level at a tax rate of 50 per cent; further tax increases would actually decrease revenues. Feldstein's work might to some extent be viewed as an attempt to give some academic respectability to the supply-side arguments of the 1980s. Nonetheless, it provides a useful tool that may help make old arguments about efficiency more meaningful and palatable to policymakers.

Recently, several authors have used similar tools to study the effects of taxation in Canada, providing robust evidence of tax avoidance behaviour. Silaama and Veall (2001) apply a refined version of Feldstein's method to Canadian data and find evidence of much smaller, though still substantial, responsiveness of taxable income to marginal tax rates. Analogous to Feldstein's approach, they look for changes in the reported incomes of a group of taxpayers following the 1988 personal tax reform, which flattened marginal tax rate schedules. Their point estimate of the elasticity for Canada is 0.25.[2] Silaama and Veall also find evidence of far greater responsiveness to taxes for the self-employed, for workers nearing retirement age, and for high-income taxpayers. Gagné, Nadeau and Vaillancourt (2001) adopt a different approach. They measure the response to tax rate changes of total taxable income in each province and in a number of income ranges for the 1972–96 period. While their results are not directly comparable to Silaama and Veall's, they also find robust evidence that taxable income responds to tax rate changes. Despite this empirical support for the "economists' prescription" of an optimal income tax rate structure sketched above, it is far from clear that such arguments have as yet had any significant influence on the tax policy debate in Canada. The average MTR has certainly come down over time, but the structure of MTRs hardly accords with what analysis suggests.

A second major change in Canadian personal income taxation during the 1990s was the introduction of substantial income-tested tax credits for families with children, now known as the National Child Benefit (NCB)

---

[2]Cast in the same "Laffer curve" terms as the Feldstein estimate cited earlier, this implies a revenue-maximizing tax rate for Canada of 80 per cent.

system. These child tax benefits are "clawed back" from families with incomes between about 50 and 80 per cent of median family income at rates as high as 30 per cent before applying standard personal income tax rates. The result is that high marginal tax rates are no longer the exclusive province of high-income taxpayers in Canada. Somewhat similar "claw-back" systems are applied to both Employment Insurance (EI) and Old Age Security (OAS) payments.

The refundable credit system seems to have been conceived at least in part as an attempt to integrate the tax treatment of children with provincial social assistance and, in the process, dismantle the "welfare wall" that created work disincentives for poor families with children. While the policies may have such salutary effects — there appears to be no clear evidence one way or the other — they may at the same time be bringing the problems of traditional welfare programs into the tax system and, increasingly, subjecting the average Canadian family to the perverse incentives that were once reserved for welfare recipients.[3] Poschmann and Richards (2000) argue forcefully that this is indeed the case. They analyze the clawbacks associated with various federal and provincial family benefit programs and show that marginal tax rates typically range from 50 to 70 per cent (and are, in some cases, even higher), even for moderately low family incomes.

If clawbacks are indeed driving MTRs too high, two very different directions of reform might be contemplated. First, the clawback rates might be reduced, mitigating the disincentive effects and spreading them over a greater number of taxpayers.[4] Alternatively, and perhaps paradoxically, clawback rates could instead be *increased*, thus concentrating disincentive effects on a narrower income band and therefore affecting fewer taxpayers. Enhancing the targeting of family benefits in this way might achieve desired redistribution while confining MTRs to the places in the income distribution where they would do the least harm, in economic (if not necessarily political) terms.

Economists appear divided on this issue. A recent study by the C.D. Howe Institute, for example, calls for reductions in clawback rates (Robson,

---

[3]See Battle and Torjman (1994) on the implicit tax rates facing welfare recipients in Ontario.

[4]This strategy is implicit in the government's recent decision to raise the break-even threshold for the NCB to $35,000, which will reduce MTRs for an affected family with two children by about eight percentage points.

Mintz and Poschmann, 2000). Others have expressed caution about this tendency for the clawbacks to creep their way up the income distribution (Boadway, 1999; Davies, 1999). This debate leads to few definitive conclusions. One reason may be because the focus of the recent debate on marginal tax rates misses some important complexities in the analysis of disincentive effects.

A high MTR discourages an individual from working additional hours (and may have other effects as well, such as on work in the informal or underground economy, self-employment, and so on). But the decision as to whether to participate in the labour force — and the choice between full-time and part-time work — depends more on the difference in *average* tax rates between low and middle income levels than on the MTRs levied at specific points in the distribution. A policy that clawed back more benefits from low and middle income families might have undesirable effects on participation, particularly of secondary earners. This may be especially true now that the federal Working Income Supplement has been abolished.

The trade-off between disincentives to hours worked and disincentives to participation thus needs to be evaluated carefully in designing the tax system. Which effect is more important is fundamentally an empirical matter. Unfortunately, there is little evidence for Canada that might inform the current debate. In particular, the literature provides no hard evidence about the effects of the reforms of the 1990s on the labour supply patterns of affected families in Canada. *Faute de mieux* — and not for the first time — policy analysts in Canada must rely on research into the effects of similar programs in the United States to assess the impact of family tax benefits. Fortunately, the U.S. Earned Income Tax Credit (EITC) closely resembles Canada's child tax benefits, with a maximum benefit of about C$5,500. The EITC generated MTRs in the clawback range in excess of 50 per cent, high by U.S. standards, but well below the tax rates currently induced by the corresponding Canadian programs.

To assess the behavioural consequences of the EITC, Eissa and Liebman (1996) examined its effects using the "natural experiment" approach that is now the workhorse of empirical policy evaluation. In this instance, the idea is that the policy change should affect single women with children (who were eligible for EITC), but not single women without children. These two groups should be affected in about the same way on average by changing labour market conditions or other changes during the reform period. The data thus provide "treatment" and "control" groups, on the basis of which the separate effects of the policy can be discerned. Eissa and Liebman found substantial effects on participation by single women with children, relative to that of single women without children. At the same time, there was no discernible drop in hours worked by mothers already in the labour force, despite the disincentives associated with the clawback and the income effects of the transfer.[5]

One must of course be careful in applying these results to Canada.[6] For example, the labour supply of women is often estimated to be more responsive to after-tax wage rates in the United States than in Canada. Moreover, the U.S. policy is directed at single mothers, and married women with children might respond very differently to the Canadian policy. For example, the clawback might influence their choice between full-time and part-time work. Nevertheless, there does appear to be good evidence that participation responds to tax incentives more than do hours. If so, the high MTRs in the current system may be less important than the effects on participation that might result from a badly designed targeting system.

As provincial governments reform their own earned-income supplements, following the introduction of the National Child Benefit system and the abolition of the federal Working Income Supplement, the need for a closer look for concrete evidence about the costs and benefits of this strategy seems obvious. This is one area in which policymakers are obviously groping for a workable and acceptable solution, and good analysis and empirical evidence may well have a beneficial impact on policy.

Payroll Taxes

In part perhaps because many people do not really think of them as taxes, governments in Canada have come to rely increasingly on payroll taxes to the point where they are now the third most important source of revenue, after personal income and sales taxes. Indeed, as Dahlby (1993) reported some

---

[5]More recently, Meyer and Rosenbaum (2000) found even greater increases in participation by single mothers (relative to the appropriate control groups) following much larger reforms in incentives during the 1990s.

[6]For a more extensive review of this literature and its implications for Canada, see Mendelson (1997).

years ago, payroll taxes have for some time created a larger "tax wedge" for workers below median income than do personal income taxes. This trend seems certain to continue. Payroll tax rates will be ramped up in future years as contribution rates for the Canada and Quebec Pension Plans (CPP/QPP) and for provincial workers' compensation programs are increased. Although contribution rates for Employment Insurance, in contrast, are still near cyclical highs and are likely to decrease in future, a net increase in payroll taxes seems inevitable.[7]

Perhaps in part because tax lawyers and accountants have not been much concerned with payroll taxes, economists have, unusually, played a leading role in the debate over payroll taxation. Fortunately, payroll taxes are particularly amenable to empirical analysis. Much of the work which has been done has focused on determining the economic incidence of payroll taxes and their effects on employment. In the simplest terms, a payroll tax reduces employers' demand for labour, which may result in a fall in after-tax wages, if labour is supplied inelastically, or in a fall in employment, if labour supply is relatively elastic.

Business groups in Canada have tended to stress the employment effects of the tax, decrying payroll taxes as "job killers". In his work for the Ontario Fair Tax Commission, Dahlby (1993) pointed out that this effect was often overstated, however. Surveying previous evidence on the elasticities of labour supply and demand, he argued that labour likely bears more than 80 per cent of the burden of payroll taxes in the long run. In other words, the total compensation costs paid by employers are largely unaffected by payroll taxes, so that the employment effects of such taxes should be correspondingly small.

Direct empirical evidence for Canada reaches a more mixed conclusion. Di Matteo and Shannon (1995) used annual time-series data to estimate the impact of all taxes, including payroll taxes, on real wages and employment in Canada. According to their estimates, the burden of payroll tax increases is approximately equally shared between labour and employers. A 1 per cent rise in the payroll tax rate would cause real after-tax wages to fall by 0.44 per cent and employment to fall by 0.32 per cent. While these estimates may not be particularly robust, they suggest a greater impact of payroll taxation on employment than Dahlby's study.

---

[7] In addition, several provinces (particularly Quebec) levy payroll taxes on employers. These taxes too may creep up over time.

Richard Bird and Michael Smart

Of course, the economic effects of payroll taxes are unlikely to be much different on average than those of personal income or, for that matter, sales taxes (although there is no evidence that this thought has influenced tax policy). All these taxes drive a similar wedge between the cost of labour to employers and the return to employment of workers. In some respects, however, payroll taxes seem likely to have effects not shared by other taxes on labour and are worthy of further study.

The ceiling provisions in the major federal payroll tax systems (CPP/ QPP and EI), for example, imply the taxes are distortionary only for workers with below-average earnings. For workers above the ceilings, although contributions are still a tax on employment, they act as lump-sum taxes, with no impact on the return to additional hours worked. Coupled with the evidence on wage and employment effects cited above, this suggests that the current structure of payroll taxes may be one factor contributing to rising wage inequality among Canadian workers. In addition, it may also encourage employment of high-wage, full-time workers, at the expense of low-wage and part-time workers (Lin, Picot and Beach, 1996).

On the other hand, some payroll taxes act to a certain extent as benefit taxes, in that the benefits accruing to workers from additional hours of employment are roughly commensurate with additional tax liabilities. If the link from benefits to contributions were exact, then such taxes would in principle have no distortionary effect on employment decisions. In practice, however, some distortions inevitably persist, since contribution rates are not actuarially fair for individual workers and tax increases are often not linked to corresponding benefit increases. Nevertheless, some payroll taxes, where the link between contributions and benefits is strongest, may have different effects than others owing to this benefit connection. For instance, Vaillancourt and Marceau (1990), found some evidence that the incidence of workers' compensation taxes was different than for other payroll taxes, a finding which they attributed to its benefit tax element. This line of thought also suggests that a case can be made for earmarking payroll taxes for con-tributory social insurance programs, a practice that has otherwise received little support from economists.[8]

One way or another, payroll taxes seem likely to constitute a larger part of the tax mix in Canada in future years, regardless of the findings of economists. In the future, however, such findings may perhaps play a more

---

[8]For a discussion of earmarking in Canada, see Thirsk and Bird (1994).

important role than they have in the past in determining the magnitude of the increases and the design of further reforms.

Taxes on Corporations

Since corporate tax policy in Canada has recently been discussed in detail in the Mintz report (Canada, 1998), not to mention its many supporting technical papers, and since Professor Mintz himself is contributing a paper on taxes and savings to this volume, we shall not dwell on this subject here. We simply note that recent economic discussion of the corporate income tax has strongly supported on efficiency grounds the move towards base broadening and rate flattening advocated in the Mintz report and that these recommendations have been further urged by the growing concern with international tax competition. While the latter argument seems stronger in rhetoric than in evidence, Canada, like most countries, appears to have largely accepted these recommendations in principle, if not yet fully in practice.

It is easy to show that at the margin investment decisions with respect to industry, location, risk-taking, asset mix, and timing may be influenced by variations in effective tax rates. It is equally easy to show that choices with respect to organizational form, financial structure, and dividend policy may be equally distorted by tax policy. Many economists (e.g., Vickrey, 1991) have drawn the conclusion from such considerations that there is no place for a separate tax on corporate income in a sensible tax system, as indeed did the Carter report.

The case against taxing corporations has not been accepted so far in any country. Close examination (e.g., Bird, 1996) suggests that there are several good reasons to maintain separate taxes on corporations. Nonetheless, the case for reducing and to some extent restructuring such taxes has generally been accepted in recent years at both the federal and provincial levels. It is interesting to speculate whether this acceptance reflects the persuasiveness of economic argument, the politically powerful interests of capitalists, or some other factor. Suggestions have also been made that, while rates may continue their downward trend, bases may again be narrowed through incentives as governments continue their ceaseless search for instruments by

Richard Bird and Michael Smart

which to satisfy their apparent need to be seen to "do something" for politically influential groups.

More interesting, and more peculiar to Canada, has been the growth of non-income taxes on corporations, notably capital taxes, over the last decade or so. As the Mintz report shows, for many firms such taxes are now often more important than corporate income taxes, especially in years in which profits are not rising rapidly. One way in which Canadian governments have made up for the relative decline of corporate income tax revenues has been by imposing new, less profit-sensitive taxes on corporations. While Bird and Mintz (2000) have noted that there may be arguments supporting such taxes in some instances, it is hard to understand the rise of capital taxation in Canada other than as another proof of the adage that the easiest taxes to impose are those of which most people are not aware, those that can, if discovered, be said to penalize the rich and large, and those that no one is really sure who pays. Ignorance, it appears, may at times play as important a role as knowledge in determining tax policy.

Other Taxes

In terms of public perception, if not in revenue terms, undoubtedly the major change in Canadian tax policy in the last decade was the introduction of the Goods and Services Tax (GST) to replace the old Manufacturers' Sales Tax (MST). Economists entered fairly vigorously into the discussion preceding the GST, as usual expounding various views. While most economists, unlike most other participants in the debate, seemed generally sympathetic both to consumption taxes and to the less distorting effects of the GST compared to other forms of indirect taxation, some favoured payroll taxes instead (Kesselman, 1993), some appear to have favoured some other form of reformed sales tax (Whalley and Fretz, 1990), and some were concerned mainly to show that the GST would be either more or less regressive than some other tax to which it was compared.[9]

---

[9]See, for example, Grady (1990, 1991); Gillespie (1991a); and Ruggeri, Van Wart and Howard (1994a).

Unusually, the contribution of economists to the GST was, in the end, decisive. After all, despite the many deficiencies in the GST as finally adopted (Bird, 1994), the evidence seems incontrovertible that the GST was economically less distorting than its predecessor the MST (Kuo, McGirr and Poddar, 1988). Indeed, since this was the only clear gain from introducing the GST, it may be argued that the Mulroney government was the first — and probably the last — in Canadian history willing to sacrifice itself on the altar of economic efficiency. As usual, of course, much of the public discussion of the GST focused not on efficiency issues, but on equity issues. While economists argued on both sides of this issue also, it seems fair to say that their contribution in showing, on the basis of plausible assumptions, that the tax was not seriously regressive helped carry the day.[10] All in all, regardless of what thinks of the GST, its adoption stands as probably the single most important example to date of the influence of economists on Canadian tax policy.

The situation is quite different with respect to property taxes. Although relatively little serious economic research has been carried out in Canada with respect to this tax in recent years,[11] such research has continued to be a major industry below the border, to the point where lengthy review articles debating the significance and interpretation of the results have recently appeared (Zodrow, 2001; Fischel, 2001). One conclusion to be drawn from these reviews is that there is still much to learn about this oldest of taxes. Another, however, is that it is hard to detect much, if any, effect on actual tax policy either south or north of the border as a result of all this research. None of the major changes that have taken place in property tax policy in provinces such as Ontario in recent years, for example, seem to reflect any concern for the issue at the heart of the academic discussion of property taxation — the question of the benefit linkage between local property taxes

---

[10]The importance of the distributional issue is illustrated by the "double whammy" of offsetting policies introduced when the GST was implemented. Although the refundable GST credit allowed under the income tax was sufficient to offset the estimated regressivity of the tax, political pressure led to the exemption also of so-called "basic foods" on distributive grounds, thus substantially reducing the efficiency gains from the tax.

[11]For a review of earlier studies, see Bird and Slack (1978).

Richard Bird and Michael Smart

and local public services, for example — or to demonstrate any knowledge of that literature.[12]

The failure to consider research results in developing tax policy is equally marked with respect to the other ancient tax that still generates significant revenue for governments in Canada, namely, excises. Countless studies — though again few in Canada — have considered the efficiency effects of taxes on alcoholic beverages and tobacco,[13] but such studies have had little perceptible effect on either the level or structure of these taxes. Much the same is true with respect to taxes on vehicles and fuel, despite the substantial economic literature suggesting alternative designs of these levies on efficiency grounds. In this, as in most fields of taxation, it appears that perceived effects on equity and political considerations have trumped, and probably always will trump, efficiency analysis — even if, as has, alas, seldom been true of academic studies, the latter is presented to policymakers in both language and a context to which they can relate.

A last example may be mentioned. While it appears that the advice of economists counted for nothing when Canada led the way in the world by abolishing all estate and inheritance taxes,[14] it seems to have been heeded amazingly quickly recently with respect to the capital gains taxes, the introduction of which was the stated rationale for abolishing taxes on wealth at death. In particular, Mintz and Wilson (2000) was hardly in press when its major recommendation, to reduce the capital gains inclusion rate, was put into place — and then a few months later strengthened. As in the case of the corporate income tax, however, one may question the extent to which such economic advice influenced the outcome, compared to the politically attractive rhetoric with respect to encouraging savings and investment on one

---

[12]In the Ontario case, this is particularly striking because the issue was thoroughly discussed in, for example, Kitchen and Slack (1993).

[13]For a recent survey of the latter, see Cnossen (2001). A rare Canadian example is Raynauld and Vidal (1992).

[14]For the most recent Canadian review of the issues, see Mintz and Pesando (1991). The rest of the world continues to find this subject worthy of study, however, as evidenced in Pestieau and Poterba (2001).

hand and the political importance of the interests thus favoured on the other.[15]

Conclusion

What lessons do we draw from the preceding rather dismal tale of the apparent lack of success of the dismal science in influencing Canadian tax policy in recent years?

The first lesson is, of course, that the tale is not really all that dismal. The glass, it may be argued, is at least half full. The downward pressure on personal and corporate income tax rates has certainly been supported, if not initiated, by the increasing evidence of the distortions caused by high marginal tax rates. Equally, the adoption of the GST can be explained only by the (possibly irrational) acceptance of the federal government of the economic argument that Canada had to change to a value-added tax to reduce economic distortions.[16]

A second lesson, however, is that too much weight should not be attached to the first lesson, because equally convincing (or unconvincing) economic studies of the damage done by poorly-designed excise, property, and payroll taxes do not seem to have met with a similarly receptive audience. It is hard to avoid the conclusion that the adoption of the flatter-rate broader-base income tax strategy is probably better explained by more fundamental political economy considerations than by simple acceptance of the advice of economists. If so, as we have already suggested, the GST stands as the major evidence of successful economic advice in the tax area in recent decades — a conclusion that may not make everyone happy and that, to say the least, does not augur well for future success. Politicians who

---

[15]One rationale for the first reduction in the inclusion rate (in February 2000) was to level out the taxes on dividends and capital gains and hence to restore a certain logic to the personal taxation of corporate-source income. Of course, the further reduction in July 2000 created an imbalance in the other direction and again made the system analytically incoherent.

[16]Admittedly, politicians may have been more influenced by the mercantilist argument that the former sales tax "taxed exports".

saw the fate of the Progressive Conservative party in the post-GST election will probably be even less likely in the future than in the past to pay much attention to the advice of "efficiency technicians".

More positively, however, three other lessons may perhaps be drawn from the broader post-war experience.[17] The first such lesson is that tax economists who want to influence public policy must pay more attention to the issues that motivate policymakers, even if this means that they may pay somewhat less attention to the techniques that lead to publishable academic papers. This is not a plea for "dumbing down" policy analysis. On the contrary, it is a plea to smarten it up.

In particular, analysis that assumes distributional considerations are either unimportant or can easily be accommodated by (unspecified) adjustments somewhere else in the tax-transfer system simply does not resonate in the policy context. Distributional issues matter in tax policy. In fact, often such issues dominate in the minds of those who shape that policy. From this perspective, the general failure of policy economists to say anything very useful about distributional issues has often relegated them, and their evidence, to the sidelines in policy discussion.

Distributional studies such as those in papers by Vermaeten, Gillespie and Vermaeten (1994); and Ruggieri, Van Wart and Howard (1994b) are decidedly out of academic fashion. This is understandable because they are both conceptually and empirically difficult and, as Whalley (1984) memorably demonstrated, extremely assumption-sensitive. But equity continues to lie at the heart of public economics, and unless and until economists can deal more explicitly and satisfactorily with this issue, their success record in influencing public policy seems unlikely to improve much.

A second lesson, as Winer and Hettich (1999) set out at length in theoretical terms and to some extent demonstrate empirically (see also Gillespie, 1991b), is that tax policy is not just about economics but about politics. We must understand the political economy of taxation if we are to understand how economic analyses of tax issues are likely to be perceived to affect policy outcomes. Scholars such as Persson and Tabellini (2000) and Besley and Coate (1997) have made major contributions to this field of study

---

[17]For a more comprehensive review of postwar experience, see Bird, Perry and Wilson (1998).

in recent years.[18] But there is clearly much more that can and should be done to understand both how the present system works and how it might be altered to improve policy outcomes in economic terms.[19] Some years ago, for example, St. Hilaire and Whalley (1985) made a number of interesting suggestions with respect to how tax reform might be institutionalized to make better use of evidence and produce better results. It seems past time to return to this line of inquiry and to attempt to apply some of the political insights of such Canadian scholars as Winer and Hettich (1999); Hartle (1988); and Breton (1996) to the problem of formulating tax policy in a democratic setting in light of the best scientific knowledge instead of leaving it, as is now generally the case, to the shifting winds of political fashion.

Finally, it may not be out of place to note that if one wishes to affect policy, one must normally write in a way, and in a forum, that will come to the notice of policymakers. Scholars such as Hartle and Mintz, to mention only two prominent examples, have not hesitated to engage in public discussion of key policy issues and to attempt to convince wider audiences of the cogency and importance of the economic analysis of taxation. While not everyone — the present authors, for two — may be constitutionally up to the personal costs imposed by this approach — and, of course, current academic mores render such involvement virtually *ultra vires* for those aspiring to tenure in academic departments of economics, it is, we think, only through such efforts to communicate to policymakers directly or indirectly by engaging with the (small) informed public with which policymakers interact that progress is likely to be made.[20]

Like the scholars we have mentioned, David Slater has for many years epitomized the best of this tradition in his scholarship, in his willingness to

---

[18]McKenzie (2001) has recently reviewed this literature from a Canadian perspective.

[19]See, for quite different perspectives on the Canadian tax policy process, Good (1980); and McQuaig (1987).

[20]To put this another way, we are in effect supporting the view of Harberger (1993) that economists need to pay more attention to their role as policy practitioners if they are to play that role more effectively. Of course, some very deep waters are being skated over rather quickly here: see, for example, the fundamental study of Lindblom (1990) on the role of social scientists in the policy process.

be involved in the policy process, and, not least, in his role in recent years in developing the important policy forum that Canadian Business Economics has become. It is only through such efforts that the gap between scholarship and policy action will ever be bridged in the area of taxation, or any other area of public policy.

References

Battle, K. and S. Torjman (1994), "The Welfare Wall: An Analysis of the Welfare/Tax System in Ontario", in A. Maslove (ed.), *Taxation and the Distribution of Income* (Toronto: University of Toronto Press).

Besley, T. and S. Coate (1997), "An Economic Model of Representative Democracy", *Quarterly Journal of Economics* 112, 85-114.

Bird, R. (1994), *Where Do We Go from Here? Alternatives to the GST* (Toronto: KPMG Centre for Government).

_____ (1996), "Why Tax Corporations?" Working Paper No. 96-2, prepared for the Technical Committee on Business Taxation (Ottawa: Department of Finance).

Bird, R. and J. Mintz (2000), "Tax Assignment in Canada: A Modest Proposal", in H. Lazar (ed.), *The State of the Federation 2000-01: Toward a New Mission Statement for Canadian Fiscal Federalism* (Montreal and Kingston: McGill-Queen's University Press for School of Policy Studies, Queen's University).

Bird, R. and E. Slack (1978), *Residential Property Tax Relief in Ontario* (Toronto: University of Toronto Press).

Bird, R. and T. Wilson (1999), "The Legacy of the Carter Commission", in R. Bird, M. Trebilcock and T. Wilson (eds.), *Rationality in Public Policy: Essays in Honour of Douglas G. Hartle* (Toronto: Canadian Tax Foundation).

Bird, R., D. Perry and T. Wilson (1998), "Canada", in K. Messere (ed.), *Tax Systems in Industrialized Countries* (Oxford: Oxford University Press).

Boadway, R. (1999), "Retain Targeting, but Make Credits Refundable", *Policy Options* 20, 18-19.

Breton, A. (1996), *Competitive Governments* (Cambridge: Cambridge University Press).

Canada (1998), *Report of the Technical Committee on Business Taxation* (Ottawa: Department of Finance).

Cnossen, S. (2001), "Taxing Tobacco in the European Union", paper presented at Conference on Public Finance in Developing and Transition Countries, Atlanta, April.

Dahlby, B. (1993), "Payroll Taxes", in A. Maslove (ed.), *Business Taxation in Ontario* (Toronto: University of Toronto Press).

Davies, J. (1998), "Marginal Tax Rates in Canada: High and Getting Higher", Commentary 108 (Toronto: C.D. Howe Institute).

_____ (1999), "Control Spending to Cut Both Taxes and Tax-Backs", *Policy Options* 20, 20-21.

Davies, J. and J. Zhang (1996), "Measuring Marginal Income Tax Rates for Individuals in Canada: Averages and Distributions Over Time", *Canadian Journal of Economics* 29, 959-975.

Di Matteo, L. and M. Shannon (1995), "Payroll Taxation in Canada: An Overview", *Canadian Business Economics* 3 (Summer), 5-22.

Eissa, N. and J.B. Liebman (1996), "Labor Supply Response to the Earned Income Tax Credit", *Quarterly Journal of Economics* 111, 605-637.

Feldstein, M. (1995), "The Effects of Marginal Tax Rates on Taxable Income: A Panel Study of the 1986 Tax Reform Act", *Journal of Political Economy* 103, 551-572.

Fischel, W. (2001), "Homevoters, Municipal Corporate Governance, and the Benefit View of the Property Tax", *National Tax Journal* 44, 157-173.

Gagné, R., J.-F. Nadeau and F. Vaillancourt (2001), "Taxpayer's Response to Tax Rate Changes: A Canadian Panel Study", University of Montreal.

Gillespie, I. (1991a), "How to Create a Tax Burden Where No Tax Burden Exists: A Critical Examination of Grady's 'An Analysis of the Distributional Impact of the Goods and Services Tax' ", *Canadian Tax Journal* 39, 925-936.

_____ (1991b), *Tax, Borrow and Spend: Financing Federal Spending in Canada, 1867-1990* (Ottawa: Carleton University Press).

Good, D. (1980), *The Politics of Anticipation: Making Canadian Federal Tax Policy* (Ottawa: School of Public Administration, Carleton University).

Grady, P. (1990), "An Analysis of the Distributional Impact of the Goods and Services Tax", *Canadian Tax Journal* 38, 925-936.

_____ (1991), "The Distributional Impact of the Goods and Services Tax: A Reply to Gillespie", *Canadian Tax Journal* 39, 937-946.

Harberger, A. (1993), "The Search for Relevance in Economics", *American Economic Review, Papers and Proceedings* 83, 1-16.

Hartle, D. (1988), *The Expenditure Budget Process of the Government of Canada: A Public Choice Rent-Seeking Perspective* (Toronto: Canadian Tax Foundation).

Helliwell, J. (1999), "Checking the Brain Drain: Evidence and Implications", *Policy Options* 20(7), 6-17.

Kesselman, J. (1993), "Payroll Tax in Lieu of GST?" *Canadian Tax Highlights* 1, 89-90, and 2, 5-6.

Kitchen, H. and E. Slack (1993), *Business Property Tax*, Government and Competitiveness Paper No. 93-24 (Kingston: School of Policy Studies, Queen's University).

Kuo, C.-Y., T. McGirr and S. Poddar (1988), "Measuring the Non-neutralities of Sales and Excise Taxes in Canada", *Canadian Tax Journal* 36, 655-670.

Lin, Z., G. Picot and C. Beach (1996), "What Has Happened to Payroll Taxes in Canada Over the Last Three Decades?" *Canadian Tax Journal* 44, 1052-1077.

Lindblom, C. (1990), *Inquiry and Change* (New Haven: Yale University Press).

McKenzie, K.M. (2001), *The King, His Courtiers, and the House of Cards: Political Institutions and Fiscal Policy Outcomes from a Canadian Perspective*, Benefactor's Lecture (Toronto: C.D. Howe Institute).

McQuaig, L. (1987), *Behind Closed Doors* (Markham: Viking).

Mendelson, M. (1997), "The WIS That Was: Replacing the Canadian Working Income Supplement", Discussion paper (Ottawa: Caledon Institute of Social Policy).

Meyer, B. and D. Rosenbaum (2000), "Making Single Mothers Work: Recent Tax and Welfare Policy and its Effects", NBER Working Paper No. 7491 (Cambridge, MA: National Bureau of Economic Research).

Mintz, J. and J. Pesando, eds. (1991), "The Role of Wealth Taxes in Canada", *Canadian Public Policy/Analyse de Politiques* 17, supplement.

Mintz, J. and T. Wilson (2000), *Capitalizing on Cuts to Capital Gains Taxes*, Commentary No. 137 (Toronto: C.D. Howe Institute).

Persson, T. and G. Tabellini (2000), *Political Economics* (Cambridge, MA: MIT Press).

Pestieau, P. and J. Poterba, eds. (2001), "Bequests and Wealth Taxation", *Journal of Public Economics*, Special Issue, 79.

Poschmann, F. and J. Richards (2000), *How to Lower Taxes and Improve Social Policy*, Commentary No. 136 (Toronto: C.D. Howe Institute).

Raynauld, A. and J.-P. Vidal (1992), "Smokers' Burden on Society: Myth and Reality in Canada", *Canadian Public Policy/Analyse de Politiques* 18, 300-317.

Robson, W., J. Mintz and F. Poschmann (2000), *Budgeting for Growth: Promoting Prosperity with Smart Fiscal Policy*, Commentary No. 134 (Toronto: C.D. Howe Institute).

Ruggeri, G., D. Van Wart and R. Howard (1994a), "Equity Aspects of Sales Taxes and Income Taxes", *Canadian Tax Journal* 42, 1263-1274.

_____ (1994b), "The Redistributional Impact of Taxation in Canada", *Canadian Tax Journal* 42, 417-451.

Silaama, M.-A. and M. Veall (2001), "The Effect of Marginal Tax Rates on Taxable Income: A Panel Study of the 1988 Tax Flattening in Canada", *Journal of Public Economics* 80, 341-356.

St. Hilaire, F. and J. Whalley (1985), "Reforming Taxes: Some Problems of Implementation", in D. Laidler (ed.), *Approaches to Well-Being* (Toronto: University of Toronto Press).

Thirsk, W.R. and R.M. Bird (1994), "Earmarked Taxes in Ontario: Solution or Problem?" in A.M. Maslove (ed.), *Taxing and Spending Issues* (Toronto: University of Toronto Press).

Vaillancourt, F. and N. Marceau (1990), "Do General and Firm-Specific Employer Payroll Taxes Have the Same Incidence? Theory and Evidence", *Economics Letters* 34, 175-181.

Vermaeten, F., I. Gillespie and A. Vermaeten (1994), "Tax Incidence in Canada", *Canadian Tax Journal* 42, 348-416.

Vickrey, W. (1991), "The Corporate Income Tax and How to Get Rid of It", in L. Eden (ed.), *Retrospectives on Public Finance* (Durham, NC: Duke University Press).

Whalley, J. (1984), "Regression or Progression: The Taxing Question of Incidence Analysis", *Canadian Journal of Economics* 42, 654-682.

Whalley, J. and D. Fretz (1990), *The Economics of the Goods and Services Tax* (Toronto: Canadian Tax Foundation).

Winer, S. and W. Hettich (1999), *Democratic Choice and Taxation* (Cambridge: Cambridge University Press).

Zodrow, G. (2001), "The Property Tax as a Capital Tax: A Room with Three Views", *National Tax Journal* 44, 139-156.

Taxing Future Consumption

Jack M. Mintz

Introduction

David Slater has always had a keen interest in taxation issues, especially in relation to savings.[1] Perhaps one of the most important contributions made by the Economic Council of Canada during his tenure as chairman was to initiate a detailed study of taxation entitled *Road Map for Tax Reform* (Economic Council of Canada, 1987). This document was the first Canadian major study outlining the impact of adopting a consumption (or expenditure) tax in Canada as a replacement for the income tax.[2] Like most documents recommending substantial changes to the tax system, it did not result in a

---

[1]David shows continued interest in this subject. In the past two years, he has sent me several papers on taxation of retirement savings (see two of these contributions in Slater, 2000a,b).

[2]More details below will be provided on the expenditure tax concept. Two important international studies preceding the Economic Council of Canada's report were the Meade Report (Institute for Fiscal Studies, 1978) and David Bradford's report (United States. Department of Treasury, 1977). A study by Boadway, Bruce and Mintz (1987) and Davies and St-Hilaire (1987) also looked at issues related to the adoption of a consumption tax in Canada.

major change. However, it did lay the groundwork for greater discussion of the consumption tax principle as a basis for taxation in Canada.

Two moves towards consumption taxation occurred in the early 1990s. The first was the replacement of the Manufacturers' Sales Tax by the Goods and Services Tax (GST) on January 1, 1991 (the GST was initially proposed in 1987 by the Conservative government). The second was a major revision of the tax treatment of retirement savings in 1991 to provide more equal treatment of holders of pension and registered retirement savings plans, including an expansion of the limits for contributions made to these plans. Studies like that of the Economic Council of Canada made it more acceptable for governments to increase the contribution of consumption-based taxes as part of the overall system.

Canadian policymakers have an ambivalent attitude towards taxation of savings. While there is strong acceptance of consumption taxation in the form of the GST and providing tax-assistance for retirement savings, governments have been reluctant to embrace fully the principle of consumption taxation. There are some important reasons for this ambivalence towards the taxation of savings, which I shall discuss below. Nonetheless, economic circumstances have changed since 1990 making it more fashionable to entertain the idea of introducing greater reliance on consumption taxation in Canada. As I believe that tax reform is very much a process for change, I shall discuss two economic developments that could give rise to a greater role for consumption taxation in Canada. These questions should be a focus of tax research in the future.

The Case for and against a Consumption Tax

Economic theories explaining savings behaviour can be classified according to three motives for savings:

- *Life-cycle savings*: Typically, savings in earlier years of their life provide resources for consumption after retirement (Summers, 1981).

- *Bequest savings*: Accumulated savings are passed on to heirs through bequests to support their consumption (Altonji, Hayashi and Kotlikoff, 1992).

- *Precautionary savings*: Savings are built up to provide consumption when resources are insufficient to cover contingencies (Deaton, 1992; and Skinner, 1988). An important element of precautionary savings is related to liquidity constraints in that a person may not be able to borrow funds to cover shortfalls in earnings.

The strongest argument made for consumption taxation is related to the life-cycle model, although the case for consumption taxation can still be made, taking into account other theories of savings behaviour (Bernheim, 1999).

I titled this paper "taxation of future consumption" for a deliberate reason. Tax research in the past several decades has recognized that a failing of the annual income tax, which applies to earnings and capital income derived from saved earnings, results in a heavier tax on future compared to current consumption. If two people have the same lifetime earnings, but one saves some earnings for future consumption, the saver pays more tax than the consumer does over a lifetime. Therefore, under an income tax, people pay more tax on future consumption derived from their savings than they do on current consumption. Thus, the annual income tax falls more heavily on those who wish to consume more in the future.

Yet, the Carter Report (Canada, 1966), still the bible of Canadian tax policy at the Department of Finance and among practitioners, argues that annual income is the most efficient and fair base for personal taxation.[3] However, the non-uniform taxation of consumption under the annual income tax is troubling. If a person's welfare depends on consumption of goods and services throughout all periods of life, what rationale is there for taxation of annual income that results in higher taxes on future consumption relative to current consumption? Taxation of the return on savings does not seem efficient or fair under these arguments.

On the other hand, a consumption tax, however, treats consumers and savers equally. Once a person has earnings, the same amount of tax is paid on a present value basis no matter whether the earnings are consumed immediately or deferred until a later time. Two approaches are possible to use for consumption taxation. First, governments could simply tax consumption

---

[3]Even the tax expenditure accounts, often cited in the press and expert analysis, rely on annual income as the benchmark for evaluating the value of such expenditures. See Bruce (1988) for a comprehensive review of the problems inherent with tax expenditures and alternative characterizations.

each year by applying the tax to goods and services sold (as in the case of a sales tax) or on expenditure expressed as the difference between earnings and savings (as in the case of registered pension [RPP] and retirement savings [RRSP] plans). Second, consumption taxes could be imposed by simply exempting the return to savings (above normal returns would be subject to a rent tax). This latter approach is referred to as the exempt-yield approach.

Without trying to review in depth a large literature, suffice it to say that experts have gained a much greater understanding as to how taxes on capital income might affect economic welfare. An important point made by Feldstein (1978), that even if savings remain constant, future consumption can decline if the return on savings is taxed. In fact, the welfare costs of taxing future consumption more heavily than current consumption can be quite significant, well approaching 20 per cent of revenue on income (ibid.) even though savings may not be responsive to changes in the after-tax interest rate.[4] Other estimates of welfare costs of taxing savings compared to a uniform consumption tax vary from 11 cents to over one dollar per dollar of revenue (Bernheim, 1999). Although models have had different assumptions and characterization of preferences, the overall view provided by most economists is that there is a significant welfare gain that would be derived by replacing the income tax with a consumption tax.

The efficiency and equity arguments for consumption taxes are further buttressed by administrative and compliance issues. Income taxes are not easy to apply (Bradford, 1984). In principle, income taxes should be levied on incomes, indexed for inflation. Depreciation of assets has to be measured appropriately. Capital gains should be taxed on an accrued, not realized basis, to make sure that the present value of taxes on capital gains is the same as on other investment income. The latter is especially difficult since accrual taxation requires periodic valuation of assets even though many are not frequently traded and taxes are assessed even if the asset is not sold (thereby raising issues of liquidity).

Given these views, then why are governments not jumping at the opportunity of eliminating the tax on savings in favour of a consumption-based tax? I would argue that there are at least five reasons why governments are so reluctant to move in this direction:

---

[4]Feldstein assumes that the uncompensated supply of savings is virtually zero in his calculations.

- *Equity.* The usual argument stated against consumption taxes is that they are not fair. Since savings rise proportionately with annual income, consumption tax critics suggest that the exemption of savings from tax results in a regressive tax (regressivity implies that taxes proportionately decline in relation to the base). Consumption-tax advocates argue, however, that consumption taxes can be made progressive if desired. The first part of the argument notes that savings simply defer taxes on consumption to future years; therefore, one should calculate the present value of taxes paid on savings and add this value to current taxes to measure the total amount of taxes paid by individuals on their earnings. Thus, a consumption tax levied at a flat rate is at least proportional to earnings, once taking into account deferred taxes on savings. The second part of the argument rests on the implementation of consumption taxes. If a refundable tax credit is provided, the consumption tax is made progressive in the sense that the average tax rate on consumption rises with consumption levels (income-testing the credit will surely make the consumption tax more progressive). As discussed above, an alternative approach is to levy a personal tax on expenditure, defined as the difference between earnings and savings (savings are deductible from the base and withdrawals are added to the base) or on an exempt-yield basis (savings are not deductible and withdrawals are exempt). One could apply a progressive rate schedule with increasing marginal tax rates that would accomplish desired equity objectives.

- *Continued use of Keynesian models.* With Keynesian macroeconomic models, using assumptions of fixed prices and wages, employment and incomes rise with greater aggregate demand in the short run. An important component of aggregate demand is current consumption. Therefore, taxation of savings is viewed as "helpful" to the economy since it has less impact on aggregate demand compared to a pure consumption tax, even though savings ultimately can affect the amount of investment available in the long run. Although Keynesian models are less fashionable among academic economists, they are still the hobby horses of many economic forecasting models used for fiscal policy analysis. The exemption of savings from tax looks inferior to equal-yield sales tax cuts when analyzed in these models. However, long-run models with flexible prices and wages would suggest a different conclusion where gains in welfare arise from greater growth in capital stock over time.

- *Concerns about wealth accumulation.* Since the accumulation of savings is equal to the stock of wealth held by people, proponents of annual income taxes argue that savings should be subject to tax (see, for example, Ontario Fair Tax Commission, 1993). Wealth provides opportunities for people to enjoy more untaxed consumption goods including leisure (the landlord's son who does not work) and political power. Therefore, it is appropriate to tax savings for these two reasons.

The first argument — the consumption tax is applied on a narrower base compared to an income tax — is an important criticism since an equal-yield consumption tax as a replacement for the income tax would result in a heavier tax on labour earnings. However, the argument does not support the rationale for an annual income tax; it is not a foregone conclusion that the return on savings should be taxed at the same rate as labour earnings. In the end, it becomes an empirical matter for assessment as to whether there should be some positive tax on the return to savings. Many studies on consumption taxation have incorporated labour supply (such as the seminal study by Auerbach, Kotlikoff and Skinner, 1983) and suggest that a consumption tax is superior to an annual income tax. The results in these studies find significant efficiency gains from applying a consumption tax as a one-time wealth levy on accumulated savings held by the elderly. In the absence of the efficiency gains from the wealth levy, the gains achieved from alleviating the tax on savings can be offset to a certain extent from the higher tax on labour supply. Much depends on the responsiveness of a labour supply and the characterization of preferences (some forms of preference functions lead to a result in which consumption taxes are superior).

The second argument made against consumption taxation is that wealth accumulation provides political power. Little research has modelled wealth as a source of political power and therefore provided special gains to certain individuals. One would need to provide an explicit model of political decision-making to understand the role of wealth, an area that should be open to greater analysis with new models of political economy that are now fashionable. Not all forms of wealth lead to greater political power — housing and retirement assets, the most significant forms of wealth for many people, are unlikely to play an important role in polit-ical influence. Instead, a tax on the very wealthy might be appropriate, as some consumption advocates have argued. One could then consider the imposition of a wealth or wealth-transfer tax with a consumption tax (see the excellent discussion of wealth taxes in the Meade Report [Institute for Fiscal Studies, 1978]).

- *Taxes and savings behaviour.* Although consumption-tax advocates argue that a consumption tax improves economic welfare, many empirical studies have suggested that taxes on savings have little or no impact. Thus, many critics of consumption taxes have argued that a shift to consumption taxation would have little impact on savings, but a negative impact on labour supply as discussed above. Theoretically, a tax on interest could reduce savings but, as Summers (1981) points out, taxes on the return to savings could increase the present value of human capital (with a lower discounting of future incomes) and therefore raise savings. Past estimates suggest that the elasticity of savings with respect to changes in interest rates is unlikely more than 0.5. However, Beach, Boadway and Bruce (1988) find that the savings elasticity could be as high as 2 for older taxpayers (for older taxpayers, human capital effects are small). Bernheim (1999) points out that studies using time series of savings likely underestimate the impact of taxes on savings since high effective tax rates were accompanied by low or negative rates of return to savings in the 1970s. Other recent studies have looked at the impact of tax-assisted retirement savings on aggregate savings (RRSPs in Canada and 401(k) or IRAs in the United States). Some studies have suggested that savings are not affected by IRA or 401(k) plans (Gale and Scholz, 1994) while others suggest that there is little substitutability and aggregate savings rise (Venti and Wise, 1990; Poterba, Venti and Wise, 1995). Bernheim's (1999) review of U.S. studies on the substitutability of tax-free savings for taxable savings suggests that contradictory results can be reconciled by heterogeneous preferences for savings among taxpayers. Canadian studies on RRSP behaviour are limited. Milligan (2001) reviews the literature and provides some new results on the impact of carry-forward provisions on RRSPs in Canada for taxpayers of different types and over time. However, in terms of the impact of taxes on savings, there is still much to be done in Canada that would incorporate panel data sets of taxpayer behaviour over time.

- *Transition problems.* Although there might be good arguments for the adoption of any major change to the tax system, any change could flounder in the face of transition problems. By shifting from an income to consumption tax, old assets and accumulated wealth of the elderly would be subject to new levies and there would be a desire to provide some tax relief for low-income individuals. Transitional relief that would make it more politically acceptable to adopt a new form of taxation could possibly reduce some of the efficiency gains from adopting a consumption tax as a replacement for the income tax. One very recent study (Altig *et al.*, 2001) has modelled transitional measures for the adoption of a flat tax on consumption in the United States and found that most efficiency gains would be lost from adopting a consumption tax that provides offsets for low income and elderly taxpayers. No similar study has been conducted in Canada, incorporating the current features of the Canadian income tax.

• *Open economy considerations.* Critics of consumption taxes argue that relief for savings will not have a favourable impact on investment in Canada. The argument is based on an important observation that businesses raise capital from international markets. To the extent that Canada is a small, open economy, greater domestic savings that might arise from tax cuts on savings would not translate into more investment in Canada since the international cost of financing is independent of international markets. Although Canadians might own more domestic assets, the level of business investment would be unaffected by cuts to taxes on domestic savings. Consumption-tax advocates respond to these arguments in two ways. The obvious argument is that one should not evaluate tax policy solely in terms of its impact on business investment. Personal savings rates may be of concern to policymakers in that individuals need to accumulate wealth to finance future consumption needs, including retirement, health and education. The second is that savings could have an impact on investment since capital markets in Canada, while being open, are not "small". First, most financing studies of equity markets suggest some international segmentation of markets — for example, studies have found that changes to dividend and capital gains tax rates have influenced stock prices, contradicting the small, open economy assumption (McKenzie and Thompson, 1996). Thus, cuts to personal taxes on income paid to shareholders can reduce the cost of equity finance for businesses. Second, small and medium sized businesses have little direct access to international markets (if they did they could lose certain tax benefits available only to Canadian-controlled private corporations). Thus, personal tax changes could substantially influence the cost of finance for these businesses. Third, aggregate investment-savings studies have found a correlation between investment and savings rates across countries (Feldstein and Horioka, 1980; and Summers, 1986). Helliwell and McKitrick (1999) suggests that one dollar of new investment is financed by 60 cents of new savings in Canada.

The above arguments explain much ambivalence towards the full adoption of expenditure taxation in Canada. Although several points may be raised against the adoption of an expenditure tax, consumption-tax advocates can easily refute most of the arguments. The economic case for consumption taxation is therefore pretty strong. But, in the end, political perception plays an important role in determining tax policy. To eliminate taxes on savings of very wealthy Canadians is not an easy sell. For that reason, proposals made by the Economic Council of Canada and others have floundered in the past.

New Arguments for Consumption Taxation

The above review of arguments both in favour and against consumption taxation is fairly well known and generally well researched. Given that Canada's tax system is a hybrid of consumption and income taxation, it is clear that the debate has not been resolved in a way that pushes policymakers to adopt one form of tax over the other. Canada uses indirect taxes on sales. The "income" tax contains some important features consistent with consumption-tax principles — contributions to retirement savings (registered pensions and RRSPs) are deductible from the tax base, withdrawals from registered-savings-plans income within registered plans are taxed and interest incurred with borrowed money to invest in plans is not deductible. Savings in owner-occupied housing (principal residence) are treated on an exempt-yield basis — there is no tax on imputed income and mortgage interest is not deductible. No deduction is provided for investments in housings and no tax is placed on the sale of the house. For many low and middle-income taxpayers whose primary assets are a house and pension or RRSP plan, the income tax is effectively an "expenditure" tax.

Nonetheless, significant savings could be subject to tax, whether they include stocks, bonds, rental housing or proprietorships.[5] Are there any special arguments today that might give rise to a greater use of consumption taxation beyond the traditional arguments presented above?

Two New Imperatives

Two special issues are at the forefront facing most industrialized economies, including Canada. The first is the impact of aging in society which will have a substantial impact on resources available to support the elderly. The second is continuing worldwide economic integration which has important implications on the ability of economies to grow and provide higher incomes for citizens.

Demographic Impacts

The demographic picture for Canadian and other industrialized economies is well known. According to a recent study (Organisation for Economic Co-operation and Development, 2001), the proportion of the population that is 65 years of age or older will rise from 14.8 per cent in 2000 to 24.2 per cent by 2050, with very little growth in the working age population after 2020 onwards. Life expectancy will increase further by about 3.5 years on average and fertility will continue its trend downwards. Given a similar labour force participation rate to that found today, the impact of these projected changes on public resources will be significant. While expenditures on education and child support are projected to fall by 1.3 percentage points of gross domestic

---

[5]One question that should be better analyzed is to assess the amount of taxes actually paid on savings. Poddar and English (1999) suggest that the effective tax rate on savings is close to zero, once taking into account preferences for investments, such as the Lifetime Capital Gains Exemption, and the deductibility of interest expense. Further work is needed in this area since there are difficult empirical issues to handle in estimating the effective tax rate on savings, including the proper incorporation of inflation in assessing returns and the impact of business level taxes on personal investments.

Jack M. Mintz

product (GDP) by 2050, expenditures on elderly benefits and health care shall rise by ten percentage points. Further, with a shift to more people retired who pay less tax, taxes, as a proportion of GDP, will decline by 1.2 percentage points. The net effect shall be a worsening of primary balances by 9.9 percentage points which can only be made up by major expenditure cuts, lower debt or substantially higher taxes that will be felt by the working population.

The impact of these demographic changes on public expenditures is only part of the story. The current working population will need to accumulate sufficient wealth to cover significant private expenditures when they retire in later years. Further, to the extent that governments target public support to the elderly who most need it, the elderly will need greater resources after retirement. Thus, savings today will be important to cover future needs. As the day of reckoning is not far away (beginning in two decades), governments will have to carefully plan now to ensure that future needs will be properly covered.

As Robson (2001) discusses in this volume, private provision for retirement income and health care will be a significant part of any future public program. The current registered pension and retirement savings plan system is intended to allow individuals to accumulate wealth for these purposes. Given the current limitations on tax-deductible contribution limits ($13,500 or 18 per cent of earned income), a person is able to accumulate sufficient wealth on a tax-free basis to cover about $80,000 of annual future expenditures. Although this amount may seem sufficient to cover most retirement and medical needs of today's population, it is important to gain a greater understanding of how much future expenditure must be covered as the population ages.

A critical question, therefore, is the degree to which tax policy can encourage Canadians to save for their future needs. New studies on savings behaviour would certainly help shed more light on this question. As Bernheim (1999) notes, an important element of tax-deductibility for savings is its psychological effect on individuals' proclivity to contribute to savings plans. Yet, little research is undertaken in Canada to understand what impact the tax treatment of registered pension and retirement savings plans has on Canadian savings. Reliance on U.S. studies is not helpful for Canadian research. As Milligan (2001) notes, Canada's tax treatment of retirement savings provides much more flexibility compared to that in the United States, including greater opportunity to carry forward amounts and withdraw amounts for contingencies prior to retirement. However, limits for contributing to retirement savings plans have not been keeping up with inflation in recent years, never mind with growth in wage income. Further, the role of public support — Old Age Security and Canada/Quebec Pension Plans — is much different than that found in the United States, therefore impacting differently on the incentives for Canadians to save for retirement. Further, as Shillington (1999) pointed out, income testing of the Guaranteed Income Supplement for the elderly, old age security pensions, and certain refundable credits can affect the incentive for Canadians to save for retirement.

Global Economic Integration

Although integration at the international level has not been a new phenomenon — after all, Canada has benefited from trade and factor flows throughout its history — the past two decades have witnessed unique growth in international linkages. Cross-border financial transactions have developed remarkably. Intra-firm trade by multinational companies across national boundaries has become increasingly prominent. Inbound and outbound investment has sharply increased for many countries. Although not disappearing, borders between countries are "thinning" (Helliwell, 2000).

The reduction in transportation and communication costs has allowed businesses to conduct operations more easily in several countries at a time, looking for cost efficiencies and highly skilled labour. To attract businesses and jobs, countries have been looking towards improving the quality of skilled labour, infrastructure and other factors that improve the business environment. Coupled with the demographic changes, as discussed above, capital investment is critical for improvements in productivity.

Seen in this light, the pool of domestic savings plays an important role in creating a better environment for economic growth. Increased domestic savings can provide new financing and a lower cost of capital for small and medium sized Canadian businesses. Canadian ownership of capital can provide greater returns to the Canadian economy from investments taking place either in Canada or in other countries. Such returns help Canadians accumulate wealth for future needs as well. Some recent theories suggest that the savings can also reduce income inequality. With additional resources, lower income households can benefit from increased investments in capital, including the acquisition of skills and training, and reduced levels of unemployment.

Jack M. Mintz

Nonetheless, there has been little quantification of the effect that domestic saving policies, including tax policy, could have on economic growth and income inequality, particularly taking into account increased global integration on the Canadian economy.[6]

Further, given the difficulties being encountered at the international level to tax income from savings, the administrative and compliance problems of levying income taxes are becoming more troublesome. Mintz and Chen (2000), for example, suggest that the corporate income tax, as we know it today, could wither in the next two decades given the problems involved with levying corporate taxes on income that can be easily shifted from one jurisdiction to another.

Conclusion: Potential Canadian Tax Reforms

Given demographic pressures and increased international economic integration, the tax treatment of savings becomes a more central policy focus for the medium term. Several policies have been proposed, but much more research is needed to understand their economic impacts and incidence. Several potential policies that are not difficult to achieve include:

- A sharp increase in sales tax revenues (sales and excise) to reduce reliance on income taxes.

- A major expansion of RRSP and pension limits to allow for greater accumulation of wealth to meet future contingencies of various sorts.

- The introduction of an exempt-yield tax saving plans (with restrictions on contributed amounts) that would encourage saving by individuals expecting increases in future tax rates (Kesselman and Poschmann, 2001). Like owner-occupied housing, contributions to plans would not be deductible and withdrawals would not be taxable. Income in the plan would not be taxed and borrowed interest would not be deductible. As

---

[6]Some theoretical underpinnings are provided in Frenkel and Razin (1994).

the Meade Report (Institute for Fiscal Studies, 1978) suggested, the value of this treatment of savings is to permit individuals to more effectively average their consumption base over time.

A more significant reform would be to replace fully the income tax with an expenditure tax system, continuing reliance on the other indirect forms of consumption taxation (sales taxes). The adoption of a consumption tax would certainly set Canada apart from other countries, including the United States. However, such a reform would require careful consideration of implementation issues, including transition, business level taxation and the treatment of international transactions (Bradford, 2000). However, as the literature has found in the past, the technical issues are not insurmountable. The primary issue is to consider how important future consumption is to Canada's overall development.

References

Altig, D., A.J. Auerbach, L.J. Kotlikoff, K.A. Smetters and J. Walliser (2001), "Simulating Fundamental Tax Reform in the United States", *American Economic Review* 91(3), 574-595.

Altonji, J.G., F. Hayashi and L.J. Kotlikoff (1992), "Is the Extended Family Altruistically Linked? Direct Tests Using Micro Data", *American Economic Review* 82 (December), 177-198.

Auerbach, A., L.J. Kotlikoff and J. Skinner (1983), "The Efficiency Gains from Dynamic Tax Reform", *International Economic Review* 24, 81-100.

Beach, C., R. Boadway and N. Bruce (1988), *Taxation and Savings in Canada* (Ottawa: Economic Council of Canada).

Bernheim, B.D. (1999), "Taxation and Saving", NBER Working Paper No. 7061. Forthcoming in A. Auerbach and M. Feldstein (eds.), *Handbook of Public Economics* (Amsterdam: North Holland).

Boadway, R., N. Bruce and J. Mintz (1987), *Taxes on Capital Income in Canada: Analysis and Policy*, Canadian Tax Paper No. 80 (Toronto: Canadian Tax Foundation).

Bradford, D. (1984), *Untangling the Income Tax* (Cambridge, MA: Harvard University Press).

_____ (2000), "Blueprint for International Tax Reform", manuscript prepared for the Brooklyn Law School International Tax Policy Symposium (forthcoming in the *Brooklyn Law Journal*).

Bruce, N. (1988), *Tax Expenditures and Government Policy* (Kingston: John Deutsch Institute, Queen's University).

Canada (1966), *Report of the Royal Commission on Taxation* (Carter Report) (Ottawa: Queen's Printer).

Davies, J.B. and F. St-Hilaire (1987), *Reforming Capital Income Taxation in Canada: Efficiency and Distributional Effects of Alternative Options* (Ottawa: Supply and Services Canada).

Deaton, A. (1992), *Understanding Consumption* (Oxford: Oxford University Press).

Economic Council of Canada (1987), *Road Map for Tax Reform* (Ottawa: Supply and Services Canada).

Feldstein, M. (1978), "The Welfare Cost of Capital Income Taxation", *Journal of Political Economy* 86 (April), S29-S51.

Feldstein, M. and C. Horioka (1980), "Domestic Savings and International Capital Flows", *Economic Journal* 90, 314-329.

Frenkel, J. and A. Razin (1994), *Fiscal Policies and the World Economy*, 2d ed. (Cambridge, MA: MIT Press).

Gale, W.G. and J.K. Scholz (1994), "IRAs and Household Savings", *American Economic Review* 84, 1233-1260.

Helliwell, J. (2000), *Globalization: Myths, Facts and Consequences*, Benefactors Lecture (Toronto: C.D. Howe Institute).

Helliwell, J. and R. McKitrick (1999), "Comparing Capital Mobility across Provincial and National Borders", *Canadian Journal of Economics* 32 (November), 1164-1173.

Institute for Fiscal Studies (1978), *The Structure and Reform of Direct Taxation: Report of a Committee Chaired by Professor J. E. Meade* (London: Allen & Unwin).

Kesselman, J. and F. Poschmann (2001), *A New Option for Retirement Savings: Tax Prepaid Savings Plans* (Toronto: C.D. Howe Institute).

McKenzie, K. and A. Thompson (1996), "The Economic Effects of Dividend Taxation", Working Paper No. 96-7 (Ottawa: Technical Committee on Business Taxation, Department of Finance).

Milligan, K. (2001), "Empirical Essays on Behavioural Responses to Taxation", unpublished Ph.D. Dissertation (Toronto: University of Toronto).

Mintz, J. and D. Chen (2000), "Will the Corporate Income Tax Wither?" in *World Tax Conference Report* (Toronto: Canadian Tax Foundation).

Ontario Fair Tax Commission (1993), *Fair Taxation in Changing World* (Toronto: Queen's Printer of Ontario).

Organisation for Economic Co-operation and Development (2001), "Fiscal Implications of Ageing: Projections of Age-Related Spending", *OECD Economic Outlook* 69 (Paris: OECD).

Poddar, S. and M. English (1999), "Canadian Taxation of Personal Investment Income", *Canadian Tax Journal* 47(5), 1270-1304.

Poterba, J., S. Venti and D. Wise (1995), "Do 401(k) Plans Crowd Out Other Personal Saving", *Journal of Public Economics* 58, 1-32.

Robson, W.B.P. (2001), "Pensions and Health-Care in Canada: Inspecting the Pillars", in this volume.

Shillington, R. (1999), *The Dark Side of Targeting: Retirement Saving for Low-Income Canadians*, Commentary No. 130 (Toronto: C.D. Howe Institute).

Skinner, J. (1988), "Risky Income, Life-Cycle Consumption and Precautionary Savings", *Journal of Monetary Economics* 22 (September), 23-55.

Slater, D. (2000a), "Tax Relief for Retirement Savings: Year 2000 Version", unpublished manuscript.

_____ (2000b), "Tax Relief on Retirement Savings: Year 2000 Version No. 2", unpublished manuscript.

Summers, L.H. (1981), "Capital Taxation and Accumulation in a Life-Cycle Model", *American Economic Review* 71 (September), 533-544.

_____ (1986), "Tax Policy and International Competitiveness", NBER Working Paper No. 2007 (Cambridge, MA: National Bureau of Economic Research).

United States. Department of Treasury (1977), *Blueprints for Basic Tax Reform* (Washington DC: U.S. Government Printing Office).

Venti, S. and D. Wise (1990), "Have IRAs Increased U.S. Saving Evidence from Consumer Expenditure Surveys", *Quarterly Journal of Economics* 105, 661-698.

Taxes, Efficiency and Economic Growth

Jack M. Mintz and Thomas A. Wilson

Introduction

When monetary policy is explicitly committed to maintaining price inflation targets, the scope for contra-cyclical fiscal policy is substantially reduced. While the automatic fiscal stabilizers continue to play an important role in reducing the sensitivity of the economy to shocks, discretionary fiscal policies have only a limited impact, because of induced monetary policy responses.[1] Under these conditions, the analysis of fiscal policies should focus on their effects on the composition of aggregate demand and on the growth of potential output. For example, a policy to deliberately reduce the public debt would, through its interaction with monetary policy, stimulate investment and hence raise potential output growth.

An earlier version of this paper was released as a PEAP Policy Study (Mintz and Wilson, 2000a). The financial support provided by the Canadian Chamber of Commerce is gratefully acknowledged. The authors also thank their research associates, Duanjie Chen and Steve Murphy, who carried out the analysis underlying the tables in this report; and Erin Bell, who prepared the final version of the paper.

[1]For a discussion of this issue see Fortin (2001, pp. 181-192).

As Canada entered the new millennium, the federal government had achieved a budget surplus, and conditions appeared favourable for increasing potential surpluses (the "fiscal dividend" which is the amount available to the government that can be used for tax cuts or expenditure increases within the framework of a balanced budget). Although the current growth recession will reduce the potential surplus somewhat, the medium-term outlook is for increasing surpluses.

The allocation of these potential surpluses is the most important fiscal policy question today. Our view is that, from the standpoint of efficiency and productivity growth, priority should be given to debt reduction and tax reductions designed to stimulate investment and potential growth. In addition, a large part of the remaining fiscal dividend should be allocated towards reducing the relatively large personal income tax burden faced by many Canadian families and individuals. Finally, new spending initiatives should focus on measures to facilitate long-term growth.

While planned debt reduction is an important component of a growth-oriented fiscal policy, in the short run the size of the surplus should vary with the level of economic activity. From a stabilization standpoint, it is important that the automatic stabilizers be allowed to work, so larger than normal surpluses will be realized under strong growth conditions, and smaller surpluses (and even deficits!) when economic growth is below potential (or the economy is in recession).

An Urgent Problem: Economic Growth

Economic growth is the critical issue facing Canada today. Canada's real disposable income per capita has grown little over the past ten years. Moreover, Canada's gross domestic product (GDP) per worker has grown far less quickly than in most Organisation for Economic Co-operation and Development (OECD) countries (see Fortin, 1999). The gap in after-tax per capita income between the United States and Canada has increased by over $4,500 (1998 purchasing power parity) in the past 17 years. Canada's ratio of taxes to GDP (a simple measure of the tax burden) has increased to 37 per cent from 30 per cent in the early 1980s. The tax-GDP ratio in the United States is about 30 per cent, well below that of Canada's.

Jack M. Mintz and Thomas A. Wilson

A critical factor that influences economic growth is productivity growth. Productivity growth implies that Canadians can use fewer resources and work less to produce the same output. It implies, therefore, for the same amount of time worked, Canadians can enjoy higher incomes.

Productivity can be improved in several ways. Canadians can adopt new technologies through innovation that will result in greater amounts of goods and services to be produced from the same resources. Alternatively, Canadians can improve their education so that they have the skills to produce goods and services with greater value-added. Governments can invest in infrastructure such as transportation and communication networks to improve productivity of the overall economy. While each of these strategies can improve productivity, it is also important to make sure that the tax system is not a barrier to economic growth and job creation as well.

Taxes can impair productivity in several ways:

- Taxes may distort economic decisions resulting in businesses and households taking decisions that fail to make the best use of resources in the economy. As prices are signals used by households and businesses to determine how best to allocate their funds amongst competing uses, taxes that distort prices faced by consumers and businesses result in a less efficient use of resources, and therefore inhibit our productivity.

- Taxes can discourage individuals from acquiring the skills needed in today's workforce and therefore reduce the overall productivity of the economy as a result. They can also discourage individuals from participating in the workforce and reduce work effort.

- Taxes may impair innovation in the economy by discouraging individuals and businesses to create, develop and market ideas or adopt new technologies used by others that would result in greater incomes for workers and supplier of inputs to business.

- In today's global economy, with highly mobile business inputs, taxes that are out of line with other countries that provide similar public infrastructure and training, will discourage business investments. The shift of resources to countries with lower taxes and comparable public services would reduce the productivity of the country with high taxes.

We believe that the fiscal planning issues now facing Canada are of critical importance. With new technologies and forms of business activity that are resulting in increased international integration, capital, businesses and skilled individuals are becoming increasingly mobile. Government tax, regulatory and expenditure policies help to determine how much economic growth and productivity gains can be achieved in the increasingly competitive international arena. Today Canada has an unusual, if not unique, opportunity to put in place reforms, both to the tax system and to expenditure programs, in order to stimulate economic growth and productivity over the medium term. We should plan to use the anticipated fiscal dividend wisely, and avoid squandering this opportunity through piecemeal spending increases and tax cuts.

In this paper, we evaluate how changes in tax policy can improve the productivity of the Canadian economy. In our view, the recent approach of cutting taxes selectively — paying attention primarily to personal taxes — is inadequate. There are a range of urgent and pressing issues that require a *comprehensive* approach to tax cuts — namely, tax reform. Tax reform requires substantial change to not only personal taxes, but also business taxes. An overall approach is required if Canada is to improve its productivity and competitiveness, in order for Canadians to enjoy a higher standard of living.

Tax Reform and Static Efficiency Gains

Business Tax Reforms

Although the focus of the current public debate is on the desirability of personal income tax cuts, improvements in efficiency are more likely to be generated by reform of business taxation. Most economic studies have suggested that the most distortionary revenue sources are related to business taxes, particularly the corporate income tax. Effective tax rates on capital vary by industry, type of asset, size of firm and business organization. The business tax system is not only distortionary but also quite complicated. Some studies have suggested that each additional dollar of corporate income tax levied, causes the Canadian economy to lose nearly $1 in economic output (see Whalley, 1997). Therefore the total cost of raising one dollar of corporate income tax revenue can be about two dollars, once these distortionary effects of the tax are taken into account.

An ideal business tax system would be neutral with respect to different industries, asset types, and degrees of risk. Any non-neutralities in the system should be related to mitigation of the effects of market imperfections. Examples of corrective non-neutralities in the tax system include favourable treatment of small business (to offset capital market rationing) and incentives for research and development (in recognition of the positive spillovers generated by an increase in knowledge or know-how).

In today's world, not only should business taxes be neutral but they should also be levied at rates that are competitive internationally. This is especially important for the corporate income tax. Given the relative ease with which corporations can shift income from high to low-taxed countries (without changing real economic activity), a country with a high corporate income tax rate could find its tax base eroded significantly. Recent studies have shown that as corporate income tax rates are increased, the gain in revenues is anywhere from 8 to 20 per cent less than what would be expected if the tax base did not change (see Dungan, Murphy and Wilson, 1997; and Jog and Tang, 1997).

Four years ago, the Technical Committee on Business Taxation submitted its *Report* to the Minister of Finance. This report recommended a more neutral business tax system with lower and more competitive tax rates. High effective marginal corporate rates deter investment, and inter-industry and inter-asset variations in these effective rates distort the allocation of capital. Consequently, a reduction in the level of marginal effective tax rates and a reduction in their variance are high priorities from the standpoints of growth and efficiency. The Technical Committee recommended that the general federal corporate tax rate for large corporations be reduced by 9.1 percentage points to 20 per cent and average provincial rates by one percentage point from 14 per cent to 13 per cent. For manufacturing income, the reduction would be only 2.1 percentage points, since the committee also recommended that the manufacturing and processing deduction be eliminated.

This measure above would reduce corporate tax revenues by $2.2 billion in 1997. However, the committee also recommended a reduction in the average corporate tax rate for small business, and a variety of base-broadening measures such that their full set of measures would be approximately revenue neutral.

As the base broadening measures would tend to reduce the inter-market and inter-asset variance of effective marginal rates, the combined package recommended by the committee would improve efficiency.

Since the committee's report was released, developments abroad have made the case for a further lowering of effective corporate tax rates in Canada more important. Within the G7, Japan, Germany and Italy have all reduced effective marginal rates substantially. The United Kingdom, which previously had the lowest effective marginal rate, also reduced its rate by two percentage points. As a result, Canada has become an outlier, with the highest effective marginal rates of any of the G7 countries (except Japan).

Recent reforms in Scandinavia have resulted in companies being taxed at corporate income tax rates below 30 per cent in Finland, Sweden and Norway, and 32 per cent in Denmark. However, the aggressive business tax policies of Ireland are the most important case in point, since Ireland is the fastest growing OECD country of the past decade, virtually doubling its per capita GDP in ten years. While Ireland has reduced tax rates on manufacturing and financial service income to 10 per cent,[2] it also eliminated a number of special ineffective preferences for investments. After pressure from the European Union, Ireland is implementing a corporate income tax rate of 12.5 per cent by the year 2004 that will apply to all businesses. As shown later, Ireland and Sweden have a far more favourable tax treatment of investments compared to Canada.

The *Economic Growth and Tax Reconciliation Act* passed by the new Bush administration in the United States did not contain major changes in business taxation. But if additional changes are introduced in the future, there will be increased pressure on Canada to respond as well.

Recent Federal Budget Changes. The 1999 federal budget addressed only a few of the issues raised in the *Report* — the personal tax treatment of offshore investment trusts, a civil penalty on tax advisors who promote fraud and most importantly, a reduction in the corporate tax rate for one highly taxed sector — electric utilities. The changes were fairly minor and were not significant in terms of making Canada's business tax structure more competitive.

---

[2]This rate is substantially below the 30 per cent rate for other industries, resulting in less-favourably-taxed industries growing less quickly.

The February 2000 federal budget and the October 2000 Economic Statement and budget update, however, did go much further. The government committed itself to a one percentage point reduction in corporate income tax rates for the broad service sector[3] in 2001, followed by four two-percentage point cuts. It indicated that it would reduce the corporate income tax rate from 28 points to 21 points by the year 2004–05 for active business income in non-resource, non-manufacturing sectors. It also increased capital cost write-offs for railway assets, utility equipment and manufacturing equipment subject to obsolescence. The government also introduced a few tightening provisions — tighter thin-capitalization rules for debt owed to related non-residents, the abolition of non-resident-owned companies and adjustments for research and development expense deductions for provincial deductions in lieu of investment tax credit programs.

The February 2000 budget business tax changes took many observers by surprise. The cut in corporate income tax rates, although small in the first year, are significant when fully implemented. The rate cuts, moreover, are focused on the broad service sector, thereby reducing inter-industry distortions. Tax rates on manufacturing and processing income as well as on resource profits would remain unchanged.

The impact of the February 2000 budget changes can be seen in Table 1. The small changes introduced for the year 2001 have little impact on effective tax rates on capital. Significant variation in effective tax rates remain across all sectors. But when the proposed corporate rate reductions are fully in effect in fiscal 2004–05, they have a much more dramatic impact. Most industries, except for mining, oil and gas, and manufacturing, would experience a sharp decline in the effective tax rate by over four percentage points. Although this tax reform is in the right direction, it still leaves considerable variation in effective tax rates on capital across industries and, in some cases, rates remain far too high thereby discouraging investment.

Moreover, these changes will take five years to complete. This is rather disappointing progress given the substantial reforms taking place around the world, as mentioned above. In the near term the Canadian tax system will remain non-competitive as seen in Table 2 and, as discussed below.

In 1996, Canada's effective tax rate on capital invested in manufacturing was comparable to that of the United States and lower than that found in

---

[3]The broad service sector includes all industries except manufacturing and processing and the resource sectors.

Table 1: Marginal Effective Tax Rates in Canada: Large-sized Tax-paying Firms (per cent)

	Year 2000	Year 2001	Year 2006
Forestry	32.5	31.3	26.0
Mining[a]	-13.4	-13.4	NA
Oil and gas[b]	-37.8	-34.4	NA
Manufacturing	24.2	23.5	21.0
Construction	37.3	35.9	28.7
Transportation[c]	28.2	27.1	21.7
Communications	28.5	27.8	21.9
Public utilities[d]	26.1	25.0	21.4
Wholesale trade	34.8	33.2	27.0
Retail trade	34.0	32.5	26.5
Services	28.9	28.4	21.9

Notes: [a] Our simulation shows that, by replacing the federal resource allowance with the deductibility for provincial mining tax and granting the manufacturing corporate income tax credit (CIT), the effective tax rate (ETR) for mining sector would be about 18 per cent.

[b] Our simulation shows that, by replacing the federal resource allowance with the deductibility for provincial royalty and granting the manufacturing CIT credit, the ETR for oil and gas sector would be about 25 per cent.

[c] Estimate for the transportation sector reflects the higher CCA rate for railway equipment (i.e., 15 per cent instead of 10 per cent).

[d] The estimate is made by assuming that 50 per cent of the public utility sector are in the power generating business, which started phasing in the M&P tax credit from year 2000 and may benefit from the higher tax allowance for CCA class 1 (i.e., 8 per cent instead of 4 per cent).

Jack M. Mintz and Thomas A. Wilson

Table 2: Effective Tax Rate for Domestic Firms in G7 Countries, 1996, 2000 and 2001 (per cent)

Manufacturing	Canada	U.S.	UK	Germany	France	Italy	Japan	Sweden	Ireland	(2)	(3)
1996	23.5	23.8	19.4	38.0	25.3	31.6	31.6	14.4	4.2		
2000	23.5	23.6	17.2	34.4	23.2	18.1	22.6	14.4	4.2		
2001	23.4	23.6	17.2	21.1	23.2	18.1	22.6	14.4	4.2		
Intention in 2006	21.0							(2004)	5.3		

Services	Canada	U.S.	UK	Germany	France	Italy	Japan	Sweden	Ireland	(2)	(3)
1996	29.0	25.0	19.2	37.5	27.9	35.5	33.1	14.2	4.2	8.7	16.2
2000	29.0	24.8	17.2	34.0	25.8	21.4	24.0	14.2	4.2	5.6	11.3
2001	28.3	24.8	17.2	20.8	25.8	21.4	24.0	14.2	4.2	4.3	9.1
Intention in 2006	21.9							(2004)	5.3		

Notes:
1. To single out the tax impact, we assumed that the interest rate and inflation rate are 6.8 per cent and 1.4 per cent respectively across countries and periods.
2. The Canadian METR for the service sector in 2001 is corresponding, respectively, to the federal CIT rate of 28.12 per cent (including the 4 per cent surtax), combined with the weighted average provincial CIT rate of 14.15 per cent.
3. The German METR for 2001 reflects the federal CIT reduction from the current 40 per cent to 25 per cent, starting in January 2001. The municipal trade tax (16.66 per cent on average) and the solidarity surcharge (5.5 per cent) will still apply.
4. The general CIT rate in Ireland was 32 per cent in 1996, 24 per cent in 2000 and 20 per cent in 2001. A lower rate of 10 per cent is applicable for manufacturing and the international tradable service sector (i.e., financial service sector), to which a corresponding METR of 4.2 per cent is shown in Case (1). Case (2) is for hotel services which is subject to the general CIT rate but enjoys a higher tax depreciation rate of 15 per cent for hotel buildings. Case (3) is for other services which subjects to the general CIT rate and tax depreciation allowance.

Germany, France, Italy and Japan and higher than rates in the United Kingdom, Sweden and Ireland. The broad service sector was more highly taxed in Canada compared especially to the United States and to most countries, except Germany, Italy and Japan.

In the current year and in 2001, Canada's competitive position will erode as a result of reforms in many countries. In 2000, Canada's effective tax rate in manufacturing, while still comparable to that in the United States, is below only Germany's. However, in 2001, Germany's substantial reform of its system will put its effective tax rate well below Canada's. For services, in the year 2001 Canada's effective tax rate is well above most countries.

With prospective reductions in federal and provincial statutory corporate tax rates, by 2006, Canada's effective tax rate on capital will be competitive with the United States but still above those of the United Kingdom, Sweden and Ireland. However, it is likely that many of these countries will undertake further changes to their corporate income tax systems. It can be expected that in five years further reductions in corporate income tax rates will take place in many countries combined with initiatives to broaden their tax bases.

The Need for Further Reforms. As the full implementation of the Technical Committee's recommended rate reductions would bring Canadian statutory rates well below U.S. rates, it would result in a significant improvement of the competitiveness of Canadians businesses relative to the United States and help combat base erosion. However, even at a combined federal/provincial rate of 33 per cent, the committee's recommendations would place Canada's corporate income tax rate only at the average of the OECD countries.

If all of the Technical Committee's recommendations were implemented, the dispersion of marginal effective rates of tax on capital across industries and assets would be reduced. This should entail some efficiency gains by improving the allocation of capital.

As discussed, these recommendations entail virtually *no* change in *average* effective marginal tax rates. This is not surprising, given the revenue neutral constraint faced by the committee. On the other hand, the February 2000 federal budget cut effective tax rates but failed to move aggressively in reducing non-neutralities and rates. Once the requirement of revenue neutrality is relaxed, it is feasible to design tax reductions to stimulate investment and make the tax system more efficient. We accept the committee's view that R&D already receives extraordinarily favourable tax treatment in Canada. Therefore, our focus should be on stimulating capital investment.

The Technical Committee report was partly criticized for eliminating a number of important special preferences for certain business activities in order to help cover the revenue loss arising from corporate income tax rate reductions. While general reductions in corporate statutory rates are of benefit to all forms of capital investment, they may result in greater losses in revenue compared to investment tax credits. Some investment tax credits are appropriate since they can encourage investments in specific activities without distorting the tax base used by federal and provincial governments for allocating corporate income to the provinces. In our view, it may be appropriate to consider investment tax credits for certain activities that are insufficient due to market imperfections (undiversifiable risky investments or technology-related investments) and to smooth over transitional impacts of tax reform that eliminates special preferences for specific industrial activities (e.g., new mine assets).

Using the tax evaluation model maintained at the Institute for International Business at the University of Toronto, we have evaluated the impact of reduced statutory rates and investment tax credits on marginal effective rates on investments in new capital.

Table 3 presents effective marginal rates for 2000 (the "base case") and what effective marginal rates would be under four alternatives. The first two incorporate reductions of statutory rates of one and three percentage points. The third incorporates a 1 per cent investment credit for machinery and equipment, and the fourth incorporates a 1 per cent investment credit for all plant and equipment.

The results indicate that a three percentage point reduction in the statutory rate would reduce effective marginal rates in the broadly defined service sector by about two percentage points. Effective rates in manufacturing would drop by 1.7 percentage points. Effective rates in the resource sector would actually increase, because of the interaction of statutory rates with various credits and allowances.

Investment tax credits (ITCs) would reduce the marginal effective tax rate for all industries. A general ITC of 1 per cent has a stronger effect than a 3 per cent rate cut for oil and gas, mining, and transportation and communications; has about the same effect for manufacturing and forestry; and has a weaker effect in the other service sectors and construction. Looking at the inter-industry variability of marginal effective tax rates (METRs), it would appear that a 3 per cent statutory rate cut would reduce these distortions, whereas an ITC would increase them somewhat.

Table 3: Impact of Corporate Tax Changes on Marginal Effective Tax Rates: Large-sized Tax-paying Firms Only (per cent)

	Base Case	Case 1	Case 2	Case 3	Case 4
Forestry	32.9	32.1	30.7	32.4	32.0
Mining	-10.6	-8.5	-4.5	-11.1	-12.2
Oil and gas	-19.6	-17.0	-12.2	-20.2	-20.5
Manufacturing	24.6	24.0	22.9	23.1	22.8
Construction	37.9	37.1	35.6	37.7	37.2
Transportation	29.3	28.8	27.8	26.5	26.3
Communications	30.0	29.4	28.3	29.0	27.9
Public utilities	31.8	31.2	29.9	31.0	30.3
Wholesale trade	35.6	34.8	33.4	35.1	34.9
Retail trade	35.1	34.4	33.1	33.8	33.6
Other services	30.1	29.5	28.2	29.5	28.8
Total - Resource	-15.4	-13.0	-8.7	-16.0	-16.7
Total - Non-resource	29.0	28.4	27.2	27.9	27.4
All industries	24.2	23.9	23.4	23.2	22.6

Notes: Base case = The current tax system.
Case 1 = Reduce the corporate income tax rate by one percentage point.
Case 2 = Reduce the corporate income tax rate by three percentage points.
Case 3 = One percentage point investment tax credit for machinery and equipment.
Case 4 = One percentage point investment tax credit for both buildings and machinery and equipment.

International Comparisons and International Competitiveness

In an open economy, the business tax structure must be designed with an eye to the likely response of multinational corporations (MNCs) as well as to its longer term effects on international competitiveness. Attention should be paid to both statutory and effective marginal rates. Statutory rate differentials may provide incentives for MNCs to shift expenses to and income away from high tax reductions, through transfer pricing and debt management practices. Statutory rate differences may also influence location decisions.

Current and projected corporate statutory rates for OECD countries are presented in Table 4. The corporate statutory rate for large manufacturers in Canada lies in the middle of this group of countries, but the statutory rate for large non-manufacturing firms is currently above all the other countries (except for Germany and Japan). Projected rates for 2006 indicate that the Canadian corporate tax rate will be below the level of the United States, Japan, Germany and France, but remain higher than many other countries.

Differences in effective marginal tax rates also provide incentives for MNCs to adjust their *real* capital stocks, increasing investment in countries with relatively low effective marginal rates in relation to other countries.

In order to prevent substantial revenue erosion, statutory rates should not be higher than rates typically found in other industrialized countries where MNC investments take place. In order to stimulate investment and provide economic growth, effective tax rates on capital should be lower than in other competing jurisdictions.

The implementation of the Technical Committee's recommendations regarding statutory rates would establish Canada's rates at the OECD average and well below U.S. statutory rates, thereby eliminating the principal sources of revenue erosion via debt shifting and transfer pricing. However, as noted above, the February 2000 budget will reduce effective marginal rates of tax on investment by four percentage points for service sectors but have little impact on manufacturing and resource sectors.

A reduction in the combined general corporate income tax rate to 30 per cent instead of 32 per cent accompanied by base-broadening would reduce typical marginal effective tax rates for non-resource firms by about 1 to 1.5 percentage points. The lower statutory rate would also make Canada more attractive relative to other countries, providing added deterrence to debt shifting and transfer pricing by MNCs.

Table 4: Statutory Corporate Income Tax Rates in Selected OECD Countries[a]

	July 31, 1996	January 1, 1999	Change	Intentions (year)
Australia	36	36.0	-	30.0 (2000)
Canada[b]	34.9/43.2	35.0/43.3	-	32.0 (2006)[c]
Denmark	34	32.0	↓	
France	41.7	36.7/40.0[d]	↓	37.8 (2000)
Germany	56.1	51.9[e]	↓	35.0 - 38.0 (2001)[f]
Ireland	10.0/38.0	10.0/28.0	↓	12.5 (2003)
Italy	53.2	31.3 - 41.3[g]	↓	
Japan	52.2	48.0	↓	41.0 (2000)
Netherlands	37.0/35.0	35.0	↓	
Norway	28.0	28.0	-	
Poland	40.0	34.0	↓	22 (2004)
Sweden	28.0	28.0	-	
Switzerland	35.5	25.1	↓	
Turkey	44.0	33.0	↓	
United Kingdom	33.0	30.0[h]	↓	
United States[i]	39.2	39.2	-	

Notes: [a] The 1996 rates are based on the former Coopers & Lybrand, *1997 International Tax Summaries* and the 1999 rates are adopted from the KPMG, *Corporate Tax Rates Survey*, January 1999, unless otherwise specified.
[b] The rate is a combination of the federal CIT rate (22.1 per cent and 29.1 per cent respectively for manufacturing and others) and the average of provincial CIT rates weighted by the provincial GDP by industry. The minor difference between the two years reflects some changes in provincial CIT rates.
[c] This is a weighted average of all industries. Note that the current general CIT rate of 43 per cent will still be applicable to the resources sector, which also enjoys various preferential tax treatments unavailable to any non-resource sectors.
[d] The rate is a combination of the corporate income tax rate of 33.33 per cent and the surtax of 10 per cent and 20 per cent respectively. The lower surtax is applied to smaller-scaled firms which are mainly owned by individuals. For the year 2000 and future years, the lower rate will apply to all firms. (See Ernst & Young, *1999 Worldwide Corporate Tax Guide*, for details.)
[e] Our estimate is based on Ernst & Young, *2000 Worldwide Corporate Tax Guide*. It includes a corporate income tax rate of 40 per cent, an average trade tax of 16.75 per cent

Jack M. Mintz and Thomas A. Wilson

(ranged from 13 per cent to 20.5 per cent) which is deductible for the CIT purpose, and a surcharge of 5.5 per cent on CIT payable.

[f] Refer to *Tax Notes International*, Vol. 20, No. 4, 24 January 2000.

[g] The higher rate (41.3 per cent) includes a general corporate income tax rate of 37 per cent and a regional tax of 4.25 per cent. The latter is levied on the Italian-source income from productive activities, which includes interest payments and labour cost. The general CIT rate may be reduced to 19 per cent for qualifying taxable income corresponding to the ordinary remuneration (currently 7 per cent) of the net equity increase. However, the average corporate income tax rate for a company may not fall below 27 per cent, which, combined with the regional tax rate of 4.25 per cent, resulted in the lower aggregated income tax rate of 31.3 per cent.

[h] Effective as of April 1, 1999.

[i] Our estimate based on an average state corporate income tax rate of 6.5 per cent (ranged from 1 to 12 per cent).

Because a reduction in corporate statutory rates would stimulate an increase in the tax base, the revenue costs would be somewhat attenuated. The Technical Committee estimates that the elasticity of the corporate tax base with respect to a reduction in tax rates is about 0.15. Based on this elasticity in 1998, for example, a two percentage point reduction in all corporate tax rates would involve a revenue loss of about $1.3 billion of federal corporate tax revenue (representing about 7 per cent of federal corporate tax revenues).[4] In future years, however, this relative revenue loss would be further attenuated, as the lower corporate tax rates lead to higher investment, a higher capital stock, and hence increased labour productivity and real output.

Impact of Corporate Taxes on the User Cost of Capital and Investment

The corporate tax structure is a major determinant of the "user cost" of capital.[5] Reductions in statutory corporate rates, increases in CCAs, or

---

[4] This revenue loss is less than the fiscal cost estimate derived from Department of Finance Canada (1999, p. 113).

[5] Other factors include the real rate of interest and the relative prices of capital goods.

increases in investment tax credits will each lower the user cost of capital. Except for the special case where capital is not substitutable for other inputs, a reduction in the user cost will stimulate real investment.

In the FOCUS macro-econometric model, maintained by the Institute for Policy Analysis of the University of Toronto, variations in these key tax parameters affect investment in machinery and equipment and non-residential structures. Since we recommend reductions in statutory rates, we implement these measures in the FOCUS model to incorporate their net impacts on each category of investment and on the corresponding capital stocks.

As noted earlier, higher rates of investment will gradually increase the capital stock, thereby raising potential growth and labour productivity. Higher future levels of output will affect most major revenue sources. These longer term "tax recaptures" will reduce the future revenue losses from the tax reduction measures. The results of this analysis are reported in the section below on "Allocating the Fiscal Dividend: Economic Effects".

Summary of Recommendations for Corporate Taxes

We support the implementation of the seven percentage point reduction in the general corporate rate in the February 2000 federal budget, as laid out in the October 2000 Statement. The first one percentage point rate reduction already took place on January 1, 2001 and the minister of finance confirmed in his May 2001 *Economic Update* that further cuts of two percentage points in each of the following three years will proceed as planned. These reductions are a start in reforming the corporate tax, but further changes are still required. Specifically, we recommend that the minister:

- Implement the base-broadening and other recommendations of the *Report* of the Technical Committee (including the elimination of the 4 per cent corporate surtax). This will permit additional reductions of federal and provincial statutory rates, bringing the combined rate close to 30 per cent.

- Provide selective investment credits that provide transitional relief for industries adversely affected by these reforms.

Jack M. Mintz and Thomas A. Wilson

Reducing Effective Marginal Personal Income Tax Rates

Personal taxes affect productivity in several ways. Personal taxes assessed at high marginal tax rates — the percentages of additional income that is taxed through income, sales, payroll and other taxes that affect the individual — can discourage work effort, savings, risk taking and entrepreneurship. High taxes, relative to the public services that such taxes fund, can discourage individuals from moving to Canada or encourage Canadians to move to other countries.

In international comparisons within the OECD or G7, Canada stands out as: having a relatively high rate of personal income taxes as a percentage of GDP; and having increased the personal income tax burden the most over the past decade.

These comparisons refer, of course to *average* burdens, and are related to *average* rates of tax. When one examines individuals and families in different circumstances, and when effective marginal rates are brought into the picture, the case for personal tax reform and personal tax reduction is even stronger.

Canada is unique among leading industrialized countries, in that children are not recognized as affecting the ability to pay income taxes. Rather, Canada relies solely on the so-called "Child Tax Benefit", a transfer payment system with clawbacks that reduce and eventually eliminate the benefit once certain threshold levels of income are reached. Unlike most other OECD countries, Canada's personal income tax (PIT) is basically on an individual basis. This has the consequence that a family's tax burden does not just depend on the family's level of net income, but varies with the *distribution* of income within the family. A family with a single earner therefore faces a considerably higher burden than a family with the same income earned by two or more family members.

The clawbacks of the Child Tax Benefit and other transfers and credits as well as payroll taxes raise effective marginal rates for low and moderate income families. These and other anomalies in the existing tax-transfer system have been examined in recent papers by Mintz and Poschmann (1999) and by Wilson (1998). Figure 1, reproduced from Mintz and Poschmann, shows the current effective marginal rates for a single earner family in Ontario. As illustrated, the highest effective marginal rate — about 60 per cent, is faced by a family earning about $25,000! This is the direct result of the interaction of clawbacks of transfers with the PIT.

Figure 1: Marginal and Average Tax Rates in Ontario for a Single Earner with Two Children, 1999

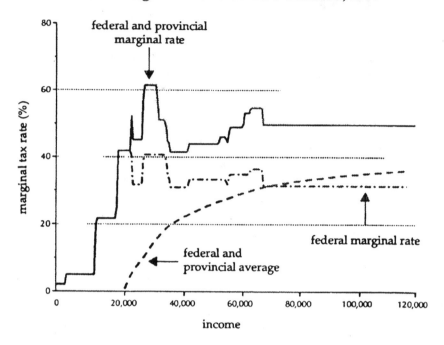

Source: Reproduced from Mintz and Poschmann (1999, p. 15, Figure 1).

Wilson examined the interaction of clawbacks of pensions for seniors with the PIT. As illustrated in Figure 2, even more anomalous rates are faced by seniors with low incomes. The interaction of the clawback of the GIS with the first bracket of the PIT produces effective marginal rates as high as 75 per cent! At higher income levels, seniors face effective marginal rates seven to eight percentage points higher than top marginal rates for other taxpayers, as a result of the 15 per cent clawback of Old Age Security (OAS).

In 1987 Canada implemented a major reform of the income tax system, which had as a major objective reductions in marginal rates and a simplified system of three rate brackets. Over time, the system has become more complex, with federal and provincial surtaxes and clawbacks creating many additional effective rate brackets (Macnaughton, Matthews and Pittman, 1998).

Figure 2: Marginal Tax Rate (%), Single Senior (Ontario), by Income ($000) Level: Current System

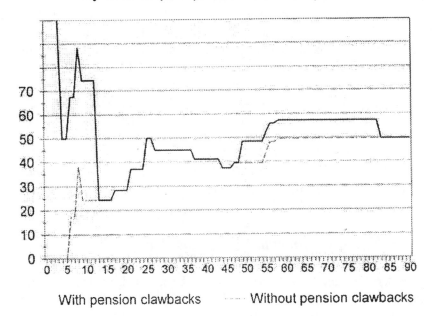

With pension clawbacks   ····· Without pension clawbacks

Source: Reproduced from Wilson (1998, p. 26:11, Figure 1).

Federal surtaxes, higher provincial tax rates, and provincial surtaxes increased the top marginal rates well above the 43.5 per cent level envisaged in the 1987 reform. As important, the effect of the partial de-indexation of the PIT — implemented in 1985 — has gradually eroded the real value of personal credits and deductions, and the real size of the income tax rate bracket thresholds.

In recent years, Ontario has implemented a major reduction in provincial PIT rates, while other provinces have put in place more modest reductions, and the general federal surtax has been eliminated. Alberta has implemented a flat tax of 11 per cent, which results in a top marginal rate of 41 per cent in 2001. While these measures represent steps in the right direction, the PIT in Canada nevertheless remains steeply progressive, with individuals earning the average industrial wage facing combined marginal income tax rates of

35–40 per cent,[6] and the top marginal rate (including federal and Ontario surtaxes) kicking in at an income level just above $63,000.[7]

The February 2000 federal budget and the October 2000 Statement have begun the process of reducing marginal rates, through the elimination of the "high income" surtax and reducing middle bracket rates. Furthermore, the restoration of full indexation will halt the "bracket creep" that was a major factor in the past increase in personal tax burdens. The measures implemented in the budget plan (including the measures in the five-year plan) would reduce personal taxes as a per cent of GDP by about one percentage point (of which indexation accounts for roughly one-half). The February 2000 budget and the October 2000 Statement therefore represent an important start. However, further measures will be needed to bring Canada's relative PIT burden closer to those of our international trading partners.

Income Taxes, Consumption Taxes and Savings

The personal income tax in Canada has long been a "hybrid" tax which has elements of a consumption base as well as an income base. The exclusion of imputed rent on housing and other consumer durables places the taxation of these consumer assets essentially on a consumption base. The deductions for Registered Retirement Savings Plan (RRSP), Deferred Profit Sharing Plan (DPSP) and Registered Pension Plan (RPP) contributions eliminate the double taxation of savings invested in these registered plans. However, as the yield on other assets held outside these plans is subject to income tax, considerable double taxation of savings remains under Canada's PIT.

The pension reform of 1990 promised to level the playing field for contributors to RRSPs and members of RRPs. Contribution levels were to be equalized and indexed. However, indexing has been repeatedly postponed, and the current RRSP limit is below the threshold for deemed equivalence to

---

[6] As noted above, when clawbacks and payroll taxes are taken into account, effective marginal rates are higher.

[7] For individuals with employment income, the top marginal rate takes effect at an income level of $63,671 in 1999 in most provinces. British Columbia, New Brunswick and Nova Scotia have surtaxes that kick in at higher income levels (see KPMG, 2000, p. 13).

defined benefit pension plans. A key savings incentive in the PIT has gradually been eroded as a result.

Indexing of RRSP/RPP contribution limits has been repeatedly postponed in various federal budgets. Currently, indexing is scheduled to begin in 2004. Furthermore, the contribution limits were rolled back below the $15,500 level originally proposed to $13,500 currently.

The steady erosion of the contribution limits in the absence of indexation has shifted the PIT more towards an income base and away from a consumption base. This erosion may have contributed to the recent declines in personal savings rates.[8] In addition, the growth of PIT revenues relative to revenues from indirect taxes on consumption (the GST and federal excise taxes) has shifted the relative weight of total federal taxes from consumption to savings.

It is important to halt, at least, this shift of taxation from consumption to savings. This can be accomplished by concentrating further tax reductions on the PIT, and increasing savings incentives within the PIT. As noted above, the February 2000 federal budget has implemented PIT reductions and has restored full indexation for credits and rate brackets. However, the budget did not increase RRSP/RPP limits.[9]

Entrepreneurship, Innovation and Risk-taking

A significant factor underlying productivity is the willingness of entrepreneurs to innovate and take risks. Innovation is the process whereby individuals (and businesses for that matter), are able to make better use of resources so that more output can be produced from the same amount of labour and capital used in the production process. Part of the innovation process is related to research and development that result in cost-saving technologies or new products. However, innovation depends on more than just research and development. It also depends on individuals acquiring knowledge and skills to develop and use new technologies. Innovation is also

---

[8]However, other factors, in particular the increased importance of capital gains relative to other income, have probably been more important.

[9]The budget did raise the foreign content limit for RRSPs and RPPs from 20 per cent to 30 per cent over two years. This measure should improve risk-adjusted rates of return within registered plans.

related to the ability of individuals to develop new forms of organization and business management, which help improve the capacity of businesses to compete in today's global economy.

It has been shown that Canada, despite having one of the richest R&D incentive systems in the world, has a mediocre rate of research and development. It has also been shown that Canada has been fairly successful at cost-savings innovations but not product development (Trefler, 1999). Is this a result of inadequate incentives for research and development (note that Canada's generous tax incentives apply equally to both forms of research and development)? Or do the lack of product development innovations reflect a wider problem in the tax system? As the Technical Committee notes in its report, innovation depends not only on the incentive for entrepreneurs and businesses to develop new products and cost-savings processes but also on the demand by business to adopt such innovations.

We believe that the business tax measures, recommended in the first part of the report, would encourage both innovation and risk-taking by reducing the overall level of taxes, especially on the knowledge-based part of the economy, while leaving Canada with one of the most generous incentives for research and development in the world through the tax credit mechanism. However, additional incentives are needed in the PIT to encourage entrepreneurs to undertake innovative activity and risk-taking. There are two key elements. The first would be a reduction in the overall personal tax rates that, as a result of high marginal tax rates, discourages investment, risk-taking and work effort. The second would be new capital gains tax incentives that do not inhibit the ability of firms to grow as well as encourage risk-taking.

There are three particular issues related to the taxation of capital gains:

- First, capital gains taxes are applied to realizations, with the consequence of encouraging investors to "lock-in" holdings rather than sell them to buy more productive assets. Although the investor is able to defer tax on capital gains by holding assets rather than selling them, the "lock-in" effect can impede dynamic efficiency by discouraging the rebalancing of portfolios from poor to better quality assets. (There are restrictive circumstances in which investors can sell assets and defer capital gains taxes to a later time through the use of the "rollover" provisions in the income tax system).[10]

- Second, capital losses generally can only be used to reduce capital gains for tax purposes. There are many circumstances in which capital losses cannot be used at all. Even if the capital losses can be used, they are carried forward at no interest, so that the time value of the losses are reduced the longer it takes to use up the losses. The lack of full refundability of losses reduces the incentive to invest in risky ventures since governments also share the gains but not the losses.[11] Although one could allow capital losses to be used to reduce other income, there are potential significant tax revenue losses if investors time the sale of their assets to shelter non-capital income from tax.

- Third, capital gains are taxed without accounting for the effects of inflation on the value of the original cost of the investment. Without indexation of capital gains for inflation, the effective tax rate on capital gains is increased. This is partly, wholly or more than wholly offset by the deferral of taxes on capital gains, since the capital gains taxes are only paid when assets are disposed of rather than on the accrued gain as the value of the assets increase year by year. The impact of inflation on the cost of holding assets subject to capital gains taxation is also offset by the degree to which individuals borrow money to purchase the asset, since the interest expense is deductible without adjustment for inflation. The degree to which the deferral of taxes on gains and the lack of adjustment for inflation affects the overall tax rate, depends on the length of time that assets are held and the rate of inflation.

Generally, the above first two issues and possibly the third suggest that capital gains should be effectively taxed at a lower rate than ordinary income. However, there is another constraint facing the government in that it is relatively easy to convert higher taxed forms of income, particularly

---

[10]Note that if the capital gains tax applied to accrued, rather than realized gains, there would be no "lock-in" effect since taxes could not be postponed.

[11]See Mintz and Wilson (2000a). We show that the incidence of capital losses relative to gains has been relatively high for investors with less that $100,000 in income.

dividends, into capital gains. Governments have tried to reduce complexity in the tax system by ensuring that dividends and capital gains are taxed at similar rates — otherwise, complex anti-avoidance rules are required to prevent dividends from being converted into capital gains. However, until the recent changes in capital gains taxation in Canada, dividends were taxed more lightly than other forms of income, since individuals received a dividend tax credit to reduce personal taxes owing on dividends. The purpose of the dividend tax credit is to integrate personal and corporate income taxes on distributed income.[12] Thus, the role of the partial exclusion of capital gains from income is also to integrate corporate and personal taxes on profits reinvested in the corporation that result in an increase in the value of the corporate equities.

In the year 2000 in Ontario, the combined federal/provincial top personal income tax rate was 48 per cent. Dividends, net of the credit, were subject to a tax rate of 32 per cent while the capital gains tax rate was 36 per cent, after applying the one-quarter exclusion rate of capital gains. Thus, to equalize taxes on capital gains and dividends, it was appropriate to increase the exclusion rate from one-quarter to one-third, assuming no other changes in the tax system. This reform was included in the February 2000 federal budget. However, if there are further reforms to lower personal tax rates or changes to the corporate income tax rate for small business income, then further adjustments in the dividend credit rate and the capital gains exclusion rate would be appropriate. As we have noted elsewhere (Mintz and Wilson, 2000a, p. 25), with general reductions in corporate and personal rates, the capital gains inclusion rate could be reduced to one-half. The October 2000 Statement reduced the capital gains inclusion rate to one-half, but did not adjust the dividend tax credit. As a result, effective tax rates on capital gains are now *below* effective tax rates on dividends, reversing the situation in effect before the February 2000 budget.

Canada also provides an incentive for individuals to hold farm property and shares in qualifying Canadian-controlled private corporations through the $500,000 lifetime capital gains exemption. Prior to 1994, a general $100,000 lifetime capital gains exemption was also available for the holding of all assets but was found to be ineffective in encouraging investment and risk-taking (Mintz and Richardson, 1994, p. 15). The current exemption is

---

[12]The dividend tax credit is set to integrate corporate and personal taxes at the small business level, which is subject to tax at a federal and provincial average rate of about 20 per cent.

provided with the aim of giving farmers and small business owners an opportunity to save income for retirement since it is not possible for these individuals to use the current RRSP system for tax-assisted retirement savings since they would need to have earned income to access the system.

The existing $500,000 lifetime capital gains exemption, however, is inefficient and unfair. The exemption can be used by owners to restructure large businesses so long as the shares qualify for the exemption. The exemption also impedes the growth of companies since it is only available for shares of private, not public corporations. Further, the exemption provides those individuals who have adequate access to the existing RRSP/RPP system from other earned income a greater opportunity to save for retirement purposes by holding qualifying farm property and private corporate shares as well as their RRSP or pension assets.

The Technical Committee on Business Taxation recommended the replacement of the lifetime capital gains exemption with an enhanced RRSP system that would give farmers and small business owners opportunities to save income for retirement by rolling over their gains into RRSPs, up to a limit that depends on the years in which the assets are held and the degree to which savings have not been invested in the RRSP system. We would endorse this proposal.

The February 2000 federal budget has introduced a rollover provision for investments in qualifying small business shares. This measure should improve small business access to venture capital. However, other incentives might be considered to encourage the growth of smaller businesses. For example, one important incentive, used in the United States, is to provide favourable capital gains treatment for small businesses that issue shares to the public for the first time (Brown, Mintz and Wilson, 2000). One could also provide greater room for individuals to save for retirement purposes by expanding RRSP limits for the ownership of certain assets, such as venture capital.

Summary Recommendations for Personal Income Taxes

A large part of the fiscal dividend should be allocated to personal income tax reforms that entail significant reductions in average tax burdens. A program for tax reform needs to be designed, and it should be gradually implemented as the potential fiscal dividend grows.

Our priorities for this program are:

- The steeply progressive rates faced by low and middle income families need to be reduced by:
    - → modifying clawbacks (and/or lowering the first bracket rate) so that no one faces a marginal rate higher than the richest Canadian,
    - → reducing the middle bracket rate,
    - → widening the first and second brackets to gradually restore their real values towards 1985 levels,
    - → restoring full indexation of the basic amounts and rate brackets, and
    - → eliminating the 5 per cent high income surtax.

- Children need to be recognized as affecting ability to pay income taxes. An indexed "amount" subject to credit should be available for each child in a family.

- RRSP limits should be increased to $15,500 and fully indexed from now on.

A start has been made in implementing many of the aspects of this program. The February 2000 federal budget reduced the middle bracket rate to 24 per cent, and an additional reduction to 23 per cent is part of the announced five-year reduction plan. The October 2000 Statement implemented a further reduction in the middle bracket rate to 22 per cent, and created an additional upper middle bracket with a rate of 26 per cent. As of January 1, 2001, the top marginal rate of 29 per cent kicks in at an income of $100,000. The budget also restored full indexation of basic amounts and rate brackets, and the five-year plan promises a modest widening of the rate brackets. In addition, following the October 2000 Statement, the 5 per cent surtax, which was to be phased out in the five-year plan, was eliminated effective January 2, 2001. However, more still needs to be done. Neither the budget nor subsequent statement did anything about the clawbacks. And the widening of the tax brackets and credits in the five-year plan is insufficient to restore them to their 1985 values in real terms.

As discussed below, the remaining required changes cannot be implemented all at once, but should be feasible within the context of a five-year fiscal plan.

More fundamental reforms should also be considered. The tax treatment of the family needs to be reviewed, with an eye towards reducing, if not

Jack M. Mintz and Thomas A. Wilson

eliminating the effects of within family income distribution on net taxes paid. The integration of personal and corporate taxes and the tax treatment of capital gains should be modified to eliminate fully the double taxation of corporate source income, and to reduce the rate of tax on dividends accordingly. Further rate reductions should be considered, particularly for the lowest income bracket,[13] to encourage participation in the workforce.

Payroll Taxes

Payroll taxes in Canada are lower than in most other industrial countries. However, it should be noted that these taxes generally finance social insurance benefits — primarily public pensions, and unemployment benefits. While the linkages from taxes to benefits may be loose for some individuals,[14] there are recognized benefits financed, in large part, by earmarked taxes. As a result, the much higher payroll taxes in Europe mainly reflect the higher social insurance benefits paid there. Similarly, higher federal payroll taxes in the United States reflect more generous U.S. social security pensions relative to Canada/Quebec Pension Plans (CPP/QPP) pensions.

In 1997, the federal and provincial governments reached an agreement to ensure the long-run financial viability of the CPP. Although there were some modest reductions in benefits, most of the reduction in the unfunded liability of the CPP was to be effected by a 65 per cent increase in CPP payroll tax rates, to be phased in over the 1998 to 2003 period. While alternatives to this approach have been put forward (Dungan, 1998; Pesando, 1997), in this paper we accept the CPP payroll tax increases as a given.

Dungan's (1998) examination of the economic effects of the scheduled CPP/QPP payroll tax increases indicates that, even when the payroll tax increase is fully shifted to workers in the long run, there are nevertheless adverse transitional effects that reduce aggregate output and cause job losses. These effects would be mitigated or eliminated if other payroll taxes were

---

[13]The October 2000 Statement reduced the first bracket rate by one percentage point, effective January 1, 2001.

[14]In Canada, for example, unemployment benefit payments are partially clawed back for individuals with income above a threshold.

reduced as the CPP rate increases take effect. The obvious candidate for this role is the EI contribution rate. At present the Employment Insurance (EI) "Fund" has a large accumulated surplus, and EI revenues exceed unemployment benefits and other outlays by $5–6 billion per year. As it is the employer portion of payroll taxes that generates the adverse transitional economic effects, and as employer EI payroll taxes are 1.4 times employee contributions, and apply to a higher income level than CPP contributions, a given CPP rate increase for employees can be offset by a smaller employee EI rate cut.

One approach, which was recommended by the Technical Committee, is to implement a limited form of experience rating via selective reductions in the employers' portion of the EI tax. We would strongly endorse this recommendation, which would improve labour-force adjustments and reduce the unemployment rate over the medium term. However, if limited experience rating is rejected, the overall EI rate should be reduced as a second-best alternative. For example, if the basic EI contribution rate for employees were reduced by 20¢ per year over the three-year period 2001–03, this would offset most of the adverse transitional effects of scheduled increases in CPP/QPP contributions (Dungan, 1998).

The Room for Tax Reductions: An Illustrative Exercise

In 1999 Finance Canada engaged four forecasting organizations to develop estimates of the potential surplus (or "fiscal dividend") that would be generated over a five-fiscal-year period (2001–02 through 2004–05). These estimates were developed on the basis of a common set of economic projections — the so-called "consensus" or average of forecasts of private sector firms and organizations — and a common set of fiscal assumptions. They have served as the base for all subsequent discussions about the utilization of the fiscal dividend and are still a useful reference point today. Beyond the fiscal measures already put in place by past budgets, these fiscal projections entail no change in basic tax rates, and program spending (other than EI and OAS/GIS payments) held constant in real per capita terms.

The average results of this exercise were published by the Department of Finance in the *1999 Economic and Fiscal Update* (Canada, Department of Finance, 1999, p. 80). We reproduce the average projected potential surpluses in the first line of Table 5. As is shown, the projected fiscal dividend steadily increases, reaching a level of $30 billion in 2004–05.

PEAP was one of the four forecasting/modelling organizations involved. The projected potential surpluses, that PEAP developed for this exercise are presented in the second line of Table 5. While these near-term estimates are close to the average, in the later years, the PEAP model generates a larger fiscal dividend, reaching $33 billion in 2004–05. This result reflects more buoyant corporate tax revenues, somewhat higher EI revenues and lower EI payouts in PEAP's analysis.

These projections, although published in November 1999, were constructed using information available in September 1999. The economic outlook improved significantly in the intervening months as reflected in forecasts published by *Consensus Economics*, and in various statements published in the financial press.

PEAP released a long-term economic forecast on November 10, 1999, which incorporated this additional information. We then reconstructed the fiscal dividend projection, using this long-term economic projection, but maintaining the same fiscal assumptions as in the September 1999 exercise. These results are shown in the third line of Table 5. The potential surplus over the first three years is increased by $1 billion to $1.5 billion per year.

Table 5: Total Fiscal Dividend ($ billion)

Fiscal Years:	2000–01	2001–02	2002–03	2003–04	2004–05
Based on September 1999 "average" forecast					
Average of 4 modelers	9.9	13.6	18.5	24.4	30.1
PEAP	10.3	14.5	20.4	26.8	33.0
November PEAP forecast (with Finance fiscal)	11.5	16.0	21.2	26.5	33.1
Pre-budget PEAP analysis[a]	12.7	16.5	22.0	29.1	35.5
Post-budget PEAP analysis	7.3	6.3	7.3	10.0	13.8

Note: [a] The projections were updated on the basis of the fourth quarter National Accounts data. Fiscal projections were based on the growth rates of the previous projection.

But in the last two years (2003–04 and 2004–05) there is little difference between the November and original estimates. This shows that projections of the out-years in a medium-term forecast are not terribly sensitive to small differences in the starting point.

With the release of the fourth quarter 2000 National Accounts data, and revisions for the previous three quarters, we updated these fiscal projections (maintaining the same fiscal assumptions). These results are shown in the fourth line of Table 5. As shown, the potential surplus is higher in every year of the analysis, but again not greatly so.

The February 2000 budget introduced a number of tax reductions. It also included spending initiatives, many of which were pre-booked to fiscal 1999–2000. There were also spending initiatives announced prior to the budget, but after the November statement, and an EI payroll tax cut on January 1, 2000. Two important measures in the budget offset the medium-term fiscal outlook: full indexation of the basic amounts, and rate brackets was restored,[15] and the five-year tax reduction plan was announced.

We have implemented all of these measures in our analysis of the budget. As no time pattern for future tax reductions was announced in the February 2000 budget, we assume that all future tax cuts are smoothly implemented over the five-year period. Consistent with the assumption in the budget (and with past behaviour) we assume that debt reduction is limited to $3 billion per year. When the budget measures are incorporated, the estimated fiscal dividend is reduced, but not eliminated, as shown in line 6 of Table 5.

A key assumption in the construction of these potential surplus estimates was that debt reduction would be $3 billion per year. Debt reduction obviously affects the magnitude of potential surpluses in the later years by reducing future interest payments to service the debt.

Table 6 presents an analysis that allows for larger debt paydowns, particularly in the early years. As a result, the potential surplus generated is somewhat larger in 2004–05 at $14.3 billion, about $0.5 billion higher than with the steady $3 billion per year debt paydown assumed in the projections of Table 5.

We believe that a strong case can be made for larger planned debt paydowns in the early years. As shown in Table 6, if debt reduction is

---

[15]In addition, various refundable tax credits, and clawback thresholds were fully indexed.

Jack M. Mintz and Thomas A. Wilson

Table 6: Derivation of Room for Additional Tax Reductions: PEAP Post-Budget Analysis ($ billion)

	2000-2001	2001-2002	2002-2003	2003-2004	2004-2005	Cumulative 5 year Totals
Total post-budget fiscal dividend (Table 5 line 5)	7.3	6.3	7.3	10.0	13.8	44.7
Debt paydown	6.0	6.0	5.0	4.0	3.0	24.0
Amount generated by additional debt reduction*	0.1	0.3	0.4	0.5	0.5	1.8
Adjusted fiscal dividend	7.4	6.9	7.7	10.5	14.3	46.5
Room for additional tax reductions	1.4	0.9	2.7	6.5	11.3	22.8

Note: *This is the interest on the additional debt reduction above $3 billion per year.

doubled in the first two years, and then gradually reduced to $3 billion by 2004–05, the future potential surplus would be increased.

We view debt reduction, particularly in the early years, as important for the following reasons.

- Larger debt reduction will generate higher national savings and lower interest rates, which are conducive to long-term growth.

- A larger budget surplus will reduce the burden on the Bank of Canada to control inflation, and

- Given the government's determination to avoid deficits, a larger planned surplus provides a more adequate "cushion" against perverse fiscal policies in the event of a recession, thereby permitting the automatic fiscal stabilizers to operate with full force.

On balance, we view the debt reduction shown in Table 6 as appropriate, and therefore must subtract these amounts from the projected fiscal dividend of the base case. As noted above, the larger debt paydown in the early years entails more room to manoeuvre in the later years because of reduced debt-servicing costs.

When the planned debt paydowns are subtracted from the fiscal dividend we arrive at our estimates of the amount available for additional tax reductions (or spending increases). The room for additional tax cuts is small in the first two years, reflecting the priority of debt repayment. But this room increases in the later years of the projection, reaching over $11 billion in 2004-05.

A Medium-Term Tax Reduction Plan

Given these projections, we believe that a medium-term tax reduction plan should be implemented. While reductions in personal income taxes will account for most of the reduction in tax revenues, it is important to include reductions in business taxes and payroll taxes in the tax reduction plan. As noted earlier, these are the taxes that have the strongest effects on efficiency and growth.

Reductions in EI payroll taxes will help to offset the adverse transitional effects of CPP/QPP payroll tax increases on employment. We have therefore allowed for five successive annual 15¢ reductions in the employee contribution rate, starting January 1, 2001. In fiscal 2004-05 this measure will cost about $5.1 billion.

A higher priority, from the standpoint of economic efficiency and growth, are reductions in business taxes. We believe that a significant reduction in corporate taxes will facilitate the implementation of the recommendations of the Technical Committee, as well as being desirable on their own. Following the February 2000 budget our tax reduction package therefore includes a seven percentage point reduction in the statutory rate for large non-manufacturing firms, to be phased in over five years. This reduction is over and above the rate reductions that could be financed by base-broadening measures. Upon full implementation, the annual *ex ante* cost of this measure would be almost $3 billion dollars. However, as the Technical Committee noted, a reduction in statutory corporate rates will likely increase the corporate tax base, thereby reducing the revenue loss. This measure would reduce the combined federal/provincial rate to about 36 per cent. Further

Jack M. Mintz and Thomas A. Wilson

reductions could be made if the base-broadening reforms recommended by the committee were implemented. It should be possible to reduce the combined federal/provincial corporate rate to about 30 per cent without additional revenue losses.

We also include a reduction in the capital gains inclusion rate from three-quarters to two-thirds, in order to bring the typical top bracket marginal rate on realized capital gains in line with the effective marginal rate on dividends. This measure was implemented in the February 2000 budget.[16] The annual net revenue costs, which would begin in fiscal year 2000–01, would be about $0.3 billion per year on an *ex ante* basis. However, a reduction in capital gains taxes will likely stimulate realizations (Mintz and Wilson, 2000b) reducing the net revenue cost of this measure.

When the payroll, business and capital gains tax reductions are deducted from the total tax room, we derive the amount available for personal income tax reductions. As shown in Table 7, there is considerable room for PIT reductions within the five-year fiscal plan.

Allocating the Fiscal Dividend: Economic Effects

The current debate is about the allocation of the fiscal dividend. We have therefore chosen to model the economic effects of the particular combination of debt paydowns, spending increases and tax reductions described above relative to an alternative allocation. In the alternative, we have limited debt reduction to $3 billion per year, and have allocated *all* of the remaining potential surplus to non-taxable transfers to persons. This particular alternative was selected since it represented the base case used in the original fiscal dividend exercise.

We then implemented our recommended package of debt reduction, spending increase and tax reductions, reducing non-taxable transfer payments dollar for dollar to "finance" these initiatives. We set monetary policy to maintain the price level approximately unchanged when our fiscal dividend allocation package is introduced.

---

[16]The inclusion rate was further reduced to one-half in the October 2000 Statement.

Table 7: A Recommended Tax Reduction Strategy ($ billion)

	Total Pre-Budget Fiscal Dividend	Expenditure* Increases	EI Rate Cuts**	Capital Gains & CIT Cuts	Room for PIT Cuts	Debt Reduction Targets
2000–01	12.7	2.3	0.3	0.0	4.1	6.0
2001–02	16.5	2.7	1.5	0.6	5.7	6.0
2002–03	22.0	3.2	2.7	1.7	9.4	5.0
2003–04	28.6	3.4	3.9	2.5	14.8	4.0
2004–05	35.5	2.9	5.1	3.3	21.2	3.0

Notes: *These are the expenditure increases announced in (or immediately before) budget 2000 (including increases in the child tax benefit).
**This is in addition to the rate cut that went into effect in January 2000.

The results are presented in Table 8. As is apparent, the package has favourable effects on employment, productivity and real output. The composition of demand is shifted from consumption to investment, net exports and real government purchases of goods and services. As the package exerts a deflationary impact on prices, monetary policy is eased, with lower interest rates and a lower exchange rate. With investment stronger, the capital stock gradually increases. The federal government surplus is increased directly as a result of our higher debt reduction targets, and indirectly because of lower interest rates and stronger economic growth. In the final year of the analysis, the federal debt-GDP ratio is reduced by 1.4 percentage points relative to the alternative.

These economic and fiscal results in this illustrative simulation are due to three of the measures in our package.

• Higher debt paydowns, which provide more room for monetary easing;

• Business tax reductions, which stimulate investment; and

Table 8: Allocating the Fiscal Dividend: The TOTAL Package Starting in 2000FY
(impacts are percentage changes unless otherwise indicated)

	FISCAL YEARS				
	2000-01	2001-02	2002-03	2003-04	2004-05
Real Output and Components					
Real Gross Domestic Product	0.48	0.24	0.30	0.59	0.69
Consumption	-0.75	-1.26	-1.18	-0.78	-0.18
Government current and capital	2.02	1.42	1.38	1.17	0.63
Residential construction	1.77	1.99	0.57	1.06	1.13
Non-residential construction	1.06	1.84	1.93	2.20	2.44
Machinery and equipment	0.89	2.22	2.33	2.18	2.01
Exports	0.32	0.50	0.65	0.82	0.81
Imports	-0.25	-0.06	-0.13	-0.10	0.21
Prices, Productivity and Employment					
Implicit deflator for GDP	-0.09	-0.05	-0.06	-0.11	0.04
Consumer Price Index	-0.07	-0.04	-0.04	-0.11	0.01
Labour productivity	0.28	-0.04	0.10	0.28	0.23
Employment	0.21	0.27	0.20	0.31	0.46
Unemployment rate (% Pts)	-0.13	-0.16	-0.09	-0.16	-0.24
Profits and Capital Formation					
Pre-tax corporate profits	3.09	1.52	2.26	3.16	2.82
Capital stock	0.03	0.21	0.44	0.64	0.82
Money and Interest Rates					
90-day paper rate (% Pts)	-0.24	-0.15	-0.17	-0.23	-0.10
Industrial bond rate (% Pts)	-0.24	-0.15	-0.17	-0.24	-0.10
Exchange Rate and Balance of Payments					
Exchange rate	-0.40	-0.50	-0.70	-0.79	-0.79
Current account balance ($b)	1.66	2.10	3.31	3.85	2.40
Deficits and Debt					
Aggregate surplus/deficit ($b)	4.72	4.26	2.67	2.57	2.71
Federal surplus/deficit ($b)	4.36	4.19	2.63	1.94	1.10
Ratio of federal debt to GDP (% Pts)	-0.42	-0.76	-1.03	-1.25	-1.37

- Payroll tax cuts, which put downward pressure on unit costs (i.e., they are like a favourable supply price shock), permitting stronger growth without inflation.

The other components of the package — PIT cuts and increased government spending on goods and services — have very similar aggregate effects as non-taxable transfers. These results therefore serve to underline the importance of debt reduction and cuts in business taxes and payroll taxes if economic growth and productivity are to be enhanced.

The additional fiscal surplus generated by our recommended fiscal package is presented in Table 9. As shown, by fiscal year 2004–05 the federal surplus would be increased by about $1.1 billion. These additions to the surplus provide some insurance that debt reduction targets will be met. Alternatively, they can be viewed as providing the opportunity for additional fiscal initiatives in the later years of the projection.

While large potential surpluses have focused public attention on tax reductions, meaningful PIT reform could also entail significant base-

Table 9: Impact of Fiscal Package on Budget Surplus

Fiscal Year	Debt Reduction Target[a]	Debt Reduction Result[b]	Additional Fiscal Surplus
2000–01	6.0	7.4	1.4
2001–02	6.0	7.2	1.2
2002–03	5.0	5.6	0.6
2003–04	4.0	4.9	0.9
2004–05	3.0	4.1	1.1

Notes: [a]From Table 6, line 3.
[b]Federal surplus reported in Table 8, plus the $3 billion Contingency Reserve.

Jack M. Mintz and Thomas A. Wilson

broadening,[17] which could finance even larger reductions in tax rates, or additional measures to improve equity and efficiency.

The macroeconomic analysis presented in this paper was carried out before the October 2000 Economic Statement and Budget Update. The additional PIT reductions announced in that statement would use up most of the estimated room for tax reductions shown in Table 6. On the other hand the federal budget surplus for fiscal 1999–2000 was $12.3 billion, about $9 billion higher than estimated in budget 2000. The federal budget surplus for fiscal year 2000–01 is $17.1 billion, about $13 billion higher than planned in budget 2000. Unless this improved fiscal position was wholly explained by transitory factors, the large surplus would provide additional room for new fiscal initiatives. In any case, the reduction in debt-service costs generated by the large surpluses of those two years will provide additional fiscal room.

Another factor clouding the picture is the deterioration of the near-term economic outlook in 2001. The slower growth experienced in the fourth quarter of 2000 and the first half of 2001 will likely reduce the federal surplus in fiscal 2001–02. However, the medium-term fiscal picture may not be significantly changed.

While the quantitative estimates provided in this paper are clearly subject to revision, our qualitative conclusions are unlikely to be affected. Consequently, we still recommend that the federal government establish a task force to evaluate the personal income tax. Like the Technical Committee's Report on Business Taxation, the report of this task force would provide the framework to guide further PIT initiatives over the medium term.

Conclusions

Our analysis suggests that the federal government should maintain its commitment to the five-year tax reduction plan and should implement this

---

[17]Above we mentioned replacing the $500,000 exemption for farmers and CCPCs with expanded access to RRSPs. Other possible base-broadening measures include the taxation of certain employee benefits, the elimination of age and pension credits, and the taxation of lottery and gambling winnings.

plan on a timely basis. While personal income tax cuts will take up most of the room for tax reductions, it is important to steadily reduce payroll and business taxes as well. Our simulations of a fiscal package involving significant debt reduction, modest spending increases and reductions in personal, business and payroll taxes, using the FOCUS macroeconometric model show that such a fiscal package should have favourable supply-side effects on output, employment and productivity over the medium term. Finally, there are still important issues of tax structure that need to be addressed. Consequently, we recommend that the government establish a task force to review personal income taxes and to consider the need for additional tax cuts.

References

Brown, R.D., J.M. Mintz and T.A. Wilson (2000), "Corporation and Taxation: A Largely Private Matter?" NBER Working Paper (Cambridge, MA: National Bureau of Economic Research).

Canada, Department of Finance (1999), *The Economic and Fiscal Update*, November 2 (Ottawa: Supply and Services Canada).

_____ (2001), *Economic Update*, May 17.

Dungan, P. (1998), *The CPP Payroll Tax Hike: Macroeconomic Transition Costs and Alternatives*, Commentary No. 116 (Toronto: C.D. Howe Institute).

Dungan, P., S. Murphy and T.A. Wilson (1997), "The Sensitivity of the Corporate Tax to the Statutory Rate", Working Paper No. 97-1 (Ottawa: Technical Committee on Business Taxation, Department of Finance).

Fortin, P. (1999), "The Canadian Standard of Living: Is There a Way Up?" Benefactors lecture (Toronto: C.D. Howe Institute).

_____ (2001), "Fiscal Stabilization and the Allocation of the Fiscal Dividend: An Assessment", in P.A.R. Hobson and T.A. Wilson (eds.), *The 2000 Federal Budget: Retrospect and Prospect* (Kingston: John Deutsch Institute, Queen's University), 181-192.

Jog, V. and J. Tang (1997), "Tax Reforms, Debt Shifting and Tax Revenues: Multinational Corporations in Canada", Working Paper No. 97-14 (Ottawa: Technical Committee on Business Taxation, Department of Finance).

KPMG (2000), *Tax Facts 1999–2000* (Toronto: KPMG).

Macnaughton, A., T. Matthews and J. Pittman (1998), "Stealth Tax Rates: Effective Versus Statutory Personal Marginal Tax Rates", *Canadian Tax Journal* 46(5), 1029-1066.

Mintz, J.M. and F. Poschmann (1999), *Tax Reform, Tax Reduction: The Missing Framework*, Commentary No. 121 (Toronto: C.D. Howe Institute).

Mintz, J.M. and S.R. Richardson (1994), *The Lifetime Capital Gains Exemption: An Evaluation* (Ottawa: Department of Finance).

Mintz, J.M. and T.A. Wilson (2000a), "Taxes, Efficiency and Economic Growth", PEAP Policy Study 2000-1 (Toronto: Institute for Policy Analysis).

_____ (2000b), "Realization and Revenue Effects of Capital Gains Taxes in Canada", unpublished paper, March.

Pesando, J. (1997) *From Tax Grab to Retirement Saving: Privatizing the CPP Premium Hike*, Commentary No. 93 (Toronto: C.D. Howe Institute).

Trefler, D. (1999), "Does Canada Need a Productivity Budget?", *Policy Options* (July-August), 66-71.

Whalley, J. (1997), "Efficiency Considerations of Business Tax Reform", Working Paper No. 97-8 (Ottawa: Technical Committee on Business Taxation, Department of Finance).

Wilson, T.A. (1998), "The Proposed Seniors Benefit: An Evaluation", *Report of Proceedings of the Forty-Ninth Tax Conference* (Toronto: Canadian Tax Foundation).

Pensions

The Canada Pension Plan:
Looking Back at the Recent Reforms

James E. Pesando

Introduction

In 1998, after extensive consultation, the federal government and the provinces implemented a package of reforms to the Canada Pension Plan (CPP). Two particularly significant reforms were included.

First, there was a sharp increase in the combined employer-employee contribution rate, from 5.85 per cent in 1997 to the steady state rate of 9.9 per cent in the year 2003 and beyond. The steady-state contribution rate is the rate necessary to fully fund new benefits and to service the existing unfunded liability.

The sharp increase in contribution rates will result in a much larger reserve fund — estimated to rise to about five years' worth of benefits. In light of this fact, the second major reform was to establish an independent, trusteed CPP Investment Board with a mandate to invest in marketable securities, including equities, in order to obtain a higher rate of return on the enlarged CPP reserve fund.

Importantly, the benefit reductions were relatively modest. The benefit reductions consist of:

- using a five-year rather than a three-year average of the year's maximum pensionable earnings (YMPE) to calculate retirement pensions (and the earnings-related portion of disability and survivors' benefits);

- freezing the maximum death benefit at $2,500; and

- tightening eligibility conditions, as well as reducing payments for disability benefits.

The primary thrust of the reforms designed to improve the funded status of the CPP is thus to increase contributions. In fact, the schedule of steep increases in the employer-employee contribution rate is accompanied by the freezing of the year's basic exemption (YBE) at $3,500. Due to inflation, the freeze on the YBE serves to expand the base of contributory earnings with the passage of time.

In this paper, I offer an economist's perspective on several aspects of the reform package. In particular, I address the following questions:

- With the benefit of hindsight, what were the economic arguments that proved successful in the political arena and ultimately led to the reform package?

- Is the steady-state contribution rate of 9.9 per cent likely to prove sufficient to finance the promised level of retirement (and disability) benefits?

- What are the prospects that the new investment strategy for the CPP fund will produce a higher real rate of return over the long run, as is assumed in the estimate of the steady-state contribution rate?

- What about "the path not taken"; that is, possible reforms to the CPP that were not undertaken, including those that have been considered in prior studies of the possible reform of Canada's public retirement income system?

The Economic Arguments Used to Achieve Reform

The economic argument used to "sell" the package of CPP reforms was one-dimensional: that of intergenerational equity.

The federal government emphasized the sharp increase in the pay-go contribution rate that would accompany the aging of the Canadian population. The implicit rate of return on required CPP contributions, by age cohort, was calculated and shown to be dramatically lower for new entrants (i.e., the younger generation) than, for example, those Canadians approaching the retirement age of 65 established by the CPP.

In *An Information Paper for Consultations on the Canadian Pension Plan*, released by the federal, provincial and territorial governments of Canada in February 1996, the importance of intergenerational equity to the consensus-building exercise is unmistakable. The *Information Paper* notes that:

> If pay-as-you-go financing is left in place, future generations of Canadians will be paying 14.2 per cent of contributory earnings for their CPP benefits — much more than the 5.6 per cent that today's workers are paying. The advantage of pay-as-you-go financing would be that the increase to 14.2 per cent could be gradual — taking place over many years. However, it fails to deal with the fundamental challenge of whether it is either reasonable or fair to expect younger generations to pay such high contribution rates. (1996, p. 25)

Less quantitatively, but with more obvious political appeal, the *Information Paper* emphasizes that:

> The basic challenge facing Canadians today is one of fairness and equity. If no changes are made to the CPP and the way it is financed, our children and grandchildren will be asked to pay two to three times more than we are paying for the same pensions from the CPP. For the past 30 years, we have not paid our way. Even today, we are not paying our way. Today's CPP pensioners have paid much less than their benefits are worth. In contrast, future generations will be asked to pay considerably more than their benefits are worth. (ibid., p. 4)

This concern with intergenerational equity is especially relevant, given the fact that the other pillars of the public retirement system in Canada —

Old Age Security (OAS) and the Guaranteed Income Supplement (GIS) — are financed on a pay-go basis.[1]

Surprisingly, any discussion of the economic efficiency issues, which have concerned professional economists at least since 1974, when Feldstein wrote his now classic paper on the possible impact on private savings of pay-go public pension programs (Feldstein, 1974), have been virtually absent from the recent public debate.

In the standard life-cycle model of consumption, the existence of a pay-as-you-go public pension plan will depress personal savings and thus reduce the stock of domestic capital. The reasoning is straightforward. With the promise of public pension income during retirement, households have less need to save from their disposable income, in order to provide for their consumption needs during retirement.

There are two important caveats to these predictions of the standard life-cycle model. First, under a pay-as-you-go public pension plan, households may reduce their consumption and increase their savings (and ultimately their bequests) in order to offset the higher "tax burden" their children face. To the extent that the behaviour of households conforms to the Ricardian equivalence model popularized by Barro (1974), the existence of a pay-as-you-go public pension plan will not depress personal savings, and the decision to increase the degree of funding of such a plan will not lead to an increase in personal savings.

Second, Canada is a small, open economy, and international capital flows are likely to limit the extent to which a higher domestic savings rate translates into an increase in the stock of domestic capital. In the extreme case of perfect capital mobility, there would be an increase in the ownership

---

[1]The security of public pensions is ultimately linked to the willingness of future generations to provide the pensions that are promised to today's workers. This willingness will depend on two considerations: first, the share of national income required to meet the pension obligations, which depends on the level of national income and on the ratio of pensioners to workers; and second, the perceived likelihood that the pension system will be perpetuated, so that future generations of Canadians will be supported in turn during their own retirement. In other words, the viability of today's pensions depends on both long-term economic considerations and future generations' acceptance of the pension "rules of the game" established by the current generation. If the perception is that the rules of the game have been singularly unfair to the now-working generation, it is reasonable to conjecture that promised benefits could be placed at risk.

by residents of Canada of an unchanged domestic capital stock, as well as an increase in the ownership of foreign assets by residents of Canada. However, as noted in a recent contribution by Gordon and Bovenberg (1996), empirical studies confirm that there is a high correlation between domestic savings and investment — that is, that international capital is not perfectly mobile. There is, not surprisingly, disagreement among economists as to the magnitude of any reduction in private savings that accompanies the existence of a pay-go public pension program. Perhaps this disagreement explains the complete absence of attention to this issue in the *Information Paper*.[2]

Nonetheless, it seems likely that the scheduled increase in CPP contribution rates will yield an increase in personal savings and in the domestic capital stock. An increase in CPP contributions, with no change or reduction in retirement benefits, will reduce the wealth of households. This will lead to a reduction in consumption, and thus to an increase in personal savings (public plus private).

Both Ricardian equivalence and open economy considerations, however, make it difficult to offer a precise estimate of the extent to which higher CPP contribution rates will translate into higher savings and ultimately into a higher stock of real capital.[3]

Professional economists have also studied the efficiency implications of the link between the payroll taxes used to finance public pension programs and the perceived benefits of such programs to individual taxpayers.

The economic rationale for using payroll taxes to finance social security benefits depends on a close association between an individual's contributions and his or her benefits. Assume, for example, that an individual's

---

[2]In prior studies of the role of the Canada/Quebec Pension Plan, the issue of its impact on savings and capital formation is accorded serious attention. For example, the Task Force on Retirement Income (Canada, 1979, p. 242) writes: "One objection often registered against enlarging the C/QPP is that it would affect adversely the level of saving in the economy and would reduce the amount of capital available to the private sector, retarding future economic growth. The validity of this argument was considered in Chapter IV. It was indicated there that both the empirical and theoretical bases for this objection are at least open to serious question."

[3]To the extent that higher savings are used to acquire foreign assets (rather than to increase the domestic capital stock), consumption needs in retirement will be financed by imports — that is, by claims to goods and services produced in other countries.

contribution to a public pension plan pays for the pension benefit that the individual earns during the period. Assume, as well, that the individual is content to save this (or a larger) amount towards retirement. Then there should be no distorting impact on the individual's labour supply. The individual's contribution to the public pension plan is just the "price" of the pension benefit to which he or she becomes entitled during the period.

In contrast, consider the case of an individual who perceives there to be no benefit associated with the pension contribution. To this person, the contribution to the public pension plan is simply a tax on earned income. Like other such taxes, the pension contribution discourages work and thus adversely affects the long-run labour supply. For those with earnings less than the YMPE, contributions raise the marginal tax rate on income that is already subject to a high marginal rate, thus discouraging additional hours of work. For those with earnings above the YMPE, CPP contributions raise the average tax rate. This may also adversely affect the long-run labour supply by, for example, encouraging individuals to work in the underground economy.

Economic studies suggest that the ultimate burden of employer payroll taxes falls mostly on employees (i.e., these employer costs are shifted back to the worker, through lower cash wages or other benefits). If this is so, a close linkage between pension contributions and pension benefits will eliminate the disincentives to long-run labour supply associated with payroll taxes. This is an important consideration, as long as there is some long-run elasticity of labour supply with respect to the net-of-tax real wage.[4]

There is no reference to this line of reasoning in the *Information Paper*. However, to the extent that the higher contributions rates are seen by younger Canadians as enhancing the security of the CPP retirement benefits promised to them, this efficiency rationale could also have been invoked as part of the motivation for reform.[5]

---

[4]The prevailing view among economists is that the long-run elasticity of labour supply is small, but not zero.

[5]In Pesando (1997), I argue that this efficiency issue favours the partial privatization of the CPP.

The Steady-State Contribution Rate of 9.9 Per cent

To calculate the required contribution rate for the CPP, one must adopt assumptions regarding a broad set of economic and demographic factors. These include, but are not limited to: fertility, migration, mortality, disability, employment wage increases, price increases and the rate of return on investment.

The fact that the estimated steady-state contribution rate is slightly *less* than 10 per cent (i.e., 9.9 per cent) invites the question of whether the actuarial and economic assumptions used to calculate this rate are reasonable and appropriate, or have been adopted to produce a politically attractive result.

David Slater and his co-author Bill Robson have raised some important concerns regarding this possibility. After reviewing the *Canada Pension Plan: Seventeenth Actuarial Report as at 31 December 1997*, they conclude that:

> As for the key question — whether public confidence in the CPP's promises will increase commensurately with its improved financial condition — the sustainability of the 9.9 per cent rate will probably be crucial in determining the answer. Although the Seventeenth Report's bottom line indicates that the 9.9 per cent rate is more than enough, the details of its projections give rise to some cautions.
>
> The balance of risks appears negative with respect to several key assumptions; those about disability benefit, immigration, earning growth, and inflation stand out as problematic. The reliability of these assumptions needs review in future reports. (Slater and Robson, 1999, p. 15)

As an economist, I find the assumption about the long-term inflation rate to be of particular interest and of instructive value.

The Chief Actuary, in the *Seventeenth Actuarial Report*, assumes that the long-term inflation rate will be 3 per cent. This figure is lower than the assumed inflation rate of 3.5 per cent adopted in the *Fifteenth* and *Sixteenth Actuarial Reports*.

The higher is the assumed inflation rate, the lower will be the estimate of the steady-state contribution rate. In the main, this is due to changes instituted on the benefit side of the CPP as part of the reform package. In particular, the calculation of the retirement benefit is now linked to a five-year, instead of a three-year, average of the YMPE. The death benefit is now fixed, in nominal terms, at $2,500.

Further, the YBE is now frozen, in nominal terms, at $3,500. As a result, the higher is the inflation rate, the lower is the real value of the initial earnings which are excluded from required CPP contributions.

Since 1991, the Bank of Canada — in agreement with the minister of finance — has committed monetary policy in Canada to the sole objective of achieving an inflation rate that lies between 1 and 3 per cent. Moreover, since 1993, the Bank of Canada has succeeded in achieving this objective.

Further, signals from the financial market indicate that market participants believe that the Bank of Canada will succeed in keeping the inflation rate below 3 per cent for the foreseeable future. At present (June 2001), the explicit real interest rate on the principal Real Return Bond of the Government of Canada (the 4.25s of 1 December 2021) is 3.6 per cent. In conjunction with the current interest rate of 5.9 per cent on conventional Government of Canada bonds with 30 years to maturity, the implicit "market" expectation of the long-term inflation rate is 2.22 per cent.[6]

In light of the above, the adoption by the Chief Actuary of a long-term inflation rate of 3 per cent seems problematic. As noted by Slater and Robson (1999), the use of the mid-point of the target range (i.e., 2 per cent) would increase the steady state contribution rate by 0.2 of a percentage point.

The Projected Real Return on the CPP Investment Fund

In the *Seventeenth Actuarial Report as at 31 December 1997*, the real rate of return on new fund investments is assumed to equal 4 per cent. This figure, although the same as in the *Sixteenth Report*, is far above the assumed rate of 2.5 per cent in the *Fifteenth Report*.

Prior to the reform, CPP funds were invested primarily in 20-year, non-marketable securities of the provincial governments, at an interest rate that reflected the cost of funds to the federal government. After the reform, the

---

[6]Note that (1.0590) ÷ (1.0360) less 1.0, times 100, is equal to 2.22 per cent.

newly established CPP Investment Board (a Crown corporation created by an Act of Parliament in December 1997) has a mandate to manage new CPP funds prudently with a view to achieving a maximum rate of return without undue risk of loss. The CPP Investment Board is currently authorized to invest in domestic equities, and it is to be allowed to actively invest (as opposed to replicating a broad market index) 50 per cent of its domestic equity portfolio.

The decision to permit the CPP Investment Board to invest in domestic equities is worthy of comment on several accounts.

First, the business community in Canada has historically opposed the move towards fuller funding for the CPP, in large part because of the possible "politicizing" of the investment decisions of the enlarged reserve fund. During the discussions that preceded the 1998 reforms, this concern was much attenuated. In sharp contrast, the potential for political interference with the investment decision of an enlarged reserve fund remains a focal point in discussions of a possible increase in the degree of funding for U.S. social security.

Second, investment in equities — especially in the United States — has produced very high realized returns for the past decade, except for the past year or so. The sharp run-up in stock prices, as reflected by price-earnings ratios that remain very high by historical standards, invites the concern that the CPP Investment Board may be directing a portion of funds into equities at a particularly inopportune time. Indeed, the CPP Investment Board, in its March 31, 1999 *Annual Report*, acknowledges this possibility:

> Stock markets, most notably in the United States and Europe, have generally produced the strongest investment returns in the 20th century during the past few years. While there is some risk that the Investment Board may be initiating its passive equity program towards the "top of the market", history suggests that better returns can still be expected from equities over the long term compared with most other investment opportunities.

In light of the existence of the large portfolio of provincial and government bonds as well as the short-term operating reserve that are both administered by the federal government,[7] the CPP Investment Board has been

---

[7]As at December 31, 2000, the market value of assets invested by the CPP Investment Board was $6.4 billion. As at this same date, the CPP had total assets

allocating 100 per cent of new investments to equities. In the first three-quarters of the current fiscal year, as a result of declines in equity markets in Canada and around the world, the CPP Investment Board incurred a net loss on its investments.

The returns to a diversified portfolio of equities will, of course, fluctuate from year to year and may on occasion be negative. The interesting question, from an economist's perspective, is whether the high level of equity prices that currently exists has any implications for anticipated returns over the longer term. To address this question, it is useful to note several insights from the modern literature in financial economics.

First, the high historical rate of return on a diversified portfolio of equities relative to "safe" assets like Treasury bills has posed a puzzle for economists. Simply stated, the observed excess of the real rate of return on equities over the real rate of return on Treasury bills (about 5 per cent, which is the difference between a real rate of return on equities of 7 per cent and a real rate of return on Treasury bills of 2 per cent) appears to be too large to be explained by any reasonable degree of risk aversion of rational economic agents. Indeed, this historical evidence has become the source of what is now referred to as the "equity premium" puzzle (Mehra and Prescott, 1985).

It may be that the sharp run-up in equity prices (as reflected by historically high price-earnings ratios) is due to the "unwinding" of this puzzle. Investors may now be willing to hold equities at a much lower than historical anticipated rate of return; that is, at a much smaller premium relative to the rate of return offered by low-risk alternatives. If so, the implication is that the expected real rate of return on equities in the future is significantly less than the historical rate of return.

Second, it may be that the sharp run-up in equity prices is due to a fad or bubble. (This argument seems particularly well-suited to the recent collapse in share prices of "new economy" stocks, as evidenced by the dramatic decline in the Nasdaq index from its March 2000 high.) If so, the present level of stock prices is vulnerable to a significant correction for a different reason: the possibility of the bursting of this bubble.

Empirical evidence from the U.S. market suggests that, over mid-term to long-term investment horizons, the real rates of return on a diversified portfolio of stocks are negatively correlated over time (Cochrane, 1999).

---

of $41.6 billion, including $29.8 billion (at cost) of provincial and federal government bonds.

This evidence is consistent with either the "overreaction" of equity prices (i.e., to mis-pricing) or to simple mean reversion in equilibrium returns. Whichever explanation is entertained, the message is again clear. The very high rates of return observed over the past five to ten years do imply, in light of this negative serial correlation, that rates are more likely than not to be relatively low in the next five to ten years.

The Path not Taken

As noted, the 1998 reform package contained only a modest reduction in CPP retirement benefits. Nevertheless, the public debate in the period leading up to the reforms focused solely on whether, and to what extent, CPP benefits should be reduced.

The nature of this discussion contrasts sharply to the public debate only 20 years earlier. At this time, the Canadian Labour Congress, and others, were aggressively campaigning for a doubling of the target replacement rate for the CPP, from 25 per cent to 50 per cent of the Average Industrial Wage. In 1979, in its joint review of public and private sector pension arrangements, the Task Force on Retirement Income Policy observed:

> The fourth and last option to be considered as a means of dealing with the multiplicity of problems surrounding the present employer-sponsored pension system is to replace a substantial portion of it with expanded benefits under the Canada/Quebec Pension Plans (C/QPP) ... If the objective of such an enlargement of the C/QPP were to ensure that most of the elderly maintain pre-retirement living standards after retirement, this would entail an increase in the replacement income provided by the C/QPP from the present level of 25% of average adjusted lifetime earnings to between 40–45%, and an increase in the ceiling on maximum pensionable earnings covered by those plans from the average level of wages and salaries — the present statutory target — to 1.5 times that level. (Canada, 1979, Vol. 1, p. 242)

Further, the task force characterized this possible reform in very sympathetic terms: "Therefore, a powerful case can be made for expanding the C/QPP" (ibid., Vol. 1, p. 243).

Of the possible retrenchments in CPP benefits that were not pursued, raising the age of entitlement or the "normal" retirement age merits particular note.

The possibility of raising the normal age of retirement to beyond age 65 (as is being done with U.S. social security benefits) is raised in the 1996 *Information Paper*. Raising the normal age of retirement from age 65 to (say) 67, with advance notice of five to ten years, would significantly reduce the steady-state contribution rate for the CPP. Further, the combination of the aging of the Canadian population and the increasing longevity of older Canadians suggest the potential attractiveness of this initiative.[8]

In fact, there was no political interest in raising the normal retirement age under the CPP. In part, this is understandable, given the continuing trend towards earlier retirement among Canadian males.[9] Of less persuasiveness, at least to professional economists, is the continued reliance of those who oppose this initiative on the "lump of labour fallacy"; that is, the claim that encouraging or requiring later retirement for older workers will mean fewer jobs for younger workers.

In the *Information Paper*, there is an attempt (although modest) to overcome this concern:

> Today, there are concerns that delaying the age of eligibility for pensions would keep people in the workforce longer, making it harder for young people to find jobs. It is important to note that when the baby boomers start to retire, it is expected that there will be no shortage of jobs, so delayed retirement would not hurt young people. (Canada, Provinces and Territories, 1996, p. 36)

Finally, it merits note that the "partial privatization" of the CPP was never a part of the mainstream reform agenda. In a previous paper, I have

---

[8]In 1966, when the CPP was introduced, the remaining life expectancy of Canadians aged 65 was 15.3 years. By 1995, the remaining life expectancy of Canadians aged 65 had risen to 18.4 years. By the year 2015, this figure is anticipated to increase further, to 19.4 years.

[9]The participation rates of males aged 55 to 64 and aged 65 and above have declined steadily for the past 25 years. Because of the dramatic increase in the participation rates of married females, one cannot simply inspect the participation rates for older females to determine if there is a corresponding trend for females.

James E. Pesando

reviewed the economic case for the partial privatization of future retirement benefits (Pesando, 1997).

In brief, the scheduled increase in contributions would be directed to a system of mandatory retirement savings accounts. This scheduled increase represents most of the cost of fully funding the retirement benefits currently provided by the CPP. The existing CPP contributions would finance the disability, death and survivors' benefits provided by the plan, and also service the unfunded liability.

Privatization would have several key advantages. Working Canadians would perceive the higher contributions as purchasing a pension benefit, not simply as a tax increase. This would reduce both the short- and long-term distortions otherwise associated with a payroll tax. Privatization could also serve as a catalyst to further reform, such as servicing the existing unfunded liability through general tax revenues rather than through a regressive payroll tax.

In May of this year, President George W. Bush — implementing a campaign promise — appointed a bipartisan commission to report back to him in the fall with specific plans for creating personal investment accounts within the U.S. social security system. Recently, Sweden allowed its citizens to invest a portion of their government pension contributions themselves, in mutual funds or other savings plans. Germany's government has recently proposed a similar idea.[10]

Concluding Comment

The "next wave" in the ongoing debate about reform of public pension programs, driven worldwide by demographics and the continuing concern with rising costs, is already in motion. Although discussion of further reform of the CPP has quieted down, at least for the near term, one can confidently predict that this issue will again surface on the political agenda.

---

[10]For a sample of the rapidly-expanding literature in this field, see, for example, James *et.al.* (1999); and Feldstein and Samwick (2000).

References

Barro, R.J. (1974), "Are Government Bonds Net Wealth? *Journal of Political Economy* 82, 1095-1118.

Canada. Task Force on Retirement Income Policy (1979), *The Retirement Income System in Canada: Problems and Alternative Policies for Reform* (Ottawa: Supply and Services Canada).

Canada, Provinces and Territories (1996), *An Information Paper for Consultations on the Canada Pension Plan* (Ottawa: Supply and Services Canada).

Canada. Office of the Chief Actuary (1998), *Canada Pension Plan: Seventeenth Actuarial Report as at 31 December 1997* (Ottawa: Supply and Services Canada).

Cochrane, J.H. (1999), "New Facts in Finance", NBER Working Paper No. 7169 (Cambridge, MA: National Bureau of Economic Research).

Feldstein, M. (1974), "Social Security, Induced Retirement and Aggregate Capital Accumulation", *Journal of Political Economy* 82(5), 905-926.

Feldstein, M. and A. Samwick (2000), "Allocating Payroll Tax Revenue to Personal Retirement Accounts to Maintain Social Security Benefits and the Payroll Tax Rate", NBER Working Paper No. 7767 (Cambridge, MA: National Bureau of Economic Research).

Gordon, R.H. and A.L. Bovenberg (1996), "Why is Capital so Immobile Internationally? Possible Explanations and Implications for Capital Income Taxation", *American Economic Review* 86(5), 1057-1075.

James, E. *et al.* (1999), "Mutual Funds and Institutional Investments: What is the Most Efficient Way to Set Up Individual Accounts in a Social Security System?" NBER Working Paper No. 7049 (Cambridge, MA: National Bureau of Economic Research).

Mehra, R. and E.C. Prescott (1985), "The Equity Premium: A Puzzle", *Journal of Monetary Economics* (March), 145-161.

Pesando, J.E. (1997), "From Tax Grab to Retirement Savings: Privatizing the CPP Premium Hike", *The Pension Papers* (Toronto: C.D. Howe Institute).

Slater, D.W. and W.B.P. Robson (1999), "Building a Stronger Pillar: The Changing Shape of the Canada Pension Plan", *The Pension Papers* (Toronto: C.D. Howe Institute).

James E. Pesando

Poverty among Senior Citizens: A Canadian Success Story

Lars Osberg

As Patrick Grady's appreciation in this volume notes, throughout his career David Slater has balanced "a deep commitment to markets and the key role of the private sector with an equally deep commitment to social policies designed to create equality of opportunity and provide support for those who are disadvantaged". In recent years, his work (e.g., Slater, 1995) has especially emphasized the sustainability and design of Canada's retirement security system. As an appreciation of his work, this chapter therefore asks:

- What are the achievements of the retirement security system which his generation of policymakers built in Canada?
- What design elements are responsible for its successes?
- What problems are there for the future?

Although it may now be the case that Canadian economists take a social safety net for granted, David Slater's generation had the opportunity to observe what a society without social security really looks like. At the time

I would like to thank Andrew Sharpe for his helpful comments, Lynn Lethbridge for her excellent work on this project and the Social Sciences and Humanities Research Council of Canada for its ongoing financial support under Grant 410-2001-0747. All remaining errors are my responsibility.

when David was taking undergraduate economics at Queen's University, Paul Samuelson was writing the first version of his best-selling text, *Economics*, in which he welcomed the fact that within the United States

> a more or less comprehensive social security system had been set up within the past decade ... which will provide more generously for the old age of the bulk of our people than individual savings and interest earnings ever were able to in the past. In fact, we shall see in our later discussion of social security that one of the crushing indictments of the capitalistic system has been the well-authenticated charge that the vast majority of citizens have been unable — even after a lifetime of effort — to provide adequately for their old age. (Samuelson, 1948, p. 76)

At the time, of course, Canada lagged well behind the United States in social policy. In 1947 in Canada a means-tested old age pension was available for the destitute at $30 per month (equivalent to about $289 per month at 2001 prices), but that was all.[1] Not until 1952 was it replaced by Old Age Security (OAS). OAS was a universal payment of $40 per month, worth about $274 per month at today's prices. With income support at this level, the result was widespread and acute poverty among Canadians over 65. Canada had to wait until 1967 for the introduction of the Guaranteed Income Supplement and Canada Pension Plan[2] (for details, see Perry, 1989, pp. 701-709).

The next section begins by describing the long-run trend in poverty among senior citizens (those aged 65 and over) in Canada, while the following section discusses some of the problems of poverty measurement that are peculiar to the over 65 population. The third section looks at the Canadian Old Age Security system in an international perspective. It examines the income changes of Canadian, American, Swedish and British households as they move into their retirement years, with particular emphasis on the income of poorer households. The final section concludes with some

---

[1] The *Old Age Pension Act* of 1927 was legislated by the minority Liberal government of MacKenzie King, in order to obtain the support of the "Ginger Group" of United Farmer and Labour Members of Parliament (who later formed the nucleus of the CCF).

[2] The minority Liberal government of Lester Pearson needed the support of the New Democratic Party (who succeeded the CCF) at this time.

discussion of the challenges facing the design of retirement security in the new millennium.

Poverty Reduction for Senior Citizens — A Major Canadian Achievement

In order to appreciate what the Canadian retirement security system has achieved in reducing poverty among senior citizens, historical context is essential. However, data on the recent past are much more easily available and easier to work with than data on the 1950s and 1960s. Since micro data which enable analysts to calculate the size of the poverty gap or to adjust money incomes to reflect the cost of living of families of different size only became available in the 1970s, data on earlier years are limited to that available in published tables.

Nevertheless, there can be no doubt that Canadian senior citizens were much more likely to be poor than the general population during the 1950s and 1960s. Table 1 is taken from the work of Podoluk (1968). A consistent theme in Statistics Canada publications has been the use of the term "low income" rather than the more easily understandable term "poverty", and Podoluk's work was instrumental in persuading Statistics Canada to adopt the Low Income Cut Off (LICO) methodology for assessing its extent. In this methodology, to be "low income" is to have "very little" left over after expenditure on items of basic necessity (food, clothing and shelter). Consequently, the 1968 LICO classified a family as low income if more than 70 per cent of pre-tax income would normally be spent on necessities.

Panel A of Table 1 presents the incidence of low income in 1961 among all Canadian families, those families with head aged 65 or over and unattached individuals. Among families whose head was aged 65 or more, the poverty rate was substantially greater (43.9 per cent) than among all Canadian families (25.3 per cent). Furthermore, the single elderly (mostly women) who survived their spouses were almost certain to be poor. The incidence of low income for unattached individuals 70 or more was an astonishing 72.5 per cent. As Panel B of Table 1 notes, older families were substantially overrepresented in the bottom ranges of the income distribution, with 36.2 per cent of families headed by someone aged 65 or more having an

Table 1

A

Incidence of Low Income* – 1961	
	%
All Canadian Families	25.3
Families: Head ≥ 65	43.9
Unattached Individuals	
60 – 64	50.7
65 – 69	64.1
70+	72.5

B

Per cent of Families by Income Group – 1961
(converted to 2001 dollars)**

	≤6,200	6,201-12,399	12,400-18,600	Median	Average
All Families	3.3	7.9	10.8	30,154	32,954
Head ≥ 65	8.8	27.4	16.8	17,407	23,158

Notes: *Original "Low-Income" criterion: > 70 per cent income spent on food, clothing and shelter.
** Original income ranges = < 1,000, 1000–1,999, 2,000–2,999.
All items CPI (1992 base) 2001 = 115.9; 1961 = 18.7.
Source: Podoluk (1968, pp. 188, 194, 247, 257).

income less than $12,400 (in 2001 dollars), compared to 11.2 per cent of all Canadian families.[3]

---

[3]Today, analysts would typically make an assumption about the economies of scale involved in household consumption, calculate an equivalence scale and examine the incidence and depth of low equivalent income among *individuals* of different ages. Older data are, however, presented in terms of the incidence of low income among families with a *head* of a given age, and no correction for family size. To retain comparability, we follow the older conventions. Appendix Table A1 demonstrates that these measurement conventions make little difference.

Although Americans received Social Security benefits beginning in 1935, Canadians had to wait until 1967 for the introduction of the Canada/Quebec Pension Plan (CPP/QPP) and the Guaranteed Income Supplement (GIS). Over time Canada Pension Plan benefits have increased in importance as individuals have been able to retire with longer histories of covered working years. Hence, as the CPP/QPP system matured in the 1970s, poverty among senior citizens fell dramatically. Table 2 examines poverty among all Canadians and among those in households headed by an individual aged more or less than 65 years.

Although the most commonly used statistic on poverty is the poverty rate, since Sen (1976) many authors have recognized that the poverty rate, by itself, is a poor index.[4] Simply counting the number of poor, as a percentage of all people, ignores any consideration of the depth of their poverty. As Myles and Picot (2000) have noted, some social policies transfer income to groups (such as single parents) whose incomes are well below the poverty line. *Because* their incomes are so far below the poverty line, policy changes which affect these groups may have large impacts on their well-being, but not show up in the poverty rate statistics if few individuals are actually moved over the poverty line.

On the other hand, an index such as the average poverty gap ratio, which looks only at the average percentage shortfall of income below the poverty line, has the defect that it ignores the issue of how many people are poor. This paper therefore uses the Sen-Shorrocks-Thon (SST) index of *poverty intensity*, which combines consideration of the poverty rate, average poverty gap ratio and inequality among the poor.[5] This paper also takes the view that poverty in Canada should be assessed in terms of *Canadian* social norms,

---

[4]For surveys of the literature see Foster (1984); Hagenaars (1991); or Zheng (1997).

[5]The Sen-Shorrocks-Thon (SST) index of poverty intensity can be calculated as I = (rate)*(gap)*(1+G(x)) where "rate" is the percentage of the population with incomes below the poverty line (sometimes called the head count ratio), "gap" is the average percentage gap between the incomes of the poor and the poverty line and G(x) is the Gini index of inequality of the poverty gap among all people. For further details on the SST index, and its trends over time in Canada, see Osberg and Xu (1999) or Myles and Picot (2000). For international comparisons, see Osberg and Xu (1997, 2000).

Table 2: Poverty Intensity and its Components, Canada, 1973–1997

	All			Head of Family < 65			Head of Family >= 65		
	Poverty Intensity	Poverty Rate (%)	Poverty Gap (%)	Poverty Intensity	Poverty Rate (%)	Poverty Gap (%)	Poverty Intensity	Poverty Rate (%)	Poverty Gap (%)
Money Income before Taxes and Transfers									
1973	22.1	21.1	56.1	15.6	16.8	49.1	67.0	59.0	73.7
1979	23.3	21.3	58.8	16.3	16.3	52.6	68.2	61.8	72.6
1989	24.5	22.8	58.3	17.8	17.8	53.1	61.7	56.6	69.3
1994	30.3	26.3	63.3	23.7	21.1	60.5	65.3	60.8	69.8
1997	29.7	26.2	62.3	23.1	21.0	59.2	64.3	59.8	69.2
Money Income after Taxes and Transfers									
1973	8.4	13.6	32.1	7.8	12.0	33.7	13.6	28.4	26.2
1979	8.6	13.9	32.2	8.1	12.0	34.8	12.6	29.6	23.4
1989	6.1	11.0	28.4	6.5	11.0	30.5	3.2	11.4	14.7
1994	6.4	11.8	28.3	7.2	12.8	29	1.5	5.0	15.0
1997	7.6	12.5	31.8	8.6	13.6	32.7	1.7	5.4	15.8

Notes: The Sen-Shorrocks-Thon (SST) index of poverty intensity is calculated as I = (rate)*(gap)*(1+G(x)) where "rate" is the percentage of the population with incomes below the poverty line (sometimes called the head count ratio), "gap" is the average percentage gap between the incomes of the poor and the poverty line and G(x) is the Gini index of inequality of the poverty gap among all people. Since the term (1+G(x)) is nearly constant, it is not presented explicitly.

The poverty line used is one-half the median equivalent income where the equivalence scale is the square root of the total number of people in the family.

Source: Author's calculations using the Survey of Consumer Finance, Economic Families.

Lars Osberg

and therefore calculates the poverty rate and poverty gap for each individual with reference to a Canada-wide norm of living standards.[6]

The top panel of Table 2 reports poverty intensity, the poverty rate and the average poverty gap ratio counting only income from labour market earnings and capital, before taxes and before government transfers. As one can note from the last three columns, there is really very little trend over time in the amount of income poverty among senior citizens in Canada *before government taxes and transfers*. For the entire quarter-century from 1973 to 1997 the poverty rate (before taxes and transfers) for seniors is stuck in the region of 60 per cent and the average poverty gap is about 70 per cent.

However, poverty outcomes among senior citizens *after* taxes and transfers are an entirely different story. Ideally, one would have comparable micro data from the period before the introduction of CPP/QPP and GIS, in order to assess the impact of the introduction of these programs. In reality, the first micro-data is available in 1973, and therefore misses the introduction effect of CPP/QPP and GIS in 1967. However, it is clear that the maturing of the CPP/QPP system has had a huge impact. Overall, poverty intensity for seniors in 1973 was 13.6. Poverty intensity declined by roughly an order of magnitude — to 1.7 — in the 24 years leading up to 1997. The decline in the poverty rate after taxes and transfers from 28.4 per cent in 1973 to 5.4 per cent in 1997 is more dramatic than the decline in the average poverty gap ratio (from 26.2 per cent to 15.8 per cent) — but either trend represents *very* substantial progress, and combined they represent a huge and lasting improvement.

To appreciate the progress in poverty reduction among senior citizens in Canada, one only has to contrast their outcomes with the rising intensity of poverty among younger households, particularly in the 1990s. Prior to 1989, adverse trends in the distribution of market income were reversed by the

---

[6]In the main body of the text, the poverty line norm adopted is one-half the median equivalent income of all Canadian individuals, since this concept of poverty has been widely used in the international literature and can therefore be compared to international data. A disadvantage of this approach is that it does not recognize the differences in the cost of living that accompany residence in urban and rural areas. Appendix Table A1 therefore presents the results obtained when the before-tax Statistics Canada Low Income Cut Off (LICO), which builds in city size and urban/rural cost of living differentials, is used as the poverty line. Unfortunately, the LICO methodology is unique to Canada and cannot be directly compared internationally.

tax/transfer mechanism, so limiting the extent of poverty increases was a social achievement. However, there is no evidence among younger Canadians of the lasting decline in poverty observed among the elderly.

In 1973, poverty *intensity* on a pre-tax, pre-transfer basis among the under 65 households was 15.6, increasing to 17.8 in 1989 (i.e., by about 14 per cent). Since after-tax, after-transfer poverty intensity for the non-elderly actually declined until 1989 by about 17 per cent (from 7.8 to 6.5), it is clear that until the 1990s the operation of the Canadian tax/transfer system was quite successful in reversing a trend to greater poverty in market incomes. However, the 1990s were a different story. For those under 65, poverty intensity before taxes and transfers rose substantially from 17.8 in 1989 to 23.1 in 1997 — an increase of about 30 per cent. From 1989 to 1997, poverty intensity in post-tax, post-transfer income among those under 65 rose from 6.5 to 8.6 — an increase of slightly greater magnitude (32 per cent). As a result, the gains of the 1973 to 1989 period were erased and reversed.

Looking at the 1973 to 1997 period as a whole, the poverty *rate* in market income rose from 16.8 to 21 per cent and the average poverty *gap* rose from 49.1 per cent to 59.2 per cent, so the increase in poverty intensity in market income was large — about 48 per cent (from 15.6 to 23.1). After taxes and transfers for the period as a whole between 1973 and 1997, the increase in poverty intensity (from 7.8 to 8.6) was much less, about 10 per cent. However, the achievements of the tax/transfer mechanism in offsetting trends in market income were largely a phenomenon of the period before 1989, and it is useful to look separately at changes in the 1990s and before.

To provide a more intuitive idea of the magnitude of poverty reduction among senior citizens and in the general population, Figures 1 and 2 present the "Poverty Box" for seniors and non-seniors in 1973 and 1997. These figures make use of a theoretical decomposition, combined with an empirical generalization.

Theoretically, poverty intensity can be calculated as:

Poverty Intensity = (rate of poverty)*(average poverty gap)*(inequality of poverty)

where "rate" is the percentage of the population with incomes below the poverty line, "gap" is the average percentage gap between the incomes of the poor and the poverty line and "inequality of poverty" is measured by one plus the Gini index of inequality of the poverty gap among all people.

Figure 1: Poverty Box — Pre-fisc and Post-fisc Seniors (>= 65 years of age) and Non-Seniors (Canada 1973)

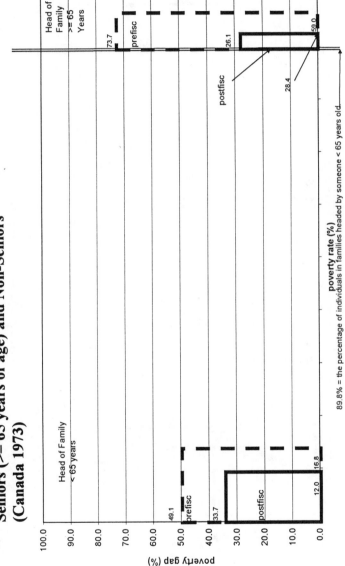

Note: The poverty line is one-half the median income (pre-fisc and post-fisc) for the entire country. The equivalence scale is the square root of the total numbers of persons in the family.

Figure 2: Poverty Box — Pre-fisc and Post-fisc Seniors (>= 65 years of age) and Non-Seniors (Canada 1997)

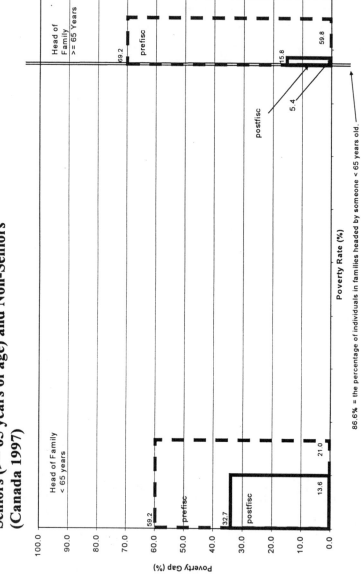

Note: The poverty line is one-half the median income (pre-fisc and post-fisc) for the entire country. The equivalence scale is the square root of the total numbers of persons in the family.

86.6% = the percentage of individuals in families headed by someone < 65 years old.

Lars Osberg

The empirical generalization is that the third term, measuring inequality of poverty gaps, is nearly constant. Empirically, it turns out that changes over time (or differences between countries or Canadian provinces) in the inequality of poverty gaps are very small, especially when compared to differences in the poverty rate and average poverty gap.[7] Since the inequality of poverty gaps is nearly constant, the implication is that for practical purposes poverty intensity is proportional to the product of the poverty rate and the average poverty gap. Graphically, total poverty intensity can therefore be represented as the area of a Poverty Box — a rectangle whose base is the poverty rate and whose height is the average poverty gap ratio.

Figures 1 and 2 present the Poverty Box for Canadians under 65, and aged 65 or more. Each figure compares poverty intensity before taxes and transfers (the dashed lines, labelled "pre-fisc") to poverty intensity after taxes and transfers (solid lines, labelled "post-fisc"). Using these figures, one can easily see whether it is the impact of taxes and transfers on the poverty rate or the poverty gap that is driving over all poverty intensity trends.

Since it is often useful to see how much of the total poverty of the nation is contributed by poverty in different groups, in both Figure 1 and Figure 2 the double vertical line divides the total population into the proportion aged 65 or more and the fraction under 65. Graphically, if one wants to look only at poverty among younger Canadians, one can simply cover up the right hand side of the figure to visualize the impact of government (through taxes and transfers) on the poverty rate (horizontal axis) and average poverty gap (vertical axis) of Canadians under 65 years of age. On the other hand, if one wants to look just at poverty among senior citizens, one should cover up the

---

[7]Across LIS countries the coefficient of variation of poverty rates is 0.493, and for average poverty gap ratios it is 0.185. However, the coefficient of variation of $(1+G(x))$ is only 0.014 (Osberg and Xu, 2000, p. 72). For Canadian provinces and U.S. states in 1997 the CV is 0.341 for the SST index, 0.384 for the poverty rate, 0.141 for the poverty gap ratio and 0.011 for $(1+G(X))$, see also Osberg and Xu (1999). The "common sense" verbal explanation for the unimportance of inequality among the poor in an aggregate measure of poverty intensity is that the differences in income among the poor are small when compared to income differences among the non-poor. The upper bound on the incomes of poor people is the poverty line. The lower bound (leaving aside measurement error), is subsistence. The dollar value of the difference is not large, particularly when compared to the dollar differences among the non-poor population. See Osberg and Xu (2000, p. 57) and Xu and Osberg (2000) for geometric proof.

left hand side of Figure 1 or 2 to see the impact of government on the poverty rate[8] and average poverty gap of Canadians 65 years of age and over.

The total amount of poverty in Canada is, of course, the sum of poverty among all Canadians, both senior citizens and those under 65. In Figures 1 and 2, total poverty intensity is proportional to the sum of the area of both Poverty Boxes — the Poverty Box for seniors plus the Poverty Box for younger Canadians. By adding the two boxes outlined with dashed lines, and comparing them to the total area of the two boxes outlined in solid lines, one can see how much total Canadian poverty is reduced by taxes and transfers — particularly for the those 65 and over.

Figure 1 illustrates how much stronger in 1973 the impact of taxes and transfers was on the poverty rate and the poverty gap among seniors than among non-seniors. Figure 2 presents the same poverty box analysis for 1997, and illustrates the quite dramatic impact which taxes and transfers had on poverty among senior citizens in Canada over the last quarter century. If one goes a little further back in time and compares the outcomes of 1997 with those of 1961, it is even clearer that poverty reduction among senior citizens has been one of the great success stories of Canadian social policy.

Problems in Poverty Measurement among Senior Citizens

Paradoxically, the success of Canada's retirement security system in putting a floor under the incomes of senior citizens has a flip side — an increased potential sensitivity of poverty measurement among seniors to "technical" measurement issues. Although there is little doubt as to the *trend* in poverty among senior citizens in Canada, assessment of the *level* of poverty in Canada is complicated a bit by the fact that many seniors now have much the *same* money income. Because analysts may draw the poverty line at slightly different income levels, small differences in the poverty line may imply large changes in the measured poverty rate.

---

[8]For each group, the poverty rate is expressed as a fraction of that group, for example, the poverty rate for seniors is a percentage of Canadians aged 65 or more.

Because they have retired from the labour force, often without private pensions or appreciable savings, in Canada (as in all the advanced countries) many of the elderly depend *entirely* on social transfers.[9] Their income determination process is therefore totally unlike that of the non-elderly, who mix transfers and earned income and have wages and hours of work which vary with different jobs and fluctuate over the course of a year. Precisely because the elderly typically have no earnings and the retirement security system provides their income, many of them have much the same income because it is derived from the same source and calculated by the same benefit formula.

When that basic income is close to the poverty line, small variations in either the poverty line or the level of basic seniors' benefits has the potential to reclassify large numbers of people — either pushing them into, or out of, poverty. Up to this point, this paper has used the common practice, in the international literature, of drawing the poverty line at one-half the median equivalent after-tax/after-transfer income of individual Canadians (where household economies of scale are assumed to be captured by the LIS equivalence scale). This measurement choice implies a significantly lower poverty rate for Canada as a whole (11.57 per cent in 1994[10]) than the use

---

[9]Luxembourg Income Study data indicate that in 1994, among households composed of seniors the percentage whose only income was government transfers was 21.6 per cent in Canada, 16.3 per cent in the United States, 22 per cent in Australia, 50.1 per cent in Germany, 52.9 per cent in Luxembourg, 18.2 per cent in France, and 14 per cent in the Netherlands.

[10]The poverty line used in this paper is conceptually similar to the Low Income Measure (LIM) of Statistics Canada, which sets the over-all 1994 poverty rate at 14.7 per cent (see Statistics Canada, 1999, p. 17) compared to the 11.8 per cent poverty rate for all ages reported in Table 2. The difference arises because the LIM uses pre-tax, post-transfer income (while we use after-tax, after-transfer income), calculates the median across families (we take the median across individuals, assuming that income is pooled within households) and does not exclude people with negative incomes (we do). The fact that such "technical" statistical choices produce variation in the poverty line, and the implied poverty rate, is a pointer to the ambiguity and imprecision surrounding exact statements about the level of poverty. In most cases, statements about poverty trends are little affected, but the reason why the "spike" in the incomes of seniors matters is that small variations in the poverty line have the potential to reclassify large numbers of people.

of the Statistics Canada Low Income Cut Off (15.9 per cent in 1994). (The reason is that a relative poverty line, like half the median, may decline with a decrease in general living standards such as that which occurred in Canada in the early 1990s; the LICO, on the other hand, remains fixed in real terms.)

In the Appendix, Table A1 reports the poverty intensity, the poverty rate and poverty gap using as the poverty line the before-tax LICO of Statistics Canada. The debate on which poverty line is more appropriate clearly affects the perceived *level* of poverty for all groups, but for the non-elderly population there is little impact on *trends*. However, poverty among the 65 and over population is potentially more sensitive to measurement choices.

Because there is likely to be a "spike" in the income distribution of the elderly, which has the potential to affect poverty measurement, the empirical issue is whether different choices of the poverty line lie on opposite sides of that spike. Figures 3, 4 and 5 therefore use Luxembourg Income Study data to graph the income distribution of one- and two-person elderly and non-elderly households in Canada, the United States and Australia in 1994. In each graph, the frequency distribution of incomes in the modal interval is presented, as well as the frequency of observations of incomes lying above and below the mode. Australia has a very significant spike in the income distribution of elderly persons, with 50.6 per cent of one-person households in the $2,000 modal interval. In Canada, 30.1 per cent of one-person elderly households are in the same interval, while in the United States the spike is much less pronounced, with only 16.3 per cent in the modal interval.[11]

These national differences are easily explained by the structure of the retirement security systems in the three countries. Australia has historically had a flat rate, means-tested pension; the spike in the income distribution is simply the maximum pension benefit (which applies when the individual has no other source of money income). The Canadian system combines a flat rate federal OAS payment with income supplementation through the Guaranteed Income Supplement, but the general availability of CPP benefits tied to earlier earnings builds in some differentiation among those persons with an earnings history. In the United States, there is no universal component, and pension entitlement under Social Security replicates in old age more of the dispersion in incomes that occurred during the working years.

---

[11]For persons under 65, the percentage in the comparably defined modal interval of the income distribution was in 1994: Canada, 9.4 per cent; United States, 8 per cent; Australia, 11.3 per cent.

Figure 3: After-Tax Income Distribution, $1,000 Intervals One- and Two-Person Households (Canada 1994)

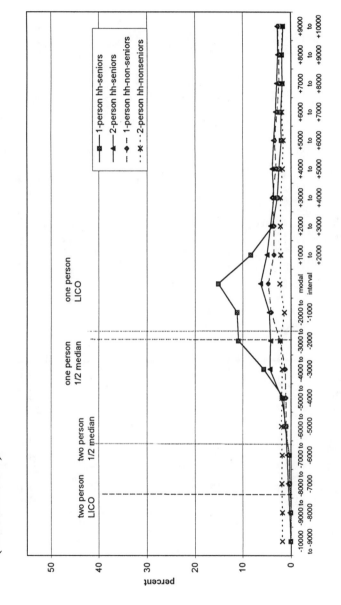

Note: The modal interval is the mode +- $1,000. The remaining intervals are the +- from the mode.

Figure 4: After-Tax Income Distribution, $1,000 Intervals One- and Two-Person Households (United States 1994)

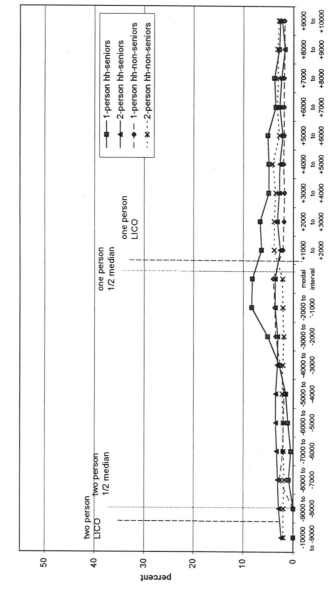

Note: The modal interval is the mode +- $1,000. The remaining intervals are the +- from the mode. The LICOs are converted to U.S. dollars using purchasing power parities (0.79).

Figure 5: After-Tax Income Distribution, $1,000 Intervals One- and Two-Person Households (Australia 1994)

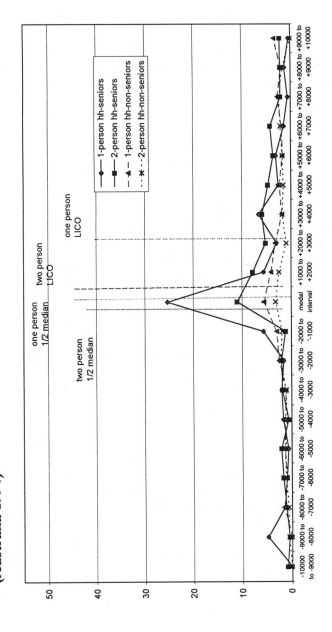

Note: The modal interval is the mode +- $1,000. The remaining intervals are the +- from the mode. The LICOs are converted to Australian dollars using purchasing power parities (1.044).

Figures 3, 4 and 5 illustrate, therefore, how much the income distribution of the elderly depends on the details of design of public pensions for the elderly. In Australia and Canada there is a spike in the income distribution of the elderly which is rather close to commonly used definitions of the poverty line. In Canada, the income distribution spike is above both the after-tax LICO and half-median equivalent disposable income conceptions of the poverty line, implying that conclusions about poverty trends are robust to these particular choices of poverty line. However, since the income distribution spike is close to the poverty line, it is fair to say that many seniors are "near-poor". As well, the more commonly used pre-tax Low Income Cut Off of Statistics Canada generates a significantly higher poverty rate than the after-tax LICO. Since Figures 3 to 5 are drawn in terms of after-tax income, it cannot be represented directly there, but it appears to lie very close to the income distribution spike.

In both Australia and the United States, the elderly are a group for whom small changes in money income or equivalence scale or the poverty line are more important. Because the official U.S. poverty line is so low, it is well below the income distribution spike. However, if the poverty line is set at the international criterion of one-half median equivalent disposable income, or at the real value of the after-tax Canadian LICO, the U.S. income distribution mode for the single elderly is just below the poverty line. Because, in these countries, many of the elderly have incomes that are quite close to reasonable specifications of the poverty line, small changes in the definition or measurement of that poverty line can appear to have large poverty consequences.

The spike in the income distribution of the elderly is very pronounced in Australia, but not nearly as much in the United States. Canada (like most other countries) is an intermediate case. Hence, since comparisons over time or across countries are affected by this spike to differing degrees in different countries, for Canadian seniors the point to remember is the clustering of many people's retirement income in a fairly narrow range, which is above, but not very far above, reasonable definitions of the poverty line.

In thinking of the social context of income flows, of course, one must also consider the adequacy of the definition of "income" which is used as an indicator of economic well-being. Thus far, this paper has looked at income poverty and the concept of poverty used has been based on the calculation of equivalent family money income, which is based in turn on the Survey of Consumer Finance definition of measured family money income. This ignores the economic well-being entailed by the ownership of wealth, the

Lars Osberg

receipt of in-kind income, the time cost of earning income and exposure to economic insecurity.

In the comparison of birth cohorts of Canadians, a particularly important issue is the imputed rent and capital gains arising from home ownership. The cohort of Canadians who were fortunate enough to purchase their homes during the era of low real interest rates and low housing prices (i.e., pre-1975) benefited significantly from capital gains in the housing market of the late 1970s and early 1980s. However, the stagnation of real housing prices since the early 1980s has meant that younger cohorts have not received comparable capital gains, meanwhile paying substantially higher real interest rates on their mortgage indebtedness. Although the realization of such capital gains is subject to significant transactions costs (in real estate fees and the loss of neighbourhood social ties) older cohorts who have retired their mortgage debt do benefit annually from a stream of housing services, which is not counted as part of money income. Since most of the members of younger cohorts are either paying rents or mortgage interest, inter-generational comparisons of money income may not accurately reflect well-being.

As well, cohorts differ in the type and amount of public services that they receive. Since senior citizens are at a stage in life when they are very likely to need medical care, they benefited disproportionately from the general increase in economic security that came with the introduction of universal medicare in 1968–70 in Canada. In general, the perceived relative well-being of senior citizens is particularly affected by the value assigned to the medical and hospital services they receive from the public sector. However, despite the fact that household money income omits consideration of the value of these services, it does not seem appropriate to add their cost to money income, since one would not want to argue that the sick have more income than the healthy, just because they receive more medical services.[12] Hence, this paper makes no adjustment to money income to account for the value of in-kind services received.

The calculation of household money income also ignores the opportunity cost of the time supplied by households to the paid labour market in order to

---

[12]If one calculated the total income of Canadians as their money income plus the value of in-kind services received, a resident of the intensive care ward would appear to have an extremely high total income, which would be greatest for those with the longest stays. This way of calculating "total income" would be a very poor guide to their well-being.

earn income. The retired population do not have these costs, but the population of working age do. Furthermore, the relative differential in costs has changed over time. Over the 1975 to 1994 period, married women substantially increased their labour force participation rates, implying that although working-age families have had more money income, they also have had less leisure, and less opportunity for home production.

Comparison of the well-being of senior citizens and those under 65 is also affected by the increase in economic insecurity, which has been greatest among youth during the period 1975 to 1994 (see Osberg, Erksoy and Phipps, 1998). Retirees have graduated to a status that is no longer affected by the ups and downs of the labour market, but working-age Canadians still face labour market risk, although their exposure differs markedly. Those who entered the labour market during the 1960s and 1970s entered a labour market in which unemployment was relatively low and jobs with contractual guarantees of continued employment were relatively abundant. After 1971, the potential costs of unemployment were cushioned by a relatively generous unemployment insurance system. In the 1990s, however, double digit unemployment rates were common, jobs with employment security became rarer and unemployment insurance was drastically cut in benefits, coverage and eligibility. Many older Canadians have worked their way up the seniority ladder into positions of relative job security, but younger Canadians were highly exposed. For much of the 1990s, the combination of higher unemployment, decreased private sector guarantees of job security and decreased income protection from unemployment insurance produced a pervasive sense of economic insecurity in the Canadian labour force.[13]

In successive cross-sectional samples from the population, such as the SCF, one cannot observe either the *ex post* realized fluctuations of money income over time or any *ex ante* anxieties about possible future income fluctuations. Nevertheless, risk averse individuals are willing to pay an insurance premium for greater income certainty, and rising levels of income uncertainty can be expected to have a utility cost, which this paper does not attempt to measure.

---

[13]Graves (2001) notes that in the late 1990s lower unemployment produced a substantial decline in survey measures of economic insecurity. The importance of macro-economic policy for such social outcomes is a lesson that I first learned in David Slater's course on Money and Banking at Queen's University in 1965–66.

Important aspects of economic well-being which are unmeasured in this paper's calculation of poverty trends include implicit income from home ownership and public services, plus the greater relative benefit from freedom from the increasing time pressures and the greater economic insecurity that affect working-age Canadians. Although these are important issues, in a very real sense their omission from this paper only serves to strengthen the general message that the relative well-being of Canadian seniors has, on average, improved markedly over the last 30 years.

If the issue is trends in deprivation, however, averages can also be highly misleading, and particularly so when age cohorts are compared. In his article in this volume, Malcolm Hamilton compares average incomes of retirees and those of working age. He also notes that using the concept of "income" as an indicator of well-being excludes from consideration the utility derived from consumption which is enabled by depletion of capital. Since the elderly have, *on average*, substantial assets, they could *on average* consume from the disposition of those assets. However, the problem with that mode of analysis is that it ignores the inequality in incomes and the high and rising level of inequality in wealth ownership.

In general, there is more inequality in the wealth distribution than in the distribution of annual income; and the rich and poor differ in the type of assets they own, as well as in the amount of assets. In 1999, as in previous years, the basic picture was "30-60-10". The poorest 30 per cent of the population have essentially no assets (except perhaps automobiles, which are the most equally distributed type of asset) and that changes little over their lifetimes. For the 60 per cent who are "middle class", the key asset is the family home — as families gradually pay off the mortgage, their net worth increases and they gradually work their way up the distribution of wealth. As they age, they also acquire more consumer durables, and often some financial assets such as RRSPs.

However, although there has been some increase in the percentage of the population who own financial assets such as stocks, bonds and mutual funds, only a few people have major money. Most financial assets are owned by the top 10 per cent of households, who in total owned 55.7 per cent of total net worth in 1999, up significantly from 51.8 per cent in 1984 (Morissette, Zhang and Drolet, 2001).

The "bottom line" is that fungible wealth is very narrowly held in Canada. A substantial fraction of the population make the transition into retirement with essentially no marketable assets, while the main possession of the broad middle class is the family home, which is indivisible and illiquid.

Hence, when it concerns those at risk of deprivation in old age — that is, the lower half of the income distribution — money income retains its importance.

The Transition to Retirement

What happens to people's incomes, particularly those at risk of poverty, as they age into retirement?

Since income and wealth in later life reflect the cumulative influence of many factors which can be strongly and mutually self-reinforcing (e.g., life events such as divorce or ill health, professional success or failure, ability to acquire and retain home ownership, etc.), trends in average incomes can be very misleading as a guide to trends in deprivation. As already noted, the details of the design of retirement security systems can have a major impact on the income distribution of seniors, and since countries differ significantly in the design of their retirement security systems, it is useful to examine comparative international evidence.

This section of the paper uses Luxembourg Income Study micro data to follow the fortunes of the birth cohort which moved into retirement as they aged from approximately 1979–81 to 1994–95. The data present point estimates[14] of income distribution trends over time for Canada (1981 and 1994), Sweden (1981 and 1995), United Kingdom (1979 and 1995), and the United States (1979 and 1994). Although the exact dates of the data for individual countries are determined by the availability of comparable micro data in LIS, the essential thing we want to make use of is the fact that the cohort born between 1915 and 1929 moved from pre-retirement to retirement over this period — someone born into this group was 51 to 65 in 1980 and 65 to 79 in 1994.

The focus is on the distribution of equivalent income among individuals, but the statistical starting point is the LIS definition of total household money

---

[14]Although estimates of the confidence intervals surrounding these point estimates are not presented here, interested readers can find such estimates (for the population as a whole), as calculated using a bootstrap methodology, in Osberg and Xu (1997).

income after tax (disposable income)[15] as the basis for calculation of the "equivalent income" of all individuals within households. We examine all national residents, as listed by LIS, excluding only those economic families or unattached individuals who reported a zero or negative before-tax money income.

Of course, comparing the experience of birth cohorts across different years in LIS data is not a substitute for actual panel data. The sample of people born 1915 to 1929 who responded to the Canadian Survey of Consumer Finance in 1981 are not, for example, the same people as the respondents in the survey of 1994 who were born in the same period. However, both samples are drawn from the same population of individuals (subject to the attrition of mortality and the impact of net migration), and both samples can be used to estimate characteristics of the distribution of income of that population. In the discussion that follows, the income of deciles of the income distribution will be compared over time. To the extent that individuals change their rank in the income distribution, these deciles of the income distribution will consist of different persons, but if one wants to assess trends in inequality, the issue is whether income mobility within cohorts has increased or decreased over time.[16]

---

[15]Disposable income consists of the sum of gross wages and salaries, farm self-employment income, non-farm self-employment income, cash property income, sick pay, disability pay, social retirement benefits, child or family allowances, unemployment compensation, maternity pay, military/veteran/war benefits, other social insurance, means-tested cash benefits, near-cash benefits, private pensions, public sector pensions, alimony or child support, other regular private income, and other cash benefits; minus mandatory contributions for self-employed, mandatory employee contribution and income tax.

[16]In the United States, Mishel, Bernstein and Schmitt conclude that: "the rate of mobility appears to have declined since the late 1960s" (1999, p. 89). Dickens' conclusion for the United Kingdom is similar: "earnings mobility has fallen since the late 1970s" (1999, p. 223). On the other hand, Baker and Solon (1998) use income tax data to conclude that the year-to-year instability of income in Canada has risen over the period 1975 to 1993. Since trends in the average income of income deciles represent shifts in the pattern of ultimate economic rewards across individuals *given* the degree of individual mobility from year to year, and since there is some evidence of *decreased* mobility in the two countries

Over the period 1980 to 1995, the cohort born between 1915 and 1929 aged from being 51 to 66 to being 66 to 81. Although most households in this age bracket had a member in the paid labour force in 1980, almost all had retired by 1995. As earnings were replaced by pensions, the money incomes of most deciles of the income distribution in all countries fell. However, the structure of the income support system for the elderly matters a great deal. In some countries (especially Canada) the presence of a floor to old age security benefits which is higher than social assistance for the non-elderly has meant that the poorest decile are actually better off in their retirement years than in their working years.

Countries differ in the extent to which the old age security system emphasizes earnings-related pensions over flat rate, needs-based benefits. In the United States, there are broadly similar declines in the income of all but the poorest and richest deciles, as the Social Security system replicates for the pensions of the retired much of the inequality in earnings that they experienced as workers. This tendency is less marked in other countries. In both Canada and the United Kingdom the bottom quintile was better off in retirement than during their working years. Despite much media comment in the United States on the affluence of the elderly, it is notable that the decline in income of the cohort moving into retirement is significantly larger in the United States than it is for most other countries.

Figures 6 and 7 present the income distribution of the pre-retirement and retirement cohorts. In these figures, the average equivalent income (after-tax, after-transfer) of each decile of individuals in the income distribution is expressed relative to the poverty line for a single person. Figure 6 uses the relative concept that the poverty line is one-half the median equivalent income of all persons, while Figure 7 adopts the absolute poverty line methodology of the U.S. Social Security Administration (converted to national currencies using the OECD purchasing power parity calculations).

In terms of absolute poverty, the Canadian and Swedish systems clearly do much more for the worst off than the U.S. or U.K. systems. Just prior to retirement, in Canada the bottom tenth have incomes that are on average 73 per cent of the U.S. official poverty line in real terms, while in Sweden the bottom decile have incomes that average 79 per cent of the U.S. poverty line. After retirement, the bottom 10 per cent of Swedes and Canadians are

---

that have demonstrated the greatest increase in income inequality, these trends in inequality of outcomes may understate tendencies to greater inequality of opportunity.

Lars Osberg

Figure 6: Ratio of Mean After-Tax Income by Decile to Poverty Line*

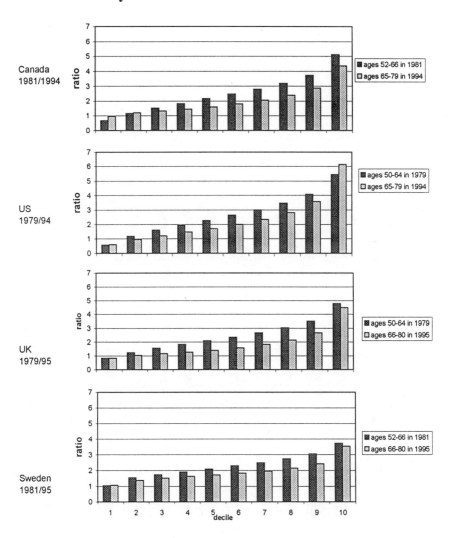

*Note: The poverty line used is one-half the median equivalent after-tax income for each country. The equivalence scale used is the square root of the total number in the household.

Source: Author's calculations using the Luxembourg Income Study.

Figure 7: Ratio of Mean After-Tax Income by Decile to Poverty Line*

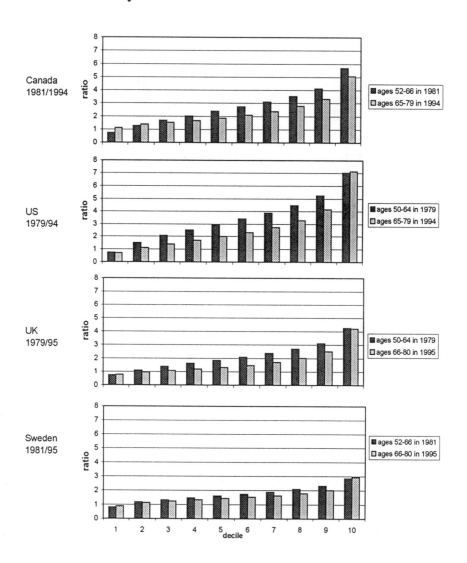

*Note: The poverty line used is the Social Security Administration (U.S. Official line — before tax) for a one-person household.
Source: Author's calculations using the Luxembourg Income Study.

Lars Osberg

actually better off than in their pre-retirement years — Swedes are closer to the U.S. poverty line (at 89 per cent) while the bottom decile of Canadians are 12 per cent above the line. By contrast, in the United Kingdom the poorest tenth of the pre-retirement cohort are only marginally better off in their retirement years (moving from 74 per cent of the U.S. poverty line to 77.5 per cent). In the United States, the poorest decile are worse off when they retire. The bottom tenth of American 50 to 64 year olds had incomes in 1979 that were, on average, only 71 per cent of the U.S. official poverty line while in 1994, the poorest tenth of the retirement cohort of 65 to 79 year olds had even lower incomes, averaging only 68 per cent of the poverty line.

It is notable that although the United States is the richest nation in over-all average income terms, the bottom decile of seniors are absolutely worse off in the United States than in any other country examined, and by a large margin, especially compared to Canada (expressing it in terms of the U.S. official Social Security poverty line, the difference between being at 112 per cent for worst-off seniors in Canada and being at 68 per cent in the United States is equal to about 44 per cent of the poverty line).

Canadian success in reducing the poverty of seniors is much the same if one uses a relative poverty line. Since drawing a poverty line at one-half the median equivalent income implies a higher poverty line in all countries than the real value of the U.S. official poverty line, and since that relative poverty line has changed over time (unlike the fixed absolute level of the SSA poverty line), Figure 6 is not quite the same as Figure 7, but the conclusion is similar.

Measuring poverty in relative terms, Canada clearly does the best job in pulling retirees up to the poverty line, since the bottom decile of 52–66 year olds in 1981 had incomes that averaged only 66 per cent of the poverty line, while the bottom tenth of 65 to 79 year olds in 1994 were at 96 per cent of the relative poverty line. In the other three countries, the bottom decile of the 1915 to 1929 cohort stayed in much the same place in relative poverty terms — marginally above the relative poverty line in Sweden (moving from 104 per cent to 107 per cent), somewhat below in the United Kingdom (84 per cent in 1979 compared to 83 per cent in 1995) and well below in the United States (55 per cent in 1979 and 58 per cent in 1994).

Conclusion and Implications

Canada has done a remarkable job in ensuring that senior citizens receive, in their retirement years, an income sufficient to prevent poverty. In comparison with outcomes in the past, or with those in other countries today, Canada's retirement security system has been relatively successful in protecting the elderly from deprivation. The contrast with the United States is particularly striking. Although the poorest Canadian seniors were much worse off than American seniors 40 years ago, they are now much better off.

Canadian transfer programs for those 65 and over have combined a universal demogrant (Old Age Security), a Negative Income Tax (the Guaranteed Income Supplement) and an earnings-related pension (CPP/QPP). The demogrant and NIT components serve to establish an income floor that is available to all, regardless of whether they have been in the paid labour force or not during their earlier years. Historically this feature has been especially important for women who have spent many years working in the home, without acquiring entitlements to an earnings-related pension in their own name. As time passes and the cohort of women who have been in the paid workforce more continuously ages into retirement, this feature can be expected to decrease in relative importance, but it will always be a necessary backstop for those with significant interruptions in their earnings histories.

The CPP/QPP system has the enormous advantages of complete coverage of the workforce, portability, low administration costs and indexation. However, it is not designed as a full income replacement scheme. In 1999, maximum benefits were \$ 9,020 per year, for retirees aged 65 (with the possibility of enhancement or reduction for early or late retirement over the age range 60 to 70). Since benefits are designed to be a maximum of about 25 per cent of the average industrial wage, it is clear that the focus of the plan is preventing deprivation in old age, and it is equally clear from the data that the retirement security system has had major success in reaching that objective. The maintenance, for the population as a whole, of working-age consumption patterns during the retirement years is a different issue — one that Canadian policy leaves more to the savings decisions of individuals (albeit assisted by the tax treatment of RRSPs and Registered Pension Plans).

By contrast, the U.S. Social Security system replicates in old age much more of the inequality in earnings observed during the working years. The

U.S. system aims at providing coverage for a significantly higher fraction of earnings, and in that sense is more clearly oriented to benefit a "middle class" constituency. Although the benefit formula is relatively advantageous to low-wage workers, they still, in the end, only receive a percentage of a low number as their retirement income. Samuelson's remark that "one of the crushing indictments of the capitalistic system has been the well-authenticated charge that the vast majority of citizens have been unable — even after a lifetime of effort — to provide adequately for their old age" is no longer true for the majority, but it remains true for a significant minority.

As Canada enters the twenty-first century and a higher fraction of the Canadian population ages into retirement, the policymakers of David Slater's generation have much to be proud of in Canada's retirement security system. The challenge for current policymakers will be how best to build upon the major success story of Canadian social policy in the twentieth century — the reduction of poverty among Canadian senior citizens.

References

Baker, M. and G. Solon (1998), *Earnings Dynamics and Inequality Among Canadian Men, 1976-1992: Evidence from Longitudinal Tax Records* (Ottawa: Statistics Canada).

Dickens, R. (1999), "Wage Mobility in Great Britain", in P. Gregg and J. Wadsworth (eds.), *The State of Working Britain* (Manchester: Manchester University Press).

Foster, J.E. (1984), "On Economic Poverty: A Survey of Aggregate Measures", *Advances in Econometrics* 3, 215-251.

Graves, F.L. (2001), "The Economy through a Public Lens: Shifting Canadian Views of the Economy", in *The Review of Economic Performance and Social Progress — The Longest Decade: Canada in the 1990s* (Ottawa: Centre for the Study of Living Standards and the Institute for Research on Public Policy), 63-88.

Hagenaars, A.J.M. (1991), "The Definition and Measurement of Poverty," in L. Osberg (ed.), *Economic Inequality and Poverty: International Perspectives* (Armonk, NY: M.E. Sharpe), 134-156.

Mishel, L., J. Bernstein and J. Schmitt (1999), *The State of Working America 1998-99* (New York: Economic Policy Institute; Ithaca: Cornell University Press).

Morissette, R., X. Zhang and M. Drolet (2001), "The Evolution of Wealth Inequality in Canada 1984–99", paper presented at the Annual Meetings of the Canadian Economics Association, mimeo, May.

Myles, J. and G. Picot (2000), "Poverty Indices and Poverty Analysis", *Review of Income and Wealth* 46(2), 161-180.

Osberg, L., S. Erksoy and S. Phipps (1998), "How to Value the Poorer Prospects of Youth in the early 1990s?" *Review of Income and Wealth* 44(1), 43-62.

Osberg, L. and K. Xu (1997), "International Comparisons of Poverty Intensity: Index Decomposition and Bootstrap Inference", Working Paper 97-03 (Halifax: Department of Economics, Dalhousie University). Available as Luxemburg Income Study Working Paper No. 152.

_____ (1999), "Poverty Intensity: How Well Do Canadian Provinces Compare?" *Canadian Public Policy/Analyse de Politiques* 25(2), 179-195.

_____ (2000), "International Comparisons of Poverty Intensity: Index Decomposition and Bootstrap Inference", *Journal of Human Resources* 35(1), 51-81; errata corrected 35(3).

Perry, J.H. (1989), *A Fiscal History of Canada: the Post War Years*, Canadian Tax Paper No. 85 (Toronto: Canadian Tax Foundation).

Podoluk, J.R. (1968), *Incomes of Canadians*, 1961 Census Monograph Program (Ottawa: Dominion Bureau of Statistics).

Samuelson, P.A. (1948), *Economics: An Introductory Analysis* (Toronto and New York: McGraw-Hill Book Company).

Sen, A.K. (1976), "Poverty: An Ordinal Approach to Measurement", *Econometrica* 44, 219-231.

Slater, D.W. (1995), "Reforming Canada's Retirement Income System", *Canadian Business Economics* 4(1), 47-58.

Statistics Canada (1999), *Low Income Measures, 1997*, Cat. No. 13-582-XIB (Ottawa: Supply and Services Canada).

Xu, K. and L. Osberg (2000), "The Social Welfare Implications, Decomposability and Geometry of the Sen Family of Poverty Indices", Working Paper (Halifax: Dalhousie University).

Zheng, B. (1997), "Aggregate Poverty Measures", *Journal of Economic Surveys* 11, 123-161.

Appendix Table A1: Poverty Intensity and Components Using the Before-Tax LICO as Poverty Line (Canada)

	All			Those < 65 Years Old			Those 65 and Older		
	Poverty Intensity	Poverty Rate (%)	Poverty Gap (%)	Poverty Intensity	Poverty Rate (%)	Poverty Gap (%)	Poverty Intensity	Poverty Rate (%)	Poverty Gap (%)
Money Income Before Taxes and Transfers									
1973	21.9	21.1	55.7	15.5	16.8	48.6	66.9	59.2	73.4
1997#	31.8	29.1	60.6	25.1	23.9	57	66.5	62.4	70
1997*	31.8	29.1	60.6	25.6	24.4	57.2	68.4	64.2	70.4
Money Income After Taxes and Transfers									
1973	9.8	16.3	31.7	9.1	14.4	33	15.8	33.1	26.6
1997*	12.2	20.1	32.3	13.1	20.3	34.3	6.6	19.1	18.4
1997**	12.2	20.1	32.3	12.9	20.2	34.2	6.8	19.9	18.1

Notes: The Sen-Shorrocks-Thon (SST) index of poverty intensity is calculated as $I = (rate)*(gap)*(1+G(x))$ where "rate" is the percentage of the population with incomes below the poverty line (sometimes called the head count ratio), "gap" is the average percentage gap between the incomes of the poor and the poverty line and $G(x)$ is the Gini index of inequality of the poverty gap among all people. Since the term $(1+G(x))$ is nearly constant, it is not presented explicitly.
In 1997, the actual number of people aged 65 years or more is available. In 1973, households are classified by the age of the household head.
* Maintains comparability with 1973.
** Weighted using the (actual number aged 65 years or more ** sample weight) for seniors and (actual number < 65 years ** sample weight) for those under 65.
Source: Author's calculations using the Survey of Consumer Finance, Economic Families.

Six Pillars of Social Policy: The State of Pensions and Health Care in Canada

William B.P. Robson

Introduction and Overview

This paper surveys the state of Canadian economic policy in two key areas: pensions and health care. The occasion for this volume provides one justification for what might appear an over-ambitious survey. The impressive range of topics that David Slater has tackled over his career includes important work in both areas. In view of his consistent attention to the big picture and the long term in his work, it seems probable that if Dr. Slater were just starting now, the *festschrift* he could look forward to in 60 years' time would make reference not just to his contributions to understanding and management of pensions and health systems separately, but also to their complementarities and interactions.

As government involvement in pensions and health care in Canada has expanded, a second reason for exploring the two topics together has become

I thank Patrick Grady, Malcolm Hamilton, Jack Mintz, Finn Poschmann and Andrew Sharpe for comments and queries on an earlier draft, and Shay Aba for research assistance and helpful discussion. Remaining defects are my own responsibility.

more compelling. Pensions and health care are major spending programs that are strongly related to the life cycle of citizens. An aging population and rising ratio of program beneficiaries to workforce participants presents each with important challenges. And, especially in the face of demographic changes, design issues in each and in their interaction need attention if Canada is to provide beneficiaries with money and services while encouraging behaviour that will support a strong economy and keep the programs sustainable.

There are, of course, also key contrasts. Income support through pensions is formally closely tied to old age, whereas many government-supported health services are available on much the same terms throughout life. Pensions are money income, whereas health-related indemnity payments are relatively small relative to the services that are provided in kind. These contrasts affect the targeting of benefits and give provider groups a different influence on policy. As this review will attempt to show, however, these contrasts are often questions of degree rather than kind, and do not prevent an examination of interactions between the two that makes parallel treatment fruitful.

The Three Pillars Framework

For Canadians, there is one further justification for attempting a parallel discussion of pensions and health care. Commentary on pensions around the world makes much use of a metaphor of three pillars in describing a comprehensive system: a safety net to guard against destitution in old age, a mandatory employment-related system to provide basic replacement income, and a voluntary system supported by provisions that reduce double-taxation of saving. The distinction among different objectives of pension programs that inspires this metaphor is helpful in evaluating the performance of national systems (World Bank, 1994; ACPM, 2000).

In Canada, the main elements of public policy related to pensions — the Old Age Security and Guaranteed Income Supplement (OAS/GIS) and various provincial transfers for low-income seniors; the Canada and Quebec Pension Plans (CPP/QPP); and tax rules and regulations related to employer-sponsored and individual retirement saving plans (RSPs) — address these different objectives with an efficacy and precision that many other countries might envy.

The same precise matching of objectives with instruments, however, is not evident in health care. The 2000 federal election campaign provided a vivid example of Canadians' preoccupation with a confused debate over public versus private financing and public versus private provision of health services.[1] So a joint survey that discusses health care with respect to the three objectives that inspire the pillars metaphor — a safety net for those who need it, a contributory system that obliges those who can provide for themselves up to a basic level to do so, and a voluntary system that reduces double-taxation of saving — might accomplish two things. It might facilitate constructive responses to the pressures that will confront Canada's health system in the future. And it might illuminate some interactions between the pension and health systems that require attention if both systems are to be sustainable.

Outline of the Paper

The rest of the paper has four main parts. The first part provides background. It gives an overview of the pillars' concept, discussing its application to pensions and health care, and outlining the implications of each pillar's objectives for the way it is financed.[2] It also discusses the challenges of Canada's current situation, in particular the aging of the population and the need to ensure that the incentives the pension and health-care systems create — both individually and together — are compatible with long-term sustainability.

---

[1]This confusion is partly deliberate, with advocates for government-produced services arguing that private production goes with private financing. In fact, physician services in Canada are nearly exclusively privately produced, as are the bulk of inputs such as drugs and laboratory services. Hospitals are still nominally independent not-for-profit organizations, although many would argue that they have become *de facto* arms of provincial health ministries.

[2]Some commentary uses the term "tiers" to distinguish different elements of pension systems (Robson, 1997). In connection with Canadian health care, however, the term "tier" has become so politically charged as to inhibit intelligent discussion. So it seems prudent to forestall some of the more reflexive, less reflective reactions by avoiding the word.

The second section turns to a more detailed discussion of the pillars of Canada's pension system, covering the motivations of the programs, their financing, recent developments and future prospects. The third section discusses health care in the same framework.

The fourth section draws out some parallels between the two systems, discusses gaps in our understanding of how they affect behaviour, and speculates about how future policy changes, especially in health care, may affect their interaction. One observation is that more pre-funding to cover the cost of the aging baby boom is desirable, both in government budgets generally and in specific pension and health programs. A second is that gradual increases in the normal age of eligibility for pension benefits makes sense, and to the extent that health benefits become available at the same age, a coordinated approach would be desirable. A third major point is that allowing the current generous and largely non-means-tested health system to evolve into an equally generous but strongly means-tested system would exacerbate disincentives for many Canadians to work and save; creating a second pillar in the health system is likely a better route to long-term sustainability. Similar considerations underlie a fourth recommendation: creation of a new type of saving vehicle that provides tax-relief on distributions rather than contributions, so that modest-income Canadians can save in a form that avoids the high marginal effective tax rates that means-tested pension and health programs will otherwise impose on them.

In summary, parallel treatment of pensions and health in the three-pillars framework highlights some useful steps Canadians can take to ensure that the two systems work together in the service of solid and sustainable benefits.

Concepts and Context

This section gives an overview of the pillars concept: the objectives of each pillar and their implications for its design and financing. It also discusses the challenges of interactions among elements of each pillar and between the pillars themselves. It then surveys the continuing transformation of Canada's population to older, more intensive users of the pension and health systems, a transformation that makes decisions about how the pillars of each system will evolve all the more important.

Distinguishing Pillars

Classifying different elements of public policy towards transfer payments and in-kind services in the pillars framework is useful because it forces attention to their different motivations.

The First Pillar: The Safety Net. The first pillar is most straightforwardly thought of as a safety net. Like social assistance and in-kind services for the destitute, first-pillar programs seek to protect citizens from circumstances that are so miserable as to threaten life itself, or would be widely regarded as intolerable.

From a traditional public finance point of view, government involvement in safety net programs arises for two main reasons.[3] In the case of the currently needy, such as the disabled, free-riding may prevent a private charity providing support on the scale that collective utilitarian motives would suggest. And in the case of potential recipients, who would insure themselves against disaster if they could, information failures — adverse selection and moral hazard — may prevent private insurers from providing the necessary coverage.[4] Students of public choice will point out also that actual and potential recipients of such programs have an interest in voting for them, as do actual and potential providers of services and transfer intermediaries.

Design of safety net programs inevitably requires trading off competing imperatives. One key question is the level of support. Programs that are relatively generous will relieve hardship more effectively. Their higher expense, however, will typically impose efficiency costs through the tax

---

[3]Rosen *et al.* (1999, chs. 10 and 9) provide a helpful overview of positive and normative considerations in these areas.

[4]Adverse selection refers to the fact that potential insurers against misfortunes with a likelihood closely bound up in the personal characteristics of the potential buyer typically know less about the likely payout than the buyers do themselves. They may, therefore, only be able to offer policies at average prices that will be unattractive to the best risks, with the result that no market develops. Moral hazard refers to the possibility that purchasers of insurance will change their behaviour in ways that increase the likelihood of a claim, but which the insurer cannot observe — another obstacle to widespread provision by private insurers.

system. More generous programs are also likelier to raise concerns about horizontal equity, both between less fortunate members of society who do or do not qualify for the program, and between those who do or do not pay for it.

Targeting, whether through means-testing (by income, or assets, or both), provision of in-kind services,[5] or characteristics such as age that serve as proxies for need, is also a key conundrum. Programs that are broadly targeted are likelier to provide support to all intended beneficiaries and will reduce incentives to change behaviour to create entitlement. Narrowly targeted programs, by contrast, are likelier to exclude people who are not intended to benefit. They thus make less acute the efficiency and horizontal equity issues just noted, and — to the extent that targeting is accomplished through providing services in kind — respond to paternalistic desires to constrain the use recipients make of their support.

Their redistributive motivation makes first-pillar programs strong candidates for financing from current general government revenue. Pay-as-you-go tax financing reflects the dual nature of judgements about deprivation. Most people would not wish relief of absolute deprivation — a level of well-being so low as to threaten life itself — to be contingent on the existence of, say, a pool of dedicated income-earning assets. Giving such relief a high-priority claim on general public sector resources makes sense. Deprivation is also a relative concept, however: the material living standards of the average Canadian family four generations ago would be widely regarded as intolerable for a poor person (particularly a poor, elderly, sick person) today. Gearing support for safety net programs to current general prosperity through pay-as-you-go financing makes adjusting its level as society-wide living standards change relatively straightforward.

These considerations do not rule out pre-funding these obligations indirectly by raising governments' net worth through general budget surpluses. If the rate of return on financial assets exceeds the rate of economic growth, pre-funding new or enriched programs will impose lower taxes for a given level of benefits.[6] In situations where an initiative is intended to

---

[5]For an exploration of type 1 and type 2 errors — inadvertently excluding intended beneficiaries and inadvertently including unintended ones — as factors in the design of redistributive programs, see Boadway and Keen (2000).

[6]Moving an ongoing program from a pay-as-you-go to a pre-funded footing is a trickier call. In present value terms, the first-round impact of such a

William B.P. Robson

transfer resources from the young to the old and/or from a presumably more prosperous future to a needier present, however, policymakers and potential recipients may not give that consideration much weight.

The Second Pillar: Mandatory Income/Lifestyle Maintenance. The second pillar is a mandatory contributory social insurance system that requires all eligible citizens to purchase a basic package of benefits, such as insurance against unemployment. Traditional public finance perspectives stress two reasons for extensive government involvement in such systems.

One of them is moral hazard created by the first-pillar safety net. It is hard for administrators of safety net programs to deny benefits to people whose deprivation is of their own making. Such judgements are always contentious, and when the deprivation results from irrevocable past choices, the desire to set a good example for others may be too weak to produce time-consistent policy. So it is attractive to force all who could provide for themselves at least up to the level of first-pillar support to do so.

Even if the safety net did not affect behaviour and people would be willing to buy insurance against misfortune at an actuarially fair price, adverse selection may mean that such insurance is not widely available. Individuals are worse off without a kind of insurance they would like to buy, and their defensive behaviour may have further adverse consequences.[7] Compulsory pooling overcomes this difficulty. As far as efficiency is concerned, it is not clear that the gains from compulsory pooling outweigh the cost of increasing the scope for moral hazard to operate within the second-pillar system. Deductibles and co-payments can curb moral hazard, however, and if a desire to shift costs among participants is a key motive for establishing a social insurance program. The resulting externalities are an intentional product of policy.

Another often-cited justification for second-pillar programs is that individuals may judge their needs poorly. They might, for example, be

---

change imposes costs on losers that are equal to the benefits to winners, making second-round impacts and judgements about the appropriate sharing of costs and benefits among generations key to the decision (see Sinn, 2000, on the inter-generational point).

[7] A frequently provided example is the possibility that without insurance against unemployment, over-hasty job-search will impede good matching of employer needs and employee skills.

myopic, underestimating their future requirements and failing to save enough on their own. They might save in inappropriate forms. Or recipients might respond to plans that provide unrestricted indemnity payments rather than restricted ones or in-kind services by spending foolishly. Whether policymakers are better at looking after participants' interests than the participants would be on their own is bound to be a matter of debate. Since compulsory participation on similar terms is a general feature of social insurance programs, experiments that would allow judgements about, say, relative time horizons among private and public decisionmakers tend not to occur.

The financing of second-pillar systems reflects their insurance aspects. Most such plans collect contributions from participants (often through their employers) whose benefits are related in some fashion to their history in the plan. Many second-pillar systems can produce records of individual participation that resemble those that private insurers would provide. To the extent that participants see their contributions as actuarially fair — no different, say, from deductions from pay to finance fringe benefits — they will impose no tax and provide no subsidy, promoting an efficient labour market.

This mimicking of private insurance policies or retirement plans does not typically extend to the handling of assets inside the plan. The usual approach is a government-administered fund. If such a fund is administered separately from other government assets and liabilities, and the program's cash flows are segregated from other items in a government's budget, there may be economically meaningful pre-funding of the program's obligations. As noted earlier, such pre-funding may be desirable when returns on financial assets exceed economic growth rates or — as is likelier with second- than first-pillar programs — when policymakers wish to keep each cohort's costs in line with its benefits. At the other extreme, the fund may be a meaningless bookkeeping entry that signifies no segregation of plan cashflows and assets from the rest of the government's budget — a misleading mask on a pay-as-you-go system.

The Third Pillar: Tax-Recognized Saving. Third-pillar systems are sets of tax laws and regulations that provide a framework for individuals, either on their own or pooled (generally through employers), to self-insure.[8] Their key

---

[8]The presumption here is that contributions to such plans are from participants themselves, although the possibility of government top-ups exists.

feature is relief from double-taxation of saving. There are two principal approaches. The more common one exempts contributions to and earnings within a saving plan from the tax base, but includes distributions. This approach is often referred to as EET — for "exempt", "exempt" and "taxed". The other, less often used, includes contributions to a plan in the tax base, but exempts accumulations and distributions. This approach is often referred to as TEE.

From a public finance point of view, these systems serve several ends. They reduce distortions in the current-salary/deferred-benefit balance of employee compensation by evening out the tax treatment of, say, pension-plan contributions and wages.[9] Relatedly, they mitigate the bias that a pure income tax creates in favour of consumption over saving (see Mintz, 2001). Although such plans may pay taxes or receive subsidies, they are usually self-funding. Tax deferral in third-pillar systems also promotes horizontal equity by making it easier for private sector employees to obtain pension and insurance arrangements like those enjoyed by public sector employees, whose employers — being formally or effectively non-taxable — find provision of generous deferred benefits less costly. They can also level the playing field between employees and the self-employed.

The voluntary nature of these systems weakens the case for restricting the services that participants can buy or the indemnities they can enjoy. Nevertheless, paternalism in third-pillar systems finds expression in regulations that, for example, attempt to ensure that saving ostensibly undertaken for retirement is actually used for that purpose.

From a public choice point of view, third-pillar plans might be seen to respond to the desire of citizens for deferred compensation under their own control. Some observers see the forward-looking behaviour such control induces as a source of positive externalities, and count this effect as a benefit of such plans. A less favourable assessment, typically reflecting a view that annual income is a suitable metric for assessing well-being, sees these plans as undermining vertical equity — allowing savers, who in a given year will tend to have higher incomes than non-savers, to avoid tax on part of their incomes — and may consider some kind of *quid pro quo* on the part of

---

[9] If the third-pillar framework promotes employer-sponsored or other private pooling arrangements that have an insurance element, it can reduce the problems that public finance economists point to in justifying second-pillar programs.

participants, such as an obligation to invest their savings in certain ways, to be appropriate.

Conundrums

As this brief review reveals, programs in each pillar present challenges: the first pillar's trade-off between generosity and efficiency; the second pillar's overcoming of adverse selection at the cost of increasing the scope for moral hazard; the third pillar's conflict between horizontal and vertical equity. The fact that developed democracies typically have a number of programs that provide safety-net, social insurance, and self-insurance services, moreover, means that sorting out the combined impacts of and interactions among different programs can be a major challenge.

Interactions. Where first-pillar benefits are geared to assets or income, for example, problems can arise when benefit-reduction schedules — popularly known as clawbacks — affect a given recipient overlap. The "welfare wall" encountered by people moving from social assistance to work who lose various transfer payments and in-kind benefits is a well-known instance. Interactions among different pillars are also important. If clawbacks in first-pillar programs create confiscatory marginal effective tax rates, for example, they will hurt incentives to work and save in general. Discouraging work is unhelpful to the contribution base for second-pillar programs, while an expectation of higher marginal effective rates in retirement may outweigh the encouragement that third-pillar programs provide for individuals in the relevant income range to save.

Finally, interactions among entire systems can matter. If the income and substitution effects of systems in one area discourage workforce participation, for example, the consequent reduction in output will adversely affect the financing of other systems.[10] Alternatively, improvements in well-being as a result of one safety-net or social insurance program may have favourable repercussions for others.[11]

---

[10]The lower workforce participation may have implications for the spending side of other programs as well.

[11]Interactions that help shape the parameters of the systems are also possible. For example, Bethencourt and Galasso (2000) investigate the possibility

Demographic Change and Fiscal Sustainability. Of course, the functioning of pillars and the interactions among them occur in real time, and the evolution of these programs and the changing circumstances that surround them have tended to confront countries with specific types of challenges.

The second half of the twentieth century was remarkable for a number of developments in the developed democracies. The first 25 years were a period both of rapid productivity growth that gave rise to unprecedented prosperity, and of dramatically higher fertility amid a long-term downward trend. Governments grew rapidly, with first- and second-pillar programs playing major roles in the expansion. Then the second 25 years witnessed a reversion to the historically normal growth rates and a resumption of the previous trend towards fewer children.

Canada shared in this experience. The boom gave rise to economic growth rates well in excess of rates of return on financial assets, encouraging pay-as-you-go financing and government deficits. The expansion of government obligations and an end to the productivity boom then created large fiscal deficits. When the historically more common situation where rates of return on financial assets exceed economic growth rates returned, high debt levels kept tax rates up even as program spending came under control. Ever since, accumulating obligations in the areas of both pensions and health care have created concern about fiscal sustainability and inter-generational fairness (Robson, 1996, pp. 3-4 and 7-9).

The central fact underlying current concern about Canadian pension and health systems is that the aging of the baby boom and the post-boom return to a longer term downward trending fertility rate is on the verge of changing the ratio of older to working-age Canadians in a massive, unprecedented fashion. Over the years from 2000 to 2020, the share of the total population that is 65 or over will go from its current level of 12.5 per cent to more than 18 per cent, while the ratio of working-age people to seniors will drop from 5.5 to 3.6.[12] More speculatively, with constant fertility rates and age-specific mortality rates continuing to decline at the rates suggested by experience from 1971 to 1991, the share of the population that is 65 or over will rise to

---

that redistribution through public health expenditures will increase the size of the constituency that supports redistribution through the pension system.

[12]Consistent with the usual labour-force definition, the working age is defined here as from 15 to 64.

25 per cent, and the ratio of working-age people to seniors will fall to 2.4 by 2040 (Robson, 2001, pp. 4-6).

Since the older population is likelier to receive payments and services from the pension and health systems, while the working-age population is likelier to contribute to them, Canada's fiscal and economic future will be highly sensitive to the interactions and overlaps among the various pillars of pension and health policy.

Pensions

The current structure of Canada's retirement income system conforms closely to that suggested by the pillars framework. The safety-net, mandatory income-replacement, and voluntary components of the system are easily distinguishable. These separations have assisted Canadians in adjusting these programs in the past, and should prove helpful in making adjustments that will keep the system functioning well in the years ahead.

Old Age Security and the Guaranteed Income Supplement

Together, Old Age Security (OAS) and Guaranteed Income Supplement (GIS) payments make up the bulk of the income-supporting safety net for older Canadians.[13]

The OAS was Canada's first national income-support payment for the elderly. It started as a modest flat transfer to all Canadians aged 70 or over in the early 1950s, grew in real value through enrichment and lowering of the eligibility age to 65, and then shrank again through inflation until being indexed to the consumer price index in the early 1970s. It is taxable and since 1990 has been subject to a special clawback of 15 per cent that reduces it to zero for seniors with net incomes above about $80,000.

---

[13]The spouses' allowance introduced in 1975 also falls under this heading, but is too small to rate separate discussion. See Burbidge (1996) for a fuller description of these programs and their history.

The GIS was introduced in the mid-1960s as a non-taxable income supplement for Canadians who would receive little or no benefit from the Canada and Quebec Pension Plans (CPP/QPP) established at the same time. It was enriched at intervals during the 1980s, and is indexed to consumer price inflation. It is clawed back at a rate of 50 cents per dollar of (most) other income.[14]

The OAS and GIS are clearly first-pillar programs, providing a floor below which no senior's income will go. They are largely responsible for the virtual elimination of severely low incomes among Canadian seniors (Osberg, 2001). Together, they represent a compromise between the objective of a lightly distorting, but less generous, universal safety-net program, and the more heavily distorting and more generous alternative. The durability of this compromise was evident when the 1996 federal budget proposed to combine the two programs into a new "seniors benefit" that would have enriched benefits marginally at the lower end and clawed back transfers to higher-income recipients more energetically. This proposal attracted a number of criticisms, among them dislike of the higher effective marginal tax rates it would have imposed on middle-income seniors (Slater, 1998), and was quietly dropped in the summer of 1998.

The OAS originally had some trappings of a contributory plan, with a notional allocation from both the personal and corporate income taxes into a dedicated account. For some early participants, this cosmetic gesture created a sense that the transfer was an earned entitlement along second-pillar lines. These earmarked taxes and the account disappeared in the early 1970s, however. Since then, the OAS and the GIS have been financed from general federal taxation — a pay-as-you-go approach that gives these programs a high-priority claim on core government resources and effectively gears them to general prosperity. Since the ratio of federal government debt to gross domestic product (GDP) has risen from around 20 per cent in the mid-1970s to more than 50 per cent currently — and the last enrichments of the GIS in the mid-1980s occurred when the federal deficit was running around 8 per cent of GDP — this financing approach can be reasonably seen as a deliberate transfer of resources from the young to the old.

Looking ahead, two contrary forces affect the claim of these plans on national resources. The more rapid growth of the recipient than the working-age population will exert upward pressure on OAS and GIS payments as a

---

[14]Importantly, OAS payments are not included.

share of the economy. But since benefits are indexed to prices rather than wages, productivity growth tends to reduce their share of GDP. Recent projections from the Chief Actuary (OSFI, 1999) showed expenditures under these plans falling from around 2.6 per cent of GDP at the time to 2.4 per cent after a decade, then climbing again, regaining their then-current share by 2015, and peaking at 3.3 per cent of GDP by 2030.[15]

Discounted over the next 50 years at 6 per cent, the net increase in the share of GDP projected to flow through these plans represents a liability of about 9 per cent of GDP.[16] The fiscal consolidation that has brought the ratio of the federal government's net debt to GDP down by nearly 20 percentage points from its peak above 70 per cent in the mid-1990s might be seen as, in part, a move to offset this liability and the associated resources transfer.

Except for the aborted seniors benefit just mentioned, the only significant attempt to rein in growth of the first-pillar programs was a proposal in the 1985 federal budget to limit the indexation of OAS payments to inflation over 3 per cent — a measure also dropped in the face of opposition from seniors. Many observers have suggested that the increase in the average healthy life expectancy of Canadians since these programs were introduced makes it reasonable to expect people to work for longer, and that some increase in the age of eligibility for receipt would make sense. Although many developed democracies, including the United States, have recently undertaken or scheduled such moves (OECD, 1998, p. 53), no such moves are currently in view in Canada.

One equity-oriented concern about the generosity of the OAS/GIS system is that, especially combined with provincial supplements, it provides

---

[15]The Chief Actuary illustrated the potential impact of ad hoc increases to keep the generosity of these programs more closely in line with the income of the working population by calculating that indexing benefits to inflation plus 60 per cent of the difference between wage growth and inflation would raise the ratio of their expenditures to GDP by about two-thirds of a percentage point above the base case by 2030 (OSFI, 1999, pp. 86 and 102).

[16]Fifty years is roughly the average life expectancy of every living Canadian. A 6 per cent nominal interest rate is equal to the roughly 4 per cent real interest rate used by the Chief Actuary in the most recent projections for the CPP, plus the 2-per cent inflation rate specified in the Bank of Canada's targets. This rough-and-ready valuation is used for the sake of consistency with the valuation of the health-care liability below (as in Robson, 2001).

William B.P. Robson

an after-tax income guarantee that is quite high relative both to the safety nets available to younger Canadians and to the levels at which working individuals and families begin paying taxes (ACPM, 2000, pp. 12-13). With indexation to prices rather than wages eroding the relative value of these payments, and increases in tax thresholds and reductions in bottom tax rates easing the burden on lower-income workers, these concerns will likely become less acute over the next few years. For the foreseeable future, then, the first pillar of the Canadian pension system is unlikely to change significantly.

The Canada and Quebec Pension Plans

The Canada and Quebec Pension Plans are second-pillar programs: mandatory social insurance, income-replacement plans that cover most employed Canadians.[17] They provide a variety of benefits: a retirement pension that, at the normal retirement age of 65, starts at roughly one-quarter of covered earnings; widow and orphan benefits; disability benefits; and a small death benefit. Contributions are levied as a proportion of earnings between $3,500 and the lower of actual earnings and a maximum roughly equal to the industrial average. Participants receive periodic statements of their status in the plans, and benefits are linked, albeit somewhat loosely, to contribution history.

The CPP/QPP have many trappings of funded plans, but they were originally intended to be largely pay-as-you-go. The CPP began paying full benefits after a decade in operation, and although the QPP's phase-in was two decades, the larger pool of assets this delay allowed was desired more for industrial policy and provincial-government financing purposes than to secure the benefits of pre-funding (Vaillancourt, 2000, p. 24). The assets under administration in both plans were dramatically short of the actuarial liabilities of the plans by the mid-1990s, and since the CPP's assets were at that time almost exclusively provincial government debt paying below-market rates of interest, one can argue that there was no economically meaningful pre-funding at all.

---

[17]The principal exceptions, as is common in this type of plan, are for certain government employees: members of the armed forces and the Royal Canadian Mounted Police are not required to belong.

The fact that the CPP does have some assets under administration, however, meant that when financial market returns moved back above growth rates in the 1980s, the plan's financial projections readily highlighted the advantages of pre-funding. As at year-end 1997, the Chief Actuary estimated the total accrued entitlement of the CPP's participants to date at $465 billion, versus assets of $37 billion, for a funding ratio of about 8 per cent, and an unfunded liability of $428 billion (OSFI, 1998, p. 191). The Quebec government does not produce comparable actuarial valuations of the QPP, but if the ratio between the QPP and CPP liabilities is proportional to the respective covered populations, the unfunded liability of both plans at the end of 1997 would have been $566 billion.

By the mid-1990s, concern that the existing plan would require contribution rates above 15 per cent by 2030 inspired action to shore up the CPP. The reform package implemented in 1998 trimmed benefits slightly and ramped up the contribution rate markedly. The actuarial projections on which the reforms were based suggest that the CPP's funding ratio will rise to about 20 per cent over the next 20 years, allowing the contribution rate to stay at a politically palatable 9.9 per cent of covered earnings for the foreseeable future.[18] The package also created an arm's-length CPP Investment Board (CPPIB) to manage the CPP's assets, an institution that represents a state-of-the-art attempt to deal with some of the well-documented problems of government-run provident funds (Slater, 1997b; Robson, 1998).

The 1998 reform package also provided for more frequent reviews of the CPP's financial state than previously.[19] More frequent scrutiny will encourage faster adjustments in the face of adverse developments. The assumptions underlying the 1998 reform package were reasonable on the whole, and positive surprises, with regard to productivity growth, for example, are possible. Importantly, however, inflation of 3 per cent — significantly above the Bank of Canada's target of 2 per cent — was needed to make the package work. Moreover, the formula used to calculate the "steady-state" contribution rate will, even if the projections on which the 1998 package was

---

[18] A coherent theoretical case can be made that the additional saving in the CPP/QPP will be offset by reduced saving outside it, and that the reform package will therefore produce no net increase in national saving. As Pesando (2001) notes, however, such an offset is unlikely in actuality.

[19] The results of the first triennial review will be out shortly after this volume is published.

based are borne out, tend to yield higher rates during the next few reviews,[20] increasing the chances that one of them will inspire fresh ideas about better funding the plan. Further reforms are not beyond the realm of possibility in the coming decade, and proposals to raise entitlement ages (see Pesando, 2001) can and should get a hearing.

More frequent review — especially following a strong economic performance such as occurred during the 1998–2000 period — might also expand the opportunity for enriching current or soon-to-be beneficiaries at the expense of later participants. Another threat to the plan's integrity may be industrial-policy advocates attracted by the growing pool of financial assets under CPPIB administration. Importantly, however, the CPP Act provides for other provinces to follow Quebec's lead and establish their own plans, and the province of Alberta has shown interest in doing so if the principles of the reform package are threatened, a threat that may help keep the package intact. To the extent that confidence among younger CPP participants that they will actually receive future benefits remains low, repackaging part of the plan into individual retirement accounts may be an attractive option (Robson, 1996; Pesando, 1997).

Pension Plans and RRSPs

The modern shape of Canada's registered pension plans emerged from two forces. One was the desire to ensure that private employer-sponsored pension plans were properly funded. The other was the desire to level the playing field between employees who had such plans and those who did not. Accomplishing these goals meant removing the obstacles to employer funding of

---

[20]The current formula for calculating the "steady-state" rate is an odd one. It specifies essentially that the rate should make the ratio of CPP assets to annual expenditures the same 63 years after the evaluation date as it is 13 years after it. Since the asset-expenditure ratio peaks between those two dates — and therefore is on its way up at the 13-year mark and on its way down at the 63-year mark — the next few evaluations will use progressively higher 13-year benchmarks for the ratio, and will therefore find that higher contribution rates are needed to push the 63-year ratios up to that level (Slater and Robson, 1999, pp. 14-15). Of course, another possible reaction to this problem would be to change the regulation that specifies the formula, and choose two new dates that yield a 9.9 per cent rate.

pension plans, and then providing analogous provisions for individuals who wished to contribute to their own.

The essential characteristic of Canada's third pillar is that it relieves contributions to employer-sponsored or individual retirement plans from current taxation, and does the same for income earned inside the plans. Withdrawals are taxed at regular personal income tax rates.

Concern about the possibility that higher income earners will avoid too much tax on contributions, as well as the federal government's fiscal difficulties in the mid-1990s, resulted in limits on contributions that in recent years have become tighter.[21] Withdrawals from and conversions of the assets in these plans into annuities or combined return-on/return-of capital arrangements (registered retirement income funds) are regulated in several ways and are obligatory after age 69.

As noted already, a key rationale for relieving contributions to pension plans from current taxation is that failing to do so would discourage employers from funding their pension promises. Passing the bill for the first cohort of recipients forward in time through pay-as-you-go financing is attractive to private companies as well as to governments, but unless growth in company revenues and profits out-paces returns on financial assets indefinitely, such arrangements tend to lead to defaults. Unfunded private defined-benefit plans have essentially been illegal since the 1960s; nowadays, the obligations of defined-benefit plans are by and large completely backed by assets. Full backing of defined contribution plans, whether employer-sponsored or individual, is of course intrinsic to their structure.

In general, the third pillar of Canada's pension system appears, like the other two, to be well suited to its purpose of facilitating voluntary retirement saving. Slightly over one-half of Canadian families have claims on defined-benefit plans (Statistics Canada, 2001), and some one-third of Canadians have Registered Retirement Saving Plan (RRSP) assets. Contributions to contributory Registered Pension Plans (RPPs) dropped somewhat between

---

[21]See Slater (1997a). Income-tax provisions concerning Canadian RSPs limit foreign investments by their owners. This restriction is unusual among developed countries, and seems to reflect a view that those enjoying deferred taxation should pay a price for the privilege. If binding, such limits can force savers into inferior risk-return positions (Fried and Wirick, 1999). For large plans with cost-effective access to derivatives, circumventing these limits is easy and inexpensive; for small individual savers, on the other hand, vehicles offering above-the-limit foreign exposure tend to be relatively costly.

1986 and 1997, but increased contributions to RRSPs more than offset the decline (Morissette and Drolet, 2001, p. 115). By international standards, the assets held in Canada's third-pillar Registered Saving Plans (RSPs) are large, amounting to some $730 billion, or almost three-quarters of GDP, in 2000 (Andrea Davis, 2001).

There is ongoing debate over the justification for RSP contribution limits. Those who dislike seeing individuals with higher annual incomes defer tax tend to argue for lower limits, an argument that has recently carried the day. The maximum contribution for which tax deferral is available has been frozen at the lesser of 18 per cent of income or an amount sufficient to provide $1,722 per year of pensionable service (to a maximum of 35 years) for defined-benefit pension plans, and 18 per cent of income or $13,500 annually for defined-contribution plans or RRSPs. After allowing for inflation over the period of the freeze (1996 to 2004), these provisions will reduce the opportunity to save 18 per cent of income in this manner to individuals with annual incomes under about twice the average, although unlimited carry-forwards of unused room reduce the impact of these limits on taxpayers whose incomes are volatile (Slater, 1997a). Those who favour consumption taxation, on the other hand, tend to favour higher limits (Mintz, 2001), and many would also favour liberalization of the terms under which funds from these plans can be withdrawn.[22]

A further area of concern that has, as yet, attracted less attention relates to the fact that income-based means-testing in the pension system's first pillar — and, as is discussed further below, in the health-care system — results in marginal effective tax rates for modest-income older Canadians that are typically far higher than the tax rates they faced while working (Davies, 1998). For these people, especially when they are older and the period of tax-free accumulation is less significant, EET-type vehicles that defer taxes may be an unwise choice (Shillington, 1999).

To judge from current behaviour, the implications of this problem are not yet clear to many of those affected: the share of income devoted to pension contributions increased more among low- than high-income workers from 1986 to 1997 (Morissette and Drolet, 2001, p. 116). Many of these contributors, especially the younger ones, are undoubtedly people whose low-

---

[22]Age limits on receiving pensions or converting the assets in a plan to an annuity or Registered Retirement Income Fund would also need re-examining in the event of an increase in eligibility ages in the first- and second-pillar systems.

income status is temporary. For those whose long-term prospects for income gains are not good, however, the disadvantages of saving in this form raise two concerns. First, it would make sense to create a TEE-type vehicle, in which contributions would be taxed but accumulations and withdrawals would be tax-free, in which lower income Canadians could more effectively save (Kesselman and Poschmann, 2001). Second, if more of the lower income population comes to understand the implications of high future-clawback/current-tax-saving ratios and save less as a result (as Hamilton, 2001, suggests they should), the first-pillar system and the taxes that pay for it will both be adversely affected.

Health Care

In contrast to the pension system, the formal organization of Canadian health care scarcely reflects a three-pillar framework. It is nevertheless straight-forward to distinguish safety-net, mandatory basic lifestyle maintenance, and voluntary saving motivations behind different components in the system.

Distinguishing these components is helpful for two reasons. It breaks the system's successes and challenges down more clearly than does the confused debate over public versus private financing and delivery that currently dominates health-care discussions. And it highlights features of the health-care system that can interact with features of the pension system in desirable and undesirable ways.

Coverage against Medical Catastrophe

Public financing of hospital treatments and other responses to life-threatening conditions is the clearest mechanism by which Canadian health systems provide safety nets to citizens. Hospital insurance was the first area of extensive public financing of health care in Canada, being brought almost entirely into a system where services are free at the point of delivery, with no co-payments or deductibles, by the early 1960s. Hospitals remain both the single biggest category of public health expenditures and also the category of health expenditures in which the share of public money is largest.[23] Both motivations for safety-net programs — ensuring that free-riding does not limit the resources available for rescue, and compulsory pooling to provide insurance of a type that adverse selection and moral hazard make it difficult for private insurers to cover — are evident in this arrangement.

Since the early 1970s, most physician services have also been effectively part of the safety net. Like hospital treatments, physician services have first-dollar coverage under provincial medicare plans. To a lesser but still considerable extent, many services that are ancillary to hospital and physician treatments, in particular laboratory services and pharmaceuticals, often come into the safety-net category. But the extent to which this type of coverage corresponds to what most people would think of as safety-net functions is erratic: while patients' hospital stays are covered, the ambulance that takes them there may not be.

For the most part, Canadian safety-net health services are targeted only in the implicit sense that, after the point of first contact — the primary-care physician, walk-in clinic or hospital emergency room — their provision is contingent on a medical condition that warrants treatment. Unlike the common practice in other countries, access to hospital and physician services in Canada is not subject to means-testing and there are no mechanisms for cost-recovery after the fact.

Some targeting of first-pillar-type services, however, does exist. Tax credits for out-of-pocket medical expenses provide full relief from taxation of income devoted to health care above specified limits (3 per cent of net income or a prescribed amount, $1,637 in 2000) for people in the bottom tax bracket, but less than full relief for those in higher brackets. The provinces that still charge health-related premiums — British Columbia and Alberta for hospital, physician and pharmaceutical services; Nova Scotia for pharmaceuticals alone — provide partial or complete relief from premiums based on factors such as age, income, or medical condition. Access to provincial pharmacare programs is also contingent on age, income and/or medical

[23]Figures on the public and private shares of health spending by use of funds are available from the Canadian Institute for Health Information at <www.cihi.ca/facts/nhex/nhex2000/NHEX_Fig1-5.shtml#figure%205> (as of 10 July 2001).

condition.[24] And importantly for subsequent discussion, public subsidies for long-term care are typically subject to income-based means tests and fierce clawbacks.

When hospital and physician services were first covered by public insurance programs, individual or family premiums notionally related to the insurance programs were common. As with the OAS, this approach appears to have responded to a sense in the population that these were, to some extent, second-pillar-style contributory programs.[25] In many cases, these provincial revenues were directed into special accounts, and the terminology of pre-payment suggested at least a minimal level of pre-funding.

Federal subsidies to the provinces — at first under cost-sharing agreements and later through block-funding — were always from general revenues, however, and over time, provincial health programs became largely or completely tax financed. Nowadays, as just noted, only Alberta and British Columbia charge premiums in respect of hospital and physician services, and the amounts raised amount to some one-eighth to one-tenth of health-envelope spending.[26] As with first-pillar pension programs, it seems reasonable to view the increase in provincial government net debt — from around 5 per cent of GDP in the early 1970s to around 27 per cent more recently — as indicative of an implicit desire to transfer resources to current recipients of these services.

Tax-financed medical services that are a *de facto* part of the Canadian safety net currently amount to some 6 per cent of Canada's GDP. Because older people absorb medical services in larger amounts than younger

---

[24]Drug plans for seniors typically involve income-tested co-payments and deductibles.

[25]The fact that packaging them this way enabled governments to levy special taxes to cover their costs made the fiscal decisions easier.

[26]In 1999–2000, Alberta raised $653 million in health-care insurance premiums, and spent $5.1 billion in the "health and wellness" envelope (Alberta, 2001). In British Columbia, medical services plan premiums were $868 million, and $8.1 billion was spent under health (British Columbia, 2000, pp. 79 and 81). In Alberta, premiums are collected by large employers. Certain categories of citizens are exempt from premiums, including seniors in Alberta; low-income families in both provinces are eligible for lower premiums.

William B.P. Robson

people,[27] the intensity of their use will likely rise in the future even as the number of working-age Canadians so important to their financing grows more slowly and then shrinks. Unlike the price-indexing that provides some automatic offset to the upcoming shrinkage of the share of the population that is working, most observers expect current trends to increase the cost to taxpayers of the health safety net.

Projections that assume constant relative age-specific utilization rates, moderate increases in age-adjusted utilization and costs, and historical increases in output per person of working age suggest that the claims of provincial health spending on the economy will rise markedly in the coming decades. Expressing these increases over current shares of GDP — or equivalently, if governments' tax shares of GDP stay constant — over current own-source revenues in present-value terms over a 50-year period yields a measure of the liability represented by higher health spending ranging from $500 to $800 billion (Robson, 2001, pp. 11 and 16).[28] Although governments have reduced their debt-to-GDP ratios since the mid-1990s, the *de facto* prefunding provided by these reductions is fairly small alongside a liability of some 50–80 per cent of GDP.

The fiscal pressures of the 1990s resulted in some narrowing of the variety of medical services covered by the tax-financed safety net, and mostly informal quantitative limits on the supply of covered services. The current period of buoyant fiscal results has eased these pressures but, while there is doubtless room for more efficient use of resources in the system through more adept planning (Evans *et al.*, 1994; Donaldson *et al.*, 2001b) or internal markets (Jérôme-Forget and Forget, 1998; Donaldson *et al.*, 2001a), it is safe to predict that they will mount again in a few years' time.

When they do, the outcome of choices about what services to continue covering in the tax-financed system will doubtless largely reflect the same desire to protect Canadians against catastrophic events — which, if paid for

---

[27]Estimates from the Canadian Institute for Health Information for 1998 show per capita use of provincially funded health goods and services some 5.4 times higher for those 65 and over than for those under 65 (Robson, 2001, pp. 4-5).

[28]Projections that assume that mortality, rather than age per se, is the key driver of costs produce figures that are somewhat more challenging. In a typical projection, the number of deaths rises more slowly than the number of seniors, but more quickly than a utilization-by-age weighted index of the entire population.

privately, would be financially ruinous — that led to hospital and physician services being covered publicly in the first place. The process of choosing might be somewhat less contentious if the safety-net motivation behind this pillar were more explicit in the debate. Age will doubtless continue to be a criterion for eligibility for certain types of services; a straightforward way of adjusting this type of targeting to cope with financial pressure and acknowledge the trend towards longer life expectancy and healthier old age would be to raise the eligibility age for such coverage.[29]

As far as moves towards means-testing are concerned, the dilemma familiar from the discussion of first-pillar systems generally and the OAS/GIS system in particular — between providing a generous level of support and avoiding punitive effective tax rates — will come to the fore. Thus far, the fierce clawbacks that generous but tightly targeted safety-net programs create have been mostly limited to the area of long-term care, where they already create powerful incentives not to save or to convert assets to forms that are immune from clawbacks. The recent increase in the importance of drugs in treatments means that provincial drug programs, which typically gear deductibles, co-payments and (where they exist) premiums to income, increasingly raise the same type of concern.

More general co-payments geared to income are one possible response to financial pressure. Recovering part of the cost of medical services through the personal income tax (Reuber, 1980, ch. 8) would be less problematic than adding to the existing panoply of income-tested benefits. Provided that the recovery was at the same tax rates that would apply to individual income in the relevant range, such recoveries would push some taxpayers into higher tax brackets, but would not create effective marginal effective rates higher than those in the personal income-tax system itself.

Mandatory Coverage

As just noted, when health "premiums" were relatively more important in funding hospital and physician services in Canada, one might have argued

---

[29]It would be more elegant if eligibility ages for pensions and health care rose in tandem. Since both systems are essentially areas of shared federal-provincial jurisdiction, some lead by the federal government would be necessary in both areas.

William B.P. Robson

that these programs reflected, at least in part, second-pillar motivation. The public systems had replaced private not-for-profit pre-paid insurance, with the explicit objective of making coverage universal and compulsory.[30] In this respect, Canada might have been said to have a second-pillar system that provided medical services in kind, funded on a largely pay-as-you-go basis by individual and family levies.

By now, most publicly funded services are financed almost completely from general revenue.[31] The sort of second-pillar system that is common in other countries — by which people who are able to protect themselves against foreseeable health risks are obliged to do so in either a social insurance program or through mandatory private insurance — scarcely exists in Canada. There are, however, examples of this type of program: workers' compensation programs, sickness benefits under the employment insurance (EI) program, and the disability components of the CPP/QPP.

With the exception of workers' compensation programs, which purchase medical benefits that they provide their participants in-kind — effectively a little-noticed second tier within the publicly funded system — Canada's second-pillar programs essentially provide indemnity payments: income replacement in the event of ill-health. About three-quarters of workers' compensation expenditures are indemnity payments, and EI sickness and CPP/QPP disability benefits are entirely provided in cash.

All three of these programs are run exclusively by governments, and depart in important ways from insurance principles. Workers' compensation programs, which are financed exclusively through payroll taxes levied on employers, resemble insurance programs most closely in that they are partially experience-rated on the basis of employers' accident records, and

---

[30]Taylor (1978, ch. 6) discusses the gradual displacement of non-government insurers of physician services after the coming into force of the *Medical Care Act* in 1968.

[31]Newfoundland, Manitoba, Ontario and Quebec levy payroll and other taxes with names that include the word "health". This, however, is no more than an attempt to make these taxes more palatable to the population: they are in no sense hypothecated for health-related spending, and there is no link (as there still is in provinces that charge premiums for certain health services) between payment of the levy and access to health services.

have *de facto* deductibles in the form of waiting periods.[32] EI and CPP/QPP are financed by taxes on wages and salaries the obligation for which is formally split between employers and employees: neither is experience-rated in any meaningful way, and neither has co-payments.[33] The two-week waiting period for sickness benefits under EI constitutes a token deductible; the four-month waiting period for CPP disability benefits constitutes a more substantial one.

For the most part, these programs have been run on a pay-as-you-go basis. By the mid-1990s, all three had sizeable unfunded liabilities. Part of the concern over Canada's fiscal predicament at that time was directed at these liabilities, with the result that workers' compensation programs have become better funded, the EI program has built up a substantial cumulative surplus, and the CPP and QPP are, as noted already, on a path to partial funding.[34]

Canada's second-pillar system is unusual in international terms, both in its relative thinness, and in its exclusion of private insurers. While workers' compensation in the United States, for example, is a state monopoly in some

---

[32]Being provincial programs, they pool risk over smaller populations than the EI program, but involve less chronic regional cross-subsidies that does EI.

[33]The EI program's provision of longer benefit periods in high-unemployment regions acts, in fact, as a kind of reverse experience-rating. There is a special clawback of EI payments to higher-income earners through the personal income tax.

[34]On the wisdom of fuller funding for workers' compensation programs, see Vaillancourt (1995, p. 84); and Bogyo (1995). CIA (1996); and Robson (1996) were among the advocates of a more fully funded CPP. The EI program is a more debatable example of fuller funding. The contribution the EI Account has made to the federal government's fiscal turnaround since the mid-1990s is so large — a cumulative swing of around $33 billion since 1995, during which time the entire reduction in federal debt has been only $26 billion — that it seems unlikely that the turnaround could have occurred without it. For that reason, one might regard it as incremental saving. A contrary view, however, would see the fiscal turn-around as driven by necessity: if the EI program had not played its part, other parts of the budget would have made up the difference. For that reason — and noting also that the EI account is consolidated with the rest of the budget and its assets are simply federal debt — one might argue that there is no meaningful pre-funding in the program.

William B.P. Robson

states, it is provided by private or a mix of private and public insurers in most (Thomason, 1995, p. 59). Many European countries and Japan go much further, obliging most or all citizens to enroll in sickness funds that pool risks by industry, geographic area, occupation, and/or in self-selected categories.[35] These programs have safety-net features — they often provide relief from premiums, deductibles and/or co-payments to those with low incomes, and there is coverage from general government revenues for treatments too expensive for the normal insurance system to cover — but in much of the world, the second pillar represents the principal source of health coverage for the typical citizen.

Not surprisingly, given the state of Canada's current debate over health care, there appears to have been very little discussion of the merits, or even the possibility, of establishing a second pillar in the health system. In the early 1980s, the Canadian Medical Association floated a proposal that each Canadian family pay $1,000 a year in premiums to support what would have amounted to a substantial second-pillar system carved out of what is now the first-pillar system (Begin, 1984, p. 82). That proposal died a quick death, however; Canadians are largely unaware that their health system contains a second pillar, and do not — especially now that the last period of liberalization of CPP/QPP disability benefits is well in the past — much debate the possibility of expanding it.

Total indemnity benefits paid under workers' compensation, EI sickness, and CPP/QPP disability are significant — at nearly $8 billion annually, they amount to close to 1 per cent of GDP, and equal about 13 per cent of the value of health services provided in-kind by provincial and territorial governments — and administrative practices have tended to increase the generosity of these systems over time. But the expansion of EI and CPP/QPP benefits related to health problems has rarely been explicitly advocated as a supplement to or substitute for the general-revenue-financed safety net, and

---

[35]See Globerman and Vining (1996, p. 25). The Swiss system is remarkable for its lack of conformity with much of the economic theory that justifies social insurance generally and a government monopoly on it particularly. Swiss ambulatory care insurance is privately provided, and not only differs by region within each canton, but offers a choice of four deductibles (with premiums adjusted accordingly) above the mandatory minimum (Schellhorn, 2001, p. 13). Japan mandates participation in medical insurance plans organized in a variety of ways, including employer-based plans financed from payroll taxes and regional (municipal) plans financed from income and wealth taxes (Blomqvist, 2001).

the possibility of their becoming significant buyers of health services along WCB lines would strike most Canadians as peculiar.

Another way of carving a second pillar out of part of the existing first pillar, and possibly out of part of the existing third pillar as well, would be to require Canadians not currently covered, or not well covered, by private insurance to buy more. Despite the extensive use of this approach abroad, this suggestion might appear beyond the pale in Canada's current political climate — as was noted above, non-government insurance in Canada has been historically associated with the principle of voluntary purchase, and was supplanted by compulsory government coverage as a matter of policy.[36] But the *Canada Health Act's* prohibition of private insurance extends only to coverage of services that are provided by provincial health programs. In that sense, there is nothing that would prevent a province from requiring, for example, that all citizens purchase a basic package of insurance for drugs, dental care, or other services outside the currently defined safety net.

The usual justifications for preferring single public plans to competing private ones are the greater ease of integrating public plans with other public services (Vaillancourt, 1995, p. 83), the administrative costs of private plans (Evans *et al.*, 1989), and the ability to hold costs down with monopsony power (Richards, 1997, pp. 123-124; Hurley, 2000). Against these advantages can be cited the benefits of competition among private insurers in providing better coverage at lower cost (Globerman and Vining, 1996, pp. 82-83), and the advantages of involving the consumer of services more directly in treatment decisions — a motivation lying behind the suggestion that a mandatory second-pillar system might be organized around individual medical saving accounts.[37] The stakes in allowing such an experiment outside the safety-net system might seem sufficiently low to permit this type of approach in some of the more entrepreneurially minded provinces.

A notable feature of Canada's second-pillar health system is that — being either oriented around working people (workers' compensation and EI)

---

[36]It would have been possible, as is done in other countries, to subsidize low-income purchasers of private insurance, but the federal government was unenthusiastic about such subsidies and designed its cost-sharing proposals to discourage them (Blomqvist, 1994, p. 409).

[37]Ramsay (1998) presents some arguments for and against mandatory MSAs. Gratzer (1999, pp. 189-208) surveys a variety of options for MSAs, most of which are voluntary.

William B.P. Robson

or providing benefits to working-age people and seniors that are mutually exclusive (CPP/QPP) — it contains no provisions that are specific to the elderly.[38] As the Quebec Commission of Study on Health and Social Services (the Clair Commission) recently noted, Canada is increasingly out of step with international practice in this regard.[39] The Clair Commission proposed a new provincial plan in Quebec that would cover a range of home and institutional care services — providing either indemnity payments or buying services directly — for people suffering from long-term incapacity. The plan would be pre-funded from a dedicated tax on personal income, through an account administered by an arm's-length body.[40]

Private Saving for Health-Related Consumption

Turning to the third pillar, Canada's tax system has no widespread systematic provisions relieving saving for health-related expenses from double taxation. This absence is not currently a major concern. The *de facto* incorporation of hospital treatments, physician services, and many drug and specific-disorder-related expenses in the safety-net system, and the effective prohibition of private purchase of many of these services or insurance to cover them, makes dedicated saving vehicles a low priority for most people.[41]

---

[38]Although premium-based drug coverage for seniors is available in some provinces, there is no obligation to enroll.

[39]The Clair Commission cited Austria, Germany, France, Luxembourg and Japan as examples of countries that established compulsory plans to fund various home support services, residential and long-term care services for the elderly (Quebec, 2000, p. 183). The most familiar example for Canadians is probably U.S. Medicare, which provides coverage for hospital services from a payroll-tax-financed trust fund similar in structure to the U.S. Social Security system. (This is Part A; Part B, supplementary medical insurance, is financed by user fees and general revenues.)

[40]Quebec (2000, pp. 181-185). The commission left open the possibility that the new plan would cover all people suffering from long-term incapacity, rather than seniors only.

[41]Around half of Canadians have at least partial insurance coverage for eye-wear, closer to 60 per cent have it for dental care, and around three-quarters have it for prescription drugs (CIHI, 2000, p. 21).

Indeed, the idea that there is a third pillar in Canada's health system would strike many as a novel one.

Nevertheless, a discernable third pillar does stand alongside the first and second pillars just outlined. Favourable tax treatment exists for some saving that is implicitly or explicitly for medical purposes. RSPs, for example, can clearly be used for medical expenses. Some health insurance pays for services that are essentially outside the safety-net system, such as dental care. Other insurance provides complementary inputs, such as drugs. And — remarkably, in view of the reductionist all-or-nothing debate over public versus private financing — other insurance supplements services covered by the first pillar, such as semi-private or private hospital rooms, or by the second pillar, such as disability indemnities.

As already noted, public policy might relieve saving for health-related expenses from double taxation for several reasons. Exempting employer contributions to health, life or disability insurance from taxation by allowing employers to deduct them as a cost of compensation but not including them in employees' taxable income makes sense if the distributions from such plans are subject to tax (the EET model). Otherwise, employers will be discouraged from funding such plans, and private sector employees will be at a disadvantage relative to their public sector counterparts whose employers do not pay tax. Alternatively, governments might grant no tax relief in respect of contributions to such plans, but exempt distributions from tax (the TEE model).

Some of Canada's existing provisions for health-related saving conform to this motivation. Disability insurance, for example, is available in either EET or TEE form. As noted already, to the extent that RSPs are used for medical expenses, they fit the pattern as well. Other provisions, however, do not. Some vehicles, such as employer-paid health and dental insurance (and their equivalents for the self-employed), attract no tax on either contributions or distributions, and others, such as life insurance, are taxed only above certain thresholds or in part — although recent changes to the personal income tax have tended to reduce the importance of these exemptions.[42]

---

[42]In passing, it bears noting that the treatment of social insurance premiums by the tax system reflects incoherent thinking about double taxation. Despite the fact that EI and CPP/QPP benefits are taxable, with the former also subject to a special clawback, the employee-paid part of the premiums is not deductible from income, but instead earns only a credit at the lowest tax rate.

William B.P. Robson

The financing of current contractual health-related saving does not raise any special concerns. Regulation and actuarial oversight of private defined-benefit plans appears to be sufficient to ensure that they are properly funded, and defined-contribution plans by definition promise no more than they can pay. Because the safety-net component of Canadian health care is so broad and deep, employer-funded health plans are relatively modest, and the continuity of coverage of retirees in the event of an employer's bankruptcy, which has been a concern in the United States, is less so in Canada. The prospect of a larger elderly population, however, and the inability of employers to tax-effectively fund post-retirement benefits, may result in pressure for more accommodative policies in the future.

Privately purchased health goods and services are quite important in Canada — at about 2.7 per cent of GDP, or $850 per person (CIHI, 2000, pp. 18-19) the private share of health spending is relatively high in international terms. It grew steadily during the 1990s while public spending was more constrained, and on recent evidence, it will continue to rise.[43] If this is so, and this increase is reflected in greater demands for saving vehicles related to health, at least two issues merit note.

First, the RSP system already provides the infrastructure for a substantial expansion of the "indemnity" part of the health system's third pillar. Such an expansion would be easier to achieve if long-delayed increases on the amounts of income for which tax sheltering is available finally came about. Liberalization of the provisions regarding withdrawals could also help convert RSPs into a third-pillar type of medical saving account.[44]

Finally, even without measures to facilitate its use for medical purposes, the rising stock of pension savings is a harbinger of an older population that is likely to be willing and able to pay for medical services that, while covered by the public safety net, are not available in a timely way or in a customer-

---

[43]There is some debate about the relationship between public and private spending on health care as revealed by international experience (Tuohy *et al.*, 2001). Canada's unique practice of prohibiting private insurance for, and effectively purchase of, services covered by the safety net, however, means that offsetting movements evident in other countries may be misleading as signals of what Canadians can expect, since publicly and privately purchased health services are less ready substitutes.

[44]As is noted below, however, EET vehicles are not suitable for many modest-income Canadians.

friendly setting. If the legislative response is to seek to erect tighter barriers to private provision, some likely short-term consequences will be more cross-border shopping, recourse to the courts by patients and providers chafing under the restrictions, and under-the-table purchases. Longer term, some have questioned whether support for the current framework of medical care in Canada will erode among such a population (Globerman and Vining, 1996, pp. 38 and 66).

Design Issues, Interactions and Challenges

Looking at pensions and health care together highlights some key design issues, especially interactions between the pillars of the two systems that may need attention as larger numbers of older Canadians draw more heavily on them, or contemplate actively the time when they will do so.

Motivation and Design

Starting with first-pillar systems, it is clear that the balance between generosity and tolerable marginal effective tax rates is easier to strike when policymakers are monitoring the combined effects of different safety-net programs. Like the "welfare wall" that eliminates immediate financial rewards from leaving social assistance for paid employment, overlapping income-tested transfers in the pension system's first pillar already subject low-income seniors in provinces such as Ontario to effective marginal rates of 100 per cent or even more.

Income supplementation programs for the elderly are reasonably well monitored, and the decision to supply a fairly generous level of support at the cost of imposing punitive tax rates on those with private incomes below it, while open to question, can reasonably be regarded as a choice Canadians have deliberately made.[45] Absent policy changes, the projected evolution of

---

[45]It is important not to overstate the coherence of policy in this area. Effective tax rates of over 100 per cent result from the calculation of the GIS clawback on the basis of grossed-up dividend income, which means that seniors

the first-pillar pension programs offers some comfort in this regard — increases in other incomes are projected to increase the share of relatively lightly clawed-back OAS payments in the total from 77 per cent recently to 83 per cent by 2030 (OSFI, 1999, p. 9), which will make the punitive effective tax rates under GIS less important.

There is, on the other hand, very little monitoring of the health system's impact. For more than 15 years, targeting of the safety-net health services has occurred almost exclusively through control of access to in-kind benefits. But there are areas where means-tested health services and subsidies are producing problems. In some provinces, income-tested drug and long-term care subsidies create marginal effective tax rates that, stacked atop other means-tested programs, impose confiscatory tax rates on the private income of seniors who use them. Ontario's nursing-home fee scale, for example, imposes effective tax rates of 100 per cent on modest-income seniors.[46]

We currently know little about how Canadians respond to the incentives these programs create, and comments about how they may respond in the future are necessarily highly speculative. Intuition and casual empiricism suggest that generous safety-net and income-replacement programs have tended to lower the participation rates of older people from the workforce. Efforts to calculate marginal benefits from staying in the workforce longer suggest that modifications to first- and second-pillar pensions might raise the average age of retirement (Baker *et al.*, 2000). The United States, where Medicaid covers nursing-home expenses only for those with very low financial assets and incomes and insurers have designed annuities to allow seniors to qualify for this coverage,[47] provides hints about what more

---

such as GAINS recipients in Ontario experience marginal effective tax rates well over 100 per cent on dividend income. Lack of concern about this inequity among policymakers might be attributable to their supposition that few GIS recipients have dividend income. In fact, across the country, almost 70,000 do so (Shillington, 1999, p. 7).

[46]Horizontal inequities also arise in situations where, for example, assets in an RRSP would disqualify a senior from receiving a subsidy while a defined-benefit plan of equivalent value would not.

[47]For couples, the annuities transfer income from the spouse requiring care to the one not requiring care; in the case of singles, the mechanism is a "balloon" annuity that pays small monthly amounts and one large final payment at the end (Ann Davis, 2001).

widespread understanding of health- and pension-related clawbacks might produce in Canada. Prudence suggests that policymakers should monitor carefully the impact of further changes to the medical safety net that target it to the less well-off, in order to avoid discouraging the work and saving that the Canadian pension and health systems will both require in the future.

One way of muting the disincentives created by heavily means-tested first pillars, of course, is to oblige those who can provide for themselves to do so through a second-pillar system. The CPP and QPP show that Canadians accept such arrangements in the pensions and disability areas. WCBs and EI are further testimony to the acceptability of contributory schemes that at least look pre-funded, even if the economic reality is somewhat different. Outside these plans, however, Canada has almost nothing by way of a second pillar in its health system.

For the sake of building on existing foundations, it is tempting to suggest expanding one or more of the CPP/QPP, WCB and EI to accommodate the foreseeable increase in health-related demands by an older population in the future. But entitlement to the benefits of these programs and the obligation to fund them are contingent on workforce participation, and the prospect of a relatively scarce workforce is what makes the fiscal implications of an aging population so daunting.

An attractive, if institutionally more challenging, alternative is to think — along Clair Commission lines — of new provincial social insurance programs funded by, say, individual or family premiums. Such programs could provide participants with health coverage up to a threshold close to the current average per-capita amount spent by provincial governments on health services.[48] In the current period of reduced fiscal pressure, creating room for the required premiums by cutting personal income taxes would be straightforward. The extent to which entitlements in such plans would be earmarked for individual or family accounts would presumably vary depending on the proclivities of each provincial government.

---

[48]Nationally, per-capita spending on health services by provincial governments is around $2,000 annually. If entitlement cumulated in such plans, as it does in the CPP and QPP, older participants would, over time, build larger claims, matching in direction, if not in precise magnitude, the tendency for older people to use more health services.

Funding

The question of how much pre-funding makes sense for Canada's first- and second-pillar pension and health systems is another area where gaps in knowledge make definitive judgements impossible. The current margin of rates of return on financial assets over rates of economic growth suggests that higher national saving would be good in general and that pre-funding is appropriate for new entitlement programs in particular.

If this margin persists or widens as aging populations in Canada and abroad lower saving rates and slow economic growth, continued general budget surpluses and accumulation of funds in existing and new programs makes sense. If, on the other hand, an aging population reduces the demand for new capital investment, lowering rates of return and allowing higher current consumption, pre-funding would be less attractive.[49] In view of these uncertainties, total elimination of regular government debt and full funding of all pension and health programs would be inappropriate goals. But prudence and equity considerations — matching costs and benefits more fairly among generations (Sinn, 2000) — make pre-funding the extra costs associated with the baby boomers' old age attractive.

As noted already, some such pre-funding is arguably occurring with regard to OAS/GIS and the health safety net, and is definitely occurring in the CPP/QPP. Setting aside a portion of future budget surpluses in a designated health account could, if the saving in these accounts were not offset in other parts of the budget, extract some of the resources for their future health care from the boomers in advance, reducing the burden that would otherwise fall on their successors.[50] Similarly, ensuring that any new second-pillar health programs were pre-funded would ensure that they did

---

[49]Elmendorf and Sheiner (2000) provide a recent survey of U.S. debate over this issue, as well as some simulations. Their analysis is pertinent to Canada not only because U.S. and Canadian demographic prospects are broadly similar, but because the outcome of these forces in the United States will be critical in determining the environment in Canada.

[50]Robson (2001) suggests that the federal government set up a Seniors Health Account in which to set aside part of its budget surpluses. In that proposal, income from these assets would flow to the provinces to help cover the health-related costs of their aging populations.

not simply become a vehicle for the boomers to vote themselves new benefits at the expense of their descendants and immigrants.

Prospects

Two other foreseeable challenges for public policy in connection with pensions and health in the coming decades have to do with moving the age of eligibility for various transfers and services up from the current 65 benchmark, and managing the incentives surrounding voluntary saving.

Raising the standard age of eligibility is easy to envision, though overlapping programs and jurisdictions would make it complex to implement.[51] As other jurisdictions have done, Canada should prepare for a staged increase in the standard age of full eligibility for first- and second-pillar entitlements — two months per year over a 30-year period, say, or three months per year over a 20-year period, to increase it to age 70.[52] Matching increases would be appropriate in provisions affecting RSPs. Such a coordinated increase would reduce disincentives to work for those approaching or past the age of 65, and should mitigate saving disincentives as well, by postponing the period of life when overlapping clawbacks essentially confiscate wealth.

The second challenge is more multifaceted. Even more so than in the case of raising the eligibility age, there is a prior need for policymakers and Canadians generally to recognize the nature of the problem that looms. In private conversation, this author has encountered dismissals of the seriousness of his and others' calculations of the implicit liability of future health care on the grounds that it is roughly offset by the stock of pension assets — a line of argument that implicitly assumes that those assets will be

---

[51]For the sake of completeness, it is worth noting that a philosophically coherent case for eliminating all reference to age in pension and health programs exists. Age has proved, however, to be such a useful marker of eligibility for all manner of benefits and privileges, that it is hard to imagine doing away with it in the foreseeable future.

[52]As was suggested by the Canadian Institute of Actuaries in the early 1990s (CIA, 1993, pp. 17-19). Calculations using summary weighted dependency ratios to create an intergenerational wealth transfer index suggest less aggressive increases (Brown, 1995; Brown *et al.*, 2001).

effectively confiscated by taxes and means-tested clawbacks of health benefits when they are converted into income. Effective tax rates close to 100 per cent already affect many individuals: it would be a grave mistake to increase their numbers. And if the bulk of services currently covered by the medical safety net continue to be effectively unavailable for private purchase, a key motive for saving — the desire for a reasonable level of consumption of health goods and services in old age — will be undermined by the fact that there will effectively be nothing to buy.

A multifaceted challenge naturally requires a multifaceted response. A good way of avoiding high and thick welfare walls for low- and middle-income Canadians is to seek, as much as possible, to recover health-related benefits through the personal income tax at standard rates. Establishing a TEE alternative to the existing EET saving vehicles would allow modest income earners who are too old to enjoy a long period of tax-free compounding to save in a form that makes sense for them, foregoing tax relief on contributions during their working years when their marginal effective rates are comparatively low for the sake of relief on distributions during retirement when their marginal effective rates may be very high (Kesselman and Poschmann, 2001).

As for the debate over private purchase of health care, suffice it to note again that patients can buy services the same as the public system covers, and providers can sell their services to both public and private purchasers, in many other countries where governments fund a larger share of total health-related expenditures than they do in Canada. The extraordinary alarm these prospects raise among many Canadians inhibits intelligent debate. There are legitimate concerns about crowding out and cross-subsidization under these circumstances. Many Canadians are going to want to buy services they see as medically necessary, however, and at the time of writing, the coincidence of chronic labour unrest in the publicly funded system and sizeable funding increases makes it hard to see them accepting existing prohibitions indefinitely. Under those circumstances, learning how other countries control these problems makes more sense than simply insisting that no modifications to the current arrangement are possible.[53] For potential purchasers of medical services, moreover, an early start to refining the

---

[53]The often-heard argument that any "two-tier" system will inevitably lead to wholesale privatization ignores the obvious fact that dual systems exist everywhere, and that the dominant trend of the past half-century has been for the share of health spending that is financed by governments to increase.

border between services that are publicly and privately purchased would be helpful for the simple reason that it will help them save wisely for their future needs (Globerman and Vining, 1996, p. 57).

Concluding Thoughts

Rather than attempting a detailed summary of this joint exploration of Canadian pension and health policy in a three-pillars framework, it seems best to close with a straightforward, perhaps obvious, observation. A good mixture of support and incentives in each of the pension and health systems is likely to produce beneficial effects in the other. Lifestyle maintenance programs that boost saving and encourage workforce participation will add to the resources that pay benefits and buy services. And a tax system that avoids penalizing saving for retirement or future health needs is likely to increase the proportion of the population that is willing and able to provide for themselves.

Canada's pension and health systems are currently a source of pride to policymakers and citizens alike. The pension system has over the past several decades benefited from ample resources and also from a precise matching of its various elements to its different objectives. The health system has benefited from even more ample resources and, as a result, has not undergone close scrutiny about the different purposes such social programs serve. Refocusing the debate over health care in a framework that distinguishes, as pension policy already does, three key objectives — a safety net, mandatory basic social insurance, and a framework for voluntary saving — offers two benefits. It promises a more fruitful resolution of current conundrums than does the confused and artificial debate over public versus private financing and delivery. And it can help ensure that the future evolution of Canada's pension and health systems work in complementary fashion to deliver effective benefits in a sustainable way.

References

Alberta (2001), *Budget 2001* (Edmonton: Government Printers).

Association of Canadian Pension Management (ACPM) (2000), *A Retirement Income Strategy for Canada* (Toronto: ACPM).

Baker, M., J. Gruber and K. Milligan (2000), "Income Security Programs and Retirement in Canada", unpublished NBER paper (Cambridge, MA: National Bureau of Economic Research).

Begin, M. (1984), *Medicare: Canada's Right to Health* (Montreal: Optimum Publishing International).

Bethencourt, C. and V. Galasso (2000), "On the Political Complementarity between Health Care and Social Security", unpublished paper (Universidad Carlos III de Madrid).

Blomqvist, A. (1994), "Conclusion: Themes in Health Care Reform", in A. Blomqvist and D. Brown (eds.), *Limits to Care: Reforming Canada's Health System in an Age of Restraint* (Toronto: C.D. Howe Institute).

_____ (2001), "Health Care Reform in Canada: Lessons from the U.K., Japan and Holland", mimeograph.

Boadway, R. and M. Keen (2000), "Redistribution", in A.B. Atkinson and F. Bourguignon (eds.), *Handbook of Income Distribution*, Vol. 1 (Amsterdam: North-Holland).

Bogyo, T.J. (1995), "Workers' Compensation: Updating the Historic Compromise", in J. Richards and W. Watson (eds.), *Chronic Stress: Workers' Compensation in the 1990s* (Toronto: C.D. Howe Institute).

British Columbia (2000), *Public Accounts 1999/2000* (Victoria: Government Printers).

Brown, R.L. (1995), "Paygo Funding Stability and Intergenerational Equity", *Transactions of Society of Actuaries* 47.

Brown, R.L., R. Damm and I. Sharara (2001), "A Macro-economic Indicator of Age at Retirement", *North American Actuarial Journal* 5(2).

Burbidge, J. (1996), "Public Pensions in Canada", in J. Richards and W. Watson (eds.), *When We're 65: Reforming Canada's Retirement Income System* (Toronto: C.D. Howe Institute).

Canadian Institute for Health Information (CIHI) (2000), *National Health Expenditure Trends, 1975-2000* (Ottawa: CIHI).

Canadian Institute of Actuaries (CIA) (1993), *Canadian Retirement Income Social Security Programs* (Ottawa: CIA).

_____ (1996), *Report of the Task Force on the Future of Canada/Quebec Pension Plans* (Ottawa).

Davies, J. (1998), *Marginal Tax Rates in Canada: High and Getting Higher* (Toronto: C.D. Howe Institute).

Davis, Andrea (2001), "Seventh Annual Special Report on Custodial Services", *Benefits Canada* (April).

Davis, Ann (2001), "Insurers Find Way to Help the Elderly Get Medicaid to Pay for Nursing Homes", *Wall Street Journal*, 6 June.

Donaldson, C., G. Currie and C. Mitton (2001a), *How the Rest of the World Reforms Health Care: Integrating Canada's Dis-Integrated Health-Care System* (Toronto: C.D. Howe Institute).

_____ (2001b), *Managing Medicare: The Prerequisite to Spending or Reform* (Toronto: C.D. Howe Institute).

Elmendorf, D. and L. Sheiner (2000), "Should America Save for its Old Age? Fiscal Policy, Population Aging, and National Saving", *Journal of Economic Perspectives* 14(3), 57-74.

Evans, R.G., J. Lomas, M.L. Barer, R.J. Labelle, C. Fooks, G.L. Stoddart, G.M. Anderson, D. Feeny, A. Gafni, G.W. Torrance and W.G. Tholl (1989), "Controlling Health Expenditures — The Canadian Reality", *New England Journal of Medicine* 320(9), 571-577.

Evans, R.G., M. Barer, G. Stoddart and V. Bhatia (1994), "It's Not the Money, It's the Principle: Why User Charges for Some Services and Not Others?" Discussion Paper (Toronto: The Premier's Council on Health, Well-Being and Social Justice).

Fried, J. and R. Wirick (1999), *Assessing the Foreign Property Rule: Regulation without Reason* (Toronto: C.D. Howe Institute).

Globerman, S. and A. Vining (1996), *Cure or Disease? Private Health Insurance in Canada* (Toronto: Centre for Public Management, University of Toronto).

Gratzer, D. (1999), *Code Blue: Reviving Canada's Health Care System* (Toronto: ECW Press).

Hamilton, M. (2001), "The Financial Circumstances of Elderly Canadians and the Implications for the Design of Canada's Retirement Income System", in this volume.

Hurley, J.(2000), "Medical Savings Accounts: Approach with Caution", *Journal of Health Services Research and Policy* 5(3), 130–132.

Jérôme-Forget, M. and C. Forget (1998), *Who Is the Master? A Blueprint for Canadian Health Care Reform* (Montreal: Institute for Research on Public Policy).

Kesselman, J. and F. Poschmann (2001), *A New Option for Retirement Savings: Tax-Prepaid Savings Plans* (Toronto: C.D. Howe Institute).

Mintz, J. (2001), "Taxing Future Consumption", in this volume.

Morissette, R. and M. Drolet (2001), "Pension Coverage and Retirement Savings of Young and Prime-aged Workers in Canada, 1986–1997", *Canadian Journal of Economics* 34(1), 100–119.

Office of the Superintendent of Financial Institutions (OSFI) (1998), *Canada Pension Plan: Seventeenth Actuarial Report, as at 31 December 1997* (Ottawa: Supply and Services Canada).

_____ (1999), *Old Age Security Program: Fourth Actuarial Report, as at 31 December 1997* (Ottawa: Supply and Services Canada).

Organisation for Economic Co-operation and Development (OECD) (1998), *Maintaining Prosperity in an Ageing Society* (Paris: OECD).

Osberg, L. (2001), "Poverty among Senior Citizens: A Canadian Success Story", in this volume.

Pesando, J. (1997), *From Tax Grab to Retirement Saving: Privatizing the CPP Premium Hike* (Toronto: C.D. Howe Institute).

_____ (2001), "The Canada Pension Plan: Looking Back at the Recent Reforms", in this volume.

Quebec, Commission of Study on Health and Social Services (2000), *Emerging Solutions: Report and Recommendations* (Quebec: The Commission).

Ramsay, C. (1998), *Medical Savings Accounts: Universal, Accessible, Portable, Comprehensive Health Care for Canadians* (Vancouver: Fraser Institute).

Reuber, G. (1980), *Canada's Political Economy: Current Issues* (Toronto: McGraw-Hill Ryerson).

Richards, J. (1997), *Retooling the Welfare State: What's Right, What's Wrong, What's to Be Done* (Toronto: C.D. Howe Institute).

Robson, W. (1996), *Putting Some Gold in the Golden Years: Fixing the Canada Pension Plan* (Toronto: C.D. Howe Institute).

_____ (1997), *The Future of Pension Policy: Individual Responsibility and State Support* (Toronto: British-North American Committee).

_____ (1998), "Making Ponzi a Prudent Man: Establishing the CPP Investment Board", *Backgrounder* (Toronto: C.D. Howe Institute).

_____ (2000), "Precarious Pyramid: The Economics and Politics of the Canada Pension Plan", in P. Boothe (ed.), *A Separate Pension Plan for Alberta: Analysis and Discussion* (Edmonton: University of Alberta Press).

_____ (2001), *Will the Baby Boomers Bust the Health Budget? Demographic Change and Health Care Financing Reform* (Toronto: C.D. Howe Institute).

Robson, W. and W. Scarth (1997), *Out Front on Debt Reduction: Programs and Payoffs* (Toronto: C.D. Howe Institute).

Rosen, H., P. Boothe, B. Dahlby and R. Smith (1999), *Public Finance in Canada*, 1st Canadian ed. (Toronto: McGraw-Hill Ryerson).

Schellhorn, M. (2001), "A Comparison of Alternative Methods to Model Endogeneity in Count Model: An Application to the Demand for Health Care and Health Insurance Choice", paper presented at the 2001 meetings of the Canadian Economics Association, McGill University, Montreal (May), <www.econ.queensu.ca/cea2001/papers/schellhorn-paper.pdf>.

Shillington, R. (1999), *The Dark Side of Targeting: Retirement Saving for Low-Income Canadians* (Toronto: C.D. Howe Institute).

_____ (2001), "The Great RRSP Rip-Off", *This* (March/April).

Sinn, H.-W. (2000), "Why a Funded Pension System is Useful and Why It is Not Useful", *International Tax and Public Finance* 7, 389–408.

Slater, D.W. (1997a), *The Pension Squeeze: The Impact of the March 1996 Federal Budget* (Toronto: C.D. Howe Institute).

_____ (1997b), *Prudence and Performance: Managing the Proposed CPP Investment Board* (Toronto: C.D. Howe Institute).

_____ (1998), *Fixing the Seniors Benefit* (Toronto: C.D. Howe Institute).

Slater, D.W. and W.B.P. Robson (1999), *Building a Stronger Pillar: The Changing Shape of the Canada Pension Plan* (Toronto: C.D. Howe Institute).

Statistics Canada (2001), *The Assets and Debts of Canadians: An Overview of the Results of the Survey of Financial Security*, Catalogue No. 13-595-XIE (Ottawa: Supply and Services Canada).

Stritch, A. (1995), "Homage to Catatonia: Bipartite Governance and Workers' Compensation in Ontario", in J. Richards and W. Watson (eds.), *Chronic Stress: Workers' Compensation in the 1990s* (Toronto: C.D. Howe Institute).

Taylor, M. (1978), *Health Insurance and Canadian Public Policy: The Seven Decisions that Created the Canadian Health Insurance System* (Montreal: McGill-Queen's University Press).

Thomason, T. (1995), "The Escalating Costs of Workers' Compensation in Canada: Causes and Cures", in J. Richards and W. Watson (eds.), *Chronic Stress: Workers' Compensation in the 1990s* (Toronto: C.D. Howe Institute).

Tuohy, C., C. Flood and M. Stabile (2001), "How Does Private Finance Affect Public Health Care Systems? Marshalling the Evidence from OECD Nations", Working Paper No. 14 (Toronto: University of Toronto).

Vaillancourt, F. (1995), "The Financing and Pricing of WCBs in Canada: Existing Arrangements, Possible Changes", in J. Richards and W. Watson (eds.), *Chronic Stress: Workers' Compensation in the 1990s* (Toronto: C.D. Howe Institute).

_____ (2000), "The Québec Pension Plan: Institutional Arrangements and Lessons for Alberta", in P. Boothe (ed.), *A Separate Pension Plan for Alberta: Analysis and Discussion* (Edmonton: University of Alberta Press).

World Bank (1994), *Averting the Old Age Crisis: Policies to Protect the Old and Promote Growth* (New York: Oxford University Press).

The Financial Circumstances of Elderly Canadians and the Implications for the Design of Canada's Retirement Income System

Malcolm Hamilton

Introduction

Canadians have recently been presented with two seemingly conflicting views of the financial circumstances of elderly Canadians. The conflict is captured in the press release that accompanied Statistics Canada's publication of *The Assets and Debts of Canadians: An Overview of the Results of the Survey of Financial Security.*

> Families in which a senior was the major income recipient had the highest net worth of any type of family unit, $202,000. The fact that many seniors live in their own mortgage-free home accounts for this to a large extent. However, this net worth should not be interpreted to mean that all senior families have relatively high net worth, nor relatively high incomes. The median after-tax income of senior families was $32,000, almost $14,000 lower than for younger families.

One can sympathize with Statistics Canada's dilemma. Seniors have high net worths and low incomes, therefore they must be both rich and poor at the same time. Alternatively, and more to the point, comparing the incomes and net worths of seniors to the incomes and net worths of younger Canadians is a pointless exercise which says next to nothing about whether seniors are rich or poor. The fact that seniors have lower incomes than younger Canadians does not mean that they are poorer than younger Canadians. The fact that seniors have higher net worths than younger Canadians[1] does not mean that they are richer than younger Canadians. It is natural for seniors to have lower incomes and higher net worths than younger Canadians because seniors are at a different stage in their lives.

Few things are more studied than the incomes of Canada's senior citizens. Baldwin and Laliberté (1999), Gower (1998) and Myles (2000) are recent examples. Most studies build upon the work of Statistics Canada which follows a long but unhelpful intellectual tradition of equating economic well-being with annual income. Income is studied by source, by province of residence, by family type, by gender, by age and by year of receipt. It is studied before- and after-tax, with and without transfers. We compare the incomes of young and old, rich and poor, male and female. We compare the incomes of those who live alone to those who live as families.

From this work, sweeping conclusions are drawn about the economic well-being of senior citizens. We celebrate the fact that the incomes of elderly Canadians have grown faster than inflation and faster than the incomes of younger Canadians. We celebrate shrinking Gini coefficients (among senior citizens) as evidence that our world is becoming more fair. We study the incidence, intensity and depth of poverty and/or low income as if these measures said something important about the lives of elderly Canadians. Yet most of these studies leave two important questions unanswered.

- Is income (before- or after-tax) a good measure of the economic well-being of senior citizens?
- What relationship should we expect between the incomes of senior households and the incomes of younger households with similar standards of living?

---

[1]The differences will be even more pronounced when pension wealth is added to Statistics Canada's analysis, as has been promised for future releases.

This paper looks at these questions and concludes first, that income is not a good measure of economic well-being, particularly for seniors, and second, that senior citizens can have significantly lower incomes than younger Canadians and yet enjoy a similar standard of living. As such, it is not clear that the incomes of senior citizens are in any way deficient, nor is it clear that recent increases in their relative incomes are desirable.

The Limitations of Income as a Measure of Economic Well-Being

The limitations of income as a measure of economic well-being are best illustrated by example. Take the simplest of all worlds; a world without inflation or interest rates or income taxes; a world where equal numbers of people are born each year; where everyone works for 30 years and earns $100 per annum; where people save $50 per annum during their working lives and accumulate $1,500 of capital (30 x $50) by the time they retire; a world where people draw $50 of capital each year during a 30 year retirement and where everyone spends $50 per annum. Let's call this world Egalitaria and its citizens Egalitarians.

In Egalitaria:

• there are equal numbers of working and retired citizens,
• all working people have $100 of income and $50 of expenditures, and
• all retired people have no income and $50 of expenditures.

Statistics Canada, unleashed on such a world, would conclude that retired Egalitarians are impoverished or, more accurately, the victims of low income. The perfect equality of income within the working and retired populations would be lauded, but the ugly gap between the income of working Egalitarians and the income of retired Egalitarians would be deplored. Yet there would be no difference between the standard of living of working Egalitarians and the standard of living of retired Egalitarians because, in Egalitaria, income says nothing about economic well-being. Working Egalitarians spend only 50 per cent of their income because they need to save for retirement. Retired Egalitarians support themselves comfortably without any income because they have large amounts of capital on which to draw.

Now, suppose Egalitaria adopted a more modern social security model for its retirement system. Each working Egalitarian would pay $50 of social security tax instead of saving $50, while each retired Egalitarian would collect $50 of social security benefits which, following the normal convention, would be counted as income. Egalitaria would still have an income equality problem before-tax (working Egalitarians have $100 of income while retired Egalitarians have only $50) but not after-tax (both working and retired Egalitarians have $50 of income, after-tax).

Alternatively, Egalitaria might build its retirement system on RRSPs. Each year, working Egalitarians would contribute $50 to an RRSP and retired Egalitarians would draw $50 from an RRSP. Withdrawals would be considered income, just as RRSP withdrawals in Canada are considered income. Working Egalitarians would then have $100 of income, before- or after-tax. Retired Egalitarians would have only $50.

Finally, Egalitaria could use occupational pension plans as the vehicle for organizing its retirement income system. Each working Egalitarian would be paid $75 per annum and would contribute $25 to an occupational pension plan. Employers would match these $25 contributions, bringing each employee's total compensation to $100. In retirement, each Egalitarian would receive $50 per annum of pension income. In such a system, working Egalitarians would have $75 of income,[2] before- or after-tax, while retired Egalitarians have only $50.

The four alternatives are summarized in Table 1.

From an Egalitarian's perspective, these four systems are indistinguishable. Each allows an Egalitarian to consume $50 per annum throughout his or her working and retired lives. Yet while there is no difference in the economic well-being of working and retired Egalitarians, there are significant differences in their incomes.

To make Egalitaria more recognizable, assume now that savings earn a 4 per cent *real* rate of return. This does not affect the social security model (since there are no savings to invest), but it significantly lowers (from $50 to $24[3]) the savings required to support the other models while simultaneously increasing the level of consumption for working and retired

---

[2] Employer contributions to pension plans are not usually included in personal income.

[3] $24 is the amount of saving required to balance pre- and post-retirement consumption at $76.

Malcolm Hamilton

Table 1: Impact of Retirement System Design on Income (Real Interest Rate = 0%)

Type of Retirement System	Annual Per Capita Consumption for Working and Retired Egalitarians	Income of Working Egalitarians		Income of Retired Egalitarians	
		Before-tax	After-tax	Before-tax	After-tax
Normal savings	$50	$100	$100	$0	$0
Social security	$50	$100	$50	$50	$50
RRSPs	$50	$100	$100	$50	$50
Occupational pensions	$50	$75	$75	$50	$50

Egalitarians (to $76 per annum). The four alternatives are summarized in Table 2.

The analysis of the "normal savings" system is particularly complicated. Pre-retirement, the incomes of working Egalitarians include the income earned on savings. This income does not increase consumption, as it is simply reinvested. In a system based on RRSPs or occupational pensions, the

Table 2: Impact of Retirement System Design on Income (Real Interest Rate = 4%)

Type of Retirement System	Annual Per Capita Consumption for Working and Retired Egalitarians	Income of Working Egalitarians		Income of Retired Egalitarians	
		Before-tax	After-tax	Before-tax	After-tax
Normal savings					
0% inflation	$76	$122	$122	$32	$32
2% inflation	$76	$132	$132	$47	$47
4% inflation	$76	$143	$143	$63	$63
Social security	$50	$100	$50	$50	$50
RRSPs	$76	$100	$100	$76	$76
Occupational pensions	$76	$88	$88	$76	$76

same investment income is earned and reinvested, but it does not usually appear in studies of personal income. In the absence of income tax, the inflation rate does not affect a worker's savings rate or the level of real consumption (since we are assuming a rate of return 4 per cent higher than the underlying inflation rate, whatever it may be), but incomes will be affected, both pre- and post-retirement, by the level of inflation due to the way income is measured (interest includes the inflation element of nominal interest rates).

All of these examples ignore income taxes, so normal savings plans perform just as well as tax-sheltered plans. The model simply demonstrates that if one defines income in the usual way, the manner in which a retirement system is organized can produce income inequalities where there are, in fact, no differences in economic well-being. Conversely, if the objective is to equalize economic well-being, unequal incomes are an unavoidable consequence of the way income is defined and measured.

The Canadian retirement system is much more complicated than any of the Egalitarian systems. We have progressive income taxes which, by their design, favour the elderly. We have a large number of government programs that provide income and services to elderly Canadians. We have RRSPs and pension plans. We have people who save outside tax shelters, either directly or through inheritance or by accessing home equity in their retirement years. As will be seen later, our senior citizens have income from many sources, suggesting that each of the aforementioned vehicles plays an important role in Canada. To use income as a measure of economic well-being in such an environment is, at best, hazardous.

For example, Baldwin and Laliberté (1999), in comparing the incomes of senior households and prime age households, produced the following numbers (Table 3).

Table 3: Relative Income of Senior and Prime Age Households

	Total Income (1996 $)		Change (%)
	1989	1996	
Senior households	$32,667	$31,834	-3
Prime age households	$55,678	$52,214	-6

Malcolm Hamilton

Baldwin and Laliberté conclude:

This general pattern of long-term increase (in the income of senior households) peaked around 1989 as the average senior household income decreased to $31,834 in 1996, a decline of about 3 per cent from 1989. However, senior households still improved their relative situation as households headed by Canadians between the age of 25 and 54 saw their income go down even further (6 per cent) during the same period. All told, in 1996 the average senior household stood at 61 per cent of the 25-54 group. (1999, p. 10)

As an arithmetical observation, the statement is accurate. But the inference that readers are invited to draw from it — that seniors were less well off in 1996 than they were in 1989 — is wrong. The decline in the income of senior households between 1989 and 1996 was largely fuelled by a reduction in investment income (from $7,014 in 1989 to $4,113 in 1996) caused by a reduction in interest rates (from 10 per cent in 1988–89 to 6 per cent in 1995–96) and other factors. The reduction in interest rates was accompanied by a reduction in inflation (from 5.2 per cent in 1989 to 2.2 per cent in 1996). A senior citizen in the 40 per cent tax bracket[4] is better off earning 6 per cent in a year when prices rise by 2.2 per cent than 10 per cent in a year when prices rise by 5.2 per cent, as demonstrated below (Table 4) for an individual with $70,000 invested at the start of the year.

Table 4: Adjusting Investment Income for Taxes and Inflation

	1989	1996
1. Opening balance (1996 dollars)	$70,000	$70,000
2. Interest rate	10%	6%
3. Interest income, before-tax ([1] x [2])	$7,000	$4,200
4. Tax on interest income (40% of [3])	$2,800	$1,680
5. Closing balance, after-tax ([1] + [3] - [4])	$74,200	$72,520
6. Inflation rate	5.2%	2.2%
7. Purchasing power of closing balance ([5] ÷ {1 + [6]})	$70,532	$70,959
8. Real income, after-tax ([7] - [1])	$532	$959

[4] Investment income is skewed to higher income households.

Thus, what appears at first to be a sizeable reduction in investment income ($7,000 − $4,200 = $2,800) could more accurately be described as a modest increase in real, after-tax income ($959 − $532 = $427).

Baldwin and Laliberté's conclusion that senior households experienced a 3 per cent reduction in family income between 1989 and 1996 is correct but misleading, because unadjusted investment income says nothing about the economic advantages derived from investing capital in a world with taxes and inflation. Adjusted for this one distortion, the income of senior households actually grew by 6 per cent between 1989 and 1996, while the incomes of prime age households declined by 6 per cent. Using after-tax incomes does not solve the measurement problem, as there is no adjustment for the erosion in the purchasing power of accumulated capital.

As a measure of economic well-being, income may be good enough to permit conclusions to be drawn from comparisons of the after-tax incomes of similar households in a given year. But comparing the incomes of senior households to the incomes of prime age households and comparing the incomes of senior households in one year to the incomes of senior households in another year with materially different interest and inflation rates should only be done with the greatest of care.

Looking Beyond Income

More generally, there are five reasons why the unadjusted incomes of senior households should not be compared to the unadjusted incomes of younger households.

• Younger households often support children.

• Younger households devote a significant portion of their income to acquiring capital that senior households already possess (a home, one or more cars, furniture, appliances, etc.) and to the related financing costs (mortgages, car loans, etc.).

• Younger households have employment-related expenses (union dues, the cost of travelling to and from work, life and disability insurance, etc.).

Malcolm Hamilton

- Younger households need to save for retirement and/or contribute to pension plans; senior households have already saved for retirement and some of their dis-saving (i.e., drawing down unsheltered capital accumulations) is not included in their incomes.

- Younger households have significantly higher taxes. They contribute to the Canada Pension Plan (CPP) and Employment Insurance (EI) and are subject to higher effective income tax rates.[5]

Of course, there are other differences between senior and prime age households. Were it not for medicare, provincial drug plans and employer-supported post-retirement medical insurance, senior households would have much larger medical expenses than prime age households. Even with these programs, seniors appear to spend more on health care than younger Canadians, but the differences are relatively small (a few hundred dollars per household per year). At advanced ages, seniors may need to pay for services that younger Canadians can provide for themselves. On the other hand, seniors have more time to do things for themselves than do younger households where one or both spouses work. Finally, seniors are the beneficiaries of many programs designed to support the elderly or those with low incomes (public housing and nursing homes with rents geared to income; seniors' discounts for services like banking and public transit).

The traditional analysis of family or household income adjusts for relatively few of these differences. Statistics Canada has, until recently, emphasized statistics that adjusted only for the number of people in the household. In comparing elderly couples to younger families, Statistics Canada used scaling factors to take into account expenditures on children, but did not adjust for taxes, capital accumulations, employment expenses or retirement savings. These studies often concluded that seniors had low incomes (which is true but not surprising) and, by inference, that seniors were financially more vulnerable than younger Canadians (which may or may not be true, but which cannot be determined from straightforward comparisons of income).

---

[5]Senior households benefit from special age and pension credits and from a progressive tax system that burdens those who have (and need) high incomes much more heavily than those who do not have (or need) high incomes.

More recently, Statistics Canada has placed greater emphasis on after-tax income. However, the tax adjustments are incomplete, ignoring CPP and EI contributions, both of which fall predominantly on younger Canadians.

To perform a proper analysis of economic well-being requires more information than would usually be available in a study of income. This is particularly true if the objective is to meaningfully compare groups that are fundamentally different. The remainder of this paper uses the *1997 Survey of Consumer Spending* to construct financial profiles of senior and prime age households, and then to compare the two. Specifically, the following items were extracted from the survey for each household:

- income by source
  → employment earnings,
  → investment income,
  → RRSP withdrawals,
  → transfers (CPP/QPP, OAS, EI, GIS, etc.),
  → pensions and other;

- taxes (income tax, CPP/QPP and EI contributions);

- mortgage payments (interest and principal);

- savings defined broadly to include RRSP contributions, non-mortgage debt repayments, interest on non-mortgage debt, pension contributions (other than CPP/QPP), additions to non-sheltered savings, insurance premiums, etc.;

- gifts (charitable donations, net gifts to or from family members, etc.);

- union dues, professional dues and day-care costs; and

- descriptive information (household type, age of reference person and spouse; number of person weeks as a member of the household, weeks worked).

These are areas where the behaviour of seniors and the behaviour of prime age households are markedly different. Items have been grouped under a few broad headings to simplify the analysis. For example, "savings" includes interest paid on debt,[6] insurance premiums and the reinvestment of investment income on non-sheltered assets; it excludes (because the survey excludes) employer contributions to pension plans and the reinvestment of investment income from tax-sheltered assets. Taxes include income taxes and employee contributions to the CPP and EI, while excluding employer contributions to CPP and EI (which do not directly consume employee income) and the goods and services tax (GST), sales and property taxes (which consume the incomes of prime age households and senior households alike, and hence do not contribute significantly to differences between the two).

To estimate the amount spent on children,[7] a conventional equivalence factor was used. Specifically, I assumed that if 1.0 represents the cost of providing a particular standard of living to an adult living alone, the marginal cost of providing a similar standard of living to an additional adult in the same household is 0.4 and the marginal cost of providing a similar standard of living to each child in the household is 0.3. While there are many other equivalence scales in use, most are quite similar and would lead to similar conclusions.

To simplify the comparisons, households with the following features were excluded:

- households with no income;

- households submitting information for less than a full year;

- households other than
  - unattached adults living alone,
  - couples, with or without children, and
  - unattached adults with children;

---

[6]If this were a study of savings behaviour, the inflation element of interest payments should be considered savings while the real element would be considered an expenditure. Since the purpose of this paper is simply to compare the ways in which seniors and prime age households use income, the important thing is that prime age households pay significant amounts of interest on debts incurred to acquire assets that senior households own outright. Whether the interest payments are characterized as savings or expenditures makes no difference to the analysis.

[7]More properly, the marginal cost to the adults in the household of supporting children.

- one person households with fewer than 52 person weeks;[8] and

- two or more person households with fewer than 104 person weeks.

Profiles from the 1997 Survey of Consumer Spending

Sample Sizes

Table 5 summarizes the data used in the principal comparisons.

Table 5: Summary of Data Extracted from the 1997 Survey of Consumer Spending

	No. of Records	No. of Represented Households[a]	Average Gross Income	Average After-tax Income
Senior couples, reference spouse over 65	1,264	836,000	$39,100	$32,700
Senior couples, both spouses over 65	987	642,000	$38,500	$32,500
Fully retired[b] senior couples, both over 65	849	553,000	$35,600	$30,600
Prime age[c] couples; with children	4,309	2,608,000	$70,500	$51,900
Prime age[c] couples; without children	952	594,000	$66,100	$47,400
Fully retired[b] unattached seniors	1,396	883,000	$19,200	$16,900
Prime age[c] unattached adults				
· With children	907	542,000	$31,600	$26,100
· Without children	1,178	799,000	$35,200	$25,600

Notes: All averages are calculated using the population weights.
[a] The total weight for the selected records.
[b] No income from employment.
[c] Reference spouse between the ages of 30 and 49, inclusive.

---

[8]A household formed during the year in question might have less than 52 weeks of survey participation in its current configuration; households of this kind were excluded.

A 65 year old adult was not considered "senior" because he or she would have been under 65 at the start of 1997 and would not have qualified for government benefits for the entire year.

While "prime age" usually refers to those between the ages of 25 and 55, in this instance the term applies to households where the reference spouse is between 30 and 49, inclusive.

By ignoring young households (under age 30), households transitioning into retirement (reference spouses between the ages of 50 and 65) and unusual households (seniors with employment income; seniors supporting children; families with dependent parents or unrelated adults in the home) the comparisons focus on the differences between typical prime age families and typical retired seniors.

For each group, Table 5 gives the sample size, the number of represented households, the average gross income and the average after-tax income. The averages in this and other tables are weighted averages, calculated by applying the population weight to each of the records in the category and rounding the result to the nearest $100. By excluding senior households with one spouse under 65 and senior households with employment income, we obtain a truer picture of the circumstances of the fully retired majority. As Baldwin and Laliberté (1999) point out, working seniors have above average incomes (even ignoring their employment earnings) and the inclusion of this relatively small unrepresentative group increases the average incomes of senior citizens by 5 per cent to 10 per cent.

Sources of Income

Tables 6 and 7 examine the sources of income for senior households (Table 6) and prime age households (Table 7). Transfers account for 54 per cent of the income of fully retired senior couples and 60 per cent of the income of fully retired unattached seniors. For prime age couples and prime age unattached adults, employment earnings account for 92 per cent and 83 per cent of gross income, respectively, while transfers account for only 4 per cent and 11 per cent, respectively.

As can be seen from Table 6, senior households draw income from many sources. RRSP withdrawals are not a significant source of income for this generation of retired Canadians. Senior households have significant amounts of investment income (four times as much as prime age households). Since interest rates were relatively low in the years leading up to 1997, at least as

Table 6: Sources of Income for Fully Retired Senior Households

Type of Income	Couples Spouse No. 1	Couples Spouse No. 2	Couples Total	Unattached
Employment	$0	$0	$0	$0
Pension and other	$6,800	$3,200	$10,000	$4,500
RRSP*	N/A	N/A	$1,400	$600
Investment	$2,900	$1,800	$4,700	$2,700
Transfers	$10,900	$8,500	$19,400	$11,500
Total			**$35,600**	**$19,200**

Note: *The 1997 Survey of Consumer Spending did not identify RRSP withdrawals by spouse, hence RRSP income is shown only for the household as a whole.

Table 7: Sources of Income for Prime Age Households

Type of Income	Couples, With or Without Children Spouse No. 1	Couples, With or Without Children Spouse No. 2	Couples, With or Without Children Total[b]	Single Adults With or Without Children
Employment	$33,000	$29,300	$64,300	$27,900
Pension and other	$500	$400	$900	$1,500
RRSP[a]	N/A	N/A	$400	$300
Investment	$700	$400	$1,200	$500
Transfers	$1,600	$1,300	$3,000	$3,600
Total			**$69,700**	**$33,700**

Notes: [a]The 1997 Survey of Consumer Spending did not identify RRSP withdrawals by spouse, hence RRSP income is shown only for the household as a whole.
[b]Total includes any income earned by children.

Malcolm Hamilton

compared to interest rates in the 1980s and early 1990s, the average senior household must have a significant amount of unsheltered capital on which to encroach, probably more than three times their annual expenditures. As will be seen later, there is little to suggest that seniors encroach on capital.[9] Many continue to save.

Income Comparisons

Table 8 compares the incomes of senior households to the incomes of prime age households.
Incomes are measured in four different ways:

- unadjusted gross income;
- adjusted gross income (income was adjusted to the equivalent for a couple without children using the equivalency scale described earlier);
- unadjusted after-tax income where after-tax income is gross income less personal income tax and (unlike Statistics Canada's calculation of after-tax income) CPP/QPP and EI contributions; and
- adjusted after-tax income (adjusted to the equivalent for a couple without children).

Table 8: Comparing the Income of Prime Age and Senior Households

	Two Adult Households			Single Adult Households		
	Prime Age	Fully Retired Senior	Ratio	Prime Age	Fully Retired Senior	Ratio
			(%)			(%)
Gross income						
· Unadjusted	$69,700	$35,600	51	$33,700	$19,200	57
· Adjusted*	$52,800	$35,600	67	$41,400	$26,900	65
After-tax income						
· Unadjusted	$51,100	$30,600	60	$25,800	$16,900	66
· Adjusted*	$38,600	$30,600	79	$31,300	$23,700	76

Note: * To the equivalent income for a couple without children.

---

[9]Other than those with the lowest incomes.

The adjusted gross incomes of fully retired senior households are low — about two-thirds of the adjusted incomes of prime age households. After-tax, senior households have 75 per cent to 80 per cent of the adjusted income of prime age households.[10] On the basis of comparisons such as these, many believe that senior citizens have inadequate incomes. Baldwin and Laliberté (1999), in assessing the extent to which Canada's retirement system has met its objectives, concludes with the following observations.

> The fact that the average income of elderly households has been rising in relation to non-elderly households suggests that the income replacement function is being met more completely. On the other hand, the fact that there is still a significant gap between the average household income of over 65 households versus under 65 households — especially for older households with no employment income, reminds us that old age still tends to be a time of relatively low incomes. The fact that elderly households are over-represented in the first and second quintiles, while being under-represented in the third, fourth and fifth suggests the same point. (1999, p. 54)

Myles concludes his examination of seniors' income by observing that,

> Seniors with low incomes have gained substantially. Conversely, it would be extremely difficult to claim that Canadian seniors have become "too rich". Although mean incomes have risen considerably since the early 1980s, virtually all of the gains have taken place at the lower end of the income distribution. (2000, p. 1)

Both Baldwin and Laliberté (1999) and Myles (2000) cite the fact that seniors are under-represented in the fourth and fifth income quintiles as proof that seniors are not "too rich". Baldwin and Laliberté adjusted for neither taxes nor children. Myles adjusted for both. Neither adjusted for mortgages, employment expenses, CPP and EI contributions, capital accumulations or retirement savings. While both may be correct in concluding that seniors have not grown "too rich", nothing in either paper supports, or is capable of

---

[10]Statistics Canada's calculation of after-tax income, which ignores CPP/QPP and EI contributions, would put the adjusted incomes of senior households closer to 70–75 per cent of the adjusted incomes of prime age households, after-tax.

Malcolm Hamilton

supporting, such a conclusion. The fact that seniors have lower incomes than younger Canadians, even after adjusting for taxes and the cost of raising children, does not mean that they are less well off.

Uses of Income: Fully Retired and Prime Age Households

Tables 9 (couples) and 10 (unattached adults) compare the uses to which senior and prime age households put their incomes. Senior households headed by someone under 75 are distinguished from senior households headed by someone 75 and over to differentiate the more recently retired from those who have been retired for some time.

Table 9: Uses of Income: Senior vs. Prime Age Couples

	Prime Age Couples			Fully Retired Senior Couples		
	With Children	Without Children	All	Under 75	75 and Over	All
Gross income	$70,500	$66,100	$69,700	$38,000	$32,900	$35,600
Tax	(18,600)	(18,600)	(18,600)	(5,500)	(4,400)	(5,000)
Mortgage	(6,200)	(5,400)	(6,100)	(200)	(200)	(200)
Savings	(5,500)	(9,000)	(6,100)	(4,500)	(2,800)	(3,700)
Gifts	500	900	500	(1,500)	(2,500)	(2,000)
Dues and day-care	(1,200)	(300)	(1,000)	(0)	(0)	(0)
Provision for children	(12,000)	(0)	(9,800)	(0)	(0)	(0)
Adult consumption	$27,500	$33,700	$28,600	$26,300[a]	$23,000[b]	$24,700[c]

Notes: [a] $32,300 ignoring gifts and savings.
[b] $28,300 ignoring gifts and savings.
[c] $30,400 ignoring gifts and savings.

Table 10: Uses of Income: Senior vs. Prime Age Unattached Adults

	Prime Age Unattached Adults			Fully Retired Unattached Seniors		
	With Children	Without Children	All	Under 75	75 and Over	All
Gross income	$31,600	$35,200	$33,700	$21,300	$17,500	$19,200
Tax	(5,500)	(9,600)	(8,000)	(2,600)	(2,000)	(2,300)
Mortgage	(2,100)	(1,900)	(2,000)	(200)	(100)	(100)
Savings	1,300	(2,800)	(1,100)	(1,000)	100	(400)
Gifts	600	(0)	300	(1,100)	(1,600)	(1,400)
Dues and day-care	(600)	(200)	(300)	(0)	(0)	(0)
Provision for children	(8,500)	(0)	(3,500)	(0)	(0)	(0)
Adult consumption	$16,800	$20,700	$19,100	$16,400[a]	$13,900[b]	$15,000[c]

Notes: [a] $18,500 ignoring gifts and savings.
 [b] $15,400 ignoring gifts and savings.
 [c] $16,800 ignoring gifts and savings.

From these tables, it would appear that:

- senior households consume less than prime age households even after adjusting for the consumption of children,[11]

- older seniors consume less than younger seniors,

- differences between prime age households and senior households are more pronounced for unattached adults than for couples,

- were it not for amounts saved and/or given away, senior couples could support a higher level of consumption than prime age couples, and

---

[11]Which, of course, says nothing about how their consumption compares to what it was when they were younger.

- prime age adults without children have a higher level of consumption than the other groups.

On the whole, fully retired senior households appear to live slightly more modestly than prime age households, but this is largely a tribute to their frugality, not to financial constraints. Fully retired senior couples save, or give away, almost 20 per cent of their after-tax income. Fully retired unattached seniors save, or give away, more than 10 per cent of their after-tax income. These percentages are comparable to the percentages of after-tax income that prime age households devote to mortgages, savings and debts.

Sources and Uses of Income by Age: Fully Retired Senior Households

Tables 11 (couples) and 12 (unattached adults) look at the impact of age on the sources and uses of income for fully retired seniors. Note that the results for any given five-year age group are subject to potentially large sampling errors, and must be interpreted accordingly.

Table 11: Sources and Uses of Income: Fully Retired Senior Couples, by Age

	Ages					
	65 – 69	70 – 74	75 – 79	80 – 84	85+	All
Transfers	$19,600	$19,800	$19,800	$19,300	$16,200	$19,400
Investment income	4,200	4,100	4,800	4,700	9,400	4,700
Pension, RRSP and other	13,600	14,300	10,300	5,200	5,700	11,500
Gross	$37,400	$38,200	$34,900	$29,200	$31,300	$35,600
Tax	(4,900)	(5,800)	(5,300)	(2,700)	(3,900)	(5,000)
Mortgage	(300)	(200)	(300)	(0)	(0)	(200)
Gifts	(1,700)	(1,500)	(2,000)	(4,000)	(1,600)	(2,000)
Savings	(2,600)	(5,400)	(3,200)	(800)	(5,300)	(3,700)
Consumption	$27,900	$25,300	$24,100	$21,700	$20,500	$24,700

Table 12: Sources and Uses of Income: Fully Retired Unattached Seniors, by Age

| | Ages | | | | | |
	65 – 69	70 – 74	75 – 79	80 – 84	85+	All
Transfers	$12,000	$11,700	$11,700	$11,100	$10,100	$11,500
Investment income	2,600	2,900	2,100	2,700	3,700	2,700
Pension, RRSP and other	4,800	8,000	4,600	3,300	2,000	5,000
Gross	$19,400	$22,600	$18,400	$17,100	$15,800	$19,200
Tax	(2,000)	(3,000)	(2,300)	(1,900)	(1,500)	(2,300)
Mortgage	(200)	(200)	(100)	(100)	(200)	(100)
Gifts	(900)	(1,300)	(1,200)	(2,300)	(1,300)	(1,400)
Savings	(0)	(1,600)	(300)	(1,000)	(500)	(400)
Consumption	$16,300	$16,500	$14,500	$13,800	$12,300	$15,000

The patterns in Tables 11 and 12 are generally consistent with a view that seniors, as they age, become less able or less willing to spend their money. Income decreases gradually with advancing age (which may be generational). This, one would think, would lead older seniors to save less in an effort to maintain consumption. Yet saving and gift giving do not seem to decline much with age. Consumption does. This might be explained by a number of factors.

- Older seniors might be particularly frugal, or perhaps this generation of older seniors is particularly frugal.

- Older seniors might be prevented by poor health from spending their money.

- Older seniors might be spending the way they always did; they just do not spend much.

- Seniors might want to leave money to their children to inherit.

- Seniors might be worried about future medical and custodial costs.

- Older seniors might exaggerate their savings and under-estimate their consumption.

Uses of Income by Quintile

Tables 13 (households with two adults) and 14 (households with one adult) examine the uses to which income is put by households in the bottom, middle and top income quintiles.

Table 13: Uses of Income by Quintile: Two-Adult Households

	Prime Age Quintiles			Fully Retired Senior Quintiles		
	Bottom	Middle	Top	Bottom	Middle	Top
Income band						
Bottom	-	$56,000	$92,000	-	$26,000	$46,000
Top	$40,000	$72,000	-	$21,000	$33,000	-
Average No. of children	1.6	1.7	1.7	0	0	0
No. of weeks worked	51	86	101	0	0	0
Gross income	$27,800	$63,400	$126,800	$17,200	$29,000	$70,000
Tax	(3,700)	(15,900)	(39,500)	(300)	(2,500)	(15,800)
Mortgage	(2,500)	(6,400)	(9,300)	(300)	(100)	(200)
Savings	2,100	(4,600)	(20,200)	400	(200)	(15,100)
Gifts	800	1,300	(400)	900	(1,900)	(5,700)
Dues and day-care	(300)	(1,000)	(1,700)	(0)	(0)	(0)
Provision for children	(6,100)	(9,000)	(14,300)	(0)	(0)	(0)
Adult consumption	$18,100	$27,800	$41,400	$17,900[a]	$24,300[b]	$33,200[c]

Notes: [a] $16,600 ignoring gifts and savings.
        [b] $26,400 ignoring gifts and savings.
        [c] $54,000 ignoring gifts and savings.

Table 14: Uses of Income by Quintile: One-Adult Households

	Prime Age Quintiles			Fully Retired Senior Quintiles		
	Bottom	Middle	Top	Bottom	Middle	Top
Income band						
Bottom	-	$24,000	$49,000	-	$14,000	$24,500
Top	$15,000	$35,000	-	$12,000	$16,000	-
Average No. of children	0.5	0.7	0.6	0	0	0
No. of weeks worked	8	47	55	0	0	0
Gross income	**$9,200**	**$29,300**	**$68,500**	**$10,000**	**$14,300**	**$38,900**
Tax	(400)	(5,800)	(20,900)	(100)	(300)	(8,700)
Mortgage	(300)	(1,300)	(4,700)	(0)	(200)	(300)
Savings	1,800	(300)	(6,800)	200	900	(3,500)
Gifts	1,800	300	(2,100)	(200)	(1,100)	(3,300)
Dues and day-care	(100)	(400)	(800)	(0)	(0)	(0)
Provision for children	(1,600)	(3,400)	(4,400)	(0)	(0)	(0)
Adult consumption	**$10,400**	**$18,400**	**$28,800**	**$9,900[a]**	**$13,600[b]**	**$23,100[c]**

Notes: [a] $9,900 ignoring gifts and savings.
  [b] $13,800 ignoring gifts and savings.
  [c] $29,900 ignoring gifts and savings.

The quintiles are based on gross income, and are determined separately for senior households and for prime age households. The relevant percentiles are as set out in Table 15.

Table 15: Gross Income Percentiles

	Two-Adult Households		One-Adult Households	
Percentile	Prime Age	Fully Retired Senior	Prime Age	Fully Retired Senior
20th	$40,000	$21,000	$15,000	$12,000
40th	$56,000	$26,000	$24,000	$14,000
60th	$72,000	$33,000	$35,000	$16,000
80th	$92,000	$46,000	$49,000	$24,500

The ratios of the incomes of, and the amounts consumed by, seniors to the corresponding amounts for prime age households *in the same quintile* are shown in Table 16.

Senior households spend less than prime age households in the corresponding quintile. In some cases (i.e., middle-income unattached adults) this is of necessity. In many instances (high-income households) it is by choice.

Simple replacement ratios, before- or after-tax, say relatively little about the adequacy of retirement income. Fully retired senior couples in the middle quintile have 46 per cent of the gross income and 56 per cent of the after-tax income of the corresponding quintile of prime age couples, yet they are capable of achieving (if they spent their after-tax incomes) 95 per cent of the consumption of prime age couples. Fully retired senior couples in the top quintile have 55 per cent of the income of corresponding prime age couples, but if they spent their after-tax incomes they could achieve 130 per cent of the consumption of prime age couples.

Table 16: Income and Consumption of Fully Retired Senior Households as a Percentage of the Corresponding Amounts for Prime Age Households

	Gross Income	After-tax Income	Adult Consumption*
	(%)	(%)	(%)
Two-adult households			
Bottom quintile	62	70	92
Middle quintile	46	56	95
Top quintile	55	62	130
One-adult households			
Bottom quintile	109	113	95
Middle quintile	49	60	75
Top quintile	57	63	104

Note: *including, in the case of senior households, gifts and savings.

Fully retired single seniors in the middle quintile have 49 per cent of the gross income of corresponding one-adult, prime age households, but if they spent their money, they could achieve 75 per cent of the consumption of prime age households. Thus, for some households (middle-quintile couples) a 50 per cent gross replacement ratio is about right. For others (top-quintile couples) it is too high. For others (middle-quintile, single adults) it is too low.

Tables 13 and 14 also demonstrate the limitations of Gini coefficients as a measure of economic equality. Many authors (Baldwin and Laliberté; and Myles among them) use lower Gini coefficients for senior incomes to demonstrate that inequality is less pervasive or less severe for older Canadians. Gower (Table 17) found that low-income, working Canadians replaced a much higher percentage of their employment income when they retired than did Canadians with higher incomes. This table is generally consistent with the view that the range of income outcomes for senior citizens is narrower than for prime age Canadians.

Table 17: Gross Replacement Ratios upon Retirement

Pre-Retirement Income (1992)	Percentage of Income Replaced upon Retirement
	(%)
less than – $10,000	147
$10,000 – $19,999	69
$20,000 – $29,999	62
$30,000 – $39,999	60
$40,000 – $49,999	59
$50,000 – $69,999	56
over $70,000	45

Source: Gower (1998).

Malcolm Hamilton

Table 18 shows that the ratios of top-quintile average incomes and adult consumption to the corresponding averages in the bottom quintile is consistently higher for prime age couples than for fully retired senior couples. On the surface, this suggests that there is less inequality among seniors, but the conclusion rests on the assumption that the ratios for prime age couples are directly comparable to the corresponding ratios for senior couples, and this may not be the case. For example, the consumption ratio for senior couples (1.85) is lower than the ratio for prime age couples (2.29) because senior couples in the top quintile save or give away 38 per cent of their after-tax income rather than consuming it. Prime age couples devote about 34 per cent of their after-tax income to mortgages and savings.

It is clear why prime age couples devote a high percentage of their incomes to mortgages and savings; they need to eliminate debts and to accumulate retirement savings if they are to enjoy a comparable standard of living when they retire. It is not clear why top-quintile seniors, who already have mortgage-free houses and comfortable retirement incomes, need to continue to save almost 30 per cent of their after-tax income. Arguably, the most relevant measure of inequality in Table 18 is, for prime age couples, the consumption ratio (2.29) and, for retired couples, the after-tax income ratio (3.21). If so, then inequality is more pronounced among senior couples than prime age couples.

Transitions from Young to Old

Table 19 looks at the transition from a young adult to prime age adult to senior citizen.

Table 18: Ratios of Top to Bottom Quintile Averages

	Prime Age Couples	Fully Retired Senior Couples
Gross income	4.56	4.07
After-tax income	3.62	3.21
Adult consumption	2.29	1.85

Table 19: Income and Consumption by Age and Household Type

	Two-Adult Households					One-Adult Households				
Age	Weeks Worked	Gross Income ($)	After-tax Income ($)	Adult Consumption ($)	Gifts, Mortgage & Savings ($)	Weeks Worked	Gross Income ($)	After-tax Income ($)	Adult Consumption ($)	Gifts, Mortgage & Savings ($)
Under 25	63	35,300	28,800	24,100	(100)	25	17,100	14,400	15,600	(3,000)
25 – 29	71	46,800	36,300	27,300	3,900	33	26,800	21,200	18,000	1,300
30 – 34	73	54,800	42,000	24,300	8,700	34	31,200	23,000	19,500	900
35 – 39	76	60,200	45,500	23,900	10,500	37	32,600	25,600	18,200	3,400
40 – 44	81	65,200	48,500	27,500	9,600	40	34,200	26,300	18,800	3,200
45 – 49	86	66,800	50,000	31,400	8,800	44	36,600	27,700	20,300	3,300
50 – 54	77	63,100	47,600	31,000	10,800	38	34,400	26,500	20,500	3,000
55 – 59	61	60,500	45,600	31,500	11,300	28	31,500	24,400	19,200	3,400
60 – 64	33	50,800	37,500	30,200	5,900	15	24,500	19,200	17,900	600
65 – 69	18	46,600	37,300	28,100	8,100	6	25,200	21,300	17,600	2,900
70 – 74	10	45,100	38,000	24,800	12,500	2	23,600	20,400	17,000	3,000
75 – 79	8	36,300	31,800	23,700	7,700	2	20,800	17,700	15,100	2,000
80 – 84	2	32,000	28,200	22,800	5,000	2	19,000	16,500	14,800	1,200
over 84	7	32,600	29,200	20,100	8,700	1	17,700	15,700	12,800	2,500

Malcolm Hamilton

Unlike the other tables, Table 19 includes adults under 30 and between the ages of 50 and 65. Seniors with employment income and seniors with non-senior spouses are included in the sample.

As can be seen from the table:

- gross income and weeks worked increase significantly between the ages of 20 and 50, and then decrease significantly between the ages of 50 and 70;

- prior to age 70, adult consumption changes very little. As incomes rise, so do taxes, mortgage payments and the cost of supporting children. As incomes decline, so do these expenses, or alternatively, as these expenses decline so does the need for income and the number of weeks worked; and

- after age 70 there is a notable decline in consumption that appears to be largely voluntary, as savings and gifts continue at a relatively high level.

Implications for the Design of Canada's Retirement System

Much of Canada's retirement system, both public and private, has been built on a faulty assumption — that seniors need to replace 70 per cent of their employment income to maintain their standard of living. Most of the evidence suggests that the required ratio is 30 per cent to 70 per cent depending on an individual's circumstances, with the average closer to 50 per cent than 70 per cent. The fact that today's seniors have roughly half of the income of prime age families, but can afford a similar standard of living, supports this conclusion.

If seniors can live comfortably on half the income of working Canadians, the implications are as follows.

Government transfers will continue to dominate the income of senior citizens. Transfer payments replace about 40 per cent of the income of the typical retiring Canadian. If 50 per cent will suffice, the average Canadian needs little in the way of occupational pensions or retirement savings to live comfortably after 65.

Canada should expect to have a relatively low savings rate. Most Canadians can retire in comfort if they do two things: eliminate their debts and save a modest amount to supplement government pensions.

Those who save heavily, either because they participate in expensive pension plans (as are common in the public sector) or because they adhere to a strict savings regime, will typically find that they can retire in their 50s and live comfortably on 50 per cent of their employment income. If they keep working until they achieve the conventional 70 per cent target, they may have trouble spending their retirement income, particularly as they push into their late 70s. The recent experience of public sector plans suggests that many Canadians are prepared to retire in their 50s with pensions that are at the low end of the range that has traditionally been considered adequate.

If seniors have difficulty spending their money as they age, one must question the wisdom of deferring large amounts of income until late in life. Seniors might be better off with larger partially indexed pensions than smaller, fully indexed pensions.

While Canadians appear to abhor two-tiered systems, our current retirement system appears to be cut from this cloth. Canadians with below-average incomes will rely almost entirely on government programs. They will do so for three reasons: (i) government pensions provide most of what they need to maintain their modest standard of living[12] when they retire, (ii) taxes, mortgages and the cost of raising children make it difficult for them to save, and (iii) income taxes, clawbacks (GIS, refundable tax credits), geared-to-income programs and services make savings relatively pointless, as little of the income generated by these savings produces a benefit for the saver.

Canadians with above-average incomes will need to save reasonably heavily and/or to participate in occupational pension plans to maintain their higher standards of living. Since government programs will be relatively unimportant to those with good incomes while retirement savings plans will be relatively unimportant to those with below-average incomes, we can expect continuing disagreements about government priorities. Many will want retirement savings plans cut back to generate additional tax revenues to shore up public pensions. Others will want government pensions cut back and a greater emphasis placed on retirement savings.

---

[12]Indeed, many will find that their standard of living improves after age 65 even if they have no savings and no occupational pensions.

Malcolm Hamilton

While much is written about employment becoming the fourth leg of the retirement income stool[13] and about the presumed need for the next generation of Canadians to continue working after age 65, these views are often premised on the assumption that Canadians need to replace 70 per cent of their retirement income and that many will need to support parents with inadequate incomes. While some Canadians will want to replace 70 per cent of their employment income and while some will need to support parents, most can get by comfortably with less than 70 per cent and many will inherit significant amounts from frugal parents who save heavily even in their 70s and 80s. For many, inheritance, not employment, will be the fourth leg of the retirement stool.

The reluctance of many seniors to encroach on capital is understandable, but unwise. In the 1970s and 1980s when inflation was high, seniors encroached on their "real" capital without knowing it, that is, they spent their interest, much of which was simply compensation for the inflation-induced erosion in the purchasing power of their capital. When inflation and interest rates declined in the 1990s, seniors had lower incomes, but they were better off because the purchasing power of their capital eroded more slowly. However, if seniors are unprepared to encroach on capital, their cash flow is adversely affected by declining interest and inflation rates and their heirs, not the seniors themselves, become the beneficiaries of lower inflation.

References

Baldwin, B. and P. Laliberté (1999), "Incomes of Older Canadians: Amounts and Sources, 1973–1996", Research Paper No. 15 (Ottawa: Canadian Labour Congress).

Gower, D. (1998), "Income Transition Upon Retirement", *Perspectives* (Ottawa: Statistics Canada), Winter.

Myles, J. (2000), *The Maturation of Canada's Retirement Income System: Income Levels, Income Inequality and Low Income among the Elderly* (Ottawa and Tallahassee: Statistics Canada and Florida State University).

---

[13]Government pensions, occupational savings and personal savings being the first three.

International Economics

WTO Membership for China: To Be and Not to Be: Is that the Answer?

Sylvia Ostry

Introduction

Canada is the member of the G7 countries most dependent on trade. The rules-based trading regime under the World Trade Organization (WTO) is critical for Canada's continuing prosperity. The biggest issue currently facing the world trading system is the accession of China, which will bring a fifth of the world's population into the system. This will obviously have widespread implications for the overall system, which will be of overarching importance for Canada. Given this importance and the lifelong interest of David Slater in trade issues, this paper focuses on the myriad of issues raised by China's accession to the WTO.

The negotiations for China's accession to the WTO have gone on, albeit in fits and starts, for almost 15 years. But as the saying goes, timing is everything. If China had joined the General Agreement on Tariffs and Trade (GATT), the negotiations would have been far easier since market access under GATT was mainly about border barriers. But since the Uruguay Round the concept of market access has been extended to include not only domestic regulatory policies but also both substantive and procedural legal issues. The barriers to access for service providers stem from laws, regulations, administrative actions which impede cross-border trade and factor flows. Implicit in this shift embodied in the General Agreement on Trade in Services (GATS) is a move away from GATT negative regulation — what governments must not do — to positive regulation — what governments must do. This aspect is now apparent in the WTO's telecommunications reference paper that set out a common framework for the regulation of competition in basic telecommunications and is likely to be adopted in other sectors. In the case of intellectual property the move to positive regulation is more dramatic since the negotiations covered not only standards for domestic laws but also detailed provisions for procedures to enforce individual (meaning primarily corporate) property rights. But the Round also dealt with social regulation, which has grown so rapidly in the Organisation for Economic Co-operation and Development (OECD) countries since the 1970s that it has been termed "regulatory inflation". In the area of social regulation (covering environment, food safety, etc.) the positive regulatory approach is procedural rather than substantive and the model is the western, especially American, administrative procedures model, of which more will be said later.

The WTO rules thus involve commitments for many member countries to what is in effect systemic redesign. Further, and in my view most importantly, the overarching governing principle of the WTO trading system is the western system of law, especially its American version, and the WTO houses a supranational juridical system for settlement of disputes, a system which is becoming increasingly litigious.

But the transformation of the system is not the only aspect of timing worth noting. The political economy of post-Uruguay Round trade policy has also been transformed. The Uruguay Round was a north-south "grand bargain", GATT-type market access for the south, especially in agriculture and labour-intensive industries like textiles and clothing, in exchange for their acceptance of rules governing the so-called new issues of trade in services and intellectual property. The deal required investment in structural transformation often with uncertain, long-term returns. Unfortunately though, it turned out to be a bum deal in the view of many southern countries and has left a wide north-south divide. And that divide has been widening further with the demand for the "trade and" (environment and labour) issues by the north, largely in response to the new global actors: the NGOs (non-governmental organizations). However, not all the NGOs are the ones you see marching on TV. Some are technical/legal groups possessing a highly valuable strategic asset — policy knowledge — and a number act as a "virtual secretariat" for the south. In post-Seattle Geneva, a seemingly paralyzed north is confronted by an increasingly proactive south. The credibility and effectiveness of the WTO is under serious challenge. Thus the impact of Chinese accession must be viewed in this context.

Since Chinese accession will be arguably among the most significant events in the history of the world trading system and is bound to have a profound impact on the system surely both the WTO and the major trading countries have undertaken a careful analysis of the subject? Rather than give you a straight answer, let me recount a story. A few months age, I was at a conference at the University of Minnesota and asked a senior WTO official how many people in the secretariat were analyzing the impact of China on the operations of the WTO. He grinned (assuming I knew the answer) and said two people in the legal division were working "round the clock on technical accession matters". OK, I said, surely you have some studies from Brussels or Washington or ..... Nothing, he said, his grin fading. There are lots of studies by business groups on the benefits of opening up a market of over a billion consumers. And lots of models estimating the impact of Chinese liberalization on China and the world. These are studies of improved access for goods under the GATT, of course, and provide carefully calibrated numbers. (Many of the econometric studies are nearly breathless in admiration for the amazing extent and pace of Chinese liberalization and the bonanza of welfare gains, albeit with some costs for industries within China and many in Asia.) But studies on the WTO system? Alas, there are none.

So I am treading in unknown territory. And I want to break ranks with my fellow economists (except for the growing institutional school) and look at Chinese accession through a legal template. I will then put forward some necessarily speculative views on the implications of Chinese accession for the future of the WTO and end with a policy proposal to facilitate the full and effective integration of China into the world trading system.

China and Transparency

The WTO is a highly legalized system with a built-in tendency for further legalization.[1] It can, for example, be observed in the growing evidentiary

---

[1]Much of this discussion is from Ostry (1998, pp. 1-22). See also Groombridge and Barfield (1999).

content of all disputes: panels are now in effect preparing reports less for the parties than for the Appellate Board. The requirement for ever-increasing amounts of detailed information has only just begun. Imagine what disputes in China's services sector or food safety and risk assessment would entail in terms of evidence. Or what about a dispute on subsidies in China's state owned enterprises (SOEs), privatized or not, which could include a demand for information on non-performing bank loans or the non-existent "services" of subsidiaries or cross-subsidization in telecommunications services or, technology transfer conditions for foreign investors, or.... But this aspect of so-called transparency is by no means the only problem. Far more important over the long run is the fundamental aspect of "transparency" as a pillar of the GATT and now the WTO, a pillar as important as non-discrimination in the origins of the system. This needs some explanation.

The drafting of the Charter of the International Trade Organization (ITO), which was to have been a part of the Bretton Woods institutional architecture, coincided with a new development in the American legal system, the establishment of the *Administrative Procedures Act* (APA) in 1946. The APA stemmed from the expansion of the role of government as a result of the New Deal and the war. It was, in effect, designed to constrain the discretionary power of bureaucrats. When the ITO died, the main elements of the APA, which had been included in the Charter, became article X of the GATT entitled "Publication and Administration of Trade Regulations". No founding member objected, probably because all industrialized countries had adapted similar legislation as a result of the expanded role of government. And all therefore required the establishment of norms to control what bureaucrats do and how they do it. However, it is important to underline that the U.S. approach was different in several respects in placing more emphasis on independent regulatory agencies with quasi-judicial or quasi-legislative functions; an emphasis on the right of notice and comment; freedom of information; and judicial review. The U.S. approach (more adversarial and fact-intensive than the European) was reflected in article X, although it is weaker than the APA in speaking of the desirability rather than the necessity of independent tribunals and judicial review, probably as a result of compromise in the negotiating process. In any case, it was hardly a major item in the negotiations because the GATT's focus was on border barriers, which are more obviously "transparent".

The Tokyo Round nudged transparency and legalization a bit further but the Uruguay Round introduced a sea change. So, for example, "transparency" — the word actually appears in the Agreement on Trade-

Related Aspects of Intellectual Property Rights (TRIPS) — now requires the publication of laws, regulations and the mode of administration in services as well as detailed enforcement procedures in TRIPS. The Accession Protocol of China, of course, reflects these changes, including requirements on the administration of the trade regime and sections on transparency and judicial review.

Can China deliver on these requirements? The short answer would be not yet — and it is not clear when. Thus, transparency covers: publication of relevant laws and regulations; right of comment before implementation; enforcement only of those laws and regulations published; creation of a single inquiry point with a time limit for response. Unfortunately, while Beijing may be able to publish all central government laws, etc. it is widely agreed that many (an unknown number) of relevant state laws will not (cannot) be covered nor will the unpublished "normative documents", a leftover from the old regime, still in use by local and state officials. More broadly, the multi-layered complexity of the evolving Chinese legal system — including several administrative laws — make it impossible to conform to WTO transparency. The Chinese laws at present lack specified procedures to constrain bureaucratic discretion and include no mandatory right of comment. Finally, the requirement for judicial review, which has been watered down in recent negotiations, faces the basic problem that there is no separation of powers in the constitution and therefore no concept of an independent judiciary. Indeed the Chinese Communist Party has the final say on judicial appointments. As several Chinese legal experts have noted, the Chinese tradition regards law as an instrument to maintain social discipline or promote policy or sovereign rights — rule by law not rule of law. And while that is certainly changing, the instrumentalist approach to law is still widely prevalent.

The concept of instrumentalism is deep-seated. Thus, the pervasiveness of local protectionism stems from the decentralization of the economic reform process launched in the 1980s. There was no view of systemic reform but rather ad hoc pragmatic evolution. The same approach applies to legal reform. Law is an instrument of policy: there is a large and growing body of legal rules for domestic and foreign transactions and government administration. There is, however, no legal system, no protection against arbitrary and unpredictable government decisions.

But many, including economists and corporations, would say: So what? There will be an endogenous demand for the rule of law from Chinese business and lawyers as it becomes clear that the costs of relations-based corporate governance, the norm in China, rises astronomically with the rapid spread of economic liberalization. So *guanxi* (connections) is a wasting asset and the rule of law is far less costly and more effective. Thus it is not the demand from the WTO, but the demand from business itself that will make the rule of law the governance norm in China. This issue is now the subject of debate among institutional economists and it is all very interesting. But *guanxi* is still prevalent, foreign corporations are actively engaged in forging relations-based networks, and during the transition from one to the other there seems to be what some have described as chaos. And there is growing evidence that corruption and red tape, that is, lack of transparency and the rule of law, have a significant negative impact on foreign direct investment and on economic growth.[2] So while obviously the transition will be lengthy, the need for some clearly delineated time-certain road map will be of crucial importance both for sustained economic liberalization and sustained growth in China, and also for the WTO. I will make a proposal for such a transition mechanism before concluding, but first let us deal with the question of impact.

Impact of Chinese Accession on the WTO

In the light of the complexity and difficulty of the profound institutional change required if China is to abide by its WTO so-called transparency commitments it is worth noting that in the accession negotiations the United States, which had demanded a 16-year transition recently settled for eight years. In an article in *Fortune* magazine, Senior Statesman Lee Kuan Yew of Singapore notes the amazing transformation of China since 1978, but argues that to change the "mindset" of the Chinese rulers will require replacement by a new generation mainly educated abroad. He estimates this will take "20 to 30 years" (Lee Kuan Yew, 2000, p. 334). So maybe the WTO members know something that has escaped the notice of Lee Kuan Yew?

---

[2]See Shang-Jin Wei (2000, pp. 303-346); and Shleifer (2000, pp. 347-351) for a fuller discussion of this point.

Seen through the prism of the legal template, the most significant impact of Chinese accession on the WTO will be on the dispute-settlement mechanism. I have already noted the endogenous legalization process at work and its increasingly evidentiary-intensive nature, which could create serious problems of access to reliable information in China. But it is also worth noting that the pressure from the United States and North American NGOs for the right to present *amicus curiae* briefs to both dispute panels and/or the Appellate Board is unlikely to abate. Indeed, a new rallying cry has been provided: "participatory legalism" (Shell, 1996, p. 370). Moreover there is now a major drive by some academic lawyers and NGOs to promote the primacy of customary international law over international trade law in the field of the environment as well as human rights (Ostry, 2001). Considering that China has just over 100,000 lawyers or about one for every 11,000 people compared with one per 300 in the United States, participatory legalism and endless arcane debates over whether or not customary international law should override the WTO may be a rather difficult game for China to play, let alone to win. (Strangely enough, however, it was reported in the *Financial Times* [2000, p. 8] that last year China decided to sharply reduce the number of new lawyers because of concern over their growing potential for disruptiveness.)

So one view of the impact of Chinese accession expressed in the corridors in Geneva is that a flood of disputes could overwhelm the already over-burdened system. There is serious concern that China would likely regard these actions as political and, to save face, simply reject the process itself. Indeed, as many China scholars have underlined, Chinese foreign policy is deeply state-centric and protection of sovereignty is at its core. A Chinese rejection or attack on the dispute-settlement mechanism would seriously undermine its credibility.

But another view shared by some, especially multinational corporations with experience in China, is that there will be very few, if any, disputes. Businesses will be fearful of complaining to their governments because of retaliation by Chinese officials. They would prefer informal behind-the-scene, government-to-government talks so that some new deal could be worked out. This scenario would involve a two-track trading system: one set of transparent dispute-settlement rules for all WTO members except China and another set of opaque bilateral arrangements for China. Other countries — India, for example — are likely to regard this as unfair to put it mildly.

Both scenarios could threaten the long-term viability of the WTO. Both would involve an indefinite period of "partial integration" for the Chinese —

to be and not to be. If that is a suggested answer it should be directly confronted. Surely a longer transition period, with clearly specified monitoring mechanisms and benchmarks as well as provisions for coordinated and targeted legal training assistance would be a more effective approach? A proposal along these lines will be described below. But one final point about impact requires exploration.

What impact will China have on the north-south gridlock over a new round of negotiations? I speculate that China will be pragmatic and carefully weigh the costs and benefits for China. Given the formidable structural change that will ensue from WTO accession — especially the impact on China's 900 million rural population and the widening rural-urban and inland-coastal income inequality — it seems highly unlikely that further liberalization would be welcome, whatever the long-term welfare gains. Hence China is unlikely to be an active proponent of new negotiations. China sees itself as a leader of developing countries and there is likely to be some jousting with India over this high profile role. But on balance it seems unlikely that Chinese accession will be a positive factor in bridging the north-south divide. Perhaps a more innovation transition mechanism could help?

A New Transition Mechanism

The Chinese accession negotiations with the two great trading powers — the European Union and the United States — have focused almost exclusively on market access for their (often competing) corporations. This is understandable, if regrettable, because *au fond* institutional or systemic issues are not a high priority. The alternative to a rules-based system is a power-based system and, unlike the postwar period when a combination of idealism and the Cold War fostered the creation of the international economic architecture, in today's post-Cold War environment commercial values rule supreme. But the same is not (or should not be) true for middle powers like Canada for whom a rules-based system is crucial to providing stability or at least reducing uncertainty. Canada played a lead role in the Uruguay Round in mobilizing middle-power coalitions that were effective in both launching and sustaining the extraordinarily difficult negotiations. And it was a Canadian proposal that created the WTO. The Chinese accession will have major consequences for the WTO and the world trading system. A middle-power coalition led by Canada could help mitigate the negative impact of accession both on the WTO and the Chinese reform process.

The accession protocol in Geneva already includes the concept of transition periods of varying length for different parts of the liberalization commitments. What is required is to house these specifics in an overall transition framework which would be time-certain; include specified benchmarks for review at designated dates by a WTO committee, which might take the form of either a new committee for economies in transition or of the existing Trade Policy Review (Groombridge and Barfield, 1999, pp. 76-81); and would result in full WTO membership at the end of the period when the TPRM certified full adherence to the transition protocol. To ensure the credibility of this mechanism the committee should have the right to apply sanctions for a specified period if China failed to deliver the commitments at any of the designated benchmarks.

This approach to accession (which should also apply to Russia where the institutional underpinning is far more chaotic and other transition economies in waiting) should be coordinated with World Bank programs. The technical assistance should be jointly supplied by the two institutions although this would require an increase in WTO training and legal resources. In addition, since China's integration into the WTO will involve major restructuring of the state owned enterprises; radical reform of the banking system; and the need to create an effective social safety net, coordination with Bank programs to facilitate this massive structural change would help ensure the sustainability of both the domestic reform and the liberalization process.

In addition to this more comprehensive transition arrangement, it would also be essential to include specific mechanisms to secure relevant information and to encourage mediation and negotiation for the settlement of seriously contentious disputes. But once again, it is important not to create a two-tier system in the WTO and thus the transitional arrangements with respect to dispute settlement should be time-certain in duration. But since the issue of the increasing litigiousness of the WTO dispute mechanism is a broader issue that the Chinese accession will amplify but does not create, it is likely to be discussed in the context of negotiations along with other issues of structural reform of the institution. Perhaps China could play a more positive role in the negotiations by working with other countries, like Canada, in strengthening the first post-Cold War institution and guardian of the rules-based trading system, the WTO.

References

Financial Times (2000), "Beijing to Slash Number of New Lawyers", November 21, p. 8.

Groombridge, M.A. and C. Barfield (1999), *Tiger by the Tail: China and the World Trade Organization* (Washington, DC: The AEI Press).

Ostry, S. (1998), "China and the WTO: The Transparency Issues", *UCLA Journal of International Law and Foreign Affairs* 3(1), 1-22.

_____ (2001), "The WTO After Seattle: Something's Happening Here, What it is ain't Exactly Clear", *American Economic Association*, New Orleans, January, Preliminary Draft.

Shell, R. (1996), "The Trade Stakeholders Model and Participation by Nonstate Parties in the World Trade Organization", *University of Pennsylvania Journal of International Economic Law* 17(1), 370.

Shleifer, A. (2000), "Comment and Discussion: Local Corruption and Global Capital Flows", *Brookings Paper on Economic Activity* 2, 347-351.

Wei, Shang-Jin (2000), "Local Corruption and Global Capital Flows", *Brookings Paper on Economic Activity* 2, 303-346.

Yew, Lee Kuan (2000), "To be Rich is Glorious", *Fortune*, November 13, 334.

Doing the Right Thing: The WTO and the Developing World

Kathleen Macmillan

The prosperity of the richest countries is at an all-time high, and so is their capacity to look beyond their own immediate needs. At the same time, the crisis of the poorest countries is acute, and the shortcomings of the current strategy of globalisation painfully evident. (Jeffrey Sachs, 2000)

Introduction

Advancing the cause of trade liberalization is a tough business to be in these days. Recent attempts to resuscitate the World Trade Organization (WTO) or launch new sets of negotiations such as the Free Trade Agreement of the Americas (FTAA) have met a groundswell of opposition. Hoards of anti-globalization protesters have demonstrated at virtually every meeting of international economic leaders held in the past two years. The activists accuse international institutions like the WTO, the World Bank and the International Monetary Fund of promoting a manifesto for global corporations to the detriment of ordinary citizens. In support of the "race to the bottom" thesis, they point to the growing income divergence between countries of the developed and developing world that has occurred in recent decades despite the massive growth in world trade volumes.[1]

Economists and trade policy experts remain convinced that trade liberalization is good for countries. A link between freer trade and income growth has been established in a number of economic studies.[2] Income growth is an essential contributor to, although not necessarily a guarantee of, poverty reduction (Max, 2001). International commitments can also foster better domestic policies. Trade liberalization brings with it regulatory reform in critical areas such as telecommunications and financial services that can be an important factor in promoting economic development.

Western political leaders, no doubt frustrated by the protesters that upstage their every meeting, have seized on the potential for trade liberalization to alleviate poverty in the developing world. Their message is that improved global economic integration is not part of a grand corporate agenda but a humanitarian one. Among the items included in the Communiqué of the 2001 G8 leaders' summit in Genoa is a pledge to launch a comprehensive round of multilateral trade negotiations aimed at addressing the concerns of the developing world. Similar commitments were made leading up to the ill-fated WTO ministerial meeting in Seattle.

The developing world has some reason to be sceptical. The West has long preached the benefits of trade liberalization while selectively choosing only those elements of the liberalization agenda that it finds palatable. High barriers persist in the textiles, clothing and agriculture sectors, despite successive rounds of multilateral trade negotiations. At the same time, developing country members of the WTO are being held to commitments to introduce western-style regimes such as intellectual property enforcement measures. Issues of priority to the developing world like labour mobility are not even on the negotiating table.

---

[1]A recent report of the United Nations Committee for Trade and Development (UNCTAD) decried the increased marginalization of the world's poorest. The 48 poorest nations accounted for 13 per cent of the world's population in 1997 but only 0.4 per cent of the world's exports and 0.6 per cent of the world's imports. See Lukas (2000, p. 15).

[2]Jeffrey Sachs and Andrew Warner concluded that developing countries with open economies grew over six times faster in the 1970s and 1980s than countries whose economies were closed to trade (Sachs and Warner, 1995).

The fact that there are so many developing country members of the WTO indicates that poorer countries are not yet prepared to give up on the multilateral trading system. Developing nations account for over 100 of the roughly 140 members of the WTO. Dozens of other developing countries have indicated an interest in undergoing the WTO accession process, an undertaking that is long, demanding and with uncertain outcomes.

The key benefit developing nations see in WTO membership is the promise it holds of greater access to markets in the developed world. As major exporters of industrial goods, many strive to emulate the East Asian miracle based on export-led growth and are anxious to participate in negotiations aimed at reducing import barriers. Countries know that trade brings new technologies and practices that can make domestic industries more competitive. They also recognize that membership in international rules-making institutions can make them a more attractive location for foreign investment. The WTO's dispute settlement provisions can also assist developing nations targeted by unilateral measures taken by richer countries in areas such as intellectual property and money laundering.

This paper examines how effectively the multilateral trading system has addressed developing country concerns in the past and considers some proposals for achieving a fairer balance in the world trading system. It is organized into sections that reflect the major trade negotiating areas of concern to the developing world: market access, textiles and clothing, agricultural trade, anti-dumping, intellectual property, the new trade agenda and trade-related assistance.

Market Access

What are developing countries to make of the rhetoric in favour of rapid liberalization, when rich countries with full employment and strong safety nets argue that they need to impose protective measures to help those adversely affected by trade? Or when rich countries play down the political pressures within developing countries — insisting that their polities 'face up to the hard choices' — while excusing their own trade barriers and agricultural subsidies by citing 'political pressures'?
(Joseph E. Stiglitz, 2000)

Better market access was an overriding objective for developing countries participating in the Uruguay Round negotiations. Negotiators made important advances in reducing tariffs, disciplining the use of non-tariff measures and expanding trade in services. Developing countries participated fully in all aspects of the market access negotiations and made significant concessions, particularly on tariffs. Despite the progress made in the Uruguay Round, however, developing country exporters still remain at a disadvantage in accessing foreign markets.

Rich countries continue to impose higher tariffs on products of export interest to developing countries than they levy on products imported from other Organisation for Economic Co-operation and Development (OECD) countries. The average OECD tariff on manufactured product imports from poor countries is estimated to be four times higher than the average tariff on imports from rich countries (Hertel and Martin, 2000). Textiles, clothing, food products, and footwear continue to attract high levels of tariff protection in developed economies. Moreover, tariffs often escalate with the degree of processing, discouraging the further processing of basic commodities in developing nations.[3]

To a large extent, developed countries have relied on the duty relief they provide least-developed countries under the Generalized System of Preferences (GSP) as an excuse for not proceeding with across-the-board tariff cuts. Research has shown, however, that GSP has had only a modest effect on trade and incomes in developing nations (Whalley, 1999, p. 1091). One reason is that it is entirely up to the developed countries providing the duty relief to determine the recipient countries and the products that qualify for GSP treatment. Quite often, "sensitive" goods like textiles are excluded. Since developed country tariffs on "non-sensitive" goods are already fairly low, tariff relief under the GSP provides little extra advantage. Second,

---

[3]Studies have found that a similar bias against exports from the developing world exists with respect to non-tariff barriers. Based on 1992 data, Low and Yeats (1995) calculated that 18 per cent of the non-oil exports from developing countries encountered non-tariff measures compared to only 10 per cent of exports from OECD countries. The disparity was even greater for specific sectors such as clothing and textiles. While members committed to removing quantitative restrictions and other non-tariff barriers in the Uruguay Round, the time frame for their elimination is long; until 2005 in the case of textiles and clothing, for example. Other non-tariff barriers, notably those in the agricultural area, were replaced by prohibitive tariffs.

security of access is never assured. GSP is a unilateral tariff concession that is not bound and can be withdrawn at any time. A poor human rights record or weak enforcement of intellectual property rights can disqualify countries from eligibility. The threat of "graduation" from GSP status is always present and can be used to exact concessions from developing country recipients.

In the aftermath of the failed Seattle ministerial meeting the European Union, the United States, Japan and Canada have pledged free access to imports from the least-developed nations. Like the GSP system, the proposals do not go far enough in addressing the impediments to access. The benefits would apply to only the 48 countries on the United Nations' list of least-developed countries. Moreover, exemptions will continue to exist. For example, European members states are resisting the idea of free access for sugar and other sensitive products. Canada's initiative will still leave duties on 10 per cent of imports from least-developed countries. As Bhagwati (2001, p. 23) notes, special programs aimed at the most needy countries merely shift limited market access amongst the poorest rather than expanding access opportunities for all developing nations.

Aside from reductions in tariff and non-tariff barriers, the Uruguay Round market-access negotiations made significant strides in opening markets to trade in services. As with the case of impediments to trade in goods, however, liberalization mostly focused on areas of export interest to rich countries. Emphasis was placed on rights of establishment and on changes in domestic regulatory environments to provide access to foreign service providers. A key negotiating priority for developing countries — labour mobility — was dismissed by industrialized nations. To the extent that it was addressed at all, it was in the context of temporary access for accountants, lawyers and insurance executives, not freer entry for construction and other non-professional workers.

The import barriers of developed nations are only one aspect of the market access challenge facing the developing world. Their own import barriers is the other. As Winters (1999, p. 43) has observed: "countries are more affected by their own trade policies than by their partners', and, of course, it is the former over which they have the most influence". The largest gains from trade occur through the consumer savings that arise from reductions in domestic import barriers.

A comprehensive analysis of market access achievements made in the Uruguay Round by Finger and Schuknecht (1999) concludes that tariffs are disproportionally imposed by developing economies and the biases against exports from developing economies exist as much in developing economy tariffs as in tariffs of developed economies. Even after the reductions made in the Uruguay Round, developing country tariffs remain several times higher than rates levied by developed countries.[4]

A number of authors blame the General Agreement on Tariffs and Trade (GATT) concept of Special and Differential Treatment (SDT) for the persistence of high import barriers in developing nations (i.e., Bhagwati, 2001). The origins of SDT lie in development ideology of the 1950s and were popularized in the Singer-Prebisch thesis. It held that the protection of infant industries and preferential access to markets in the developed world was the only means to avoid a secular decline in the terms of trade of developing nations (Whalley, 1999). The extension of this idea, which was formally introduced in the Kennedy Round of GATT negotiations, was that developing countries should not have to reciprocate negotiating concessions made by other GATT members.

In many respects the SDT concept institutionalized the second-tier status of developing nations. In departing from fundamental GATT principles, it also allowed developed countries to get away with their own GATT-inconsistent practices such as the Multi-Fibre Agreement (Srinivasan, 1999, p. 1051). The result was that until the Uruguay Round, little progress was made in reducing trade barriers in developing countries. The reductions that did occur were often as a result of intervention by the World Bank, not through multilateral negotiations (Pangestu, 2000, p. 1290).

SDT is only part of the explanation for the south's reluctance to reduce import barriers. Many developing countries levy duties not for protective effect but as a second-best policy option. For countries with a rudimentary tax system, for example, customs duties are the cheapest and most effective way for governments to raise revenue. Countries that lack a competition policy regime use import duties to guard against anti-competitive behaviour on the part of foreign corporations (Whalley, 1999, p. 1091). Developing countries frequently lack the technical expertise and resources to implement the other policy changes that would make tariff reduction possible.

It was only in the latest round of trade negotiations that developing countries participated as full players in market access negotiations. Many have come to recognize the limitations of non-reciprocity and understand the

---

[4]Finger and Schuknecht (1999) have estimated the average post-Uruguay Round applied *ad valorem* tariff rate to be 2.6 per cent for developed economies and 13.3 per cent for developing economies.

Kathleen Macmillan

benefits of reducing their own import barriers. A number of difficulties remain, however, including the challenge of replacing government revenue lost as a result of tariff reductions. Developed countries can help by providing technical assistance in this area. However, the most important priority for future trade negotiations is reductions in barriers that rich countries maintain against imports from the developing world.[5] It is time to expand market access negotiations to include sectors that matter not only to rich countries but to poor countries also.

Textiles and Apparel

It is shameful for their wealthy trading partners to continue to maintain tariffs and quotas against the products for which the least-developed countries have a clear economic advantage. (Michael Moore, 2001)

In their accounting of U.S. trade barriers, Hufbauer and Elliott termed textile and clothing import restraints "the Mount Everest of U.S. trade protection".[6] The same could also be said for the clothing and textile barriers levied by other countries in the developed world. A combination of restrictive import quotas under the Multi-Fibre Arrangement (MFA) and high import duties levied by industrialized nations has frustrated developing country exporters for decades.

It is hard to find a more compelling north-south trade issue. Textile and apparel production is viewed as a critical "first" industry in the process of industrial development and accounts for roughly 20 per cent of industrialized

---

[5]Anne Krueger has advised developing countries to press for across-the-board, not zero-for-zero access in upcoming trade negotiations. This would ensure that developed countries do not resort to their traditional strategy of selecting only those sectors where they have a comparative advantage and removing the political pressure these sectors can exert for liberalization of other restrictions (Krueger, 1999).

[6]Hufbauer and Elliott (1994) estimated that clothing and apparel import barriers account for 9 per cent of the economic cost of trade protection in the United States.

exports from the developing world. Moreover, quantitative restrictions in textiles and clothing are almost exclusively targeted at products exported from the developing to the developed world. With minor exceptions, they do not affect trade between developed countries (Low and Yeats, 1995, p. 58).

Since the 1950s, developed countries have relied on "voluntary" export restraints negotiated on a bilateral basis with developing nations to limit their imports of textile and apparel products. Although it constituted a fundamental violation of GATT principles, quantitative restrictions on clothing and textile exports were formalized under GATT auspices in a series of "trading arrangements" made over the following two decades culminating in the MFA in 1974. The arrangement was extended in 1977, 1981, 1986 and 1991.

Despite the strong case for liberalization, progress has been painfully slow. Powerful producer lobbies in the OECD countries are only part of the explanation. The healthy rents accruing to MFA quota-holders in traditional exporting countries such as Hong Kong, Korea and Taiwan have made them staunch defenders of the status quo intent on keeping out newer producers from places like Bangladesh, Pakistan and India.

Although members agreed in the Uruguay Round to integrate textile and apparel products into the GATT 1994, true trade liberalization still remains a long way off. The implementation period is ten years in duration and little liberalization will occur until the very end. Phase-out requirements refer to import categories, not import volumes and countries have selected for early liberalization categories where no quota restrictions apply or import categories that face little competition from developing countries, such as yarns and fabrics. As an illustration, by January 1, 1998, 33 per cent of imports had to be brought under the GATT rules. The United States has met its obligations but in a way that eliminated only 1 per cent of its MFA commitments. The record for the European Union (EU) and Canada was somewhat better at 7 and 14 per cent respectively (Finger and Schuler, 1999).

The Uruguay Round negotiations instituted a system of transitional safeguards to cushion the effects of liberalization. The resulting mechanism to address import surges could end up being even more restrictive than the MFA quotas themselves (Hamilton and Whalley, 1995, p. 36). Developed countries have also maintained high rates of duty on textile and apparel imports and most have exempted clothing and textile products from the GSP and other tariff preferences that they offer developing nations.

Lest the combination of residual quota restrictions, high duties and transitional safeguards offers insufficient protection from textile and apparel imports from the developing world, rich countries can resort to the use of anti-dumping measures. Producers in the EU and the United States have already taken anti-dumping actions against a variety of textile products. It is expected that anti-dumping cases will multiply as the end of the implementation period approaches (Reinert, 2000, p. 41; Hamilton and Whalley, 1995).

Developed countries remain concerned that the West might renege entirely on its Uruguay Round commitments with respect to clothing and textiles (Reinert, 2000). Should this happen, it would amount to a monumental failure of the Uruguay Round in the eyes of the developing world.

Agriculture

Barriers to developing country exports in industrialized markets continue to severely disadvantage poor countries. Industrialized countries spend more than $300 billion a year on agricultural subsidies. That is roughly equal to the total GNP for all of Sub-Saharan Africa. And yet, even today developed country tariffs on meat, fruits, and vegetables — all primary exports from the developing world — can exceed 100 per cent. Debt relief without increased market access is a sham. (James D. Wolfensohn, 2001)

The notion that developing countries glean the preponderance of their earnings from farming and other primary industries is outdated. In fact, manufactured products account for over 70 per cent of the exports of developing countries and could rise to 80 per cent by 2005 (Hertel and Martin, 2000). Despite this, agriculture is perhaps the most critical sector for developing countries to address in the next round of multilateral trade negotiations. As Kym Anderson has noted, the welfare cost to developing countries of OECD agricultural policies is estimated to well exceed the cost of protection to the textile and clothing sector. For the world as a whole, agricultural policies are more damaging to economic welfare than are tariffs on industrial goods, despite agriculture's small share of global trade and GDP (Anderson, 1999, p. 3).

Farm subsidy and support programs in rich countries negate the natural comparative advantage developing countries have in the production of many basic agricultural commodities. Rice, sugar and peanuts are examples of goods that trade on world markets at prices well below domestic support price levels in industrialized nations. High trade barriers in developed countries shut out many food imports from the developing world. Domestic farm subsidies in developed nations create food surpluses that are sold in world markets, sometimes with the assistance of export subsidies, driving world prices to uneconomic levels. Food aid compounds the difficulties, particularly since rich countries are more inclined to donate food when prices are low and surpluses high, destroying any opportunity for local farmers in recipient countries to earn a fair return. The fact that many of the poor in the developing world live in farm households means that low and unstable global food prices affect a large proportion of their population.

The Uruguay Round succeeded in bringing agriculture within the general GATT framework. Theoretically, agriculture will be subject to the same general disciplines that apply to manufactured goods. In reality, however, the extent of liberalization is very limited. Average agricultural tariffs in the industrialized nations remain in the 40 to 50 per cent range while tariffs on manufactured goods have steadily fallen to the 4 per cent level over the past 50 years. Domestic subsidization is still permitted, although subject to certain constraints. While a variety of non-tariff barriers, such as Canada's import restrictions on dairy, poultry and other supply-managed commodities, were converted to tariffs, the outcome of tariffication was, in the view of one observer, "scandalous" (Srinivasan, 1999, p. 1053). The tariff on butter imports to Canada is over 300 per cent. Japan has implemented tariffs of over 1,000 per cent on some varieties of rice. Worse still, according to Hertel and Martin, is that the new tariff-rate-quotas (TRQs) are less transparent than the previous quota regimes and they generate significant quota rents. This will make future liberalization very difficult to accomplish (Hertel and Martin, 2000). Anderson (1999, p. 3) shares this view noting that the TRQs have created a new MFA — a multilateral food agreement — that could leave agricultural trade with quantitative restraints for decades to come.

Real progress on agricultural trade liberalization remains some distance away. Although the European Union made some conciliatory overtures in the lead-up to the Seattle WTO ministerial meeting, it remains committed to its interventionist Common Agricultural Policy. Governments such as the EU's and Japan's have garnered strong support at home for the notion that farm policy is critical to achieving a host of non-agricultural objectives such as the protection of rural communities, the humane treatment of animals, and proper environmental stewardship. They maintain that because of this so-called "multifunctional" dimension of farm policy, agriculture should not be subject to the same sort of disciplines that govern trade in industrial goods. Outbreaks of mad cow and other diseases have strengthened the call for border restrictions in developed countries. Concern over genetically-modified products, the so-called "frankenfoods", contribute to more trade impediments, not less. Like many other issues on the new trade agenda, developing nations view the West's concern for food safety and the "multifunctionality" of agriculture as thinly veiled attempts at protectionism.

It does not help that developing nations are not entirely agreed on the desirability of agricultural trade reform. Countries such as Brazil, Argentina and Thailand have pressed for improved access for their food exports. But importing nations, recognizing that high subsidies in developed countries lower their food costs, are more ambivalent. Preferential trade arrangements, such as the Lomé Convention that favours former European colonies, have made some privileged developing countries strong advocates for the status quo.

If agricultural trade reform is to have any success, it will need to form part of a broader package in future trade negotiations. Players such as the EU are strongly resistant to liberalization, despite the solid economic case for it. It is essentially the EU and United States that will determine the prospect and pace of agricultural trade liberalization. One would hope that they will keep the interests of the developing world in mind.

Anti-dumping

The fact that the WTO permits anti-dumping may make it sound respectable. It rarely is. (*The Economist,* October 3, 1998, p. 17)

Use of trade remedy laws, until now a prerogative of developed nations, undermines legitimate attempts to liberalize trade. In Stiglitz's view (2000, p. 439), nowhere is the hypocrisy of the developed world greater than when it comes to anti-dumping.

Dumping occurs when an exporter sells goods to a foreign market at less than the price it charges in its home market or at a price that does not fully cover its average total cost of production. The GATT allows an importing country to impose special duties on dumped imports that cause or threaten to cause material injury to its producers of the competing product. The duties remain in place for up to five years but can be renewed if a threat of injury continues to exist.

Economists have rarely understood the rationale for anti-dumping measures (see, for example, Boltuck and Litan, 1991; and Macmillan, 1995). Price discrimination is normal behaviour for profit-maximizing firms. It is only natural that price discrimination would occur across international borders, particularly since factors like tariff protection at home might warrant higher prices in the domestic market. Analyses of anti-dumping cases have concluded that only rarely would they qualify as genuine predatory pricing behaviour (Hutton and Trebilcock, 1992; Willig, 1998). Instead, anti-dumping has become a valuable weapon of corporate strategy for oligopolistic industries, particularly in the metals, chemical, machinery and textile sectors. The proliferation of anti-dumping actions by developed nations is an important factor behind Sylvia Ostry's (1990, p. 17) characterization of the 1980s as "the decade of the privatization of trade policy".

Anti-dumping measures are a highly effective protectionist tool. Typically, the duties imposed are many times higher than prevailing nominal tariff rates. It is not unusual to have anti-dumping duties in the 20 to 50 per cent range, sometimes higher. Almost always, the imposition of anti-dumping measures wipe out imports from affected countries and has a "chilling" effect on shipments from other countries. The information and legal demands for exporters hit by an anti-dumping action are extremely onerous and expensive. Quite often, developing country exporters targeted by anti-dumping actions do not even bother attempting to defend their interests.

Countries made a half-hearted attempt to address the interests of the developing world in the Uruguay Round negotiations on anti-dumping. The text of the WTO agreement stipulates that particular regard be given by developed country members to the special situation of developing country members when considering the application of anti-dumping duties. Competition policy solutions are suggested as an alternative. However, many countries, including Canada, have not even implemented this aspect of the Anti-dumping Agreement into their domestic legislation, let alone excused any developing country member of anti-dumping duties that would otherwise apply.

The use of anti-dumping measures continues unabated. According to the latest WTO Annual Report, WTO members notified 360 initiations of anti-dumping investigations in 1999, up 42 per cent over 1998. The European Union and India reported the highest number of initiations in 1999, 68 each, followed by the United States at 45 initiations. Despite the introduction in the WTO Anti-dumping Agreement of a five-year sunset clause in 1995, the accumulated stock of anti-dumping measures in existence continues to grow. In mid-2000, an estimated 1,211 final anti-dumping findings were in place worldwide, 300 of which were accounted for the United States and 190 by the European Union. Canada ranks fifth in the world for the number of anti-dumping measures levied, with 88 (WTO, 2001).

There is good reason to fear that matters will get worse before they get better. Anti-dumping has become entrenched in the world trading system with the recent introduction of legislation in many countries, including dozens of developing nations. Developing countries have learned well from their developed counterparts and have levied many actions against each other, with China being a favourite target. Anti-dumping measures, per dollar of imports, are now probably higher among developing nations than among developed nations (Finger and Schuknecht, 1999, p. 36).

An even greater concern for the future is that the anti-dumping system will be used by industrial countries as a way to escape liberalization commitments in other areas. There is already some indication that clothing and textile import restraints could be replaced with anti-dumping findings. The removal of quantitative restrictions and other non-tariff barriers could lead to a renewed interest in anti-dumping among producers in industrialized nations.

There is no shortage of creative ideas for reforming the anti-dumping system. Alternatives such as the use of import safeguards or competition policy measures have been advocated for years by trade policy analysts. What has been absent is the political will for reform, particularly in the United States. The fact that Canada and the United States with their similar domestic regulatory regimes cannot even agree to restrain the use of anti-dumping measures on bilateral trade does not bode well for the prospect of significant reforms at the multilateral level.

Intellectual Property

> The TRIPS does not involve mutual gain; rather, it positions the WTO primarily as a collector of intellectual property-related rents on behalf of multinational corporations. This is a bad image for the WTO.
> (Jagdish Bhagwati, 2001, p. 20)

Developing country members had little alternative but to go along with the WTO's Agreement on Trade-Related Intellectual Property (TRIP). WTO's "single undertaking" or "all or nothing" nature meant that members had to sign on to all its component agreements if they wanted to improve their market access in agriculture, textiles and other areas.

Developing nations also considered a multilateral agreement preferable to the unilateral pressure they were under from developed nations to enforce western-style intellectual property obligations. Under Section 301 of the U.S. 1988 *Trade and Competitiveness Act*, countries could be placed on a watch list for what was considered to be weak enforcement of intellectual property rights. The WTO's TRIP commitments had one important advantage over the unilateral U.S. measures: disputes arising under the TRIP Agreement would at least be handled by the WTO's dispute settlement provisions.

While developing nations held their noses and agreed to the TRIP commitments during the Uruguay Round, many have yet to implement the obligations. At the end of 2000, one year past the deadline contained in the WTO agreement, some 70 countries have still not brought their domestic laws and regulations into conformity with the TRIP requirements. Implementation of the TRIP commitments — or, more accurately, the failure to do so — has become an important symbol of North-South trade relations, post-Uruguay.

The South quickly began to regret its grand bargain — immediate implementation of Western-style intellectual property enforcement in return for the uncertain promise of improved market access and technical assistance sometime down the road. Many countries failed to appreciate at the time the tremendous burden involved in implementing intellectual property measures. In retrospect, it was simply unrealistic to expect that countries with little or no legal or regulatory tradition in this area could create a system within a few short years (Finger and Schuler, 1999).[7]

The very nature of the TRIP Agreement imposes an uneven burden on developing nations. Ciuriak (2001, pp. 257-258) notes that it represents a fundamental departure from the standard GATT approach in two important respects. First, unlike the old GATT which generally avoided pronouncing on matters of domestic regulation, the TRIP Agreement severs the implicit barrier between international and domestic policy. Second, Ciuriak observes that the TRIP Agreement departs from the typical practice followed in GATT tariff reductions of dictating symmetrical lowering of barriers to asymmetrical levels. Instead, it requires countries to institute asymmetrical reforms in their domestic policy regimes to achieve a uniform standard. Ostry sees this as part of a general shift from the *negative* regulation under the GATT — what governments must not do — to *positive* regulation — what governments must do (Ostry, 2001). Because they often begin with more rudimentary intellectual property policy regimes and a relative lack of policy resources, the implementation burden is especially difficult for developing nations.

The TRIP Agreement might have even more ominous consequences in the future for developing nations. In using the international trade system to address non-trade objectives, Ciuriak believes that the Agreement creates a dangerous precedent. It opens the door to embedding other non-trade matters such as labour and environmental goals in the WTO, a possibility that gravely concerns developing countries. In the view of many trade policy experts, intellectual property enforcement is a matter that might have been better left with the World Intellectual Property Organization to determine (see Bhagwati, 2001; Hufbauer, 2001; Srinivasan, 1999).

Others have asked even more basic questions about the fairness of requiring developing countries to enforce the property rights of western industrialists. According to Jeffery Sachs, a vast inequality in innovation and technology diffusion is the root cause of much of the global divide. This could be eased if rich countries showed more restraint in asserting intellectual property rights. Patent protection renders life-saving pharmaceuticals and seed varieties inaccessible to millions of impoverished citizens in the developing world. While an ad hoc solution has recently been found to make

---

[7]There are essentially three transition periods for the TRIPs Agreement: developed countries, by January 1, 1996; developing and transition economies, by January 1, 2000; and least-developed countries by January 1, 2006.

low-cost AIDS drugs available to highly infected African nations, other diseases remain untreated due to the prohibitive cost of patent medicines or because the rewards to pharmaceutical firms are too meager to interest them (Sachs, 2000).

Winters (1999, p. 59) has also expressed concern that the creation and rigorous enforcement of intellectual property rights at the WTO could discourage researchers from focusing on the problems of poorer nations. He advocates special measures to disseminate publicly funded technologies and to develop crop technologies and health products for the poor.

Developing countries are painfully aware that they often lack the necessary knowledge and technology to adequately provide for their citizens. Many view the rigorous enforcement of western intellectual property rights as limiting their access to this knowledge, perpetuating a world of "haves" and "have nots". A better balance needs to be found between the desire to reward genuine innovation and the diffusion of ideas that could dramatically improve the well-being of the world's poorest citizens. Arguably, the TRIP Agreement has not achieved this balance.

The New Trade Agenda

> Some lines will have to be drawn as to what is trade and trade-related policy — and what is not. Several, if not many, of the issues that have been brought into the realm of trade policy issues are in fact broadly *trade-unrelated*. Continuing to deal with them in a trade context is damaging to the cause of getting developing countries to support a new round. (Jagdish Bhagwati, 2001, p. 20)

A disconnect has emerged between the trade policy objectives of the developing and developed world, post-Uruguay. Developing nations are preoccupied with implementation matters and remain committed to expanding market access. The West is considering expanding the scope of trade agreements to encompass social, environmental and other "values" issues. In reaction to pressures from non-governmental organizations and representatives of civil society at home, western governments are also debating ways to make the WTO a more open and democratic institution.

One area where the developing world stands united is in opposition to the "trade and ..." initiatives. Former President Clinton's support for the idea of trade sanctions to enforce core labour standards was a major reason behind the failure of the WTO's Seattle ministerial meeting. Equally unpalatable to developing nations is the attempt to link trade and the environment. In their view, using the trading system to impose the West's environmental or labour standards is simple protectionism that is designed to undermine their comparative advantage.

Developing countries will strongly resist the introduction of labour and environmental standards into WTO Agreements and will likely object to any other "values" standards that depend on extraterritorial application of domestic norms. Their position is that these matters are best left to the relevant international body to administer. For its part, the U.S. Congress appears to consider labour and environmental standards as part of its trade agenda and has pressured the administration to include them in its recent pact with Jordan. This does not bode well for a new round of multilateral trade negotiations or, indeed, for bridging the North-South divide.

Another element of the new trade agenda that developing countries greet with scepticism is the bid to "democratize" the WTO. On the one hand, they welcome measures to improve the WTO's "internal democracy" by wrestling control over key policy decisions from the small group of western nations that previously reigned. What they decry, however, are proposals to open WTO dispute settlement and committee meetings to non-governmental representatives (Bhagwati, 2001). They fear, with some reason, that the chief preoccupation of non-governmental organizations intervening before the WTO would be social and environmental considerations. Poorer nations view the deference that countries like Canada and the United States accord representatives of "civil society" with a measure of curiosity and mistrust.

There is no doubt that the WTO needs to evolve as an institution if it is to remain relevant and effective. It is equally true that it cannot avoid addressing domestic regulation if it is to liberalize trade in important areas such as services and investment. However, the issues that divide developed and developing nations are considerably larger when it comes to the new trade agenda than in the more traditional areas of trade policy. They raise matters of governance and national values and, as such, are highly sensitive.

Trade-Related Assistance

> The transition periods for implementation for developing countries were arbitrary and not based on any analysis or, indeed, on any awareness of [the] system problem. (Sylvia Ostry, 2000, p. 6)

Developing nations have missed out on many of the benefits of participation in the multilateral trading system because they lack the resources to take advantage of them. Assistance is needed in several areas: to help implement the commitments they have already made, for trade adjustment, to represent their interests in trade disputes, to participate in future rounds of trade negotiations and to reform their policies and regulations to better capitalize on the new opportunities created by trade liberalization.

As Ostry (1999, p. 21) has written, the one common element characterizing the new WTO issues is that they all deal with the institutional structure of domestic economies. As with negotiations on competition policy, financial services, e-commerce and investment, this necessarily infringes on areas of domestic regulation. Obligations to increase institutional transparency and reform domestic regulations gravely concern developing nations. And it is more than simply an issue of resources. Developing nations often lack the long history of institutional development that OECD nations have shared. In many instances, they are required to implement in several short years western-style legal and institutional systems that evolved over many centuries in the western nations themselves.

The most immediate issue is that of implementation. Finger and Schuler (1999) estimate that the cost of implementing the WTO Agreements can easily exceed the entire development budget of a least-developed nation. It is many times greater than the burden that implementation represents for developed country members since the disciplines being imposed closely reflect the status quo in industrialized nations.

Another issue is that of trade adjustment. Rich countries agonize over trade adjustment pressures affecting their textiles, apparel, steel and agriculture sectors. These pale in comparison to the challenges facing countries in the developing world. As Stiglitz (2000, p. 440) points out, trade adjustment in developing countries is inhibited by many factors including government rigidities, rigidities in labour markets and lack of access to capital. These matters have to be addressed if trade liberalization is to succeed. The

Kathleen Macmillan

standard competitiveness paradigm that applies in OECD economies does not always work in the developing world.

Help is also needed to allow developing country members to participate in trade negotiations and represent their interests in trade disputes. More than one-half of the WTO's developing country members cannot even afford to have a full-time representative in Geneva. The WTO's dispute-settlement mechanism, while much welcomed by developing nations, is too expensive for many to access. Often, developing countries lack the money and expertise to properly defend their own interests in WTO disputes or to participate in other disputes where important issues of principle are being decided.

In recent years, international institutions have recognized that trade assistance needs to be supported by programs to back institutional and regulatory reform and development of social and physical infrastructure. Basic issues of governance need to be addressed and reforms undertaken to improve legal systems, infrastructure and private sector capabilities. The WTO's own resources for trade-assistance are meager, in the range of US$ 500,000 per year. International institutions have tried to improve coherence in recent years through initiatives such as "The Integrated Framework for Trade-Related Assistance to Least Developed Countries". Unfortunately, the resources are still insufficient and their mandates ambiguous. Moreover, many of the measures are aimed solely at the least-developed countries when it is all the nations of the developing world that require technical and institutional resources.

The failure to provide adequate trade-related assistance for developing countries was one of the greatest shortfalls of the Uruguay Round. More resources and a better appreciation of the implementation and adjustment burden facing developing countries is necessary if they are to become full partners in the multilateral trading system.

Conclusion

As many trade experts often point out, the WTO is not a development agency. That argument is true but irrelevant, because trade is not trade today. And the new focus on domestic policy and institutions creates spillover and linkages among policy domains and international institutions that never existed in the GATT. Thus, the implications of the grand bargain for the evolution of the WTO are profound and deserve far more analysis than has been provided to date. (Sylvia Ostry, 2000, p. 15)

The legitimacy of the WTO depends critically on its ability to achieve a better balance between its developed and developing country members. Multilateral trade relations have deteriorated sharply post-Uruguay with the refusal by many developing countries to implement Uruguay Round commitments and the very meagre progress in services and agricultural negotiations. It is up to developing country members, and particularly the influential "Quad" group of countries which includes Canada, to take up the challenge. Not only is a greater concern for the trade aspirations of developing countries the right thing to do from a development perspective but it is also essential to the future success of the multilateral trading system.

The challenge is particularly relevant for the Canadian government, which is already under scrutiny for cutting back the budget of the Canadian International Development Agency during the 1990s.[8] Like the other industrialized countries, Canada does not allow international development officials much, if any, role in trade policy-making. The fact that the foreign aid and trade policy realms operate in virtual isolation is one reason why development issues are rarely taken into account in the trade policy of developed countries.

There is much work to be done. Import barriers in developed country markets disproportionately penalize exports from the developing world. The West has held out promise that agricultural and textile barriers will drop sometime in the future, but only in return for the immediate implementation of intellectual property regimes and reforms in other areas such as customs valuation, import-licensing, and technical, sanitary and phyto-sanitary standards in developing nations. Poorer countries have been left largely on their own without outside technical resources to make the considerable changes to their domestic institutions and regulations that their WTO commitments require. Developed countries have steadfastly held onto their protectionist weapon of choice — anti-dumping measures — the use of which can obliterate the effects of trade liberalization in other areas. Moreover, the WTO threatens to evolve into a more transparent and democratic institution by allowing representations from NGOs, many of whom are intent

---

[8]OECD figures ranked Canada's aid budget relative to the size of its economy as seventeenth out of 22 donor countries in 2000 (*The Globe and Mail*, April 27, 2001).

Kathleen Macmillan

on expanding agreements to include non-trade considerations like social and environmental standards which could undermine the comparative advantage of poorer countries.

The elements of a fairer trade system are quite obvious: the removal of tariff and non-tariff barriers on imports from the developing world, reform of domestic agricultural programs, generous financial assistance and assistance in kind to developing nations to help them with implementation and trade adjustment, a substantial weakening of anti-dumping regimes and the refusal to include labour and other "values" standards in WTO Agreements.

Sadly, trade policy has very little to do with fairness nor, indeed, with economic efficiency. If economic principles prevailed in trade policy-making, all countries would abandon protectionism unilaterally for domestic economic reasons. Instead, trade policy-making is dominated by special interests and, up until now, has represented a balance between the demands of import-competing interests for protection and the desire of powerful exporters in industrialized nations for greater market access. The interests of developing nations have not been well served by what has essentially been a mercantilist bargaining model.

Previous rounds of trade negotiations have not been entirely devoid of non-economic objectives, however. The desire to provide a basis for a lasting peace was the major consideration behind the creation of the GATT in the postwar period. If it is to succeed, the WTO needs a unifying mission that is more persuasive than merely economics. As Ostry points out in this volume, Canada has played a lead role on many previous occasions mobilizing middle-power support for difficult negotiations (Ostry, 2001). It is hard to imagine a more worthy political, economic and humanitarian cause for Canada to champion than a WTO that better addresses the interests of the developing world. This must begin by acknowledging the degree to which trade policy in the West has disadvantaged those that are already disadvantaged.

References

Anderson, K. (1999), "Agriculture, Developing Countries and the WTO Millennium Round", paper prepared for the World Bank's Conference on Agriculture and the New Trade Agenda from a Development Perspective (Geneva: WTO Secretariat).

Bhagwati, J. (2001), "What Will It Take to Get Developing Countries into a New Round of Trade Negotiations", *Trade Policy Research 2001* (Ottawa: Minister of Public Works and Government Services).

Boltuck, R.D. and R.E. Litan, eds. (1991), *Down in the Dumps: Administration of the Unfair Trade Laws* (Washington, DC: The Brookings Institution).

Ciuriak, D. (2001), "The 'Trade and' Agenda: Are We at a Crossroads?" *Trade Policy Research 2001* (Ottawa: Minister of Public Works and Government Services).

The Economist (1998), "Survey of World Trade: Time for Another Round", October 3.

Finger, J.M. and R. Schuknecht (1999), "Market Access Advances and Retreats: The Uruguay Round and Beyond", World Bank Conference on Development Economics, April.

Finger, J.M. and P. Schuler (1999), *Implementation of Uruguay Round Commitments: The Development Challenge,* World Bank Policy Research Working Paper (Washington, DC: The World Bank).

The Globe and Mail (2001), "Canada's Development Aid Ranked among Least Generous in World", *The Globe and Mail*, April 27.

Hamilton, C. and J. Whalley (1995), "Evaluating the Impact of the Uruguay Round Results on Developing Countries", *The World Economy* 18(1), 31-49.

Hertel, T. and W. Martin (2000), "Liberalising Agriculture and Manufactures in a Millennium Round: Implications for Developing Countries", *The World Economy* 23(4), 455-469.

Hufbauer, G.C. (2001), "Trade and Coherence: Where the Major Gains Lie", *Trade Policy Research 2001* (Ottawa: Minister of Public Works and Government Services).

Hufbauer, G.C. and K.A. Elliott (1994), *Measuring the Costs of Protection in the United States* (Washington, DC: Institute for International Economics).

Hutton, S. and M.J. Trebilcock (1992), *An Empirical Study of the Application of Canadian Antidumping Laws: A Search for Normative Rationales* (Toronto: Ontario Centre for International Business).

Krueger, A.O. (1999), *Developing Countries and the Next Round of Multilateral Trade Negotiations,* Working Paper No. 2118 (Washington, DC: World Bank).

Low, P. and A. Yeats (1995), "Nontariff Measures and Developing Countries: Has the Uruguay Round Leveled the Playing Field?" *The World Economy* 18(1), 51-70.

Lukas, A. (2000), "WTO Report Card III: Globalization and Developing Countries", *Cato Institute Trade Briefing Paper* (Washington DC: Cato Institute), 15.

Macmillan, K. (1995), "Antidumping: Next on the Trade Agenda", *Canadian Business Economics* 3(3), 20-28.

Max, K.D. (2001), "Addressing Trade-Related Development Needs: Options for the Donor Community", *Trade Policy Research 2001* (Ottawa: Public Works and Government Services), 52-70.

Moore, M. (2001), "Coherence in Global Economic Policy-Making: WTO Cooperation with the IMF and World Bank", speech to WTO General Council, January 18 (Geneva: WTO).

Ostry, S. (1990), "Antidumping: The Tip of the Iceberg", in M.J. Trebilcock and R.C. York (eds.), *Fair Exchange: Reforming Trade Remedy Laws*, C.D. Howe Institute Policy Study No. 11 (Toronto: C.D. Howe Institute).

_____ (1999), "Coherence in Global Policy-Making: Is this Possible?" *Canadian Business Economics* 7(3).

_____ (2000), "The Uruguay Round North-South Grand Bargain: Implications for Future Negotiations", paper presented to conference on the Political Economy of International Trade Law, University of Minnesota, September.

_____ (2001), "WTO Membership for China: To Be and Not To Be: Is That the Answer?" in this volume.

Pangestu, M. (2000), "Special and Differential Treatment in the Millennium: Special for Whom and How Different?" *World Economy* 23(9), 1285-1302.

Reinert, K.A. (2000), "Give Us Virtue, But Not Yet: Safeguard Actions Under the Agreement on Textiles and Clothing", *The World Economy* 23(1), 25-55.

Sachs, J. (2000), "A New Map of the World", *The Economist*, July 22.

Sachs, J. and A. Warner (1995), "Economic Reform and the Process of Global Integration", *Brookings Papers on Economic Activity* 0(1), 1-95.

Srinivasan, T.N. (1999), "Developing Countries in the World Trading System: From GATT 1947 to the Third Ministerial Meeting of the WTO, 1999", *The World Economy* 22(8), 1047-1064.

Stiglitz, J.E. (2000), "Two Principles for the Next Round or, How to Bring Developing Countries in from the Cold", *The World Economy* 23(4), 438-439.

Whalley, J. (1999), "Special and Differential Treatment in the Millennium Round", *World Economy* 22(8), 1065-1093.

Willig, B. (1998), "Antidumping: What Does the Evidence Show?" in R.Z. Lawrence (ed.), *Brookings Trade Forum* (Washington, DC: The Brookings Institution).

Winters, L.A. (1999), "Trade and Poverty: Is There a Connection?" *Trade, Income Disparity and Poverty*, WTO Special Studies 5 (Geneva: World Trade Organization).

Wolfensohn, J.D. (2001), "The Challenges of Globalization: The Role of the World Bank", Address to the Public Discussion Forum, Berlin, Germany, April 2.

World Trade Organization (WTO) (2001), *Annual Report* (Geneva: World Trade Organization).

Where Are They Now?
Migration Patterns for Graduates of the University of British Columbia

John F. Helliwell and David F. Helliwell

Introduction

Records of university graduates provide a promising source of new information on domestic and international migration of the highly skilled. If it is possible to keep track of a high enough proportion of a university's graduates, then their locations, classified by degree and year of graduation, can provide a valuable history of migration patterns. When the Alumni Association of the University of British Columbia (UBC) asked us to assist

The analysis in this paper, which was prepared for the "Re-Thinking the Line" Conference, Vancouver, October 25, 2000, was initiated at the request of the UBC Alumni Association. Thanks are due to the Alumni Association for compiling the addresses of alumni, to Alan Marchant, to the UBC Faculty of Graduate Studies, and to Statistics Canada for supplementary data and advice. An earlier abbreviated report on the project was published as Helliwell and Helliwell (2000). We are grateful for research support from the Social Sciences and Humanities Research Council, and from the UBC Hampton Fund. Interpretations and opinions are those of the authors.

them in analyzing the results of a survey of graduates currently living outside Canada, we were immediately attracted by the possibilities for enriching the amount and quality of data relating to the migration of the highly educated. We concluded that the survey results could best be interpreted in the context of the overall trends and patterns of the distribution of graduates.

This paper summarizes the results of our research in several stages. First we present the location data by degree type and year of graduation, with graduates classified according to whether they are living in British Columbia (BC), in the rest of Canada (ROC), in the United States, or in the rest of the World (ROW). This first analysis of the patterns and trends evident in the data is followed by analysis using statistical models of migration to show the importance of distance, population size, income differentials and national borders as determinants of the locations chosen by UBC graduates. Then we will consider the extent to which the data for the graduates are consistent with aggregate migration patterns, and whether the UBC experience is likely to be indicative of what would be found if similar research were available for other universities. We then discuss the responses to the Alumni Association survey of UBC graduates living outside Canada. Our concluding section summarizes the results and suggests issues that seem to require or invite further research.

Geographic Distribution by Degree

The current location of all UBC bachelor's graduates by year of graduation, starting in 1930, is shown in Figure 1. There is a four-way distribution of locations in all of the figures shown in this section. We use the proportionate distribution to remove the strong upward trends in actual numbers, caused both by the growth of BC population and the increasing fraction of the population obtaining higher education.

About two-thirds of UBC graduates of the 1930s and 1940s live in British Columbia, with about 15 per cent in the United States, an equal number in the rest of Canada, and a sprinkling over the rest of the world. By 1950 a downward trend has started to appear in the share living in the United States, matched by an increasing share going to the rest of Canada. By the late 1950s the ROC share is more than twice that going to the United States. From 1960 on, there is an increase in the share of UBC bachelor's degree

John F. Helliwell and David F. Helliwell

Figure 1: Current Location of UBC Bachelor's Graduates 1930 to 1997

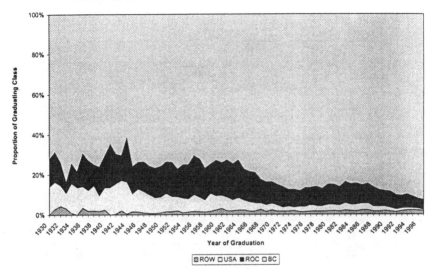

Year of Graduation

ROW □USA ■ROC □BC

holders staying in BC, so that more than 85 per cent of UBC's mid-1970s bachelor's degree graduates are still living in BC in the late 1990s, with about 10 per cent in the rest of Canada, 3 per cent in the United States, and 2 per cent in the ROW. For the 1980s graduates, there are slight increases in all of the shares living outside BC, with that trend being reversed again in the 1990s. For 1990s grads, roughly 90 per cent live in BC, 6 per cent in the rest of Canada, and 2 per cent each in the United States and the rest of the world.

Figures 2 through 15 show the current locations of the holders of UBC's undergraduate and graduate degrees. These figures start in different years, according to when each program or degree achieved sufficient numbers of graduates for each subsequent year.[1] Figures 2 and 3 show the locations of the holders of degrees from the two largest degree groups, the Bachelor of Arts and the Bachelor of Science. The figures start in 1960, since before that time the Faculty of Arts and Sciences was a single unit, with less clear demarcation between degrees in the sciences and those in the humanities and social sciences. The two degrees follow similar patterns of distribution,

---

[1]An appendix showing the total number of degrees granted for each program and each year is available from the authors on request.

Where Are They Now?   *293*

Figure 2: Current Location of UBC Bachelor of Arts Graduates 1950 to 1997

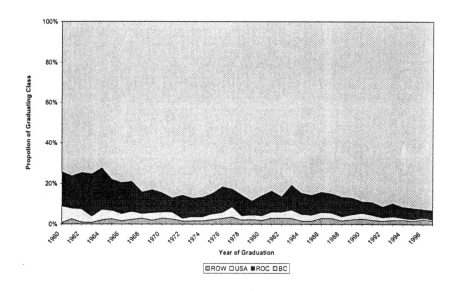

Figure 3: Current Location of BSc Graduates

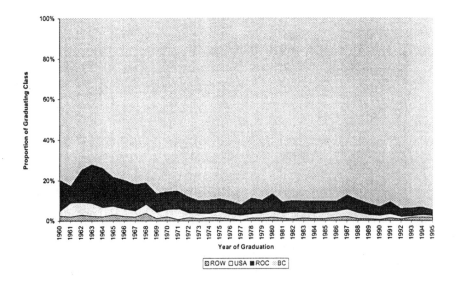

John F. Helliwell and David F. Helliwell

which in both cases are similar to those described for the totals in Figure 1. Figures 4 through 7 show bachelor's degrees in applied science, education, commerce and law. Since the number of graduates is large enough, the figures for engineering, commerce and law go back as far as 1950. For education, the number of graduates was very small in the 1950s, so Figure 5 starts in 1960. Figure 4 shows that more than two-thirds of the engineering grads of all decades still live in BC, with the proportion rising with each decade, so that more than 90 per cent of the 1990s grads are in BC. The proportion living in the rest of Canada has the largest downward trend over the decades, with the U.S. share always being small but declining only slightly over the decades. The rest of the world's share has generally been larger than the U.S. share.

Figure 5 for education shows the striking extent to which teachers, at least those trained in British Columbia, remain living and working in the province. The proportions living in the United States and the rest of the world have seldom been as high as 1 per cent each, and have generally shrunk over the decades. The proportion living in the rest of Canada has averaged about 5 per cent, with an upwards movement, to almost 10 per cent, for graduates in the first half of the 1990s.

The distribution of commerce grads, shown in Figure 6, is rather similar to that shown for engineers, with the exception of the rising ROW share in the 1990s. This is related to the increasing share of commerce students originally from Asia, and especially Hong Kong and Singapore, who have returned there to live and work after graduation.

Figure 7 shows that the large majority, averaging almost 90 per cent, of UBC LLBs living in British Columbia, with almost all of the remainder living in the rest of Canada. The proportion living in the rest of Canada shows bulges for the graduates of the 1960s and the 1990s.

Figures 8 and 9 show the main health science degrees, the bachelor's degree in nursing and the MD degree, respectively. In both cases there are substantial drops over time in the share of graduates living in the United States. However, the two health professions show quite different patterns for the shares of graduates living elsewhere. For BSNs, for which the data start in the 1960s, when the program first attained significant scale, the U.S.-resident share has dropped from 9 per cent for 1960s grads to less than 4 per cent for 1980s grads and less than 2 per cent for 1990s grads. There has been a parallel drop in the larger proportion living elsewhere in Canada, which falls from 17 per cent for 1960s grads to 4 per cent for 1990s grads. The MDs also show a large drop in the U.S.-resident share, from 12 per cent

Figure 4: Current Location of BASc Graduates

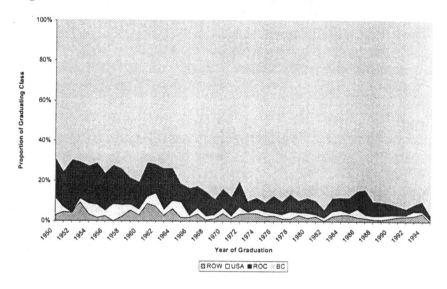

Figure 5: Current Location of BEd Graduates

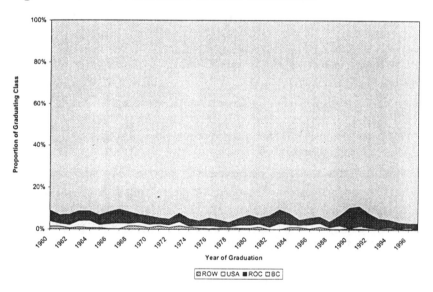

John F. Helliwell and David F. Helliwell

Figure 6: Current Location of BCom Graduates

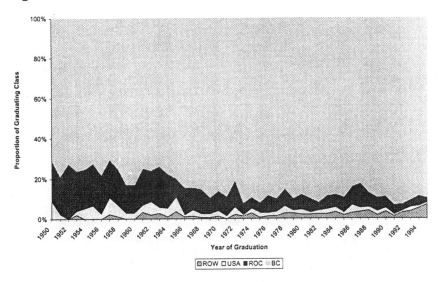

Figure 7: Current Location of LLB Graduates

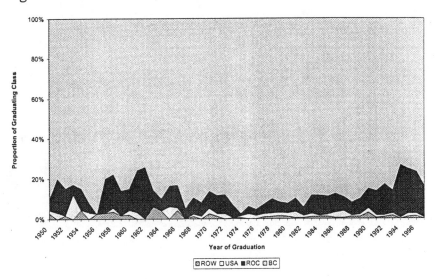

Figure 8: Current Location of BSN Graduates

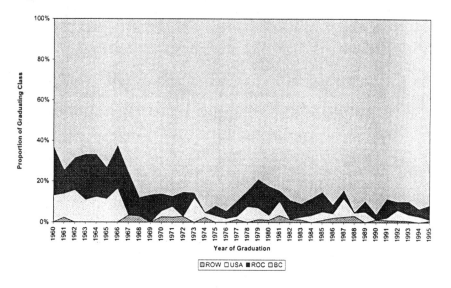

Figure 9: Current Location of Medical Graduates

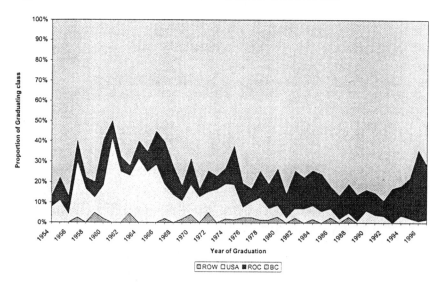

for 1950s grads to 4 per cent for 1980s grads and 3 per cent for 1990s grads. But there has been a substantial increase of the share living in the rest of Canada, which is 8 per cent for 1950s grads, rising to 15 per cent for 1980s grads and 18 per cent for 1990s grads. The pattern for MDs probably reflects, among other things, the extent to which there have been increases in the scale and quality of specialist post-graduate medical training in Canada. Students who go away for training also make contacts, friends and often families while there, and sometimes put down roots there as well. Thus the shift from U.S. to ROC residence is likely to reflect the shift from U.S. to Canadian locations for post-graduate medical training over the past four decades. The 1990s grads, of course, include many who are still in the midst of their residencies and specialist training, and have yet to choose the locations where they will practice.

In Figures 10 through 15, the spotlight turns to the graduate degrees. The graduate student populations are drawn from all over, and are correspondingly likely to go farther afield after graduation. They are also much more likely than are students in bachelor's or professional degrees to be employed in teaching and research during the course of their studies. There is a systematic database available for the citizenship of the incoming master's and doctoral classes for 1993 to 1997, but unfortunately nothing comparable for earlier years or for the bachelor's programs. The citizenship data reveal that the master's students are much more likely to be Canadian citizens than are the PhD students, and Figures 10 through 15 show that they are also more likely to be living in Canada after their graduation. Of the roughly 4,500 students who entered UBC master's degree programs 1993–98, 62 per cent were Canadian citizens, compared to 46 per cent of the 1,300 PhD entrants. Figures 14 and 15 show that similar, but slightly higher, proportions of 1990s master's and PhD graduates are now resident in British Columbia, and much higher proportions resident somewhere in Canada, roughly 85 per cent for master's grads and 75 per cent for PhDs. Figures 10 to 13 show the distribution of locations of residence for the graduates of the largest master's programs. The patterns generally match that for the total, although for engineers the decline of the U.S. and rest-of-Canada shares is most evident, just as it was for the undergrad engineers. For both master's and PhD programs there is thus a substantial net flow of foreign citizens into Canadian residence. Many of these students would have established their Canadian residence before undertaking graduate work, although the current data do not permit the extent of this to be measured. In addition, of course,

Where Are They Now?

Figure 10: Current Location of MA Graduates

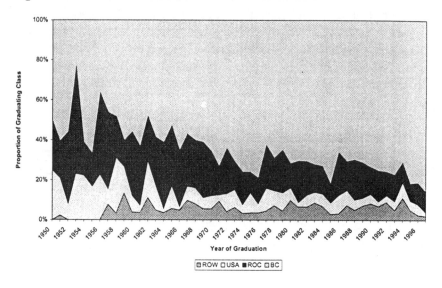

Figure 11: Current Location of MSc Graduates

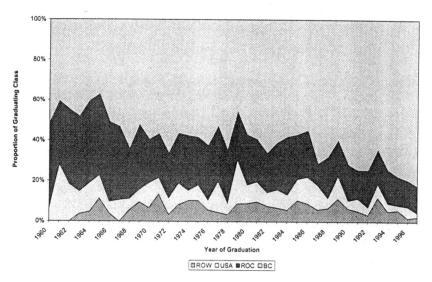

John F. Helliwell and David F. Helliwell

Figure 12: Current Location of MASc Graduates

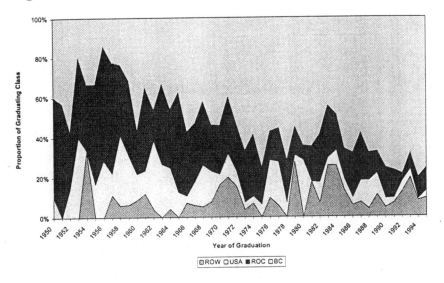

Figure 13: Current Location of MBAs 1970 to 1997

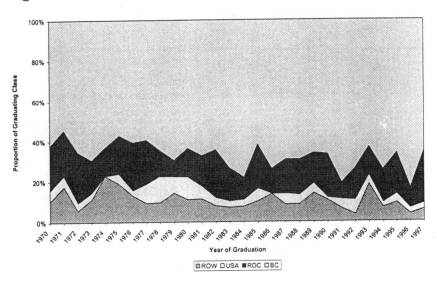

Figure 14: Location of UBC Master's Graduates

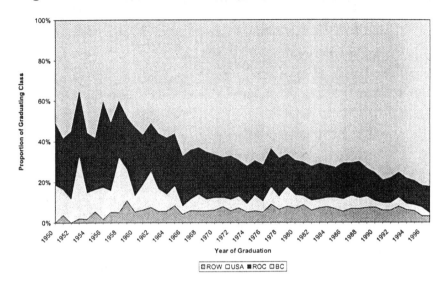

Figure 15: Current Location of PhD Graduates

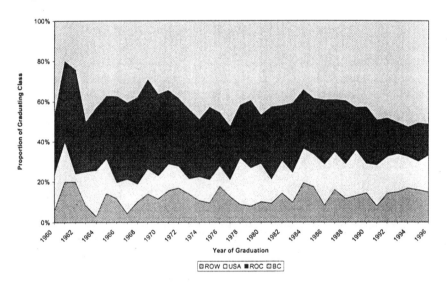

John F. Helliwell and David F. Helliwell

the students covered by the 1993–98 entry class data are not the same individuals as the 1990s graduates, since the latter generally started and finished earlier. However, there is a large overlap, and the general distribution patterns of entrants have remained fairly stable over the period for which data are available, so that the citizenship patterns for the 1990s grads are likely to match fairly closely those of the 1993–98 intake.

There is some evidence of a net pass-through effect, of foreign students receiving PhD degrees at UBC and then moving to the United States for employment. U.S. citizens represent 7 per cent of PhD entrants, while the United States is the current residence of more than 15 per cent of 1990s UBC PhD graduates. There is no similar pattern in master's degrees, where the U.S. citizenship share among entrants (6 per cent) is larger than the share of 1990s master's degree recipients now living in the United States. It is reasonable that the magnet effect of the United States should be larger for PhDs than for master's degrees, since the PhD is a specialized degree, with positions scattered widely, with concentrations in areas with many well-funded research institutions, such as in Massachusetts and California. Since the U.S. population is more than 80 times that of British Columbia, and the total of teaching and research positions much more than 100 times as great, it is remarkable that there are roughly three times as many of UBC's 1990s PhDs resident in BC as in the United States. Many PhD graduates scan the world as a whole for possible positions after their graduation, while no doubt some others set down roots where they receive their training, as was suggested earlier for the case of medical post-graduate training. Later research will analyze the extent to which graduate students' countries of origin are linked to their post-degree choices of residence and employment. For some students, the PhD is a ticket to the outside world, with no return ever planned, while others no doubt arrive, or are sent, in the expectation that they will return home at some stage to their original countries of citizenship.

Among the intake classes, there is evidence of a strong China/Hong Kong linkage, with more than 10 per cent of master's intake and 13 per cent of PhDs holding citizenship from China, Chinese Taiwan or Hong Kong. The Commonwealth ties also appear to be strong, as the per capita representation of students from Australia, New Zealand and the United Kingdom is more than three times that for the United States, even without taking account of the fact that the distances to UBC are far greater for the Commonwealth students. We turn now to consider more systematically the effects of distance and other factors in determining the place of residence of UBC grads from different degrees and decades.

Factors Influencing Migration Trends and Patterns

We have two sorts of evidence to report in this section, statistical analysis based on the data already described in Figures 1 through 15, and the responses submitted to the questionnaire aimed at non-resident UBC graduates. The statistical analysis will receive most of our attention, because it covers a large majority of all of UBC's graduates, wherever they may be living, and because the responses to the survey questions are summarized in a later section.[2]

The central device we use to explain the geographic distribution of UBC graduates is the gravity model of migration. The theory and related literature are described elsewhere (see Helliwell, 1998, especially ch. 5), but the central idea is simple, and the results are fairly straightforward to interpret. The basic gravity model of economic and social interaction, true to its Newtonian namesake, hypothesizes that the intensity of trade, social interaction and migration between two cities, countries or regions increases with their size and decreases with the distance separating them. In Newton's version, these effects are all proportional, so the interaction increases proportionately with the product of the sizes of the two bodies and decreases proportionately with the distance between them. This translates into an equation that is linear in logarithms. When this is applied to migration or trade data, the extent of the proportionality is estimated rather than assumed on theoretical grounds.

When we apply the model to the determination of place of residence of UBC graduates, we measure the size of the destination region by its population, and measure its economic attractiveness by its income per capita. Distance is measured by the distance separating UBC from the destination in question. We have restricted our analysis to UBC grads living in Canada and the United States, since those living in the rest of the world are spread among so many countries that there are generally too few observations for each country to make statistical analysis reliable. We divide the U.S.-resident grads among the 50 states and the District of Columbia, and the Canadian grads among the ten provinces. For each equation we eliminate those observations representing states or provinces where there are no resident UBC

---

[2]The detailed survey results are also available from the authors on request.

John F. Helliwell and David F. Helliwell

grads of the decade or degree in question. Our desire to keep the sample large enough to produce significant results has therefore led us to restrict our main equations presented to those covering major degree types, and by decades for the largest degree type. Our early results showed that the distribution patterns were quite different as between bachelor's, master's and PhDs. The change in distribution patterns from decade to decade proved to be significant only for bachelor's degrees. Both of these main statistical results were foreshadowed by the patterns in Figures 1 through 15. What we can gain in addition from our statistical work is some idea of the determinants of the patterns as well as measures of the extent to which the visible patterns are statistically significant.

Table 1 shows our results for the distribution of all UBC grads among states of the United States and provinces of Canada, with separate equations for each of the three major degree types.[3] The dependent variable in each case is the logarithm of the number of UBC grads of the type in question resident in a particular state or province, and the independent variables include the logarithms of distance, per capita income, and population. Because earlier research has shown that migration is much more likely within a country than across national borders, even after allowing for the effects of distance, we add a variable called Canada, which takes the value of one for each of the Canadian provinces. To test for the possibility that UBC grads also have a preference for remaining in British Columbia (perhaps reflecting their place of birth and the locus of family, social and professional contacts), we also add a variable that takes a value of one for the BC row in the matrix.

Several patterns are evident in the results shown in Table 1. We already saw, from Figures 1 through 15, that the holders of graduate degrees were more likely to be widely spread. We could not tell at that stage why this was the case, although we inferred that it was primarily because graduate students come from farther away in the first place, so that going far away after graduation is likely to be a return home. In our equation, we cannot adjust for the differing mixes of incoming students, since we do not have the necessary information. However, we can see that there is a steady decrease

---

[3]The three equations are estimated as a system, using the Zellner SUR estimator, as implemented in the SHAZAM statistical package. Since the three equations are estimated as a system, they need to have the same number of observations. Thus any destination is excluded unless it has at least one of UBC's bachelor's, master's or PhD degree holders.

Table 1: Distribution of UBC Alumni among States and Provinces (by degree type)

	ln(distance)	ln(y/capita)	ln(pop)	Canada	BC	R^2
Bachelor's	-0.97	1.74	0.92	3.84	1.50	0.91
	(7.4)	(5.0)	(11.2)	(15.4)	(2.1)	
Master's	-0.75	1.55	0.79	3.7	1.1	0.87
	(5.4)	(4.0)	(8.7)	(13.4)	(1.3)	
PhD	-0.43	0.98	0.74	3.1	1.29	0.86
	(3.4)	(3.0)	(9.5)	(12.8)	(1.8)	

Note: Absolute values of t-statistics are shown in parentheses below the coefficients. There are 54 observations for each equation.

in the effects of distance, income per capita, and population size as one moves from the bachelor's through the master's to the PhD results. We also find that the preference for other provinces relative to the United States, as indicated by the size of the Canada coefficient, drops as the level of degree increases. This could be entirely due to the more international citizenship mix of the graduate degrees, although it may also reflect differing patterns of job availability.

The results for distance, income and population are consistent, and are likely to have similar underlying explanations. As already discussed, higher levels of education tend to provide more specialized skills, with a corresponding reduction in the number of available jobs in any particular region. To obtain a job in one's specialty is likely to require a longer move the higher the degree of specialization. Thus, it is no surprise to find that the effect of distance drops steadily as the degree level rises. The distance effect for PhDs is less than half as large as that for bachelor's, with the effect for master's in between, but closer to the bachelor's effect.

The effect of income differentials is also markedly different by degree type. All three types of degree holders are significantly drawn towards states or provinces with higher per capita incomes, but these effects are much larger for bachelor's than for PhDs, with the master's in between. There are likely to be three reasons for this: many of those entering PhD programs have already opted for specialized research over higher income options, the distribution of research and teaching positions does not match per capita

John F. Helliwell and David F. Helliwell

income differences very closely, and there may also be a loose relation between research salaries and general income levels within a state or province. PhDs are thus more likely to go where their research interests take them, with relative income levels relegated to a lesser role. For bachelor's, the relative income effects are large and significant, with a 1 per cent increase in a state or province's income per capita being associated with a 1.7 per cent larger number of UBC graduates. For master's degree holders, the income differences are also large and significant, although smaller than for bachelor's. Interestingly, and supportive of the results for the PhD grads, when the master's grads are split between the more research-oriented programs (MA and MSc) and the master's degrees with a more professional focus, the relative income effect is significantly higher for the holders of professional degrees than for the more research-oriented degrees.

Table 2 shows the significance of the coefficient differences discussed above. As already noted, the differences between the bachelor's and PhD results are most marked, with all the coefficient differences except the BC border effect being significant. For the master's, the relative income and border effects are insignificantly different from the bachelor's, while for the distance and population effects the master's are part-way between the bachelor's and PhDs and significantly different from both. As for the border effect, Table 3 shows the likelihood of a degree-holder choosing to live in BC rather than the United States (in the first column), and the likelihood of choosing to live in the rest of Canada relative to living in the United States (in the second column), in both cases after adjusting for the effects of size and distance.[4]

For example, the value of 61 for the bachelor's Canada effect means that a UBC bachelor's grad (who is not living in BC) is 61 times more likely to be living elsewhere in Canada than to be living in the United States, after adjusting for the effects of population size, distance and relative incomes. The border effects are much larger for grads living in British Columbia, as foreshadowed by Figures 1 through 15. The border effects for PhDs are significantly less than for bachelor's, with a typical PhD who is not living in BC being 22 times more likely to be living in the rest of Canada than in the United States.

---

[4]The Canada effect is the anti-log of the Canada coefficient, while the BC effect is the anti-log of the sum of the BC and Canada coefficients. The sum is used in the second case because the BC and Canada variables both take the values of one for the BC observations.

Table 2: Significance of Coefficient Differences between Degree Types

Test of Equality of Coefficients	Probability of Coefficients Being Equal				
	ln(distance)	ln(y/capita)	ln(pop)	Canada	BC
Bachelor's = PhDs	0.000	0.006	0.000	0.003	0.986
Bachelor's = Master's	0.013	0.330	0.005	0.826	0.473
Master's = PhDs	0.021	0.021	0.019	0.003	0.669

Table 3: Border Effects

	BC vs. U.S.	Canada vs. U.S.
Bachelor's	240	61
Master's	161	59
PhDs	89	22

We turn now to consider trends by decade in the choices of residence by UBC grads. Analysis on a decade-by-decade basis for the graduate degrees does not show significant differences. This is partly evident in the data reported in Figures 10 though 15, but is also due to the relatively small number of graduate degrees, and hence of destinations, in the earlier decades. This is because UBC's graduate programs are of much more recent vintage than the main bachelor's degrees. Although the number of degrees has been growing rapidly, it is not adequate to support much in the way of decade-by-decade analysis.

Our results for bachelor's grads, reported in Tables 4 and 5, show that there has been a slight but not significant drop in the distance effect from the 1950s to the 1990s, and no significant change in the relative income and population effects. However, there have been significant increases in both the BC and Canada border effects, especially from the 1950s to the 1990s. We have two different samples to calculate equations for the 1990s. One includes

John F. Helliwell and David F. Helliwell

Table 4: Distribution of UBC Bachelor's Alumni among States and Provinces (by decade — each with 46 observations)

	ln(distance)	ln(y/capita)	ln(pop)	Canada	BC	R^2
1950s	-1.14	1.60	0.87	3.40	0.45	0.88
	(6.93)	(2.08)	(7.01)	(10.75)	(.53)	
1960s	-0.82	2.69	0.73	3.83	1.18	0.88
	(4.87)	(3.42)	(5.71)	(11.81)	(1.34)	
1970s	-0.91	2.54	0.68	3.86	1.65	0.90
	(5.72)	(3.44)	(5.69)	(12.64)	(1.99)	
1980s	-0.85	3.27	0.79	3.98	1.57	0.91
	(5.3)	(4.4)	(6.52)	(12.98)	(1.88)	
1990–94	-0.78	2.03	0.78	4.05	2.33	0.90
	(4.68)	(2.62)	(6.19)	(12.61)	(2.68)	
1990–97	-0.83	1.90	0.84	4.30	2.31	0.89
	(4.53)	(2.22)	(6.08)	(12.2)	(2.41)	

Note: Absolute values of t-statistics are shown in parentheses below the coefficients.

only the five years from 1990 through 1994, while the other includes 1990 through 1998. The results are different, showing that the most recent grads are more likely to show addresses in British Columbia. To some extent, however, this is likely to be due to the continued appearance of local addresses for ex-students who may have moved elsewhere without the UBC mailing records having yet been brought up to date. There will also be students who are undertaking further education in British Columbia, or are traveling with

Table 5: Significance of Coefficient Differences between Decades

Test of Equality of Coefficients	Probability of Coefficients Being Equal				
	ln(distance)	ln(y/capita)	ln(pop)	Canada	BC
1950s = 1990s	0.050	0.689	0.853	0.001	0.019

Where Are They Now?

addresses of convenience still in British Columbia, before establishing their longer-term residences. Even if the analysis is restricted to the 1990–94 grads, there is still a significant reduction from the 1950s to the 1990s in the likelihood that graduates are living in U.S. states rather than in British Columbia or elsewhere in Canada.

Table 6 shows that the relative likelihood of a UBC bachelor's graduate moving elsewhere in Canada, compared to the United States, rose from around 30 in the 1950s, to between 50 and 60 for the following decades, with some further increases showing up in the 1990s. The relative likelihood of a UBC bachelor's grad living in BC, compared to moving to the United States, has shown an even larger increase, from about 50 in the 1950s to more than 500 in the 1990s.

Table 6: Border Effects for UBC Bachelor's Graduates

	BC vs. U.S.	*Canada vs. U.S.*
1950s	47	31
1960s	150	54
1970s	246	51
1980s	246	58
1990–94	590	57
1990–98	726	79

How Do the UBC Data Compare with other Measures of Graduate Migration?

Thanks to a recent national survey of 1995 graduates of Canadian universities who have moved to the United States (Frank and Bélair, 1999, hereafter *South of the Border*), it is now possible to fit the UBC data into the national picture. If the UBC and the national data correspond well for the national survey year of 1995, then the UBC data can be used to add a valuable time dimension to the national data. Without such a time dimension, the survey of 1995 graduates provides a precise and valuable snapshot, but cannot be used to assess trends in the numbers, degree mix and fields of graduates who move.

Our data cover all UBC graduates, wherever they are from, and wherever they may now be living, while *South of the Border* deals especially with Canadian graduates who moved to the United States, leaving aside graduates who have moved to other countries, and removing graduates who were U.S. citizens at the time of graduation. As we shall see, these differences are important in the case of graduate students, while being much less important for bachelor's graduates, who are much more likely to be Canadian citizens and are much less likely to move outside Canada after graduation. We plan further efforts to obtain data from the national survey that are more exactly comparable to the UBC data, but we are already able to see that the two data sources are remarkably consistent, thus increasing their separate and joint usefulness.

One general question that might be raised is whether the migration patterns of BC graduates are likely to be very different from those of other provinces, perhaps because British Columbia has had population growth exceeding that of other provinces for most of the decades under review. In fact, *South of the Border* (Figure 3-6, page 13) reports that British Columbia is closer to the national average than any other province, providing 9 per cent of the movers to the United States as well as 9 per cent of graduates who remained in Canada. By contrast, Quebec graduates are less than half as likely to leave for the United States, compared to the national average, while Ontario graduates are almost 40 per cent more likely to move south of the border. Studies of migration show that both distance and a common language are important determinants of migration, so both of these effects are to be expected, with Ontario much closer to large U.S. centres of population, and Quebec graduates mostly having French as their first language.

When we come to consider the details of the data, we find some interesting differences arising between the UBC and national data, most of which are sensibly explained by UBC's geographic and educational position among Canadian universities. Tables 7 and 8 show the U.S.-bound graduates as measured nationally in *South of the Border* and for UBC by our data set. The most striking thing about the table is how close the two measures are, and how they contain similar levels and patterns of migration among degree types. The closest comparison is provided by using the UBC totals including

Table 7: Current Location of 1995 Graduates

Location of Graduates	Bachelor's	Master's	PhD	All Degrees
Canada				
From UBC	4,484	878	183	5,545
From Canada	134,044	20,539	2,626	157,209
UBC share	3.3%	4.3%	7.0%	3.5%
U.S.*				
From UBC	51	30	37	118
From Canada	2,376	683	359	3,418
UBC share	2.1%	4.4%	10.3%	3.5%
Canada + U.S.				
From UBC	4,535	908	220	5,663
From Canada	136,420	21,222	2,985	160,627
UBC share	3.3%	4.3%	7.4%	3.5%
Rest of World				
From UBC	108	59	42	209
From Canada**	5,654	1,845	684	8,183
Worldwide				
From UBC	4,643	967	262	5,872
From Canada	142,074	23,067	3,669	168,810
UBC share	3.3%	4.2%	7.1%	3.5%

Notes: * The Statistics Canada (National) data cover graduates who went to the United States after graduating, but may not still be there. The UBC data are for UBC graduates who are currently in the United States.
**From an unpublished estimate based on the 1997 National Graduates Survey.

Table 8: Proportion of 1995 Graduates Living in the United States

	Bachelor's (%)	Master's (%)	PhD (%)	All Degrees (%)
Share of (Can+U.S.) in U.S.				
UBC	1.1	3.3	16.8	2.1
National	1.7	3.2	12.0	2.1
Share of Total in U.S.				
UBC	1.1	3.1	14.1	2.0
National	1.7	3.0	9.8	2.0

John F. Helliwell and David F. Helliwell

only those graduates living in Canada or the United States.[5] By this measure, Table 8 shows that 1.1 per cent of UBC 1995 bachelor's graduates are living in the United States, compared to 1.7 per cent of national graduates who moved to the United States between 1995 and 1997. These figures become more equal if account were taken of the fact that 18 per cent of the national movers returned to Canada between 1995 and 1997. If this adjustment is appropriately applicable to bachelor's, it would lower the national estimate from 1.7 per cent to 1.4 per cent.[6] In addition, British Columbia is farther from U.S. centres of population, and hence less likely to have graduates move to the United States. Finally, population growth has been greater in British Columbia than in the rest of Canada, thereby increasing the share of local graduates likely to remain in the province of graduation. As shown by our gravity model equations in the previous section, the distance effect is more likely to show up for bachelor's than for master's and PhDs, since the latter graduates are much less deterred by distance. The adjustment for U.S. citizens would not make much difference for bachelor's, since the U.S. citizen share is very low at that level of study.

For master's graduates, the UBC measure of 3.3 per cent is very close to the national 3.2 per cent. Not too much should be made of a very close match, since there are noticeable year-to-year fluctuations, as evident in Figures 1 through 15, due to the relatively small number of migrants. Both sources of data show master's graduates to be two to three times more likely to move south than are the bachelor's graduates, for reasons discussed in the previous section.

For PhD graduates, the basic UBC measure for U.S.-resident 1995 UBC PhDs is 14.1 per cent, rising to 16.8 per cent if the graduates in the ROW are excluded to make our data more comparable with the reported national

---

[5]This gives a higher estimate of the share of graduates living in the United States, since the denominator excludes graduates living in the rest of the world. The difference is negligible for bachelor's, noticeable for master's, and quite substantial for PhDs.

[6]Supplementary data from Statistics Canada show that bachelor's were a slightly smaller share of the returnees (43 per cent) than they were of the original movers (51 per cent). Using this additional adjustment reduces the proportion of bachelor's returning to 15 per cent. This raises the 1.4 per cent national estimate for bachelor's movers who also stayed, but by little enough that it still rounds down to 1.4 per cent.

numbers. The number from *South of the Border* is 12 per cent. Thus both sources of data show that PhDs are much more likely to move to the United States than are either bachelor's or master's graduates. Why might the UBC numbers be higher than the national total? There are several reasons. Adjusting for U.S. citizens is important at the PhD level. As we have seen in the previous section, 7 per cent of the 1993–98 PhD intake at UBC were U.S. citizens, who are excluded from the *South of the Border* calculations. They are included in the UBC data. If 7 per cent of the 1995 UBC PhDs were U.S. citizens, and half of them returned to the United States after graduation, then removing the U.S. citizens from the UBC data would reduce the 16.8 per cent to 13.3 per cent, very close to the national 12 per cent. Our data for residence do not include citizenship, so we cannot know exactly what fraction of the U.S. citizens returned to the United States, but the factor is clearly important. The geography effect is not likely to be important, since distance was not found to be important for the subsequent location of PhDs.

Other possible reasons for greater southern mobility of UBC PhDs might include a more international and more specialized composition of UBC's PhD programs, compared to the national average. Table 7 also shows that UBC is much more than proportionately represented in national PhD production, and is thus also likely to be accompanied by a greater range of specialized programs. The more international mix of PhD students (fewer than 50 per cent of UBC PhD students are Canadian students, and citizenship is spread widely over more than 100 countries) is also likely to produce a crop of graduates who are mobile, and perhaps as likely to be attracted to U.S. as to Canadian opportunities. Offsetting these reasons for higher PhD export from British Columbia to the United States is the growing relative size of the BC population, and the rapidly expanding number of UBC PhDs resident in the province (see Figure 15).

Given the fact that the UBC and national numbers are quite similar degree by degree, with smaller UBC export of bachelor's being offset by greater PhD export, it might be thought surprising to find that for all degrees taken together, 2.1 per cent of North American resident UBC grads live in the United States, compared to 1.5 per cent as reported in *South of the Border*. The reason for this difference is that the Statistics Canada national number includes degrees below the bachelor's level. When the total is constructed, as in Table 8, for bachelor's degrees and above, the UBC share living in the United States is exactly equal to that for the national sample. The similarity for the aggregate of the degree types is made up, as Table 8 shows, of a U.S.-bound share of UBC grads that is less than the national

John F. Helliwell and David F. Helliwell

average for bachelor's, equal for master's, and higher for PhDs. Thus UBC produced 3.3 per cent of Canada's 1995 bachelor's graduates now living in North America, compared to 4.3 per cent of the master's grads and 7 per cent of the PhDs.

Another expected difference between the UBC and national results is in the distribution of graduates among the different U.S. states. In the national results, the main recipient states were Texas, California, New York and Florida, with 16 per cent, 11 per cent, 10 per cent and 8 per cent of the U.S.-resident Canadian graduates, compared to U.S. population shares for these same states of 7 per cent, 12 per cent, 7 per cent and 5 per cent. Thus Texas received more than twice its population share of U.S.-bound graduates at the national level, while California received its population share, with New York and Florida 50 per cent more than their population shares. The UBC pattern, which we have calculated for the average of the period 1990–97 to make the sample sizes usefully large, shows the effects of its western location and its higher proportion of research degrees. Thus the largest recipient states for UBC graduates are California 23 per cent (twice its population share),[7] Washington State 15 per cent (seven times its population share), New York 8 per cent (slightly above population share), and Massachusetts 4 per cent (twice its population share).

How do the UBC data compare with the national totals across different fields of study? As we have already seen in Figures 1 through 15, most degrees have fairly similar shares of U.S.-bound graduates, except that the U.S. shares are traditionally lower than average in certain professional areas, such as education and law. The national data for 1995 show unusually high proportions of south-bound migrants in the health professions, who were more than twice as likely to have moved south than were graduates in other fields. For the UBC nursing and MD grads, however, the U.S.-resident share of 1995 graduates, and of 1990s graduates in total, remained stable at slightly below 2 per cent, and thus below the university-wide average for all specializations. The over-representation of health-care professionals in U.S.-bound 1995 graduates in the rest of Canada is perhaps reflective of health

---

[7]Roughly one-quarter of both UBC and national U.S.-resident PhDs are resident in California, so the difference between the UBC and national numbers is due to a higher proportion of PhDs in the UBC total and also to California-bound migration at the bachelor's and master's levels that is greater for UBC than for other Canadian universities.

care spending and employment cuts in other provinces that were not mirrored in British Columbia.[8]

South of the Border also reports that graduates with degrees in engineering and the applied sciences were twice as numerous among the south-bound migrants as they were among the graduating class. The UBC data do not reflect this part of the national data either. For the national sample, engineers and applied scientists were almost twice as numerous among the migrants as they were among those who stayed in Canada. UBC engineering grads, by contrast, were no more likely to move south than all bachelor's taken together, with 1.1 per cent of 1995 grads, and a corresponding share of all 1990s BASc grads, now living in the United States.[9] Given the relatively large flows from UBC to Washington State, it is possible that some applied scientists appearing as BSc graduates in the UBC data, such as computer science graduates, may have been over-represented even if engineers were not. We do not have data for sub-programs within each degree, but for the Bachelor of Science degree as a whole, of which computer science is a part, 20 of the roughly 1,300 BSc graduates in 1995 in the alumni data file are now living in the United States. This is about 1.5 per cent, not materially above the average for all bachelor's programs.

In addition to the one-shot Statistics Canada data for the graduating class of 1995, there are additional cross-checks possible with some time series for total emigration of degree-holders from Canada to the United States. Zhao, Drew and Murray (2000) report sample data from the Statistics Canada reverse records check that there was an increase from the 1986–91 period to the 1991–96 period in the numbers of permanent and temporary migrants moving from Canada to the United States. For the two types of movement considered together, the annual average increased from 23,000 in the 1986–91 period to just under 30,000 per year from 1991–96.

---

[8]*South of the Border* reports that one in five of the national south-bound migrants of the class of 1995 were nurses, and suggests that this was likely to reflect dramatic changes that were taking place in the health-care sectors of several provinces.

[9]The same pattern is true for the MASc, with 3 per cent of the 1995 graduates living in the United States, the same share as for UBC master's graduates in general. We have not split the PhDs by specialty, since the annual numbers in each field are small enough to make the year-to-year changes subject to considerable random fluctuation.

John F. Helliwell and David F. Helliwell

They also report data from Revenue Canada that the number of taxfilers moving from Canada to the United States increased from something like 10,000 in 1991 to between 14,000 and 23,000 in 1997. How can we reconcile these data with the data for UBC graduates? We can probably rule out the possibility that the recent migrants are less likely than earlier migrants to have university degrees, since the post-FTA changes in immigration rules have made it relatively easier for Canadian degree-holders to work in the United States. The most likely explanation for the different trends is the fact that the UBC data show only the current locations of degree-holders, and not when they moved. Thus it is likely that the higher number of movers during the 1990s included migrants from a number of different graduating classes. There is supporting evidence for this interpretation from the U.S. CPS data, which show that almost 70 per cent of the post-1990 adult (aged over 16) Canadian-born movers to the United States were in the 25 to 44 age group. This suggests that during the 1990s there may have been an increase in the proportion of several pre-1990s UBC degree recipients now living in the United States. These increases have not, however, been large enough to reverse the general trend showing more recent graduates to be less likely to be living in the United States. However, as already noted, for the most recent years it is likely that the UBC address records will not have fully caught up with the latest addresses, especially for those who have not yet chosen long-term locations.

We turn now to a review of the UBC Alumni Association survey of UBC graduates living outside Canada.

The Survey Evidence

The UBC Alumni Association has had a survey posted on its Web page (www.alumni.ubc.ca) since early in 1998. Since then, about 300 UBC alumni have responded, answering the questions and often offering their opinions, as requested, on whether a "brain drain" is taking away Canada's "best and brightest", and, if it is, how such a problem should be resolved.[10]

---

[10]The survey is described, and answers recorded, accompanied by some responses to the open-ended questions, in an Appendix to this paper available from the authors.

Due to the low response rate, small sample size, and strong risk of self-selection bias, it is difficult to make any firm conclusions from the survey evidence. However, the answers given do seem consistent with the larger Statistics Canada survey and our regression analysis, although the sample is too small to permit us to see if there are the same differences by level of degree.

For the first question (Why did you move away?), the majority of respondents (76 per cent of U.S. residents and 69 per cent of ROW residents) cited better job or graduate school opportunities. Better pay was a distant second in terms of frequency, with 26 per cent of U.S. residents and 6 per cent of ROW. Lower taxes were an important factor to 18 per cent of the U.S. residents, 13 per cent of ROW. In general, ROW respondents in Europe (especially northern Europe) were paying more tax than they had in Canada, while many Southeast Asian ROW respondents were paying lower taxes. The net effect is that moves to the United States are more financially driven, while moves to other countries are often motivated by personal or cultural factors. This is reflected in responses to the second question (What do you like most about your new home?) where "culture" scored 25 per cent for ROW residents, but only 10 per cent for U.S. residents.

In some cases, the difference between U.S. and ROW responses can be illustrative of underlying decision factors in the migration decision. For example, in the third question (What do you dislike about your new home?) there are several answers with significantly different responses from the two groups. Residents in the ROW were more likely to not like the crowds (18 per cent ROW to 7 per cent U.S.), the pollution (18 per cent to 5 per cent) and the weather (11 per cent to 7 per cent). On the other hand, U.S. residents were more likely to not like peoples' attitudes (27 per cent of respondents living in the United States compared to 20 per cent of ROW respondents), crime and gun control (21 per cent to 3 per cent), or lack of Canadian activities such as skiing and hockey (8 per cent to 2 per cent). Thus, from the survey results there seems to be a clear trade-off between lifestyle priorities for those going to the ROW, versus financial priorities for those going to the United States.

When describing what they missed most about Canada, ROW respondents first mentioned Canada's geography and weather (56 per cent), while U.S. respondents first mentioned friends and family (41 per cent). The second most missed thing for ROW respondents was friends and family (32 per cent), and geography and weather for U.S. respondents (36 per cent). These results fit with several factors identified in this paper. First, the fact that ROW respondents are less likely to miss friends and family in Canada mirrors the fact that UBC graduates not born in Canada are much more likely to have been born in the ROW than in the United States. For example, there are increasing numbers of Asian students returning to Southeast Asia (27 of 91 ROW respondents were in Southeast Asia), where they already have established networks of friends and relatives.

Conclusion

Our analysis of the UBC graduate data, and our comparisons of the UBC data with those from the national survey reported in *South of the Border*, show a striking degree of consistency. Differences only appear where they are expected, principally due to the western position and unusually high proportion of research degrees among UBC's graduates. We found a slightly higher proportion of UBC graduates living in the United States than is true for the national sample, but this is fully explained by UBC's relatively high production of master's and especially PhD graduates, who are and have always been more mobile than bachelor's graduates. UBC's PhD students are drawn to UBC from more than 100 countries, and are widely distributed after their graduation. Some countries receive more of the completed PhDs than their citizens make up of the student body, while for others the reverse is the case. United States citizens make up about 7 per cent of incoming PhDs, while twice that many UBC PhD graduates live in the United States. This no doubt reflects the fact that research and teaching positions, especially those with high incomes and research grants, are more concentrated in high income countries, and especially in the United States, than is the citizenship distribution of incoming PhD students. This international transfer of high level students, who come from one country, obtain graduate education in another, usually contributing teaching and research assistance while so doing, and then often choosing either country, or a third country, to continue their careers, provides the potential for increasing the fluidity of the international transfer of productive ideas. When viewed from the perspective of countries that provide many of the students but receive few of the eventual PhDs, this process has been described as a "brain drain". This has frequently been the case for many developing countries, many of which do not have the resources to provide adequate facilities to even make the best use of their highly trained expatriates.[11] Under the same name, the issue was studied in the 1960s in Canada, with respect to what were then seen as large flows from Canada to the United States of those with high levels of education and skills. Our UBC data show how much the basic situation has changed between the 1960s and the 1990s. Canadian research and graduate education have expanded dramatically, leading many more undergraduates to stay in Canada for their graduate work. This is perhaps the single most important reason why the south-bound flows of bachelor's graduates has fallen so much from the early 1960s to the 1990s. The resurgence of discussion of a brain drain in the 1990s has much less basis in the data, and probably represents factors specific to a number of specific sectors where funding support has risen much less rapidly than in the United States, such as some components of health spending, research and university financing. It has also been fuelled to some extent by sharp increases in the numbers in temporary NAFTA visas to Canadians working in the United States, and in part to increasing 1990s gaps, favouring high-income earners in the United States, relative to their Canadian counterparts, in salaries and tax rates.[12]

The UBC graduate data provide a valuable time dimension to the data available from *South of the Border*, enabling us to see whether the 1995 flows are part of a rising or falling trend. This can provide at least a partial answer to the question of whether there is evidence of an increasing flow of highly skilled Canadians, and citizens of other countries trained in Canada, to the United States. The UBC graduate data show, consistently with the data from the U.S. Bureau of the Census, that the past five decades have seen continuing reductions in the shares of UBC graduates living in the United States. Neither body of data is perfect, as the accuracy of the UBC data depends on the validity and coverage of address lists, and the U.S. Current Population Surveys done during the 1990s are on a sample basis. Thus it will take the 2000 Census in the United States to show with full precision whether there has been, during the 1990s, some resurgence of Canadian university graduates moving to the United States. The UBC data do not show any evidence of this so far, because for all of the large-scale bachelor's

---

[11]For an example focused on developing countries, see Bhagwati and Martington (1976). For a summary of the evidence and issues with more attention to the Canadian situation in the 1950s and 1960s, see Grubel and Scott (1977).

[12]For evidence on both these aspects, see Iqbal (1999); and Helliwell (1999).

John F. Helliwell and David F. Helliwell

programs the proportion of graduates living in the United States has continued to fall during the 1990s.

For the graduate programs, the proportion living outside Canada is and has always been high, reflecting a very international mix of both the student intake and the available career positions. For all degrees, the proportion of 1990s UBC graduates living in the rest of the world is higher than that in the United States. For the graduate degrees, the proportion of the graduates subsequently living and working in Canada, and especially in British Columbia, is much higher than the share of Canadian citizens among the incoming students. With respect to the international distribution of those with the highest level of educational aptitude and attainments, as represented by the master's and PhD graduates of UBC, Canada and British Columbia stand in the middle ground between the United States and the rest of the world. Comparing the citizenship of UBC's graduate intake with the country of residence of the graduates, the United States is the largest proportionate net recipient (7 per cent U.S. citizen intake, 14 per cent U.S.-resident 1990s PhDs), Canada is the largest recipient in terms of numbers of PhDs (46 per cent Canadian citizen intake, 70 per cent Canadian-resident 1990s PhDs), with students from 100 other countries providing a net flow into Canada and the United States.

References

Bhagwati, J.N. and M. Martington, eds. (1976), *Taxing the Brain Drain: A Proposal*, vols. 1 and 2 (Amsterdam: North-Holland).

Frank, J. and É. Bélair (1999), *South of the Border: An Analysis of Results from the Survey of 1995 Graduates Who Moved to the United States* (Ottawa: Human Development Canada and Statistics Canada).

Grubel, H. and A. Scott (1977), *The Brain Drain: Determinants, Measurement and Welfare Effects* (Waterloo: Wilfred Laurier University Press).

Helliwell, J.F. (1998), *How Much Do National Borders Matter?* (Washington, DC: The Brookings Institution).

_____ (1999), "Checking the Brain Drain: Evidence and Implications", (<www.arts.ubc.ca/econ/helliwell/pages/papers.htm>). (An abbreviated version is in *Policy Options*, September 1999, available at <www.irpp.org>.)

Helliwell, J.F. and D.F. Helliwell (2000), "Tracking UBC Graduates: Trends and Implications", *ISUMA: Canadian Journal of Policy Research* 1(1) January. (Available at <www.isuma.net>.)

Iqbal, M. (1999), *Are We Losing our Minds? Trends, Determinants and the Role of Taxation in Brain Drain to the United States* (Ottawa: Conference Board of Canada).

Zhao, J., D. Drew and T.S. Murray (2000), "Brain Drain and Brain Gain: The Migration of Knowledge Workers To and From Canada", *Education Quarterly Review* 6(3), 8-35.

Globalization

Adjusting to Globalization: Challenges for the Canadian Banking System[1]

Edward P. Neufeld

Introduction

The forces of "globalization" are transforming virtually every industrial sector in Canada including financial services retail distribution. Observers who downplay its significance tend to take a short-run view of the matter, pointing to what has not yet been affected greatly by globalization rather than to how a continuation of current developments will change the economy and its sectors over the next decade.[2] Because of the mobility of capital, financial services sectors have already been heavily affected by globalization.

How well is the Canadian financial system including its regulatory regime, positioned to deal with globalization? This paper addresses that question, and mainly as it relates to the Canadian banking system, by: (i) referring to past evolution of the system and how current challenges differ from past ones; (ii) identifying the challenges that the current environment

---

[1]Some of the analysis included here is taken from Neufeld (2000).

[2]For an effective portrayal of current and prospect changes driven by globalization see Friedman (1999).

has generated — in part by examining the stresses and strains revealed by the Asian financial crisis and its lessons for achieving stable and efficient financial systems; (iii) appraising the extent to which the Canadian banking system and its regulatory framework, as well as current Canadian financial services policy, is in tune with addressing those challenges; and (iv) drawing some conclusions of relevance to the Canadian banking system from this perspective on globalization.

The Evolution of the Canadian Banking System

The need to adapt to changing circumstances and opportunities is nothing new for the Canadian banking system. Over its history of almost two centuries the growth and development of the system has involved: geographic expansion; industry consolidation; expansion in the range of financial services offered; and innovation in the delivery of services. The process was greatly assisted early on by innovations in transportation technology — transcontinental trains; and in communications technology — telegraph and telephone. By the end of the 1920s domestic geographic expansion and industry consolidation had gone a very long way. However, product and product delivery innovations were minimal until after the Second World War.

Currently, with the domestic market relatively mature, both in terms of geographic coverage and product offerings, the only significant frontier left for the system is that of international financial services. The most important question now is whether the Canadian legislative framework and the ingenuity of the banks will be such as to see the system survive strongly in Canada and abroad in the face of the forces of global competition that have become a permanent feature of the system and are likely to increase in intensity.

It is useful to examine these evolutionary forces in somewhat more detail.

The Period before World War II

The chartered banks first typically emerged in the larger urban centres, with smaller urban and rural communities being served by local private bankers

Edward P. Neufeld

and money lenders, including the activities of accountancy and law offices. The banks then began to extend their reach into the hinterlands — which saw the emergence of the historically important innovation of the branch system and its effective administration — the latter involving not just new accounting and control procedures and practices but new human resource policies as well, as personnel that were required to move around far-flung branch systems.

This experience and new regional opportunities combined to enable the banks to extend their reach beyond their own hinterland to neighbouring provinces and, simply following trade, to the Caribbean region. As they did so it became evident that structural changes to the banking system were necessary in order to take advantage of the inviting presence of banking opportunities in the widely dispersed regions, and to serve their communities efficiently. These structural changes took two major forms: the disappearance of local private bankers and money lenders as the more efficient bank branches began to serve local communities, and major consolidation among the banks through mergers and acquisitions as they sought to meet the new dimensions of "optimum size" dictated by a greatly expanded market.

The structural changes that emerged were quite dramatic. It would appear that in the 1890s there were close to 200 private banking offices in Canada most of which had disappeared by the 1920s; on the other hand, while in 1890 there were 426 bank branches, in 1920 there were 4,676.[3] Whereas in 1890 there were about 11,300 Canadians per branch this had declined to below 3,000 by the 1920s and represented long-term density maturity. At the same time the number of chartered banks diminished dramatically. In 1870 there were 30 active chartered banks while by 1930 these had been reduced to ten. Mergers played a very significant role in enabling the emergence of institutions of a size appropriate to the breadth of the Canadian market and to the then demands of international business.[4]

---

[3]See Neufeld (1972) for a full analysis of the development of the Canadian banking system.

[4]A significant example of this was the emergence of the Royal Bank of Canada. It began operations as a small chartered bank in 1871. From 1910 to 1925 it effected five strategically important mergers. Consequently, whereas it accounted for under 4 per cent of bank assets in 1910, by 1930 it had 27 per cent,

In Canada, in contrast to the United States, government policy did not impede these major structural changes that led to the development of national branch systems and consolidation among the banks, to the substantial benefit of the Canadian economy with its relatively small population and large territorial expanse.

While the Canadian chartered banks were highly successful in growing their institutions by increasing their geographical reach within Canada and by mergers and acquisitions, they were much less imaginative in doing so through expanding the range of their products, as indicated by the relatively static character of their liability instruments and assets over many decades prior to the Second World War, and the relative absence of non-intermediation services. On the sources of funds (i.e., liabilities) side of their activities they did begin to develop actively the simple savings deposit in the late 1860s, in addition to their chequing account business, and this turned out to be highly significant for their future growth, but no further important liability instrument innovations appeared until after the Second World War.

As for their lending activities, they saw themselves essentially as providers of short-term business loans, with peripheral activity in areas such as federal, provincial, municipal and corporate securities remaining relatively small. One bank in the 1930s found a way of circumventing the interest rate ceiling in order to develop consumer instalment credit, but the business remained small and its lead was not followed by the other banks. Not until well after World War II did they take consumer lending seriously and they waited long before starting to lobby for mortgage-lending powers.

In the meantime, their intermediary competitors moved ahead and their share of the financial intermediary business declined steadily — from 73 per cent in 1870 to 40 per cent in 1940. Their mortgage loan, trust and insurance company competitors pioneered mortgage lending, both industrial and residential, the small loan companies and money lenders developed consumer credit; while that wonderful savings instrument — the automatic periodic payment — was for long largely the preserve of the life insurance companies, it was also adopted by the mutual fund companies which emerged in the 1930s. Trust companies in the 1920s succeeded in achieving legislative changes that enabled them to enter the historic preserve of the banks — the deposit business — as did the credit unions and caisses populaires.

---

making it the largest chartered bank in Canada. See McDowall (1993, ch. 4) and Neufeld (1972, p. 99).

Edward P. Neufeld

This lethargy on the part of the banks in product development cannot be explained by legislative constraints even though such constraints did exist. Over decades, the banks had been relatively successful in achieving desired changes in the *Bank Act* during the decennial reviews. The overriding perception among the banks themselves was that they should confine themselves to gathering demand and savings deposits and this, it was felt, dictated that they confine themselves essentially to providing short-term, self-liquidating business credit.

The Period after World War II

Geographic expansion and increasing branch density had been largely exhausted as a way of growing the banking system prior to World War II. But growth through expansion of the product range had great potential. It emerged slowly and in the two very important cases of consumer credit and mortgage lending, it came as much through the desire of the government as through the lobbying of the banks. The 1937 *Home Improvement Loans Guarantee Act*, which protected the banks against losses up to 15 per cent, was followed in 1954 by the *National Housing Act*, under which the banks began to offer government-guaranteed residential mortgage loans. Not until 1962 did the banks begin to argue for broad mortgage lending powers and these emerged in the next *Bank Act*, the one of 1967.

Similarly so with consumer credit. The step taken by the Canadian Bank of Commerce in 1936 to offer consumer instalment loans under accounting that enabled them to charge more than the maximum legal interest rate, a step tolerated benignly by the government, was not followed by the other banks. The 1954 *Bank Act* permitted the banks to take chattel mortgages as security but not until 1958, when the Bank of Nova Scotia entered the consumer credit field aggressively did the rest follow.

Innovation in instruments for raising funds also came slowly. In 1959 the Canadian Bankers' Association appointed a committee of three, two bankers and one outsider (the writer) to examine the feasibility of forming an active short-term money market with emphasis on bankers' acceptances. But only gradually did a full array of term notes, debentures, bankers' acceptances and a variety of savings plans appear. In the 1960s all the chartered banks became associated with mutual fund companies and in time this evolved into a major area of activity. There then emerged a virtual explosion of innovation in how services were delivered with the move into credit cards, beginning with CHARGEX, then VISA and MASTERCARD, and some years later individual bank cards and automated teller machines (ATM), then debit cards, telephone banking and finally Internet banking.

Of great significance for achieving growth through widening the range of services offered was the permission granted to banks in 1987 to acquire investment dealers and in 1992 to acquire trust companies. This, together with their burgeoning mutual fund business paved the way for them to become major players in wealth management and related services. The acquisition of dealers was also important for their lending activities in that it enabled them to provide the full range of corporate financing services, not simply demand and term bank loans as they had done over much of their history. Special departments for loans to small and medium-sized businesses as well as separate venture capital arrangements were also developed by the banks individually.

As a result of this broadening of the range of services offered, the banks succeeded in achieving a rate of growth that maintained their relative position in financial intermediation in Canada and increased somewhat their share in the provision of non-intermediary services such as wealth management. But by the end of the twentieth century the potential for further growth in Canada through broadening even further the range of services appeared to have been largely exhausted — apart from branch distribution of life insurance and car leasing, both of which they were prohibited from entering by federal government legislation. In short, just as geographic reach and branch density had been essentially exhausted prior to the Second World War, by the end of the twentieth century the potential for growth through expansion of product range in Canada had also been largely exhausted.

The challenge for future growth and development that this has posed for the Canadian banks is clear. They can be content with serving the very mature Canadian market and accept the low rate of growth that this implies or they can begin to extend their reach seriously beyond Canada's borders just as in the late nineteenth century they had begun to extend their reach beyond their local communities and home province into Canada as a whole.

However, either is easier said than done because of a new development that exploded in the 1990s, namely globalization and global competition. On the one hand, this phenomenon has the potential for challenging the banks in their own domestic market — a new development that will reduce further the opportunities for growth in the already mature domestic market; and on the other hand it has imposed new prerequisites for banks wishing to become respectable players outside their home market. Domestically, the banks must be as efficient as possible in terms of the cost and quality of service or their market share will be eroded by international institutions; while being effective international players requires them to have a size that enables them to capture the economies of scale enjoyed by their much larger international competitors.

The issue that emerges is whether the Canadian banking system and the legislation governing it are poised to meet the challenges of globalization over the next ten years.

Implications of Globalization for the Canadian Financial System

Globalization is a permanent, non-reversible phenomenon. Canadian financial services policies based on the assumption that domestic financial systems are heavily protected from external influences, as was the case over past decades, will be ineffective and, indeed, counterproductive. They risk undermining rather than strengthening the domestic financial system. A recent book on the subject of globalization has noted that:

> the globalization system, unlike the Cold War system, is not static, but a dynamic ongoing process: globalization involves the inexorable integration of markets, nation-states and technologies to a degree never witnessed before — in a way that is enabling individuals, corporations and nation-states to reach around the world farther, faster, deeper and cheaper than ever before, and in a way that is also producing a powerful backlash from those brutalized or left behind by this new system. (Friedman, 1999, pp. 7-8)

There are a number of important implications for the Canadian financial system of this worldwide trend. How Canadian policy deals with some of them will determine whether the Canadian financial system will be "brutalized" or "left behind", its place to a significant degree taken by external players.

Increased Foreign Competition within Canada

Canada's domestic market will be challenged by non-Canadian institutions much more so in the future than in the past. Telecommunication innovations and the decline in telecommunication costs — microchips, satellites, fibre optics, the Internet — are breaking down regional, international and institutional barriers that had previously protected institutions from external forces. The nineteenth century equivalent of this was the massive improvement in transportation and decline in transportation costs, as well as the improvement in communications through the telephone and telegraph which were prerequisites for breaking down regional barriers to nation-wide banking and financial services generally. The break-down of international boundaries by rapidly developing information and communication technologies will naturally lead to an increase in the share of the Canadian financial services market going to non-Canadian financial institutions.

Increased Importance of International Competitiveness

The ability of Canadian institutions to withstand increasing foreign competition will depend on their economic efficiency relative to that of the encroaching competitors. In the past when the threat of foreign competition was unimportant it did not much matter for Canadian financial institutions if government policy impeded the move to a more efficient system, the only ones suffering being the users of financial services. But now non-Canadian institutions with greater scale advantages can use rapidly emerging technology to deliver highly reliable and competitive financial services to the home or office. Canadian clients are likely to be quite receptive to such services since they are among world leaders in the adoption of Internet services, including banking services. Therefore, it is simply a matter of time before most of them will routinely use the Internet for accessing banking and other financial services.

Not only does this mean that new non-Canadian institutions have much easier access to the Canadian market than previously, but Canadians will become increasingly indifferent as to whether they are dealing with Canadian or non-Canadian institutions. Such new competition in itself is beneficial to Canadians, but if the edge is given to non-Canadian institutions because of costly legislative constraints imposed on domestic institutions then the outcome is undesirable both for the long-term prospects of the domestic financial system and for the efficiency of resource allocation within the financial services sector. The challenge for Canadian policy is to remove such constraints, some of which, as noted later, are currently of concern.

Obsolescence of Past Measures of "Optimum Size"

The forces that have facilitated globalization of financial services have also made obsolete past measures of economies of scale and of the "optimum" size of financial institutions, and past guidelines concerning excessive domestic market concentration are no longer reliable. Month after month cases emerge in a large number of countries of already large financial institutions increasing their market reach and reducing their operating costs through mergers with other large institutions. That is, the technological revolution is changing the parameters concerning the relationship between size and efficiency so that data relating to past size/efficiency experiences are no longer a reliable guide for the future. At the same time the concern in earlier years that this would lead to problems of inadequate domestic competition are increasingly irrelevant. They are being made irrelevant because financial services clients increasingly can source a wide variety of financial services from abroad as well as from a growing range of foreign and domestic institutions within domestic markets.

Recent Canadian policy of, in effect, preventing mergers between the larger banks stands out as an exception to what is happening in most of the industrialized countries. There are already disturbing indications that the Canadian banks do not have the size to support certain large international and domestic financial activities. For example, they have all exited the payroll business and, all but one, the custodial trust business, their places taken by foreign institutions. Also in March 2001, the Royal Bank of Canada announced that it would be selling RT Capital Management, its equity management arm, the most likely buyers being foreign fund managers.[5]

---

[5]The Canadian institutions had been inhibited in building up their foreign equity management teams because of the prolonged Canadian restrictions on the foreign content of Canadian pension plans — an example of regulative restrictions causing permanent damage to the Canadian financial system.

System Growth Dependent on Competitiveness at Home and Abroad

For Canadian financial institutions to experience solid growth in the future will require them to be internationally competitive at home and abroad. Not only, as noted earlier, is the Canadian financial services market a very mature one but it will be increasingly challenged by non-Canadian institutions. Therefore the future growth of Canadian financial institutions will depend on them expanding their international activities, especially in the United States. But in order to do this successfully they will need both to be internationally competitive in their home market and to have a size that enables them to compete aggressively abroad.

The Canadian banks have already slipped a long way down the list of important international financial institutions as measured by the size of their assets and of their capital bases; and current government policy impediments to mergers among the big banks means in my view that non-interest costs are 10–20 per cent higher than they would be if mergers were permitted. The result is that current attempts by the large banks to establish a stronger presence in the United States while entirely appropriate, and indeed very necessary, are limited both by domestic operations that are more costly than they could be and by capital bases that are smaller than they need to be.

Inevitability of Increased Foreign Ownership

The forces of globalization will generate a persistent tendency towards increased foreign ownership of Canadian financial institutions as has already begun to happen, and to an increase in non-Canadian executives running them. International institutional and other investors seeking long-term profit maximization through balancing their investments over a wide spectrum, are increasingly indifferent to the national origin of the investments. This alone will lead to an increase in foreign ownership of Canadian companies. Furthermore, as Canadian institutions acquire foreign institutions through share exchanges in order to grow their business, as in a recent case,[6] the

---

[6]On January 26, 2001, the Royal Bank announced that it intended to acquire Centura Banks Inc. of North Carolina for $3.5 billion through an exchange of shares.

Edward P. Neufeld

degree of foreign ownership will increase. Also in order to be internationally competitive it will be necessary for Canadian institutions to seek executive talent where they can find it. Since Canada's own supply is much smaller than the international pool, this will inevitably mean more non-Canadians running Canadian institutions. Boards of directors will have a growing number of non-Canadian members as business activities are globalized.[7]

Neither of these developments are ones that Canadian policy can or should combat. But they increase the urgency for Canadian policy to be in harmony with enabling domestic financial institutions to be as competitive domestically and internationally as possible and to avoid actually hastening the trend towards foreign ownership and control by weakening the relative position of Canadian institutions.

Weaknesses of Financial Systems Revealed by Globalization

The Asian Financial Crisis Experience

How well, over-all, is the Canadian financial system placed to survive financial globalization? A useful way to address this question is to examine how the Canadian system stands up against the weaknesses in certain financial systems revealed by the Asian financial crisis — a crisis that was largely triggered by the forces inherent in financial globalization. For domestic financial systems to survive globalization will involve correcting or avoiding such weaknesses.

Many of the weaknesses revealed by the Asian financial crisis had existed within the various financial systems for many years. What brought them to the fore was first the easy access of official and private institutions to short-term capital brought about by the globalization of financial markets and then the shock imposed on domestic financial systems of the sudden flight of that capital at the first signs of economic difficulties. Stabilization

---

[7]The number of U.S. residents who are directors of Canadian companies increased from 10 per cent in 1995 to 15 per cent in 1999. See *National Post*, February 5, 2001, p. C1.

of conditions in those systems involved not just the historically well-known adjustment to cyclical distortions but correction of newly revealed and deep-seated structural problems — the principal reason why the crisis was as severe and long-lasting as it turned out to be.

The more important financial system weaknesses revealed by the Asian financial crisis may briefly be noted in order to judge how the Canadian system stands up against them.

Macroeconomic policies. In some cases the macroeconomic policy environment was destabilizing: monetary policy was late in taking action to restore price stability which was even more important than fiscal imbalances in as much as the latter was not a problem in most Asian countries during the crisis; and policies of fixed exchange rates resulted in exchange values being held at artificially high levels having in mind the failure of macroeconomic policies to protect their real values.

Structural deficiencies among financial institutions. Domestic policies to a substantial degree shielded domestic financial institutions from international competition. For example, while the United Kingdom introduced major reforms in 1986, Japan ignored this example until the late 1990s. Consequently system rationalization was delayed and serious "moral hazard" problems existed within it, that is, the belief among private institutions that government would rescue them in time of trouble. At the same time the detailed regulation of the systems prevented the emergence of efficiency-generating competition within them. Mergers, acquisitions and even bankruptcies were made very difficult, thereby tending to "freeze" existing system structures at a time when exploding technology and growing international pressures were making such systems obsolete and highly vulnerable to life-threatening attacks. The lesson that emerged from all this was that regulations that operate against, instead of in harmony with market forces are not likely to be effective indefinitely. In most of the industrialized countries, including most recently the United States, old structures were permitted to be transformed through the playing out of market forces and this process is continuing through seemingly endless mergers, acquisitions and even bankruptcies.

Structural deficiencies within corporate operations. In retrospect it became clear that many private sector corporations had hidden deteriorating conditions from the view of public markets. This lack of transparency in accounting, weak financial controls, deficient bankruptcy laws, and in-adequate internal risk management permitted abuses to multiply, of which investors were unaware until crisis conditions had been created.

Structural deficiencies within domestic regulatory agencies. The sudden very large flows of short-term international capital to a wide range of private financial and non-financial institutions created risks for which regulatory agencies were unprepared. Inadequate reporting requirements, as for example, exposure to short-term capital outflows and the use of derivatives, poorly trained regulators and the absence of effective international co-operation among regulators were weaknesses that suddenly stood out as the crisis developed. In addition, governments, by hiding deteriorating conditions from markets caused the inevitable adjustment to be more severe than it need have been. An important example of this was the concealment of deteriorating official foreign exchange reserve positions. Just as policies of stability required much more transparency in corporate operations so it was required of official operations.

Structural deficiencies in multilateral surveillance. One of the most significant weaknesses revealed by the Asian financial crisis was the unpreparedness of the multilateral institutions to deal with international financial system problems. Neither the International Monetary Fund nor other multilateral institutions had concerned themselves with structural problems in member country financial systems, for the most part confining themselves to issues of macroeconomic stability and industrial development projects and policies. Recent multilateral efforts, in which Canada is playing an active part, to strengthen domestic financial systems, improve the quality of domestic regulators, establish international standards in the operations of financial institutions and of regulators, constitute serious attempts at addressing these weaknesses.

How the Canadian financial system measures up against those deficiencies. The Canadian financial system measures up quite well when judged against the weaknesses revealed by the Asian financial crisis. The fundamental strength of the Canadian financial system was demonstrated by the fact that it, as were those of the other western industrial countries, was relatively untouched by the crisis. Monetary policy was unequivocally directed towards maintaining a low rate of inflation and the Bank of Canada adopted a policy of increasing transparency in its operations. Low inflation and the move towards budget surpluses provided a stable environment for the financial system and the floating exchange rate removed the risk that the rate would be out of line with market forces.

Not that the exchange rate policy was and is now without controversy. Some would attribute the weak Canadian dollar over recent years to the maintenance of relatively high taxes, excessive government expenditures and inadequate reduction of the public debt, while others would attribute it essentially to weak commodity prices. Be that as it may, the floating exchange rate regime contributed to financial system stability in contrast to the fixed rate systems in many Asian countries — systems that collapsed under pressure.

Also contributing to stability is the fact that the federal government regulatory system overseeing Canadian financial institutions, as distinct from certain regulations themselves, is of high quality by international standards, including the quality of its regulatory personnel. Canada recognized the need to greatly improve international surveillance of the international financial system because of the many-faceted implications of financial globalization. The prime minister raised the issue at the Halifax G7 summit of 1995 and the minister of finance did so at various international fora. When the Group of Twenty was formed to work towards a more stable international financial system the Canadian finance minister was asked to be its first chairman. Furthermore the chairman of the Canadian Deposit Insurance Corporation was asked to head a subgroup under the newly formed Financial Stability Forum to make recommendations on deposit insurance; and Toronto was chosen as the location for the new International Centre for Leadership in Financial Sector Supervision.

Also many, although not all, of the historic barriers between the "four pillars" of financial institutions (banks, trusts, investment dealers and insurance companies) have disappeared, thereby increasing competition between them, and there is a strong foreign presence in most areas of the system, including increasingly in the banking system.

The need for transparency in corporate operations and for strong corporate governance practices has been emphasized by official regulators and by self-regulating institutions. As a result, for example, corporate reports, including those of the banks, are more informative for investors than in past years and many, although not yet all, annual reports now include a section outlining how the corporation's governance practices match up against the guidelines laid out by the Toronto Stock Exchange.

These favourable developments lay back of the ease with which the Canadian financial system withstood the international pressures created by the Asian financial crisis and demonstrated that the system had many strengths in going against increased global competition.

In addition, there is evidence in the recent acquisition actions of Canadian banks in the United States that they understand well that their

Edward P. Neufeld

future prosperity will depend on the development of their North American base, and not just their Canadian base.[8]

Unfortunately, there is one significant aspect of Canadian financial services policy that appears not to measure up well against the lessons learned from the Asian financial crisis and so risks undermining the future competitiveness of the system. This refers to the fundamental importance of permitting structural changes of a kind that reflect the pressure of new forces generated by globalization.

Bill C-8: Canadian Policy for Confronting Globalization

Prior to the federal election of 2000 the Canadian government tabled Bill C-38, a massive bill intended to introduce a large number of changes to the law governing the operation of federal financial institutions in Canada. This legislation appeared after the publication of the *Report of the Task Force on the Future of the Canadian Financial System* in September 1998 (the Mackay Report) and the government's policy paper of June 25, 1999, entitled *Reforming Canada's Financial Services Sector: A Framework for the Future*. That Bill died with the call of an election. It, however, was reintroduced as Bill C-8 in February 2001 and received Royal Assent a few months later. Bill C-8 introduced no policy changes from Bill C-38 although it did correct a number of errors and ambiguities that hasty drafting had left in that first bill. Space does not permit a detailed review here of the merits of all the measures included in that bill. Therefore this discussion focuses on those of relevance to longer term evolution of the system.

---

[8]A few recent examples may suffice. Toronto Dominion Bank is the largest shareholder of TD Waterhouse, a leading international brokerage firm. The Bank of Montreal through its U.S. subsidiary, Harris Bank, is acquiring First National Bank of Joliet. The Royal Bank is acquiring Centura Banks Inc. with assets of $11.5 billion; prior to that it acquired Security First Network Bank, an Internet bank; also Prism Financial Corp., a mortgage company; Liberty Life Insurance Co.; and Dain Rauscher Corp., a full service securities firm.

Competition

Some measures in the bill are presented as intending to increase competition in the Canadian financial services market. But others, in practice, will have the opposite effect.

Opening up the payments system to life insurance companies, securities dealers and money market funds will tend to increase competition marginally in the payments area. But encouraging the formation of new small banks, "community-based banks" as the Department of Finance Press Release puts it, by lowering capital requirements from $10 million to $5 million goes directly against the evolution of banking systems most everywhere. Not only is it unlikely to increase competition but it is more likely to lead to future bank failures and a drain on the reserves of the Canada Deposit Insurance Corporation. If the attempt is made to offset this risk with strict regulations and higher deposit insurance premiums for the upstart banks, then the measure will likely be still-born in terms of its results.

The government wishes to facilitate the credit union movement in developing national services entities that may help the movement to survive in a market where economies of scale come from large electronic management and delivery systems. This is quite appropriate although there is little in the bill that will lead specifically to that end. Its eventual impact on competition is likely to be minimal. (It is slightly ironic that here policy recognizes that large systems are needed for survival while elsewhere the bill envisages achieving increased competition through encouraging the formation of new local banks.)

Several measures over the last few years have given increased flexibility to foreign banks in the Canadian market including the valuable ability to engage in wholesale banking through branches of the parent company instead of through the more costly route of a Canadian subsidiary. Foreign bank subsidiaries in Canada have always had all the business and investment powers of Canadian banks and all size limitations on them have been removed. Bill C-8 ensures that they will have all the new investment and business powers being granted to Canadian banks. This, taken by itself, is appropriate since more competition is better than less. However, some measures of Bill C-8, including details of policy not embedded in the bill itself, will have the effect of dampening the ability of Canadian banks to compete with foreign banks.

The discriminatory measures that will have this effect include the restrictive and politicized bank merger policy which, for some time, risks preventing Canadian banks from achieving the economies of scale that their much larger international competitors are achieving; the continued prohibition against the distribution of life insurance through bank branches, which directly restricts competition in the Canadian market and indirectly does so by making bank branches less productive than they could be; the continued exclusion of the banks from the car leasing business, a business almost completely dominated by foreign institutions — a quite incredible case of Canadian law restricting competition in a Canadian market by keeping Canadian institutions from competing with foreign institutions in the Canadian market place; the threat in the bill directed at the large Canadian banks, and not at smaller competing institutions or foreign institutions located in Canada or entering the Canadian market through the Internet, that if they do not provide certain low-cost services they will be forced to do so.

But the most glaring weakness of the new policy as concerns competition is its failure to recognize clearly that by far the most important source of future competition will be large international institutions operating directly in Canada and through the Internet from outside Canada. There is little recognition that the most important issue for Canada will be the survival of at least a few large uniquely Canadian financial institutions.

Restructuring

One of the most significant aspects of globalization and the technological revolution that is driving it is the impact it is having on what constitutes economically efficient private sector institutions. The development of large-scale electronic systems has changed what constitutes optimum-sized institutions and has facilitated enlarging the range of products and services that individual institutions can offer. In response to this, financial system restructuring is taking place in virtually all countries and the size of many international institutions has increased greatly through mergers and acquisitions.

Globalization is also changing past guidelines as to what constitutes concentration in the financial services industry. This is because of the growing importance of cross-border competitors and their ability to deliver services with ease from a wide range of out-of-country suppliers. Past guidelines as to what constitutes excessive domestic concentration are becoming obsolete.

Domestic restructuring and competition policies that fail to take these developments into account risk undermining the future competitiveness of domestic financial institutions. Some measures in Bill C-8 are helpful in this respect but other ones are not. Also, since many of the important details of the measures will emerge in regulations and many actions that institutions might want to take in response to them are subject to the discretionary approval of the minister, it is not always clear how things will work out in practice.

Holding companies and investment and business powers. A positive change is one that permits the banks and life insurance companies to structure themselves under an upstream regulated non-operating holding company. This increased flexibility recognizes the great variety of activities now undertaken by those institutions and the fact that they need not be subject to identical regulatory oversight and so can be placed in separate subsidiaries of the holding company. Of course, the existing structure where subsidiaries are run off the parent operating company will remain as an option.

Additional investment powers being granted also reflect the changing world. These include, for example, the ability of a bank to own retail and wholesale banks downstream. Also the "in-house" powers of the banks are broadened in information technology, subject to ministerial discretion, and regulations can be used to extend those powers as the government deems appropriate. However, prohibition on bank branch distribution of life insurance and bank participation in car leasing is perpetuated.

Canadian large bank merger policy. Federal government policy relating to the merger of banks with equity in excess of $5 billion is outlined in the government document *Merger Review Guidelines* released along with Bill C-8, but is not reflected in any statute. Not being part of the bill itself the guidelines can be changed by the government with ease, which is fortunate or not depending on how such discretionary policy-making will be used. However, the process itself is tortuous in nature and subject at crucial stages to strong short-term political influences. It has been presented as having three stages.

Stage 1: (a) the banks apply to the Competition Bureau, the Office of the Superintendent of Financial Institutions (OSFI) and the minister of finance for permission to merge, together with assessment information; (b) the banks must prepare a Public Interest Impact Assessment (PIIA) giving the business case, costs and benefits to clients, details on branch closings and their impact, contribution to international competitiveness, employment impact, ability to adopt new technology, transition remedial steps contemplated, and impact on the structure of the industry; (c) the Competition Bureau and OSFI will review the proposal for competition and prudential considerations; (d) concurrently with the preceding reviews, the House of Commons Standing Committee on Finance and the Standing Senate Committee on Banking, Trade and Commerce (Senate Committee) will hold public hearings using the PIIA as their focal point; (e) the Competition Bureau and OSFI will report their views on competition and prudential aspects to the minister of finance, which documents the minister will make available for scrutiny to the Finance Committee and Senate Committee; (f) the latter two committees will report to the minister on the broad public interest issues raised by the merger proposal.

Stage 2: The minister of finance, drawing in part on the information in the aforementioned reports will decide if the public interest, prudential, and competition issues raised, can be addressed. If he deems that they cannot be addressed then he will simply deny permission to merge. If he deems that they can be addressed he will authorize negotiation of remedies — the third stage. A significant flaw in this stage is that the minister must make his decision before the Competition Bureau and OSFI have spelled out the specific remedies they would regard as being satisfactory — ones that would lead them to recommend approval of the mergers. Such decision-making in the dark increases the risk that short-term political factors will predominate.

Stage 3: Competition, prudential and public interest remedies will be negotiated with the banks by the Competition Bureau, OSFI and the Department of Finance. If the minister of finance judges the negotiations to have been successful then he will approve the amended merger proposal. If not, he will reject it.

These guidelines include two improvements to those initially included in the government's policy paper of June 1999. First, the government will seek to complete the whole process in a specified period of time: five months. Unfortunately there is an easy way around this in that it is "subject to the prerogatives of Parliament". Second, the Senate Committee will be involved in the process, which is desirable in that it tends to be more professional and less political in nature than the House of Commons Finance Committee in its consideration of policy issues, particularly those relating to the banks.

This process, while possessing a certain sequential logic to it, is flawed in that it is tortuous, and therefore inevitably subject to delays along the way, and risks being hostage at several crucial stages to short-term political considerations. The Finance Committee has at times shown that its recommendations in matters of bank policy can be highly political in nature, so there is no assurance that its recommendations would be based on objective analysis. The minister has the right to reject a proposal even before the Competition Bureau and OSFI have attempted to negotiate their concerns with the banks involved, as well as after, and the short-term political pressures on him can be decisive. A slightly different problem is that the Competition Bureau has indicated that it takes a two-year time perspective when appraising competition impacts of a merger — which largely misses the emerging competitive factors arising from changing technology and with it increasing cross-border competition, and risks delays in restructuring until it is too late to meet successfully emerging competitive forces. In addition, most significant mergers take at least two years to be consummated in practice, and some more than that, another reason why a two-year perspective makes the Bureau's merger analysis irrelevant.

The restriction on mergers between large banks and large de-mutualized insurance companies is even stricter than that between large banks. They are simply forbidden. The effect is to deny the financial system the synergies in the distribution of insurance products and the utilization of large electronic systems that such integration would make possible — synergies that are being captured by competing international institutions of other industrial countries.

Degree of Regulation and the Regulatory Environment. The government's press releases accompanying Bill C-8 refer to measures that streamline the regulatory process. The bill does reduce ministerial discretionary powers relating to past permitted banking activities. A positive step is giving the Superintendent full authority to approve certain applications, with automatic approval after 30 days if the Superintendent has not raised any objection. Unfortunately these would appear to be confined to matters of a relatively routine nature, with the minister of finance retaining some discretionary authority in all the major new provisions of the legislation — investment and business powers, holding companies and consumer interests.

The body of regulations that will spell out that discretionary authority is likely to be complex and in any case it will be difficult to document clearly what will and will not be permitted by such authority in specific cases. This extensive use of discretionary authority injects a high degree of uncertainty into the regulatory process. So, having in mind the complexity of the regulations that such discretionary authority will require and the uncertainty hanging over a system depending heavily on such authority, it is not likely

Edward P. Neufeld

that the regulatory system over-all will have been made more streamlined by Bill C-8.

New compliance regulations will undoubtedly emerge from the establishment of a Financial Consumer Agency of Canada (FCAC) for enforcing the consumer provisions of Bill C-8. Branch closures will also be subject to a more burdensome regulatory process including the possibility of imposition by FCAC of a consultative process in situations to be outlined in regulations.

One of the more unhelpful and seemingly worthless parts of the new regulatory requirements is the obligation on federal financial institutions with more than $1 billion equity to publish "annual accountability statements that describe their contribution to the Canadian economy and society ... for example ... small business lending, charitable donations and community involvement, and the location of openings and closings of branches" (Finance Canada, 2001). This was first suggested in the Mackay Report. The inherent difficulty, if not impossibility, of measuring long-term economic benefits of restructuring actions taken today in response to competitive pressures means that the reports will likely be exercises in political correctness, serving no useful purposes yet costly to produce as public relations documents.

The over-all effect of Bill C-8 would appear to be an increase in micro-management of some parts of the financial system, including through widespread discretionary powers left in the hands of the minister of finance. In addition to the waste of regulatory and compliance resources and so reduced competitiveness that this appears to involve, its economic costs are magnified by its inherently discriminatory nature — aimed at the large institutions that the authorities can reach and leaving untouched many institutions that they cannot reach, including small federal institutions, all provincial ones, and foreign ones evolving through Internet operations.

Survival of a Unique Canadian Financial System?

A central issue for the future is not whether there will be a financial system in Canada that provides Canadians with necessary financial services. Rather the issue is whether that system will be made up essentially of Canadian institutions, ones that can draw on decades of experience to address effectively the needs of the Canadian economy and society. International competition, coming from all directions, will ensure that Canadians will have satisfactory financial services available to them, but it also means that with inappropriate Canadian policies non-Canadian institutions over the next decade will come to dominate the Canadian market and that Canadian institutions will slip into the role of minor players.

There is a risk that this will happen under the policy directions included in Bill C-8 and the regulations and ad hoc discretionary policies that could emerge from it.

First, the large international institutions already encroaching on the Canadian market, and which will do so increasingly in the decade ahead, can do so with competitive efficiencies through economies of scale that large Canadian banks are, in practical terms, being denied by a restrictive and politicized merger policy.

Second, increasing the limit on individual voting share holdings to 20 per cent from 10 per cent, with ministerial approval, prior to the restructuring of the larger Canadian financial institutions through mergers may make it possible for outside institutions to make strategic investments in major Canadian institutions with a view to having a preferred position when Canadian merger policy does begin to facilitate restructuring. While a Canadian institution could also make such a strategic investment, it seems highly unlikely that the minister of finance would permit two large Canadian banks to develop a relationship in that way while he might well approve a foreign bank doing so. Indeed, the government seems almost to invite this when it states in its news release that the larger shareholding "would allow these institutions to enter into substantial share exchanges, including the ability to enter into strategic alliances and joint ventures" (Finance Canada, 2001). Of course the very uncertainty overhanging such discretionary rule-making illustrates the difficulty that policy is imposing on the strategic planning of the larger Canadian financial institutions.

Third, in recent years government policy has removed restrictions on the operations of foreign banks in Canada and the current bill will continue to give them the same investment and business powers as those of the Canadian banks. At the same time, because they will not be operating through extensive branch systems in Canada and some will use electronic systems almost exclusively, they will not face the regulatory burden of the large Canadian institutions. The Canadian banks meanwhile face regulatory obstacles in creating a branch system that is as low cost as possible — by placing great obstacles to consolidation through mergers, by requiring them to offer some services at low cost and by denying them the right to deliver life insurance products.

Fourth, Bill C-8 in its impact continues to shield foreign financial institutions in the Canadian automobile leasing market, which they dominate, and prevents Canadian banks from even competing with them.

Fifth, for Canadian institutions to become effective players in the emerging global market place will require them to develop strong market positions outside of Canada — not an easy challenge keeping in mind the size and market reach of their international competitors. Some Canadian banks have already closed a number of their foreign branches in the face of such competition while at the same time concentrating on getting a foothold in the U.S. market — their only option if they wish to grow and retain some place in the international system. Canadian legislation and regulations that inhibit the Canadian banks from developing capital bases of competing size through mergers and that face regulatory obstacles for creating a system in Canada of maximum efficiency have the effect of favouring foreign institutions in both the Canadian and the international markets. Without more realistic policy in Canada their relative position is likely to continue to decline, as it has in the past several decades.

It is rather surprising that Canadian policy would discriminate against the future success of its own large institutions and in favour of non-Canadian institutions, a bias clearly not rooted in economic logic or economic research.

Short-Term Political Considerations versus Long-Term Financial System Needs

Over the last decade and a half there has been an enormous amount of research on the functioning of the Canadian financial system and its regulation; and good research is indeed a necessary condition for good policy to emerge. But it is not at all a sufficient condition because of the decisive role that short-term political considerations can play.

Political considerations have always been an important part of the process of amending banking and other financial services legislation and of government appraisal of mergers and other proposals.[9] The period 1900 to 1930 was one of major consolidation within the banking system. The most

---

[9]For a very interesting account of the interplay between the banks and the government, with emphasis on the period after the Second World War, see MacIntosh (1991).

significant example was the five mergers completed by the Royal Bank of Canada which helped it increase its size in terms of assets from just under 4 per cent of the banking system to 27 per cent (Neufeld, 1992, p. 99). The mergers attracted the close and personal attention of the then minister of finance, who had concerns of a political nature, but in the end, and without great delay, they were for the most part permitted to go forward and so the necessary restructuring of the system was not unduly impeded.[10]

What distinguishes the current period from previous ones is the extent to which political considerations are impeding restructuring of the system in the face of strong market pressures for change.

Specifically, and by way of example, it is difficult to explain the following other than by short-term political considerations:

- Canadian policy that keeps potentially competitive Canadian institutions out of the foreign-dominated Canadian automobile leasing market;
- Canadian policy that prevents Canadians from buying life insurance at their local bank branch;
- ministerial rejection of bank merger proposals outright, as happened in 1998, that is, without permitting the relevant regulatory agencies from determining if official concerns could be met by the applicants;
- introduction of very complicated bank merger policy procedures that, step by step, include major political hurdles;
- imposition of regulatory burdens on the system that are not based on serious research, that are not evenly applied across the system and that reduce the system's economic efficiency;
- introduction of legislation that is replete with discretionary ministerial powers, thereby creating great uncertainty over what is acceptable to government and what is not.

Even the two most important cases of banking industry restructuring of recent years went forward when they did largely because of the playing out of political forces and not because of coherent federal government policy relating to the needed restructuring of the system. The reference here is to the integration of investment and commercial banking and the integration of the banking and trust business.

---

[10]For a detailed account of these mergers and how they came about see McDowall (1993, pp. 123-162).

Consider first the integration of investment and commercial banking.[11] In February 1986 the federal government announced that Montreal and Vancouver would be permitted to form International Banking Centres. This was in response to local pressures for them and against the advice of a study headed by a former Governor of the Bank of Canada — and viewed by most everyone as essentially a political move on the part of the federal government.

The Ontario government and the City of Toronto were very disturbed over this discriminatory decision, worrying about its impact on Toronto as a financial centre. Quebec even in the early 1980s had permitted outside ownership of its investment dealers, wishing to build up its province-based financial sector. These moves finally pressured Ontario to change substantially its historic protectionist position concerning its investment dealers, with greater readiness to consider ways of strengthening them. Opening up that industry to more sources of capital was the most logical way to achieve this and in June 1986 the Ontario minister of financial institutions announced that they would permit banks and other financial institutions to own up to 30 per cent of an investment dealer. The chartered banks, sensing a major change in the political situation, began to lobby to be permitted to have wholly-owned dealers, but they made no immediate progress.

Then in November 1986 another decision by a government agency, and the political rivalry that followed it, in effect decided the issue. The Quebec Securities Commission announced that it would permit the Bank of Nova Scotia to have a full service dealer in Quebec. Of course, the federal chartered banks were prohibited from acquiring such a dealer but the Bank of Nova Scotia achieved it under the "temporary investment powers ..." of the *Bank Act*. The Ontario government then clearly faced the possibility of a major shift of the dealer industry out of Ontario, and so began negotiations with the federal government concerning bank ownership of such dealers and how they might be regulated. By the end of the year both governments had accepted the idea of bank ownership and had agreed on how bank-owned dealers would be regulated by the two levels of government (the "Hockin-Kwinter Accord[12]). This then led within several years to the

---

[11]For a detailed discussion of how this came about see MacIntosh (1991, ch. 14).

[12]Named after the then federal minister of state (Finance) Tom Hockin and the then Ontario minister of financial institutions, Monte Kwinter.

acquisition of the major investment dealers by the banks and a very large infusion of capital into the investment dealer industry. The interplay of federal-provincial political forces had succeeded where rational economic arguments up to then had failed — they had brought about a fundamental change in the structure of the industry.

The second example of how political exigencies rather than a clear understanding of the need for industry restructuring led to a desirable change in the structure of the industry is the integration of the banking and trust industries. A trust industry separate from banking was unique to Canada with even the United States having integrated it into the banking system at the end of the nineteenth century. Periodic failures among the smaller Canadian trust companies over the years had indicated problems in the industry, including corporate governance, economies of scale and regional diversification problems. The substantial similarity in activities between banks and trust companies because of the dominance of financial intermediation activities over trust activities in the latter, had removed any rational justification for maintaining them as a separate industry. But both federal and provincial legislation had done so until the early 1990s.

Then when the federal law was changed in 1992 making it technically possible for a widely-held bank to acquire a trust company, any merger proposal still was subject to the discretion of the minister of finance. One aspect of that discretion was the informal but firm policy of the federal government that "big shall not buy big". But then with little advance warning Royal Trust, the largest Canadian trust company, ran into financial difficulties and faced the prospect of bankruptcy. Had it failed the Canada Deposit Insurance Corporation would have faced a large financial drain because of the guaranteed deposits of Royal Trust, which in turn would probably have required loans to it from the federal Consolidated Revenue Fund. Royal Bank of Canada, after several weeks of intensive due diligence investigations, made an offer which Royal Trust accepted and which was quickly approved by the minister of finance. Thus a "big" bank had acquired a "big" trust company. Within several years the largest part of the Canadian trust industry had been integrated into the banking system — a restructuring that had made perfectly good sense for years but had been opposed by federal and provincial policies.

One aspect of this experience may still be of importance. The earlier rule "big shall not buy big" was presumably modified by the Royal Trust case to "big shall not buy big unless one of the big ones faces bankruptcy". While this rule was ostensibly replaced by the articulated bank merger process outlined above, in fact the wide discretion left with the minister in that process means that the rule may still be very much in place. Yet were one of the big banks or insurance companies to face serious financial difficulties there is little doubt that federal government approval for a merger would come quickly.

A policy that in effect stands in the way of a merger between healthy institutions and requires that one or other of them must be in financial straits before a merger is permitted would not appear to serve the system well. The merger of two healthy institutions, and the controlled integration that it permits, would preserve the strength of both; while waiting until one of the institutions finds itself in financial difficulties would risk wasting much of its valuable resources in terms of customer base and executive talent, to the advantage of other, including some foreign, institutions.

There is a serious danger in permitting major aspects of restructuring to be driven by short-term political considerations. The danger is that the credibility of and the confidence in the official direction of financial system restructuring will be undermined. The "chill" that this has imposed on integration projects of individual financial institutions is probably already an important obstacle to restructuring among the larger Canadian financial institutions, particularly the banks. It would today take courageous bank management to come forward with a merger proposal of any significance under circumstances where the project is to a substantial degree hostage to short-term political considerations.

Summary and Conclusions

Appraising the Canadian financial system against weaknesses revealed by the Asian financial crisis shows that in most respects, but with two vital exceptions, it is well positioned to survive the many challenges of globalization. Its strengths include the stable macroeconomic environment now that inflation is under control and budget surpluses permit a reduction in the public debt; a well-developed regulatory system with qualified regulators; increasing transparency in the operations of financial and other institutions; greater emphasis on corporate governance than in past decades; and a tradition of regular reviews of financial system statutes and regulations.

However, the exceptions, and major weaknesses, are the failure of current restructuring policy to take into account how global forces are reshaping competitive institutions and the dominance of short-term political considerations at the expense of long-term national interest. There appears to be a presumption in Canadian policy that it can be indifferent to its impact on the economic efficiency, that is the cost base, of the large Canadian financial institutions, particularly the banks. The most costly example of this is the practical obstacles placed in the way of mergers. It is in Canada's long-term interest to have at least a few strong and internationally competitive financial institutions, ones that know intimately the character and needs of Canada's economy region by region. This requires policy to facilitate mergers that will achieve that objective. Current policy does not appear to lead to that outcome and risks persistent erosion of the Canadian aspects of the financial system and growing dominance of it by others. This process has already begun and the rapid changes occurring in international competition mean that this trend will not become less important. A change now in Canada's restructuring policies could minimize future damage, but it could not undo damage already done.

The fact that some of the major obstacles to necessary restructuring rest not in the legislation itself but rather in regulations and in the discretionary authority of the minister of finance, means that it would be possible to remove them relatively quickly. Removing them could ensure that Canada, in the years to come, would retain something in the nature of a unique Canadian financial system with institutions that are internationally competitive and important. But this can happen only if there is policy leadership willing to put aside short-term political complications when making industry restructuring decisions and focus strongly on the long-term needs of the Canadian financial system.

References

Finance Canada (2001), *News Release 01-014*, February 9.
Friedman, T.L. (1999), *The Lexus and the Olive Tree: Understanding Globalization* (New York: Farrar, Straus and Giroux).
MacIntosh, R. (1991), *Different Drummers, Banking and Politics in Canada* (Toronto: Macmillan Canada).

McDowall, D. (1993), *Quick to the Frontier, Canada's Royal Bank* (Toronto: McClelland & Stewart).

Neufeld, E.P. (1972), *The Financial System of Canada: Its Growth and Development* (Toronto: Macmillan Canada).

_____ (2000), "What Kind of a Financial System do Canadians Want?" Discussion Paper No. 2000(1) (Kingston: School of Policy Studies, Queen's University).

North American Economic Integration and Globalization

Morley Gunderson

The June 11, 2001 cover of the Canadian edition of *Time* magazine featured "Welcome to Amexica: What's Happening on the U.S.-Mexico Border is Changing a Continent". The text inside (p. 23) declared that "the American Century could give way to the Century of the Americas and the border might as well have disappeared altogether". The text described "NAFTA prospectors" who saw the opportunity to make their fortune by opening factories along the border — factories that otherwise would have gone to Asia. It also talked of the rise of the "NAFTA manager" — the new breed of managers who are equally at home in Mexico or the United States.

The same cover featured "Canada and Silicon Valley", with the story inside showing a map of silicon circuits connecting major Canadian and U.S. cities. The story referred to the "integrated tech world of North America" (p. 61) and it highlighted numerous Canadians who interact continuously with Silicon Valley and various Canadian high-tech nodes. The approximately 80,000 Canadians who live in Silicon Valley have established invaluable networks, especially with respect to venture capital, and are "bringing home their knowledge and their contacts — either by returning to

Financial assistance from the Government of Canada funded project on Regional Aspects of Employment Relations Policy in Canada is gratefully acknowledged.

Canada or by sharing their expertise and Roladexes with U.S. and Canadian colleagues" (p. 61). Such networks are fostered by the Venture Capital Advisory Board — an informal collection of Canadians who work at some of the Valley's most powerful venture capital firms. Others are fostered by the informal "toque parties" at local bars. Perhaps the integrated aspect of this economy is best illustrated by the fact that some Canadians who have made their fortune in Silicon Valley are sharing their philanthropy between Canada and the United States. Jeff Skoll, the co-founder of the Internet auction eBay, has donated $4.9 million to his alma mater, the University of Toronto, and is also financing an inner-city craft-school program in Pittsburgh, Pennsylvania that is a springboard to college for disadvantaged children.

These Mexican and Canadian features illustrate that one aspect of globalization involves markets across North America becoming more integrated. This is true for markets for goods and services, financial capital, physical capital, human capital, labour and ideas. Such integration results from the rationalization of production to exploit the comparative advantages of different countries and to obtain the economies of scale for world production. Not surprisingly, North American market integration has implications for a wide range of issues, from income distribution to national sovereignty.

The purpose of this paper is to highlight the various dimensions of economic integration and its implications. Reflecting the comparative advantage of its author, the focus is on labour issues. The paper begins with a discussion of the various dimensions of economic integration as well as the existing and proposed forms of economic integration. It highlights the implications for internal integration as a precondition for external efficiency under globalization. The new regionalism is discussed, as is the declining importance of border effects. Issues pertaining to policy integration and harmonization across countries are discussed, as are international responses in such areas as the labour side accord in the North American Free Trade Agreement (NAFTA), social clauses in trade agreements, corporate codes of conduct, social labelling, consumer boycotts, transnational actions amongst unions, social groups and non-governmental organizations (NGOs), and union-to-union co-operation. The paper concludes with a discussion of the main policy issues that merit consideration.

Concepts of Integration

Economic integration has both a *deepening* and a *widening* dimension (see Gomez and Gunderson, 2001; Hoberg, 2000; Weintraub, 1994). The deepening dimension refers to the expansion of the different aspects or functional areas and market dimensions that are involved in expanding exchange. These aspects include:

- freerer trade in *goods and services*, usually enhanced by reductions in tariffs and non-tariff barriers to trade, leading to expanded exports and imports;

- freerer flows of short-term *financial capital* in response to investment opportunities;

- increased flows of longer-term *capital* in the form of foreign direct investment and plant location and investment decisions, often enhanced by relaxation of foreign ownership rules;

- enhanced flows of *human capital* embodied in labour sometimes through temporary visas for professional, technical and managerial personnel or intra-company transfers, and sometimes, more permanently as part of a brain drain;

- enhanced *mobility of basic labour* in general, sometimes through temporary work permits and sometimes through permanent immigration and emigration;

- *integrated operations of multinationals*, with head offices and research and development often done in one country, outsourcing to suppliers in other countries, production and assembly done in another country (sometimes through their own plants, sometimes through local companies), and warehousing in other countries, all facilitated by advanced transportation and communications systems; and

- enhanced flows of *ideas and technology transfer*, facilitated by the other aspects of integration as well as by the advanced communications systems of the new knowledge economy, and often involving issues of intellectual property rights.

The *widening* aspect of economic integration involves the expansion of these different dimensions of deeper integration across different countries and regions. In North America, examples include:

- the Auto Pact of 1965 involving integrated production in one industry,
- the Canada-U.S. Free Trade Agreement of 1989, and
- the expansion to include Mexico under the North American Free Trade Agreement, signed in 1992 and ratified by Canada in 1993.

Other aspects of widening as part of North American integration may also include:

- further expansion of NAFTA to include countries such as Chile, Argentina or Columbia, as well as possible existing regional trade blocs such as MERCOSUR (Argentina, Brazil, Paraguay and Uruguay), the Andean Pact (Bolivia, Columbia, Ecuador, Peru and Venezuela) and CARICOM (the Caribbean Basin countries); and

- complete widening through a Western Hemisphere agreement to involve North, Central and South America including the Caribbean Basin.

In theory, the different dimensions involved in the deepening of economic integration can act as complements or substitutes. Free trade, for example, can be a substitute for labour mobility since the goods can embody the labour that otherwise would move.[1] They can also be complementary, however, if immigration fosters backward linkages to suppliers and customers in the country of origin of the immigrants, as well as enhancing technology transfers and capital and investment flows (Head and Reis,

---

[1]The fact that the recent brain drain is not as large as it was earlier and that may be expected based on the large income and unemployment rate differences between Canada and the United States (Helliwell, 2001) could occur in part because free trade is a substitute for such mobility. The mobility that did occur tended to be in non-tradable sectors like health and education, reflecting the cutbacks in those areas in Canada and the tax rate differences at higher income levels.

1998). In practice, it appears that the complementarities dominate with enhanced exchange in goods, services, capital, human capital, labour and ideas increasing together in a self-reinforcing fashion.

Similarly, regional trading blocs can be a substitute for more general multilateral trade expansion. Again, however, they appear to foster expansion as other countries join the blocks or they merge.

Internal Integration and External Competitiveness

Deeper and wider economic integration can also foster the internal integration within a country since such integration is generally regarded as a precondition for external competitiveness. North American economic integration, for example, provided impetus for Canada to develop the Internal Free Trade Agreement of 1994, with the aim of fostering the internal trade and capital and labour mobility. Such an internal arrangement is designed to help rationalize production and achieve the economies of scale necessary for successful competition in the global economy. However, the extent to which it has been effective in removing internal trade barriers, especially provincial procurement policies, is open to question.

Within Canada, increased attention is being paid especially to removing barriers to the interprovincial mobility of labour.[2] Such barriers exist in various forms. Professional licensing and certification[3] requirements especially amongst self-governing professions often create barriers in such forms as educational requirements, intern training periods, licensing examinations and residency requirements. Licensing and certification can also exist for particular trade and occupational groups such as electricians (licensed) or mechanics (certified). Interprovincial mobility is often restricted by the different licensing or certification requirements, the different trades

---

[2]For an expanded discussion see Gunderson (1994) and references cited therein.

[3]Under occupational licensing only the licensed professional can practise (i.e., they have an exclusive right to practise) while under certification others can practise but only the certified professional can use the professional designation (i.e., they have an exclusive right to title).

that are licensed or certified, and the failure to recognize qualifications from other provinces. For the licensing and certification of both professionals and trades, there are also failures to recognize the qualifications of immigrants.

In addition to these constraints, preferential hiring practices can also exist whereby governments often give preferences to the hiring of local residents as public employees. Such preferential practices can also apply indirectly to the private sector through government procurement practices in the awarding of government contracts or through the granting of permits for natural resource projects. The extent to which preferential hiring practices and occupational barriers have an important impact on deterring internal mobility is open to debate in part because there is little systematic analysis of their effects.

Income security programs can also deter interprovincial mobility. They can do so directly, through residency requirements (sometimes informally through administrative practices) and limits on portability. And they can do so indirectly by reducing the post-transfer income differences that otherwise may provide the economic incentive to move. While public pensions are completely portable, private employer-sponsored occupational pensions may not be completely portable because of vesting requirements and because of the loss of service credits and benefit accruals if people leave "early".

In Canada, differences in the education system across the provinces may also deter interprovincial mobility. At the elementary and secondary level this can occur because of differences in the curriculum and testing standards. At the university level it can occur through implicit or explicit quotas as well as residency requirements for financial aid.

In many of these areas, attempts are being made to reduce the barriers to labour mobility, in part to foster the internal competitiveness that can facilitate external competitiveness in the global economy. The Red Seal program involving the mutual recognition of trade qualifications across provinces is expanding. Efforts are being made to recognize the qualifications and credentials of immigrants. Preferential hiring practices are being curbed, as are the preferences in government procurement policies. Pension regulations have required earlier vesting periods, and there has been some shift to defined contribution plans that are completely portable.

New Regionalism

The previously discussed changes were in the direction of fostering the internal mobility of labour that in turn can foster internal competitiveness as a precondition for external competitiveness under increased globalization. Thus, the external integration fosters internal integration.

The forces of integration within North America, however, are also changing the axis of integration, creating new regional alliances and shifting the traditional trade patterns and orientation of Canada from east-west to north-south. The east-west pattern was fostered by somewhat artificial factors such as the protective tariff and non-tariff barriers to trade as well as the building of the transcontinental railway, both being part of the National Economic Policy of 1878. More recently, however, new regional alliances are being formed, based on more natural economic trade and investment patterns. Examples include: the Cascadia region involving the British Columbia, Washington and Oregon triangle (Goldberg and Levi, 1993); Winnipeg increasingly regarding itself as the northern end of a transportation corridor via Interstate 29 to Mexico and a north-south rail network linking Canada and Mexico;[4] Quebec fostering ties with New England, especially for the sale of its natural resources including hydro power (Konrad, 1995); and Alberta increasingly looking south for the sale of its oil and natural resources. The Golden Horseshoe surrounding Toronto, which provided manufactured goods to the rest of Canada under the protective tariff, increasingly aligns itself south of the border. As stated by Krugman, "Industrial Ontario is aptly considered by geographers to be part of a common American manufacturing belt" (1991, p. 71). The Golden Horseshoe is essentially ten hours driving time from major U.S. markets in cities like New York, Boston, Philadelphia, Baltimore, Washington, Pittsburgh, Cincinnati, Cleveland, Detroit and Chicago. Courchene and Telmer describe the region as a new region state, replacing the old nation-

---

[4]This was recently fostered by the approval in 1999 of Canadian National's proposed US$ 2.4 billion acquisition of the Illinois Central railroad which would create a continental rail network linking Canada, the United States and Mexico. This highlights the north-south economic integration of the service market. The integration of the capital market is illustrated by the fact that the majority of shares in the expanded Canadian company are held by Americans (Handelman, 2000, p. 21).

state. In fact, they describe it as the "premier economic region state within North America" (1998, p. 2).

Whether one goes so far as to say that the new region states and city-states are replacing the now defunct old nation-states (Ohmae, 1996), the fact remains that in Canada new north-south regional alliances are forming, and the traditional east-west orientation is shifting towards one that involves more integration with the United States and Mexico.

Border Effects

This changing orientation is further illustrated by the declining importance of borders although, as Helliwell (1998, 2001) emphasizes, borders still matter with respect to various aspects of exchange. Border effects[5] are estimated via gravity models where trade flows are a function of the distance between trading partners and their size. The empirical evidence indicates that borders matter in that internal trade flows across provinces within Canada in the late 1980s were about 18 times larger than were external trade flows across the Canada-U.S. border, even after adjusting for differences in distance and size of the market. That is trade between cities within Canada was about 18 times larger than was trade between Canadian and American cities of the same size and distance from each other. This preference for internal trade compared to external trade can be attributed to a wide range of factors including familiarity, networks, exchange-rate risks, customs regulations, laws, regulations and institutions, and perhaps the legacy of earlier preferential tariffs.

What is important for the purposes of illustrating the significance of integration, however, is that border effects were reduced dramatically after the Canada-U.S. Free Trade Agreement (FTA) of 1989. That is, the east-west internal trade flows across provinces were reduced from being 18 times greater than were the north-south external trade flows with the United States in 1990, to 12 times greater by 1993. The importance of "the border" was cut by one-third over a brief three-year period of time surrounding the FTA.

---

[5]See McCallum (1995) and Helliwell (1998, 2001) and references cited therein.

The effect of the FTA seems to have been "one shot", with the ratio of internal to external trade levelling off fairly quickly in the post-FTA era.

The north-south versus east-west orientation and the change in that orientation differs substantially across the various regions of Canada.[6] Prior to the FTA, the importance of internal trade within Canada relative to external trade with the United States was greatest for Ontario and Nova Scotia, but below average in all other provinces, especially for Alberta and British Columbia. The restructuring away from internal east-west trade and towards external north-south trade was greatest in Ontario and Quebec and the least in British Columbia and Saskatchewan.

Overall, the following trends have emerged:

- a dramatic shift away from internal east-west trade to external north-south trade occurred in Canada over the brief period surrounding the FTA;

- that shift towards economic integration with the United States was most pronounced in Ontario and Quebec;

- after the shift the four western provinces were most integrated with the United States (as they generally were prior to FTA) in the sense of having the lowest ratio of internal trade within Canada relative to external trade with the United States; and

- in spite of this greater integration with the United States, as Helliwell (1998) emphasizes, borders still matter as Canadians still seem to have a preference for internal versus external trade. While borders are "coming down" throughout the world, they nevertheless remain important for a variety of markets — goods and services, physical and financial capital, human capital, and labour in general.

---

[6]Calculations given in Gunderson (1998b, p. 210) based on data from Helliwell (1998).

Policy Integration

Integration can also occur on the policy front, sometimes as part of a conscious design to harmonize or standardize policies to facilitate exchange, and sometimes as an indirect by-product of the other aspects of integration.

Adopting a *common currency* such as with the euro in the European Union, or under a North American Monetary Union[7] is a form of monetary integration designed to facilitate exchange.[8] This can also occur less formally through the increased use of the currency of a particular country for exchange purposes, as is currently occurring through *dollarization*. Other standardized policies could also facilitate exchange within a country as a precondition for external competitiveness. As discussed previously, in the labour area this can occur in such areas as occupational licensing, health and safety standards, qualification recognition, education and training standards and the elimination of preferential hiring and procurement practices.[9]

Integration on the policy front can also occur through the emulation of "best practices" (or "worst practices" depending upon one's political views!) in the policy arena. Engaging in various forms of exchange with other countries provides greater exposure to the policies of those countries, making them more obvious contenders for adoption.

Policy harmonization can also occur if particular policies could be interpreted as unfair subsidies and hence subject to trade sanctions. There would be pressure to reduce such policies to the levels of those of the trading partner, with harmonization being a natural result of this process.

The same applies to the reduction of non-tariff barriers to trade. Under the policy of "national treatment" governments are under an obligation to impose the same regulations on their domestic producers as they impose on imports, with harmonization being a natural by-product.

---

[7]For an expanded discussion see Harris (2000).

[8]Because there essentially would be no exchange rate under a monetary union, it would also make it more difficult for inefficient employer practices to prevail under the "protection" of a devalued Canadian dollar.

[9]Various articles in Bhagwati and Hudec (1996a,b) discuss harmonization of standards in other areas such as products, technology, commercial transactions, intellectual property rights, tax policies and environmental protection.

Morley Gunderson

The strongest pressure for policy integration, however, comes from the indirect effect that other forms of integration place on governments in establishing and administering their policy initiatives. With freerer trade and capital mobility, firms have a more credible threat of relocating their plants and business investment away from countries with the higher regulatory costs and into those with lower regulatory costs. Political jurisdictions are under more pressure to compete for that business and its associated jobs, with the reduction of costly legislative and regulatory initiatives being one instrument in that competitive process. Hence, there is concern on the part of some that harmonization will be to the "lowest common denominator" — that there will be a "regulatory meltdown" with Canadian labour laws and regulations conforming to those of the right-to-work states of the U.S. South, or of the Mexican maquiladoras. In essence, the concern is that our policy initiatives are also shifting from an east-west orientation to a north-south one. At this stage, however, there is insufficient evidence to determine if harmonization is leading to the lowest common denominator.[10]

The north-south shift as it relates to labour policy is an important issue — *the* most important *labour* issue with respect to integration. In fact, it may be the most important consequence of trade liberalization and globalization — more important than the conventional gains from trade. For those who eschew such government initiatives, this is, of course, a positive development. It is essentially subjecting the policy-making process to the same scrutiny of the forces of competition that apply to business and labour. This perspective is buttressed by the fact that the laws and regulations that will be under the most pressure to dissipate are those that are the most inefficient in that they protect the rents of particular interest groups and impose costs without offsetting benefits. Laws and regulations that have an efficiency rationale and foster competitiveness will not only survive, but indeed thrive under such political competition. This *may* be the case, for example, with policies that provide a social safety net or that compensate those who lose from efficient changes and hence reduce their resistance to such change. Workers' compensation can be associated with costly payroll taxes but it

---

[10]The stringent conditions for downward harmonization, and examples of mixed evidence is given in Gunderson (1998a, 1999). Studies in the political economy tradition that conclude that Canada still has considerable control over its domestic policy initiatives even in the face of greater economic integration include Banting, Hoberg and Simeon (1997); Banting and Simeon (1997); and Hoberg (2000).

may also save on the costs of the tort liability system since workers essentially give up their right to sue their employer under such a system. Advance notice requirements for plant closings or mass layoffs *may* foster efficient job search. Guaranteeing wage payments that are due *may* foster the contractual arrangements that are so important in facilitating exchange. Occupational health and safety regulations *may* offset the information asymmetries that can inhibit compensating wage premiums for risk from ensuring the optimal degree of workplace health and safety.

It is even possible that multiple equilibrium can prevail with different jurisdictions providing different Tiebolt-type combinations of regulations with their associated costs and benefits, with firms and workers sorting into the jurisdictions based on the extent to which they are affected by the costs and benefits. While such markets are likely to be "thin" given the various combinations of regulations, they likely can be packaged into combinations involving low costs and low regulations, and high costs and more regulations with their associated benefits.

One area where there can be a serious "market failure" in such political competition is with respect to distributional or equity-oriented policies that do not have positive feedback effects on efficiency (Gunderson and Riddell, 1995). Some policies may have such positive feedback effects, for example, if they reduce resistance to otherwise efficient change or save on social costs elsewhere, such as crime. But some simply do not "pay for themselves". In such circumstances, it will be difficult to sustain such equity-oriented policies under globalization even if the citizenry generally desires them. Corporations may find them laudatory, but they may find it difficult to pay the corporate taxes to sustain them when competing with other countries without such high taxes. Financial capital is seldom willing to "pay the price" except in the case of "social funds". Individual citizens may be willing to pay their share of the tax burden, but this can be compromised by the fact that individuals with a high embodiment of human capital may have the mobility to "escape" the high taxes, leaving only the immobile factor of production (middle and low-wage labour) bearing the burden of the tax. These issues are compounded if the more generous equity-oriented policies serve as a magnet to attract more disadvantaged persons. They are further compounded by the fact that increased adjustment consequences and polarization of market outcomes have occurred because of trade liberalization and especially skill-biased technological change (see Campbell, Haces, Jackson and Larudee, 1999; Jackson and Robinson, 2000). In essence, the demand for equity-oriented initiatives may have increased at the same time as the ability of governments to provide them is circumscribed.

Global problems require global solutions. However, the international institutions are largely not there to provide such solutions, and to the extent that they are present, they often have other associated problems. Nevertheless, there has been a wide range of international responses to the potential policy vacuum created by globalization and integration.

International Policy Responses

Of particular relevance to labour policy under NAFTA is the *labour side agreement* — the North American Agreement on Labour Cooperation. The agreement essentially obliges each country to enforce its own existing labour standards (Compa and Darricarrère, 1996; Diamond, 1996). As such, there is no formal loss of sovereignty since each country is simply required to do what it is legally supposed to do internally in the first place. The sanctions are minimal, and mainly involve adverse publicity in the "court of public opinion". Other trade agreements in Latin America and the Caribbean are also including side agreements on labour policy (Aparicio-Valdez, 1995).

Such side agreements can take on many faces. Depending upon the perspective of the viewer,[11] they can be regarded as:

- "toothless" token gestures designed to give the appearance of forestalling downward harmonization, but doing little in reality;

- token "bribes" designed to reduce the opposition to trade liberalization by offering minimal concessions required to obtain free trade;

- "diversion tactics" to redirect pressure from consumer advocacy groups that threaten boycotts, Internet "outing" and other publicity campaigns;

- "image advertising" to portray a good corporate image;

---

[11]This viewer regards each of these perspectives as containing a grain of truth.

- "stepping stones" for building the infrastructure for more meaningful regulations with sanctions and enforcement procedures;

- a form of "minimal protection" designed to reduce the most egregious concerns;

- "thin-edges-of-the-wedge" for ultimately establishing more costly regulations with sanctions and enforcement procedures;

- "thinly disguised protectionism" requiring the poorer countries to harmonize upwards and hence to lose some of their comparative advantage of low-cost labour; and

- a "viable adjustment strategy" that slows down the rapid adjustment that otherwise would ensue because of large labour cost differences.

Stronger sanctions can be involved in *social clauses as part of trade agreements* when there are enforcement mechanisms across the countries as is the case with the European Union.[12] Cases can be brought to the European Court of Justice, with the results binding on the parties and setting precedence for the interpretation of the laws in each country. In the case of the EU, countries like Germany and France that already had high wages and labour standards advocated such clauses. The intent was to compel "upward harmonization" of such standards in the lower wage, new entrants like Spain and Portugal as a condition of entry into the EU for those countries. This also highlights the concerns that such practices are simply thinly disguised protectionism designed to reduce competition on the basis of labour costs (Bhagwati, 1994). To assist in such upward harmonization, however, the EU also provided "social funds" to the poorer country.

Corporate codes of conduct have also been advocated for multinationals that do business across less-developed countries, and that often subcontract to locally managed operations often accused of being "sweatshops".[13] Both

---

[12]The history of including social clauses in trade agreements is discussed, for example, in Servais (1989), Swinnerton and Schoepfle (1994), and van Liemt (1989).
[13]Corporate codes are discussed, for example, in Compa and Darricarrère (1996); Erickson and Mitchell (1996); Liubicic (1998); and in various articles in Blanpain (2000).

the Organisation for Economic Co-operation and Development (OECD) in 1976 and the International Labour Organization (ILO) in 1977 set out voluntary guidelines for multinationals emphasizing that they should adhere to local laws and provide wages and labour standards at least as good as those provided locally. These are largely redundant recommendations since multinationals tend to try to be "model employers" in the first place, being particularly sensitive to the public image. The ILO and OECD guidelines also refer to freedom of association; non-discrimination in employment; consultation and information-sharing; preferences for and training of local employees; and of a greater potential constraint — refraining from threatening to transfer operations so as to influence bargaining.[14] While the latter is likely to be the most important credible threat of multinationals, it is not likely to be one that has to be overtly threatened; it is a threat that is obvious.

In 1998, the ILO also followed up with its Declaration on Fundamental Principles and Rights at Work, obliging all members to follow and promote basic core rights: freedom of association and the right to bargain collectively; the elimination of forced or compulsory labour; the abolition of child labour; and the elimination of employment discrimination.

Social labelling, the modern variant of the old "union label", has also been advocated as a way of informing consumers of the working conditions under which the product was produced (Freeman, 1994; International Labour Office, 1997). For economists, such procedures have appeal since they provide information and otherwise adhere to consumer sovereignty. Those who want to purchase that attribute, possibly paying a positive price for the "social content" of the product can do so. Some people may be willing to pay a positive price for an alligator logo on a shirt, or a Gap label, or a social label — no accounting for tastes. There is, of course, the issue of the effectiveness of such labelling given the incentive to "support the cause" but buy the cheapest elsewhere. Evidence, however, suggests that consumers are willing to pay a positive price for the "social content" of the goods they consume (Elliott and Freeman, 2001).

Consumer boycotts against products produced under sweatshop conditions can also be particularly effective especially against multinationals

---

[14]For discussion of the ILO and OECD codes of fair competition see Gunther (1992); various articles in Blanpain (2000); and at <http://oecd.org/daf/cmis/cime/mneguide.htm>.

whose products are marketed through the creation of an image.[15] In a world where image is everything, those who live by an image can die by an image. Such boycotts can be particularly effective in a world of "Internet outing" as can occur, for example, with <www.corpwatch.org>. They can also put pressure on multinationals to ensure that they cannot distance themselves through outsourcing to local suppliers — employers who can be the modern-day equivalent of the overseer under slavery in the U.S. South.

Unions have been involved in many of the previously discussed initiatives. They have also engaged in efforts to share information and co-ordinate with counterpart unions, social groups and NGOs in the other countries. With respect to NAFTA, this has taken various forms: "site visits, educational tours and workshops, meetings attended by representatives of organizations from the three countries, regular communication and exchange of information (aided by faxes and access to computer networks), joint political strategizing around NAFTA, solidarity actions around specific conflicts, pressuring of government officials and politicians to concern themselves with events in the other countries, and so on. Cross-border collaboration has taken place at both the grassroots level of people-to-people contacts and amongst organization leaders" (Cook, 1994, p. 146; see also Brooks, 1992; and Thorup, 1991).

These efforts are part of transnational actions on the part of unions, social movements and NGOs to deal with international issues especially amongst trading partners to try to fill some of the void left by the weakened role of sovereign states in dealing with these issues (Sikkink, 1993). Especially prominent are issues pertaining to human rights since they garner the most publicity and broadest political support. Some transnational union-to-union efforts have also occurred (Cook, 1994), although these have generally involved simply sharing of information and acts of solidarity over specific conflicts. Broader efforts at coordinated bargaining or international union mergers have been hampered by legal and institutional differences and traditional union rivalries that make international unionism less prominent (Murray, 2001).

In essence, to deal with the labour and social issues arising under globalization, considerable actions have occurred in various dimensions: labour side agreements; enforceable social clauses as part of trade

---

[15]Examples include campaigns against Nike, Reebok and Wal-Mart; see Elliott and Freeman (2001); Kech and Sikkink (1998); and Klein (1999).

agreements; corporate codes of conduct; social labelling; consumer boycotts; transnational efforts amongst unions, social groups and NGOs; and union-to-union cooperation. These have been designed to fill at least part of the void left by the difficulty that national governments have in dealing with labour and social issues that arise under globalization, and their reluctance to relinquish sovereignty over laws and policies to international bodies. Whether these have much more than a symbolic effect compared to the ability of governments to establish and enforce laws and policies is an open and interesting question.

Policy Implications

Clearly NAFTA and globalization in general are fostering the integration of various North American markets — for goods and services, financial capital, physical capital, human capital, labour and ideas. This is occurring through both the deepening and the widening aspects of integration.

A variety of policy implications flow from the analysis.

* Internal integration is an increasingly important precondition for external efficiency under global integration. This implies more attention must be paid to barriers to labour mobility that can be fostered by such factors as licensing and certification requirements, preferential hiring practices, lack of pension portability, and the failure to recognize credentials and qualifications.

* New economic regions more closely linked with U.S. regions are forming with particular cities becoming more important in that realignment. Local labour markets in each region are thereby becoming more important, highlighting the need for more local labour market information on a "just-in-time" basis to serve the "just-in-time" needs of the employment relationship. Such local labour market information on skills mismatches and skill shortages can be particularly important for reducing the skill bottlenecks that can inhibit meeting the emerging global challenges.

- Skills development will be increasingly important in general, given that the effective use of human resources in the knowledge economy is the new comparative advantage for higher wage countries like Canada given the declining importance of traditional sources of comparative advantage such as access to raw resources and markets. With prices of goods, capital, human capital and labour increasingly being determined in world markets, the strategic use of human resources is one of the few remaining degrees of freedom.

- While still important, borders are becoming less important, shifting the former internal east-west orientation within Canada to more of an external north-south orientation to the United States. Policy initiatives must take account of that re-orientation, with U.S. policies and practices becoming more important as a benchmark.

- This implies pressure for the harmonization of policy initiatives in the direction of those of our trading partners, the United States and Mexico. This is fostered mainly by interjurisdictional competition for business investment and the jobs associated with that investment, with businesses now having a more credible threat at the political bargaining table (as well as at the collective bargaining table).

- While this raises the spectre that the harmonization will be to the lowest common denominator (the U.S. South, and the *maquiladoras* of Mexico), it is the case that regulations that serve an efficiency rationale will survive, while inefficient regulations, and especially those that protect the rents of particular interest groups, will be under the most pressure to dissipate.

- In that vein, governments should thereby delineate their appropriate role under these circumscribed circumstances, likely focusing on dimensions that will make markets more efficient such as through providing labour market information (especially at the local level), uniformity in trades and occupational certification and licensing, facilitating pension portability, supporting active adjustment assistance programs that facilitate adjustment in the direction of market forces rather than passive income maintenance programs that can deter such adjustment, and providing the efficient delivery of their own programs.

Morley Gunderson

- The area of greatest social concern (in the view of the author) is that pure equity-oriented policies that serve an important social purpose, but which do not have positive feedback effects on efficiency, will also be more difficult to sustain. This can be particularly problematic since the polarization that is occurring because of trade liberalization and especially technological change may be increasing the need for such policies.

- In such circumstances, governments should again *focus* their more circumscribed role on policy initiatives with an equity-oriented focus to assist the disadvantaged who are being bypassed by the new opportunities under globalization.

- International responses in such areas as the labour side accord in NAFTA, corporate codes of conduct, social labelling, consumer boycotts, transnational actions amongst unions, social groups and NGOs, and union-to-union cooperation can play a role, but it is a limited role without the laws and enforcement procedures of governments, and such supranational institutions are not likely in North America since each of the three nations jealously guards their sovereignty, even if it is a more limited sovereignty.

- The interesting question that emerges from this new role of policy in a more integrated North American environment is whether this more circumscribed role of governments and greater role of market forces will, in the long run, benefit the more disadvantaged, including those in the poorest country, Mexico. So far, the greater emphasis on market forces seems to have left significant numbers of disadvantaged persons bypassed by the changes and unable to take advantage of the new opportunities that are created. Whether that will be true in the longer run, remains an interesting and open question — in fact, *the* interesting question associated with integration and globalization. The equitable sharing of the efficiency gains of deeper and wider economic integration will likely determine the long-run sustainability of this important and growing phenomenon.

- While there are grounds for optimism on this front, it is cautious optimism, based on the notion that an expanding economy will draw in the disadvantaged in the long run, and that if this does not occur through market forces, there will be a realization that the sustainability of the efficiency gains will require action on the social front.

References

Aparicio-Valdez, L. (1995), "Hemispheric Integration and Labour Laws", *International Journal of Comparative Labour Law and Industrial Relations* 11 (Summer), 99-111.

Banting, K. and R. Simeon (1997), "Changing Economies, Changing Societies", in K. Banting, G. Hoberg and R. Simeon (eds.), *Degrees of Freedom: Canada and the United States in a Changing World* (Montreal and Kingston: McGill-Queen's University Press), 23-70.

Banting, K., G. Hoberg and R. Simeon (1997), "Introduction", in K. Banting, G. Hoberg and R. Simeon (eds.), *Degrees of Freedom: Canada and the United States in a Changing World* (Montreal and Kingston: McGill-Queen's University Press), 3-22.

Bhagwati, J. (1994), "Fair Trade, Reciprocity and Harmonization: The New Challenge to the Theory and Policy of Free Trade", in A. Deardorf and R. Stern (eds.), *Analytical and Negotiating Issues in the Global Trading System* (Ann Arbor, MI: University of Michigan Press).

Bhagwati, J. and R. Hudec, eds. (1996a), *Fair Trade and Harmonization: Vol. 1, Economic Analysis* (Cambridge, MA: MIT Press).

_____ (1996b), *Fair Trade and Harmonization: Vol. 2, Legal Analysis* (Cambridge, MA: MIT Press).

Blanpain, R., ed. (2000), *Bulletin of Comparative Labour Relations.* Special Issue on Multinational Enterprises and the Social Challenges of the XX1st Century: The ILO Declaration on Fundamental Principles at Work. Public and Private Corporate Codes of Conduct, 37.

Brooks, D. (1992), "The Search for Counterparts", *Labor Research Review* 19, 83-96.

Campbell, B., M.T. Guitiérrez Haces, A. Jackson and M. Larudee (1999), *Pulling Apart: The Deterioration of Employment and Income in North America Under Free Trade* (Ottawa: Canadian Centre for Policy Alternatives).

Compa, L. and T. Darricarrère (1996), "Private Labor Rights Enforcement Through Corporate Codes of Conduct", in L. Compa and S. Diamond (eds.), *Human Rights, Labor Rights, and International Trade* (Philadelphia, PA: University of Pennsylvania Press), 181-198.

Cook, M. (1994), "Regional Integration and Transnational Labor Strategies under NAFTA", in M. Cook and H. Katz (eds.), *Regional Integration and Industrial Relations in North America* (Ithaca, NY: ILR Press), 142-166.

Courchene, T. with C. Telmer (1998), *From Heartland to North American Region State* (Toronto: University of Toronto, Centre for Public Management).

Diamond, S. (1996), "Labor Rights in the Global Economy: A Case Study of the North American Free Trade Agreement", in L. Compa and S. Diamond (eds.), *Human Rights, Labor Rights, and International Trade* (Philadelphia, PA: University of Pennsylvania Press), 199-226.

Elliott, K. and R. Freeman (2001), "White Hats or Don Quixotes? Human Rights Vigilantes in the Global Economy", NBER Working Paper No. 8102 (Cambridge, MA: National Bureau of Economic Research).

Erickson, C. and D. Mitchell (1996), Labour Standards in International Trade Agreements", *Labour Law Journal* 47 (December), 763-773.

Freeman, R. (1994), "A Hard-Headed Look at Labour Standards", in W. Sengenberger and D. Campbell (eds.), *Creating Economic Opportunities: The Role of Labour Standards in Economic Restructuring* (Geneva: ILO), 79-92.

Goldberg, M. and M. Levi (1993), "The Evolving Experience along the Pacific Northwest Corridor Called Cascadia", in R. Green (ed.), *The Enterprise for the Americas Initiatives: Issues and Prospects for a Free Trade Agreement in the Western Hemisphere* (Westport, CT: Praeger), 99-119.

Gomez, R. and M. Gunderson (2001), "The Integration of Labour Markets in North America", in G. Hoberg (ed.), *North American Integration: Economic, Cultural and Political Dimensions* (Toronto: University of Toronto Press).

Gunderson, M. (1994), "Barriers to Interprovincial Labour Mobility", in F. Palda (ed.), *Provincial Trade Wars: Why the Blockade Must End* (Vancouver, BC: Fraser Institute), 131-154.

_____ (1998a), "Harmonization of Labour Policies under Trade Liberalization", *Relations industrielles/Industrial Relations* 53(1), 24-52.

_____ (1998b), "Regional Impacts of Trade and Investment on Labour", *Canadian Journal of Regional Science* 21 (Summer), 197-226.

_____ (1999), "Labour Standards, Income Distribution and Trade", *Integration and Trade* 3 (January), 82-104.

Gunderson, M. and C. Riddell (1995), "Jobs, Labour Standards and Promoting Competitive Advantage: Canada's Policy Challenge", *Labour*, S125-S148.

Gunther, H. (1992), "The Tripartite Declaration of Principles Concerning Multinational Enterprises and Social Policy", in R. Blanpain (ed.), *International Encyclopedia for Labour Law and Industrial Relations*, Vol. 1 (London: Kluwer).

Handelman, S. (2000), "The Rise of North America Inc.", *Canadian Journal of Policy Research* 1 (Spring), 17-23.

Harris, R. (2000), "The Case for a North American Monetary Unit", *Canadian Journal of Policy Research* 1 (Spring), 93-96.

Head, K. and J. Reis (1998), "Immigration and Trade Creation: Econometric Evidence from Canada", *Canadian Journal of Economics* 31 (February), 47-62.

Helliwell, J. (1998), *How Much Do National Borders Matter?* (Washington, DC: The Brookings Institution).

_____ (2001), "Canada: Life Beyond the Looking Glass", *Journal of Economic Perspectives* 15 (Winter), 107-134.

Hoberg, G. (2000), "Canada and North America Integration", *Canadian Public Policy/Analyse de Politiques* 26 Supplement (August), S35-S50.

International Labour Office (1997), *The ILO, Standard Setting and Globalization: Report of the Director General* (Geneva: ILO).

Jackson, A. and D. Robinson with B. Baldwin and C. Wiggins (2000), *Falling Behind: The State of Working Canada, 2000* (Ottawa: Canadian Centre for Policy Alternatives).

Kech, M. and K. Sikkink (1998), *Activists Beyond Borders: Advocacy Networks in International Politics* (Ithaca, NY: Cornell University Press).

Klein, N. (1999), *No Logo: Taking Aim at the Brand Bullies* (New York: Picador).

Konrad, H. (1995), "Borderlines and Borderlands in the Geography of Canadian-United States Relations", in S. Randal and H. Konrad (eds.), *NAFTA in Transition* (Calgary: University of Calgary Press).

Krugman, P. (1991), *Geography and Trade* (Cambridge, MA: MIT Press).

Liubicic, R. (1998), "Corporate Codes of Conduct and Product Labelling Schemes: The Limits and Possibilities of Promoting International Labor Rights through Private Initiatives", *Law and Policy in International Business* 30 (Fall), 112-158.

McCallum, J. (1995), "National Borders Matter: Canada-U.S. Regional Trade Patterns, *American Economic Review* 85, 615-623.

Murray, G. (2001), "Unions: Membership, Structures, Actions and Challenges", in M. Gunderson, A. Ponak and D. Taras (eds.), *Union-Management Relations in Canada*, 4th ed. (Toronto: Addison-Wesley Longman), 79-116.

Ohmae, K. (1996), *The End of the Nation State: The Rise of Regional Economies* (New York: The Free Press).

Servais, J.-M. (1989), "The Social Clause in Trade Agreements: Wishful Thinking or an Instrument of Social Progress?" *International Labour Review* 128, 423-433.

Sikkink, K. (1993), "Human Rights, Principled Issue Networks, and Sovereignty in Latin America", *International Organization* 47 (Summer), 411-441.

Swinnerton, K. and G. Schoepfle (1994), "Labor Standards in the Context of a Global Economy", *Monthly Labor Review* 117 (September), 52-58.

Thorup, C. (1991), "The Politics of Free Trade and the Dynamics of Cross-Border Coalitions in U.S.-Mexican Relations", *Columbia Journal of World Business* 26 (Summer).

van Liemt, G. (1989), "Minimum Labour Standards and International Trade: Would a Social Clause Work?" *International Labour Review* 128, 433-448.

Weintraub, S. (1994), *NAFTA: What Comes Next* (Washington, DC: Center for Strategic and International Studies).

Regional Issues

Has Quebec's Standard of Living Been Catching Up?

Pierre Fortin

Introduction

David Slater has always been a great inspiration for me. His concern has been that economists should strive to connect deep theoretical thinking with practical affairs and public policy. This is an old view of the role of the economist in society, one that Maynard Keynes, in particular, carried to its highest accomplishment in the twentieth century. It is an old view not in the sense of being passé, but of being a firmly established and ever relevant view of what our profession is about. I get comfort in seeing the best and brightest among our colleagues still advise governments, work for governments and even engage in politics. In my generation, Olivier Blanchard, Willem Buiter, Stan Fischer, Pedro Malan, John McCallum and Larry Summers are good examples to watch.

Speaking of Keynes, David remained inspiringly Keynesian through the 1970s and 1980s, when conservative ideology came to dominate thinking in economic theory and policy and Keynes was repeatedly pronounced dead. I am referring to Friedman's monetarism, to Lucas' equilibrium business cycles based on price misperceptions and to Prescott's real business cycles based on productivity shocks. Conservative macroeconomics eventually petered out both on empirical grounds and against the counterattacks of New

Keynesians such as Akerlof, Blanchard, Grandmont and Stiglitz. As Paul Krugman (1994, p. 197) nicely put it, Keynes has proved to be the "Energizer Bunny" of economics. Greenspan's brand of success at the helm of the U.S. Federal Reserve owes almost everything to Keynes, and almost nothing to the conservative icons of those two dark decades. David had it right all along. His common sense helped many of us weather the passing storm.

David has also been helpful in a more personal way by inviting me to be a member of the Economic Council of Canada in 1985, and a member of the Board of Directors of the Centre for the Study of Living Standards in 1995. He has even guided my judgement in the preparation of this short paper. My understanding of the regional implications of Canadian military expenditures during the Second World War, which I explain below, owes much to his deep knowledge of wartime public finance (Slater, 1995).

Unsolved Mysteries

My subject is Quebec's relative growth performance since World War II. In his seminal 1971 contribution to the study of Canadian regional growth from Confederation to 1956, Alan Green stated: "In spite of its high degree of industrialization coupled with its locational advantages, Quebec has remained consistently below the national average and below that of its neighbour, Ontario. Why this divergence in Quebec and why its persistence are still largely unsolved mysteries" (Green, 1971, p. 44). He ended his study by emphasizing again: "A search for answers to this problem would seem imperative" (Green, 1971, p. 68).

The question raised by Green about Quebec is the primary motivation for this paper. While, mainly due to paucity of data, I will not answer his question about the province's lack of economic convergence towards Ontario before the 1960s, I will nevertheless show that a solid convergence process was at long last underway at the very moment Green's book appeared in the early 1970s. There is also another motivation behind this paper. In the last three years, two popular books by Jean-Luc Migué (1998) and Gilles Paquet (1999) and a widely-quoted policy paper by Marcel Boyer (2001) have produced very negative assessments of Quebec's post-Quiet Revolution economic performance. All three essays are motivated by various political agendas. I will not discuss them in detail, but essentially "do my thing". It will be clear from the empirical results I report that I am more sanguine about Quebec's economic performance and prospects than those authors are. The key difference between my view and theirs is that, where they see an empty glass, I see it as already half-full and still filling.

The Bottom Line

It is an easy matter to show that the Quiet Revolution (QR) has been accompanied by faster per capita economic growth in Quebec than in Ontario. The summary evidence is presented in Figure 1. The figure provides a "difference in differences" picture of the trend in Quebec's real domestic income per capita *as a percentage* of Ontario's back to 1926.[1] The long-term picture is clear. From the late 1920s to the late 1950s, there was decline and stagnation in Quebec's relative standard of living — exactly as observed by Green. Beginning at 78 per cent of Ontario under Taschereau in the late 1920s, Quebec's relative position ended the 1950s at 74 per cent of its neighbour under the Duplessis regime. Conversely, in the last 40 years the standard-of-living gap between Quebec and Ontario has shrunk. It fell to 14 per cent in 1999 from 26 per cent in 1960. This translates into an average gap-narrowing rate of 1.8 per cent per year over the last four decades. By international historical standards, this is neither slow nor rapid convergence, but just average speed (see Barro and Sala-i-Martin, 1999). Migué (1998) has recently stated that Quebec did relatively well in the pre-QR period, and characterizes the post-QR period as one of relative economic decline and stagnation for the province.[2] Figure 1 shows that the exact opposite is true:

---

[1] Real domestic income per capita is calculated as the linked series for provincial personal income less government transfer payments to persons (for 1926–1961) and gross domestic product (for 1961–2000) divided by the total population and the consumer price index (CPI) for Montreal or Toronto. The CPI ratio between Quebec and Ontario is multiplied by the factor 0.972, reflecting estimated purchasing power parity in the base year 1992.

[2] Migué states that pre-QR per capita growth in Quebec was "parallel" to Ontario growth. He does not realize that this defines exactly the nature of the pre-

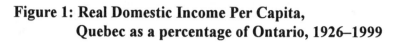

Figure 1: Real Domestic Income Per Capita,
Quebec as a percentage of Ontario, 1926–1999

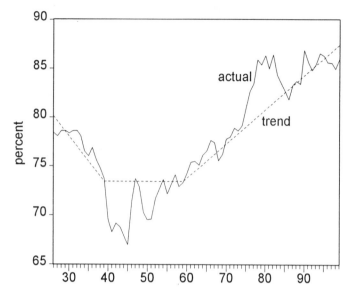

Source: Statistics Canada and author's calculations.

it is the earlier period that was one of decline and stagnation, and the more recent period that has been one of relative growth and catch-up. QED.

This does not end the discussion, however. First, two important anomalies must be recognized and explained: the sharp drop between 1939 and 1945, and the big bubble of 1975–85. Second, the sources of the long-term convergence since the late 1950s must be identified and understood.

QR problem raised by Green: lack of convergence before 1960. He omits looking at the entire 1926–60 and 1960–99 periods, but instead selects sample periods, such as 1946–58 or 1994–98, that (perhaps inadvertently) suit his argument. In making interprovincial comparisons, he sometimes neglects deflating aggregate activity by population. He compares investment, productivity and employment trends across provinces without paying attention to widely different population growth rates. He often emphasizes remaining gaps between Quebec and Ontario, but does not report whether those gaps have been widening or narrowing.

Pierre Fortin

And third, the prospects for a continuation of convergence in the future must be assessed.

First Anomaly: The Second World War

The first of the two anomalies is the big drop in the standard-of-living ratio between Quebec and Ontario during the Second World War, which can be seen in Figure 1. The ratio dropped sharply from 74 per cent in 1939 to 67 per cent in 1945, and then suddenly climbed back to 74 per cent in 1947. The likely explanation is the regional pattern of military expenditures during the war, which turned out to be highly skewed against Quebec. Military pay was about $3 million each in Quebec, Ontario and the rest of the country in 1938. By 1945, it had increased to around $100 million in Quebec and $500 million each in Ontario and the rest of Canada. Compared to a proportional sharing of military pay according to regional population, this constituted a major redistributive shock amounting to 10 per cent of Quebec's personal income. This is more than enough to explain the relative drop of the Quebec economy during the war. Quebec men paid very dearly for their reluctance to enrol in the armed forces. The lack of data by province makes it difficult to say anything about the regional distribution of other war expenditures and the regional concentration of the military-industrial complex.

Another temporary drop in Quebec's relative economic performance occurred from 1948 to 1951. This remains a puzzle. Confirming the picture in Figure 1 at the manufacturing level, Raynauld (1961, Table 26) reports that the ratio of manufacturing value-added per employee between Quebec and Ontario fell sharply from an average of 92 per cent in 1943–46 to 85 per cent in 1948–51. This was clearly not caused by a similar regional distortion of military pay during the Korean War. Such a distortion simply did not occur. Another candidate for an explanation would be some regional unbalance resulting from C.D. Howe's postwar reconstruction policies. It is not known whether these factors can account for the 1948–51 drop, or the persistent lack of convergence of Quebec's productivity towards Ontario's for the rest of the 1950s.

Second Anomaly: The Big Bubble of 1975–85

The second anomaly that stands out in Figure 1 is the big bubble in Quebec's relative performance that took place between 1975 and 1985. Over the four years, 1975–78, Quebec's real income per capita shot up from 79 per cent to 86 per cent of Ontario's. It stayed at about this level over the next four years until 1982, and then receded to around 83 per cent by 1985. Understanding what happened in this period is key to interpreting the long-term trend correctly. Does the fact that in 1999 Quebec's income, at 86 per cent of Ontario's, was no higher than in 1978 imply that the 20-year period, 1979–99, was one of relative stagnation for the province, as argued by Boyer (2001), for example? Or should the entire period 1975–85 be, for some reason, considered as an outlier, and the 1986–99 period seen as a return to the pre-existing, long-term trend established before 1975?

The big push of 1975–78 was first underlined by Gérard Bélanger (1980) and further analyzed by Paul Davenport (1981). Both authors pointed out that faster labour productivity growth in Quebec than in Ontario was the main factor behind Quebec's startling relative income performance in that four-year period. It then looked as if Quebec had escaped the worldwide slowdown in productivity that had begun around 1973. This is supported by Figure 2, which shows that Quebec's labour productivity increased from 89 per cent of Ontario's in 1974 to 98 per cent in 1978. The Quebec-Ontario ratio stayed around this level over the next three years, and then peaked at 101 per cent in 1982. Then, over the next 17 years, Quebec's relative productivity trended down, reaching 93 per cent in 1999.[3]

Bélanger and Davenport had two opposite conjectures to interpret the 1975–78 development. Bélanger thought relative productivity was high

---

[3]Labour productivity is calculated as real gross domestic product (GDP) divided by employment from the *Labour Force Survey*. The Quebec-Ontario real GDP ratio is obtained through division of the Quebec-Ontario nominal GDP ratio by the Quebec-Ontario CPI ratio adjusted for purchasing power parity. To the extent that the interprovincial CPI ratio differs from the interprovincial ratio of implicit GDP deflators, the resulting statistic is not *true* relative labour productivity, but the product of true relative labour productivity and relative terms of trade (where, by a slight abuse of language, "terms of trade" is taken to mean the ratio between the implicit GDP deflator and the CPI). In 1954–60, GDP is replaced by personal income.

because relative real wages were high. Davenport thought relative real wages were high because relative productivity was high. We all know, of course, that labour productivity and real wages are closely connected endogenous variables that reflect interactive firm and employee behaviour. This is borne out by a comparison of Figure 2 with Figure 3, which traces relative wage trends back to 1961.[4] Relative labour productivity and relative real wages tend to follow broadly similar time paths through much short-term wandering.[5]

With the benefit of hindsight, it seems that Bélanger's conjecture was the correct one. The supporting evidence is both qualitative and quantitative. The qualitative evidence is historical. The mid- to late 1970s were years of extreme tension in Quebec's labour markets and labour relations. A large number of major construction projects were proceeding simultaneously (the James Bay Project, the Montreal Olympics, the Mirabel Airport, the Montreal Metro, etc.). Very generous wage settlements were granted in the provincial public sector in 1975 and 1979. There was civil disobedience, union leaders were thrown in prison, the La Grande Dam construction site was sacked, a provincial task force was commissioned to investigate corruption and violence in the construction industry, and the province by far led the country — if not the world — for the annual number of days lost per worker due to labour conflicts. Labour reforms were very favourable to the union side, social policy was expanding rapidly, and the provincial minimum wage reached almost 60 per cent of the average wage. These developments are entirely consistent with the wage explosion that occurred in 1975–78, was sustained until 1982, and momentarily brought average weekly earnings in Quebec to *exceed* those in Ontario in both nominal and real terms (Figure 3).

---

[4]Average real weekly earnings are calculated as average weekly earnings divided by the CPI adjusted for purchasing power parity. Deflation by the CPI instead of the implicit GDP deflator justifies the same note of caution as for the definition of relative labour productivity. There is a break in the average weekly earnings series in 1983, when coverage was broadened to cover the public sector and firms of smaller sizes. The old and the new series are linked in that year.

[5]The two curves should not be expected to coincide in any given region. There is much short-term wandering, measurement error could be significant, and the degree of competition in product and labour markets as well as the technological-organizational connection between labour and output can differ significantly across regions.

Has Quebec's Standard of Living Been Catching Up?

**Figure 2: Labour Productivity (real GDP per worker)
Quebec as a percentage of Ontario, 1946–1999**

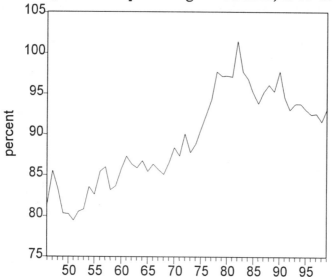

Source: Statistics Canada and author's calculations.

**Figure 3: Average Real Weekly Earnings,
Quebec as a percentage of Ontario, 1961–1999**

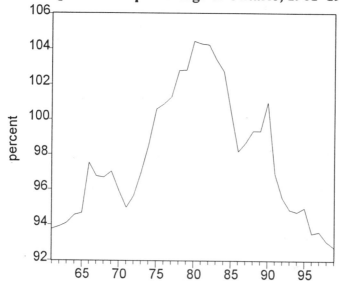

Source: Statistics Canada and author's calculations.

Pierre Fortin

The quantitative evidence is based on the identifying behaviour of the employment rate, the profit share and the capital-labour ratio. First, Quebec's employment rate dropped sharply from 90 per cent of Ontario's in 1975 to 85 per cent in 1982 (see Figure 4).[6] Second, the corporate profit share in Quebec plummetted from 93 per cent of its Ontario counterpart in 1961–73 to 72 per cent in 1981–86, once the effects of the wage explosion could no longer be masked by the pre-1981 cyclical expansion (see Figure 5).[7] Third, consistent with the slump in relative profits, Quebec's capital-labour ratio stopped rising as a percentage of Ontario's and began to decline after reaching its peak in 1982 (see Figure 6).[8] The crucial point is that in each case the medium-term trend is consistent with the occurrence of a relative wage push, and just the opposite of what one would expect from a favourable relative productivity shock. The latter would have been accompanied by *increases* in relative employment, profit share and capital-labour intensity (see Blanchard, 2000, among others). The focus on the *medium-term* trend is crucial here. Owing to the large ongoing investment projects, the cyclical expansion was much stronger in Quebec than in Ontario in the second half of the 1970s. The extent of disequilibrium introduced by the wage explosion was therefore hidden for a while.

The Bélanger hypothesis on the role played by exogenous institutional and policy developments can be extended to interpret post-1982 trends in productivity and wages, which both headed downward. Again, the evidence is historical-qualitative and quantitative. Historically, it can be argued that the 1982 recession, which was much more devastating in Quebec than in Ontario, became a sort of "day of reckoning" for the union movement and the

---

[6]The employment rate of the working-age population is the fraction of that population who are employed. For 1946–66, the working-age population is defined as the population aged 14 and over. For 1966–2000, it is the population aged 15 and over. The two series are linked in 1966.

[7]The corporate profit share is equal to corporate profits before taxes as a share of net domestic income.

[8]The capital-labour ratio is the capital stock per person employed. It is defined as net non-residential private and public capital stock in constant 1992 dollars divided by total employment. The capital stock is depreciated through the (infinite) geometric depreciation method. No adjustment for purchasing power parity is made.

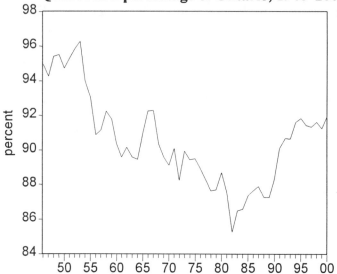

Figure 4: Employment Rate of the Working-age Population, Quebec as a percentage of Ontario, 1946–2000

Source: Statistics Canada and author's calculations.

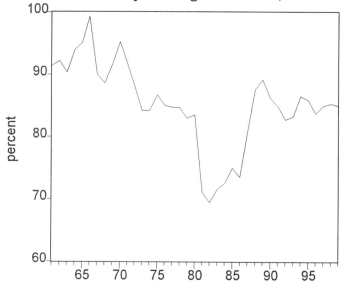

Figure 5: Corporate Profit Share, Quebec as a percentage of Ontario, 1961–1999

Source: Statistics Canada and author's calculations.

Pierre Fortin

Figure 6: Capital-Labour Ratio,
Quebec as a percentage of Ontario, 1961–2000

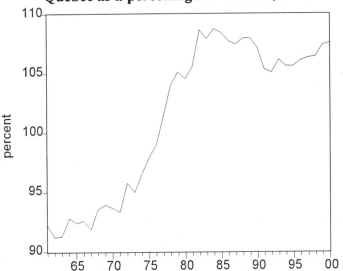

Source: Statistics Canada and author's calculations.

provincial government. The right to strike was severely restricted by the *Essential Services Act*, the 1983 public sector bargaining round brought a stinging defeat for unions with spillovers to the private sector, rank-and-file members began to require unions to focus less on wage increases and more on job security, labour conflicts suddenly became less frequent and shorter in Quebec than in Ontario, the Solidarity Fund of the Quebec Federation of Labour became an important supplier of venture capital, social policy became more prudent, and the provincial minimum wage was frozen for an extended period. Somewhat like the Netherlands after 1982 and Ireland after 1987, Quebec after 1982 entered a prolonged period of wage moderation and peaceful labour relations. Simultaneously, it seems that wages and labour relations in Ontario came under stress under the Peterson and Rae governments, which reinforced the downward trend in the Quebec-Ontario real wage ratio.

The quantitative evidence is also consistent with the hypothesis that declining relative wages caused declining relative productivity after 1982, instead of the reverse. Again, the identifying variables are the employment

Has Quebec's Standard of Living Been Catching Up?   *391*

rate, the profit share and the capital-labour ratio. There were favourable turnarounds in all three variables. First, Quebec's relative employment rate stopped declining and began to increase right after 1982. From 85 per cent in that year, the Quebec-Ontario employment-rate ratio rose to 92 per cent in the second half of the 1990s (Figure 4). This is two points higher than the 1961–74 pre-wage explosion average of 90 per cent. Figure 7 brings additional supporting evidence from unemployment behaviour. The average unemployment-rate gap between the two provinces rose from 2.2 points in 1965–76 to four points in 1977–90. It then declined again to 2.7 points in 1991–2000.[9] Second, beginning in the second half of the 1980s, the Quebec income share of corporate profits regained much of the ground lost previously against Ontario. Starting from 74 per cent in 1986, the ratio of profit shares eventually came to exceed 85 per cent in 1989. It has hovered around that level through the 1990s (Figure 5). Third, Quebec's relative capital-labour ratio finally stopped declining in 1992. Since then, it has trended upward slightly (Figure 6).

Let me summarize the argument. The "second anomaly" in Quebec's global economic performance since 1926 took the form of a temporary bubble above trend for relative income per capita around 1975–85 (see Figure 1). The proposed story is one of strong cyclical expansion accompanied by a wage explosion in the second half of the 1970s, and followed by a return to wage moderation after the 1982 recession. The wage explosion was a major economic disturbance, but its deleterious effects on employment, profits and capital formation were temporarily hidden by the short-term expansion until the recession struck in 1982. The depth of the recession forced the union movement and the provincial government to finally acknowledge the damage. At that point, they realized that a return to wage moderation and improved labour relations was essential for a recovery of employment, profitability and capital formation. Winding down the wage excesses of the 1970s was a long process. It took until the 1990s before employment, profits and capital intensity were really back on track, relatively speaking. The Quebec economy was much better prepared to weather the 1991 recession than the 1982 recession. In fact, contrary to much of what could be read at the time in the national press (including horrifying tales of Sainte-Catherine Street being literally shut down), employment took a much

---

[9]The unemployment rate of the labour force is the number of persons who want to work but are without jobs expressed as a fraction of all those who want to work.

Figure 7: Quebec-Ontario Unemployment Rate Gap, 1946–2000

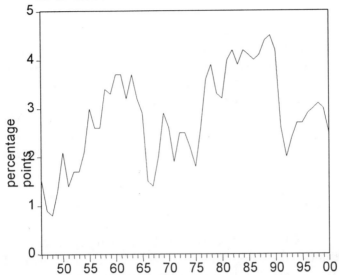

Source: Statistics Canada and author's calculations.

smaller hit in Quebec than Ontario during the 1991 recession and its aftermath.

A blind focus on the 20 years of observations, 1979–1999, in Figure 1 would seem to imply that this entire period was one of relative stagnation for Quebec. This is a mistaken view. The key implication of the discussion has been that there was a major wage explosion in the second half of the 1970s, which was later repaired by persistent wage moderation in the 1980s and 1990s. This means that the entire period, 1975–85, should be, for this reason, considered as an outlier involving a major, but temporary bubble in relative performance. In this interpretation, the Quebec economy after 1985 should be seen as reverting to its pre-1975 rising long-term relative trend, shown as a dotted line in Figure 1.

Accounting for Convergence Since 1960

Let us now return to the bottom line. Quebec's real domestic income per capita increased from 74 per cent of Ontario's in 1960 to 86 per cent in 1999. In log points, this means exactly half of the initial Quebec-Ontario gap was closed in four decades.[10] To better understand this development, it is instructive to decompose real income per capita into its three sources: productivity, employment and demographics. There are indeed three ways for a population to get richer: producing more per worker, putting more adults to work, and making less babies. In pure accounting terms, this follows from the canonical decomposition:

$$Y/N = (Y/E)(E/A)(A/N) ,$$

where Y = real GDP, E = employment, A = working-age population, N = total population. The three ratios are: Y/E = labour productivity, E/A = employment rate, and A/N = working-age ratio (the percentage of the total population who are of working age). Let us examine, in reverse order, how each ratio has contributed to the gap-narrowing process.

First, beginning in the early 1960s, the baby-boomers began to enter the working-age population in large numbers. They also made a lot less babies than their parents. The baby boom was followed by a baby bust. With more persons of working age and fewer children to feed, the working-age ratio A/N increased. This gave an automatic upward lift to income per capita Y/N. The demographic windfall was more pronounced in Quebec than in Ontario because Quebec's fertility rate started at a higher level and landed at a lower level than Ontario's. Figure 8 shows that Quebec's working-age ratio rose swiftly from 92 per cent of Ontario's in the mid-1950s to 101 per cent in the late 1970s.[11] It has stayed around this level ever since. A not-insignificant 35 per cent of the 1960–99 increase in Quebec's relative income per capita can be attributed to this demographic shift.

---

[10]Since [log(.74)]/[log(.86)] = 0.501.

[11]The working-age ratio expresses the population aged 14 and over (in 1946–65) or 15 and over (1966–99) as a percentage of the total population.

Figure 8: Working-Age Ratio,
Quebec as a percentage of Ontario, 1946–1999

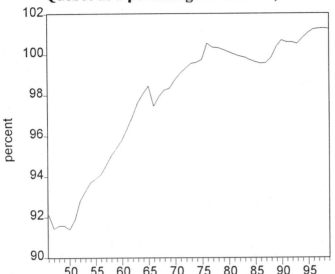

Source: Statistics Canada and author's calculations.

Making fewer babies is not the most glorious way to increase a region's standard of living, but it is an inevitable mathematical consequence. It is also a temporary one. The phenomenon will reverse itself when the baby-boomers begin to retire in large numbers around 2010. Less adults to work will tend to slow down Quebec's income growth. Moreover, the province will be harder hit by this reversal because it will age more rapidly than other regions.

Second, the trend in Quebec's relative employment rate (the E/N ratio), already reported in Figure 4, initially deteriorated from 1953 to 1960. This development owes much to the fact that women's labour force participation began to increase much later in Quebec than Ontario, but is also due to the better performance of the job market in Ontario, as underlined by the rise in the unemployment-rate gap between the two provinces in that period. Except for the spike around Expo 67, the next 15 years until 1974 witnessed some stability in the Quebec-Ontario employment-rate ratio, at around 90 per cent. Then came the big drop to 85 per cent in 1982, followed by the recovery to 92 per cent up to the second half of the 1990s, which I have already linked to the wage explosion of 1975–78 and the post-1982 climate of wage moderation.[12] Rising educational standards and the concomitant catch-up in the labour force participation rate of Quebec women were also important movers of the relative employment rate in the last two decades.

On net between 1960 and 1999, the increase in Quebec's relative employment rate was less than two points — from 90 per cent to 91.5 per cent. The four-decade contribution of the rise in relative employment to narrowing the income gap with Ontario is therefore small — about 10 per cent. However, that contribution has been of major significance in the more recent, post-1982 period. It has been strong enough to more than offset the downward adjustment in relative labour productivity (Figure 2) and allow relative real income per capita to continue to rise on trend after 1985 (Figure 1).

Relative labour productivity is the third factor that has contributed to the narrowing of the income gap. It has been responsible for the remaining 55 per cent of the process. It can be seen in Figure 2 that the Quebec-Ontario productivity ratio (which may also include a relative terms-of-trade element) increased from 86 per cent in 1960 to 93 per cent in 1999. This means the Quebec-Ontario productivity gap declined at the average rate of 2 per cent per year over the 39-year period, 1960–99. Again, this is neither slow nor fast by international historical standards (Barro and Sala-i-Martin, 1999). The growth in relative productivity has not always been smooth. Relative productivity increased rather smoothly from 83 per cent in 1954 to 89 per cent in 1974, then spiked at 101 per cent in 1982, and has since adjusted downward to 93 per cent in 1999. Just as in the case of relative employment, movements in relative productivity after 1974 can be related to the peculiar sequence of wage explosion and wage moderation observed in Quebec over the last quarter-century. One factor that has retarded the increase in relative productivity is the emigration of hundreds of thousands of highly-skilled anglophones between 1960 and 1980. Since many of them settled in Ontario, this had the effect of both reducing productivity in Quebec and increasing it in Ontario.

---

[12]Due to its slow population growth, Quebec can see its employment rate increase faster than in other regions even if its share of national employment growth is smaller than its share of the Canadian population. This continues to cause much confusion about Quebec's relative employment situation in public and media discussions.

Future Outlook

What are the prospects for a continuation of convergence in the future? The demographic outlook is for stability in Quebec's working-age ratio relative to Ontario's. Further, there are no indications that the current social peace and good industrial relations are about to end. Hence, the future behaviour of productivity and employment will be the key determinant of relative economic convergence. In turn, this will depend on Quebec's relative propensity to save and to invest in education, infrastructures and equipment, and research and development. I now survey Quebec's performance in each of these three areas.

First, concerning education, Table 1 uses data from the Canadian census and the U.S. *Current Population Survey* compiled by Lemieux (1999) to compare schooling trends in Quebec, Ontario and the United States in 1991 for three cohorts of men born in 1926, 1946 and 1966. Quebec men born in 1926 spent almost two years less in school than Ontario men of the same generation. In fact, their level of schooling was *less* than black American men of the same age. The Quebec-Ontario schooling gap began to shrink with the cohort of men born in 1946. In this cohort, Quebec men averaged

Table 1: Average Number of Years of Schooling in 1991 of Men Born in 1926, 1946 and 1966, Quebec, Ontario and the United States

Birth year	Quebec	Ontario	United States	
			White Population	*Black Population*
1926	9.0	10.9	12.1	9.4
1946	11.7	12.8	13.5	12.2
1966	14.0	13.9	12.9	12.7

Source: Lemieux (1999, p. 53).

Has Quebec's Standard of Living Been Catching Up?

about a year of schooling less than Ontario men. Incidentally, this constitutes evidence that the winds of change had already been blowing for a while in Quebec when the Quiet Revolution began "officially" in 1960. Eventually, the Quebec-Ontario gap was closed entirely with the generation born in 1966. Overall, from the 1926 cohort to the 1966 cohort, the average level of schooling increased by five years in Quebec and by three years in Ontario. In both provinces, years of schooling for the 1966 generation exceed the corresponding U.S. level by one year. Updates from Statistics Canada's *Labour Force Survey* indicate that in the fall of 2000 school attendance among the 15–19 population was 85 per cent in Quebec and 86 per cent in Ontario. Among the 20–24 population, the figures were 40 per cent in Quebec and 42 per cent in Ontario. There seems to be already near-complete educational convergence among the younger generations of the two provinces.

Given the close connection between education levels and the employment rate, the closing of the schooling gap between Quebec and Ontario since the 1950s must have played a major role in the turnaround of Quebec's relative employment rate begun in the 1980s. Further, there should be more to come. As older, less educated generations are progressively replaced by younger, more educated generations, we should see the Quebec-Ontario employment-rate gap continue to shrink over the medium to long term. In 2000, for example, the employment rate for men aged 50 to 64 in Quebec was only 89 per cent of that in Ontario. But for men aged 30 to 49, the Quebec-Ontario ratio was 95 per cent. The same kind of cohort-based evidence is available for the unemployment rate. In this case, the Quebec-Ontario gap was 3.8 percentage points for the 50–64 age group, and 2.5 points for the 30–49 group. This is indicative of future decreases in the interregional unemployment-rate gap. Of course, these are "other-things-equal" projections. The future should never be taken for granted. Much will depend on success in reducing illiteracy and dropout rates further and in improving the general quality of education.

The second area to look at is investment in infrastructures and equipment. Figure 6 can be interpreted as broad evidence that Quebec does not lag behind Ontario in equipping its labour force with non-residential productive capital. Quebec's capital-labour ratio is relatively high, in particular due to heavy investment in hydro-electric dam sites in the 1960s and 1970s. The most worrisome trend here is that the investment-to-GDP ratio has trended down both provincially and nationally since the 1950s. The main challenge for the future is to redress the situation by adopting policies

Pierre Fortin

supportive of saving and investment, such as raising **RRSP** limits, incurring fiscal surpluses, shifting public expenditures towards infrastructure development, and making the tax and general economic environment more competitive.

The third and final sensitive area for growth is investment in reasearch and development. Regional data on direct R&D spending begin only in 1979. The available time series for Quebec and Ontario are graphed in Figure 9 as percentages of GDP. The evidence they provide is that direct spending on R&D as a percentage of GDP grew faster in Quebec than Ontario between 1979 and 1997. Quebec's R&D spending-to-GDP ratio overtook Ontario's beginning in 1995. This is rather impressive, given that all federal R&D spending made in Ottawa are included in the Ontario total. There is, in particular, a strong concentration of high-tech industries in the Montreal area, supported by favourable federal and provincial tax and grant policies. This bodes well for the future, although one wonders whether enough attention has been paid so far to encouraging the *diffusion* of domestic and foreign new technology across firms and industries, as opposed to generating new technological *innovations* domestically.

Figure 9: Direct R&D Spending as a Share of GDP, Quebec and Ontario, 1979–1997

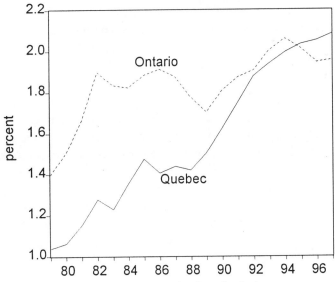

Source: Statistics Canada and author's calculations.

Has Quebec's Standard of Living Been Catching Up?

If Quebec has already caught up with Ontario in education, infra-structures and equipment, and R&D spending, one must wonder why its real GDP per capita is still less than 90 per cent of Ontario's. Part of the answer lies in the very long gestation period required before the educational revolution filters through all age groups. Part also probably lies in incomplete technology diffusion. And, as suggested by the trend in Figure 5, business profitability in Quebec could still be insufficient. Little can be done about the first problem — only waiting for time to go by — but the last two need to be investigated and addressed.

Conclusion

Thirty years ago, Alan Green (1971) wondered why Quebec had not been able to narrow the gap with Ontario's standard of living between Confederation and the mid-1950s. We still do not have a definitive answer to this question. But in this paper, I have reported evidence showing that the process of narrowing the gap did at long last begin to take place at the end of the 1950s, and was already making good progress at the time Green was writing.

In contrast, the pessimistic view has recently circulated that the Quebec economy was doing rather well before the Quiet Revolution, and has since gone through a period of stagnation and decline (Migué, 1998; Paquet, 1999; Boyer, 2001). I report evidence that shows the exact opposite is true. In terms of real income per capita, the Quebec economy was in relative decline from the late 1920s to the late 1950s, and has grown comparatively faster than the Ontario economy on average since the Quiet Revolution. Quebec's real income per capita increased from 74 per cent of Ontario's in 1960 to 86 per cent in 1999. Therefore, half of the standard-of-living gap between Quebec and Ontario observed by Green was closed over those 40 years.

By international historical standards, this is neither slow nor rapid convergence — just average speed. A standard decomposition of real income per capita into its canonical sources indicates that demographics, employment and productivity have all contributed on net to the narrowing of the Quebec-Ontario gap over the last four decades — for 35 per cent, 10 per cent and 55 per cent, respectively.

There have been major ups and down in the catch-up process. One anomaly is that Quebec's standard of living dropped sharply during the Second World War. This can be attributed to a major redistributive shock amounting to 10 per cent of Quebec's personal income. There was a huge distortion in the regional sharing of military pay, due to the reluctance of Quebec men to enrol in the armed forces.

Another anomaly is the big bubble in Quebec's relative performance that took place between 1975 and 1985. I have taken some time to show that both the qualitative and quantitative evidence point to a major wage explosion occurring in the second half of the 1970s. Its deleterious effects were initially masked by a strong cyclical expansion, but revealed clearly during the 1982 recession. After that recession, a prolonged period of wage moderation and more peaceful labour relations began, which has lasted up to this day. The 1986–99 period saw a return of Quebec's relative performance to the pre-existing, long-term trend established before 1975. This recent period has been marked by a important recovery of employment, following the trough of 1982.

Prospects for a continuation of Quebec-Ontario convergence in the future are good, but nothing should be taken for granted. Quebec's investment performance in education, infrastructures and equipment, and research and development is not very different from Ontario's. Much will depend on success in reducing illiteracy and dropout rates further and improving the general quality of education. There is also progress to be made in the area of technology diffusion. Finally, business profitability in Quebec is still comparatively low. The province would benefit from various policies that would support saving and investment, such as raising RRSP limits, incurring fiscal surpluses, shifting public expenditures towards infrastructure development, and making the tax and general economic environment more competitive.

References

Barro, R.J. and X. Sala-i-Martin (1999), *Economic Growth* (Cambridge, MA: MIT Press).

Bélanger, G. (1980), "La productivité croît-elle trop rapidement au Québec?" *Le Devoir,* October 8.

Blanchard, O.J. (2000), *The Economics of Unemployment, Lecture 1,* Lionel Robbins Lectures, London School of Economics, October.

Boyer, M. (2001), *La performance économique du Québec: constats et défis*. Rapport bourgogne (Montreal: Centre universitaire de recherche en analyse des organisations), February.

Davenport, P. (1981), "L'économie québécoise et le ralentissement de la productivité", Working Paper No. 3/81 (Montreal: Department of Economics, McGill University).

Green, A.G. (1971), *Regional Aspects of Canada's Economic Growth* (Toronto: University of Toronto Press).

Krugman, P. (1994), *Peddling Prosperity* (New York: Norton).

Lemieux, T. (1999), "Disparités de revenu et croissance de l'emploi: y a-t-il un trade-off?" in S. Lévesque (ed.), *L'après-déficit zéro: des choix de société* (Montreal: Association des économistes québécois).

Migué, J.-L. (1998), *Étatisme et déclin du Québec* (Montreal: Varia).

Paquet, G. (1999), *Oublier la Révolution tranquille* (Montreal: Liber).

Raynauld, A. (1961), *Croissance et structure économiques de la Province de Québec* (Québec: Ministère de l'Industrie et du Commerce).

Slater, D. (1995), *War Finance and Reconstruction: The Role of Canada's Department of Finance, 1939–1946* (Ottawa: D.W. Slater).

Environmental Economics

Economists, Environmental Policies and Federalism

Anthony Scott

Introduction

Canadian economists analyze environmental problems much as do American economists. They use the same tools. They are in abstract agreement with the goals of the American economists and their policy-making bosses. But there the agreement stops. Within the United States, economists presume that the selection and implementation of actual environmental policies and of tangible targets is a task for the national government. Within Canada, there is no consensus on whose task it is. Canadian economists are kept busy with plans or decisions made at provincial and at national levels of government.

I have received generous help in my informal survey of environmental economics in Canada, but it is important to stress that my opinions are my own. Edmund Blewett, Robin Boadway, Louis Cain, Brian Copeland, Rod Dobell, Diane Dupont, Kathryn Harrison, John Livernois, Stephen McClellan, Andrew Muller, Nancy Olewiler, Peter H. Pearse, Roger Reid, Fred Riggs, John Robinson, John Sargent, Claude Simard, Rob Smith, Mark Sproule-Jones, C. van Kooten and Peter Victor have all provided useful information, as did those others who a few years ago provided material for an earlier paper on a related subject (Scott, 2000). Jennifer Wood efficiently helped me to locate materials.

Sometimes this results in small-scale systems of regulation reflecting local notions about what is ideal and what is fair. Goals and standards may differ from place to place.

The standard literature reflects a large body of research and reflection by U.S. economists, forced to deal with problems of U.S. national policy and choice. As professionals, Canadian economists also become familiar with this standard analytical approach, one that leading economists constantly refine. Indeed they contribute to it. Yet they may find it only partly relevant to the actual diversity of problems, physical opportunities, preferences, distributional goals and constitutional powers facing the provincial decision-makers who look to them.

In 1985 and 1995, I reviewed the allocation of functions in a federation by examining the assignment of powers over the environment. I found that there was no reason why all the environmental powers should be assigned to one of two levels. Nevertheless, the various theories I discovered and tested suggested that when governments were competitive, there would be a tendency for the powers over one field to drift in one direction.

In this paper, I start from the other end: from public functions and policies, not from levels of government. To do this, I review some of the history of environmental activities in England, in the United States and in Canada. I then review what economists have had to say about these activities. This is followed by a review of what Canadian economists say and do, compared with what economists in the United States say and do.

Environmental economics is a young subject, only slightly younger than the environmental policy with which it is most concerned. Environmental policy is still in its infancy, especially policies dealing with pollution, in particular, global air pollution. The institutions in which policy is to be framed and enforced constitute one of its problem areas.

Policy Evolution

Britain. For centuries, efforts to escape from pollution required victims to push the doctrines of common law: nuisance actions dealt with inter-property flows of smoke and fumes, while property-law doctrines dealt with the changes in the quality of water flowing in streams. These two branches of the law were helpful mainly when there were only two parties: a single victim whose enjoyment of property was reduced by harmful effluents from a single identified mill or factory. Where several ordinary parties suffered from the effluents of many upstream factories, the common-law courts offered no remedy.

In the industrial revolution, to escape from this limitation, water-pollution victims bypassed the courts and appealed directly to Parliament. The Victorian politicians obliged, but only on a local scale: with public-health acts requiring reduction of urban sewage, and with fisheries-protection legislation banning stream pollution. But, when it came to making general doctrine about who had personal rights to pollute and who had rights to be free from pollution, the politicians seemed unwilling to go much further than had the courts. And when it came to enforcement, the government's statutes were weak. Thus, although in 1876 Britain did enact a water pollution law directed against everyone dumping wastes into rivers, the law had no national inspectorate. Local councils applied to local courts for an order to require a factory to stop polluting. The innovation was that the new law focused the courts' attention on the condition of the river not on the harm that was or was not suffered by selected victims.[1]

Air pollution policy evolved differently. In the 1860s and 1870s, Parliament enacted the Alkali Laws,[2] a series of laws focusing attention on the standards in factories within alkali industries using soda and acid products and also in copper smelters (coal was not included). Just as significantly, it established a monitoring and enforcement body, the famous Alkali Inspectorate, whose report and observations and experiences provided bases for early changes in the laws. The standards that emerged under the Alkali Laws were aimed at reducing the harmful wastes from polluters' practices in the factories. They were not directly concerned with the property or health of victims of air pollution, nor with the air or water conditions.

---

[1]Elworthy and Holder (1997, p. 64). Polluters could still rely on the defence that they were already using the "best practical means" available in that industry and place.

[2]See Elworthy and Holder (1997, pp. 62 and 217). The alkali industries, starting with salt, manufactured sodium sulphate, carbonate and hydrate, and various compounds of chlorine. Many of these were raw materials for other products, such as soap, textiles, explosives, paper and pharmaceutical alkaloids. The dangerous and unpleasant waste products included muriatic (hydro-chloric) acid and sulphur oxides.

Only minor progress was made thereafter. Britain did not pass any smoke or smog statute to match the Alkali Laws. The Great Depression discouraged new legislation so that "smokeless zones" were postponed until after World War II and, after a devastating smog incident, a *Clean Air Act* until 1952.

United States. American water-quality laws steadily built on older common-law, fishery, and public-health and sanitation powers, somewhat as in Britain. All were at the state level (see Melosi, 2000; Cain, 1978).

We do not find the American federal government addressing pollution problems until after the Second World War. It started with a clean water program. Between the wars New Deal spending had been channelled into river-basin development, financing jobs and helping farmers, as was permitted by the Constitution. The projects chosen dealt with navigation, flood prevention and hydro power. Pollution, health and sewage were left to the states, and the "environment" was not considered (see Weiland *et al.*, 1997). This distribution of responsibility continued until, in the 1960s, almost suddenly, clean water and in-stream sewage dilution were included in the national legislation. The administration's multiple-purpose, water-resource agency was authorized to make plans for improved in-stream aeration and diversion, and also to consider alternative projects for treating pollution emissions and preventing waste production. In a few years, the engineering search for river-basin projects was being transformed into a water-quality search for projects and policy instruments in aid of the "environment" with benefits for recreation, aesthetics, wildlife, and so on quickly included as national concerns.

A federal clean-air program came later. There had been a long-standing policy of leaving air pollution control in states' hands (Dewey, 2000). Coal smoke and other industrial fumes and emissions had evoked complaints which gave rise to flurries of rudimentary local and state legislation and control activity. Although at one stage Chicago built on a common-law approach by declaring smoke to be a nuisance per se, the typical state legislative approach was to impose standards of plant equipment, materials or process (as with the British Alkali Laws). In the 1930s, St. Louis introduced rules about coal quality. This regulatory method was widely applied to heavy industry during and after World War II. It might be said to have reached reach a climax when California began to make car-exhaust standards, long before there was any national standard.

To deal with smoke and pollutants drifting across their borders, the states adopted agreements or "compacts" to deal with cross-border flows of industrial wastes. Federal clean-air acts left them to it until state activities fell far behind public opinion.

In the 1970s federal agencies were given powers to intervene within states, researching and identifying local problems and also imposing standards that the states would have to meet. As Andrew Thompson wryly observed in 1980, "With an English positivist tradition, the Canadian lawyer can scarcely credit as law a statute like the *United States National Environmental Policy Act, 1969* (NEPA) which merely declares a national policy and directs government agencies [including state agencies] to establish conforming procedures. Yet NEPA is law, and has had more influence in Canada than any Canadian statute" (1980, p. 15).

Canada. In Canada, the nineteenth century courts carried on with English common law on private nuisance, and riparian principles of property law on water quality.

The provinces adapted some of the British public-health laws, including those that would now be called pollution policies. They had jurisdiction over water quality in inland waters, but shared this with Ottawa when it came to boundary waters such as the St. Lawrence and the Great Lakes. They had jurisdiction over air quality, but in fact took almost no action against smelter and sawmill emissions.[3]

The Dominion government was excluded from most public-health functions. After the 1880s it could use its fishery powers to legislate against dumping "deleterious" substances into most rivers. Later, it also found that its powers over navigation were a possible legal base for pollution law-making.

Thus in the nineteenth century, legislatures and local governments in England, the American states and the Canadian provinces began to take over environmental-quality law-making from the courts. Long tolerant of fumes, smoke and chemicals, legislatures were eventually driven by concerns about sanitation, health, and fisheries, to aid municipalities to develop clean water supplies and to make simple rules about dumping wastes in streams. As for air pollution, change was very gradual. When legislation did come, it was similar to factory and safety laws, concerned with particular practices, materials and, especially, particular items of equipment. But in most

---

[3]Two well-publicized air pollution situations were that of the smelters at Trail, B.C. and at Sudbury, Ontario.

jurisdictions, the neighbours of establishments emitting fumes and smoke just put up with dirty air until well into the twentieth century.

Reactions from Economists

Market Failure and Ideal Output

It cannot be said that these developments received much attention from economists or economic historians.[4] Even those mid-Victorian writers who did take a broad interest in "social conditions", such as Marx and Engels, Mill and Marshall, had little to say about the abatement of water or air pollution.

Sidgwick, Edgeworth and especially Pigou did mention pollution. Their references were incidental to their efforts to explain how a general equilibrium of the competitive market economy might produce a socially-optimal allocation of resources ("ideal output"). Their basic theory was that goods sold in a non-competitive market would be over-priced, bringing excessive profits to firms in such a market, so attracting excessive factors of production. Improving market competitiveness would lead to a re-shuffling of inputs and an increase in the value of total output. As a supplement to this idea of mis-allocation they considered a similar cause for a distorted allocation of *inputs* among goods and markets: excessive profits for firms that gained from "unpaid factors" and externalities or spillovers. The jobs of making markets competitive and of correcting spillovers should fall to government.

The economists rather casually mentioned pollution as an illustration of unpriced or unpaid inputs, and emissions taxes as remedies. But their writings do not suggest they had familiarized themselves with actual research

---

[4]And my casual search of one-volume modern economic histories produced almost no mention of water supplies, water pollution, air pollution or the *Alkali Acts*. In France, the elite *Ponts et Chausees* institute may have developed analyzes from an economic point of view, as may its German equivalent, but I have found little trace of them in modern secondary materials.

Anthony Scott

on pollution.[5] Pigou's insistence on the market's failure to make the best of the economy was reinforced primarily by his studies of monopoly and imperfect competition, not of the pricing or handling of water and air pollutants.[6] These theorists usually had in mind the problems of markets in a simple two-level world of consumers and manufacturers.

But in the real world, external diseconomies and spillovers were encountered where there were non-homogeneous raw materials, uncertainty, exhaustibility and unsure ownership. In 1958, Bator pointed to non-price relationships as between producer and consumer, producer and producer, consumer and consumer, and employer-employee. A feeling for the working of these relations could not be gained by considering defects in just one kind of market. Practical knowledge, experience and measurement were necessary before anything very useful could be said about the society's ideal allocation of scarce inputs to waste disposal of heterogeneous, unappropriated, raw materials. Realizing this, the economists said very little about pollution.

In the mid-1950s, attention was directed from market behaviour and failure to the problems of collective choice. Paul Samuelson, with public-expenditure theorists, suggested models of the economy in which firm-consumer markets were only a part of the economic mechanism. At first

---

[5]In 1950, K.W. Kapp made a valuable collection of the evidence on external diseconomies ("extra social costs"), directed at economists. It is striking that little if any of his material came from previous economists' studies.

[6]Theorizing about the correction of externalities had passed its peak in the 1950s. Little of it came from economists' studies. Ciriacy-Wantrup, foremost in dealing with natural-resource conservation and policy, in 1952 also referred briefly to pollution and other external effects, but concentrated on finding a role for government in resource conservation. It is interesting that, in the 1950s, he makes no mention of Pigovian taxes. One gathers politicians paid little attention to the marginal effect of taxes. They regarded charges as penalties for reinforcing regulation. Pigou's later discussion of "his" tax is disappointing (see *Public Finance*, 1947, pp. 99-100). In Baumol's 1952 thesis, the author argues that the state exists because various kinds of externality-distortion cannot be dealt with individually or in the marketplace. Although he quotes Mill, Pigou and especially Sidgwick, as prior users of natural-resource examples of environmental externalities (such as floods and pollution) to justify the collective actions of the state, Baumol himself rarely pauses to consider these problems. That is also true of most of the writings of late-1940s contemporaries in the "ideal output" debate: Kahn, Lerner, Myint, etc.

government action had been regarded as an instrument to avert or repair the damage of market failure. The new group of theorists attempted to use the same economic principles as had been used to explain the supply and demand view of the marketplace to explain the joint-supply or collective-supply view of public organization. What kinds of goods; what kinds of persons; what kinds of production processes indicate a need for public supply? Considering all the modes of public supply, which modes could be predicted to be adopted for the production of each kind of good (regulation, subsidy, public production)? To these questions had to be added the old public finance or distributional questions: given a public supply, how should the tax burden be divided, and how should individual tastes for political and governmental systems be incorporated?

For those attempting to generalize about the place of government in the economy, the intricacy of these questions was discouraging. But for those who were increasingly alert to the problems of the environment, the new models were encouraging. They at least suggested that the same public-choice mechanism that determined the individual output of goods and services was involved in the output of jointly-supplied public services, and that these public services included the management and protection of the environment. Indeed, while early theoretical discussions of public goods often revolved around the creation of *man-made* facilities such as those for national defence or transportation, early quantitative exercises often centred on the preservation of *natural* sites, such as climate modification, hunting and fishing recreation, and wildlife preservation.

Benefit-Cost Analysis of Pollution

While the economists in the externalities debate were busy adding to the list of difficulties in identifying the ideal output of an economy, and the difficulties of obtaining consent on public goods, in 1936 the United States' administration and Congress developed a standard benefit-cost (b/c) approach to water-project selection. This was quickly adapted for projects having multiple purposes[7] (not just flood control but also power, irrigation

---

[7]Engineering evaluations of public-works projects were attuned to business investment evaluation methods, such as for railways, for example. Economists concentrated on the effect of decreasing costs and of monopoly (see

and navigation).[8] William Baumol wrote that the economists involved in standardizing benefit-cost project comparisons were "doing the hard work involved in giving substance and application to the theory of externalities and public expenditure" (1969, p. 22).

Nevertheless, cleaning up a polluted river, the standard example in the externality literature, was left out of official federal benefit-cost analysis, as it was not one of the "purposes" of multiple-purpose river-basin development. Responsibility for public health, waste disposal, and sewage was still entrusted to the states and localities, not to the federal government. Consequently, it remained a subject for public-health and engineering experts, not economists.[9]

Although there may be other forerunners, much of the credit for the introduction of steady, detailed, quantitative study of water pollution policies

---

Schumpeter, 1954, p. 949). In 1952, this procedure was heavily supplemented by welfare-economics (or national-income-maximizing) concepts. Probably similar reforms were being made in other countries, but the enormous scale of almost routine spending on American river-basin projects focused attention on U.S. federal procedures (see Prest and Turvey, 1967).

[8]To help with dating, it seems that in the planning of the American side of the St. Lawrence Seaway project, stretching from the 1930s to 1955, there was never a comprehensive comparison of the Seaway package of projects with possible alternatives (see Willoughby, 1960). However, some ten years later, both American and Canadian sides of the Columbia River Treaty negotiations (1958–63) were more sophisticated. Krutilla (1967, pp. 199-201) suggests that the Canadian team may actually have done more homework regarding the economic implications of various alternative river systems than the U.S. team.

[9]There were economists specializing in local-government public finance who did work on civic enterprises such as sanitation, and Pigou and the Webbs in England did continue to consider urban enterprises. It is always a surprise for visitors from the United States and Canada to find that in the U.K. government it is to the municipal-affairs department that "environmental" problems have been assigned, reflecting the historical local-government focus on public-health policies (see Cain, 1978). In 1955, in his thesis, the splendid *Water-Resource Development: The Economics of Project Evaluation,* Otto Eckstein does not mention pollution, waste, sewage and so on. In the important Maass *et al.* report on their early 1960s work on design of water-resource systems, Maass and Dorfman do mention pollution abatement, but only in order to assume it away from their calculations and arguments.

Economists, Environmental Policies and Federalism 413

into federal benefit-cost analysis must go to economists at Resources for the Future in Washington, DC.[10] The story goes that in 1963 the Corps of Engineers proposed to create reservoirs in the Potomac River to augment low summer flows and to improve the sewage assimilative capacity of the estuary. The economists, all recreationists and canoeists, became alarmed as, in the course of the benefit-cost studies of this project, they learned the reservoirs would spoil white-water canoeing. This threat concentrated their thinking into looking for a wider range of approaches to water-quality improvement, including collective treatment, a process then beyond the Corps' range of alternatives.

After 1960, the new environmental movement, spreading alarm about the capacity of nature to support economic growth, attracted economists. They considered regulation versus property (Coase, 1960), materials scarcity and growth (Barnett and Morse, 1963); natural limits (the Club of Rome 1972) and resources and growth (Solow, 1974) and the eclectic idea of sustainable development (Brundtland Report, 1987). And they began to apply analysis to toxic pesticides (Carson, 1962), ocean pollution, endangered species, acid rain, CFCs and global warming — each of these suggesting new twists on the measurement of benefits and costs of environmental policies.

It is not clear when Canadian jurisdictions began to utilize anything like benefit-cost analysis. I have the impression that after World War II politicians, treasury boards and their consultants all devoted their efforts to improving engineering-type studies of the costs of various scales of project. An informal benefit-cost manual was produced for Canadian use in 1962, and an official volume manual a dozen years later.[11] There were plenty of postwar opportunities, including the International Joint Commission's Columbia River projects, the St. Lawrence waterway projects, and the South Saskatchewan Dam. All of these were intensively examined, of course. But

---

[10]Including D'Arge, Kneese, Krutilla, Herfindahl and Fox.

[11]The first Canadian guide took into account the U.S. water-resource benefit-cost rules that evolved through 1952 and the "Policies, Standards and Procedures" of 1962. They had been sponsored by the Bureau of the Budget, while the Canadian guide had no official standing. The Treasury Board Secretariat produced a benefit-cost analysis guide in 1976. There was then really no official Canadian doctrine to say that only increases or decreases in national income should count.

I suspect that only the Winnipeg project received anything approaching the kind of survey of "all, benefits, all costs, and all alternatives" urged in the public-finance and theory textbooks of that day.[12]

Minimal Economists: Environmental Impact Statements

The environmental impact statement or assessment (EIA) came to general attention in the United States when it was added as a requirement of the National Environmental Policy Act (NEPA) in 1969. It was intended to force an action from the agencies and states when NEPA was otherwise merely a statement of Congress' principles (Weiland et al., 1997, p. 101). Those who submitted a project proposal were required to provide the information so that professional experts could judge the effect of the project on the environment.

Soon after the United Kingdom and other countries in the European Commission[13] adopted a similar EIA requirement. In 1973 Canada also made an environmental assessment review process a main element of legislation. This step integrated environmental considerations into the government project-selection and policy-making process, whether or not the project or policy being reviewed had an "environmental" purpose. Some Canadian provinces also adopted their own EIA laws or procedures. In addition to its applicability to federal government projects, the Canadian EIA law had the surprising effect of imposing *federal* environmental concerns onto project proposals for provincial projects. For example, litigation forcing an embarrassed federal government to conduct EIAs of the Rafferty-Alameda dam (1989), and the Oldman River dam (1992) was significant in pointing out a wider federal environmental jurisdiction than the provinces or even Ottawa had realized.[14]

In many countries, making environmental impact assessments and giving them weight in project design and selection became routine procedures.

---

[12]See the report by Clarence Barber. Thanks to T. Shoyama and Robin Boadway for discussions.

[13]See Elworthy and Holder (1997, pp 388-421) for EIAs in the United Kingdom and the EC.

[14]For an up-to-date account of this litigation and its aftermath, see Field and Olewiler (forthcoming, ch. 15).

Canadian jurisdictions were not as enthusiastic, as politicians in Ottawa and most provinces endeavoured not to lose detailed control over public-works spending.[15] One time-honoured procedure was to appoint ad hoc Commissions of Inquiry or Royal Commissions. When a bridge, port, railway or other resource or environmental matter was under discussion, such inquiries could obtain information while helping to cool the disputants. One example was the 1975–77 (Berger) northern-territories pipeline inquiry, noted for its author's concern about communal and socio-economic impacts as well as purely environmental impacts. (It came quite soon after Quirin's 1962 business-like investment study of northern oil and gas prospects — one that, remarkably, had been able to avoid saying anything about social, community or ecological impacts.) Ad hoc reports such as Berger's were able to weigh social and environmental factors at some length, but they made a minor contribution to the building-up of a framework for environmental analysis — scientific, sociological or economic. I am not aware that environmental economists in Canada have given these studies, or the data in them, much attention.[16] By their uniqueness they created no precedent: the author's personal conclusions, not his approach, are remembered.

Teaching and Research: Environmental Economics beyond Benefit-Cost Analysis and the EIA

Economists who taught the subject left environmental impact to "environmental scientists". They had their hands full as old controversies about benefit-cost analysis gave way to a very wide range of topics, always including "pollution economics". They concentrated on five or six main

---

[15]Most jurisdictions began to call for EIAs to consider public policy alternatives, and their effects on the region's resources. Some suggested merging benefit-cost analyses with EIAs. Of course, there were numerous difficulties. In good benefit-cost analysis, double counting is prevented by final-product or national-income (net) concepts. The environment, however, has no final product. Everything that is impacted is as important as anything else. Thus EIA is analogous to economic *impact* where every dollar change in sales is counted, even if that dollar is already included within another item.

[16]Compare the continuing reference by Canadian fisheries economists, to the reports of the Sol Sinclair, Pearse and Kirby fisheries inquiries.

policy areas, all connected by the problem of a market and of individual property rights.[17]

Land use. This policy area is a natural, especially for economists and departments for whom it is simply a continuation of earlier work in land economics, agricultural economics, regional economics and urban economics. Today's economists are busy in related fields such as recreation (and parks and reserves) and endangered species. Many of their fields of interest are shared with geographers. Pioneering institutions like Resources for the Future were manned primarily by land-use specialists. By now all policy areas in environmental economics have borrowed land-use valuation concepts such as irreversibility, option value, existence value, travel-cost and contingent valuation, and policy approaches such as safe minimum standards, transferable development rights and land-use reserves. Perhaps relatively fewer Canadians than Americans are in this field, though that is just an impression.

The environment, total output and economic growth. From Malthus to the Club of Rome to the Brundtland report, economists have participated in asking about the influence of resources on output and growth. Since the 1960s, the condition of the environment, both as cause and effect, has attracted equal attention. The idea of "sustainable development", advanced in terms that economists could understand, promoted these inquiries.

Materials balance and input-output. Early attempts to bring environmental economics, production and wastes together into a single "spaceship

---

[17]Most curricula also include the economics of exhaustible resources, such as the calculus of forest husbandry and mine development, although these are, mainly, traditional subjects that do not involve the special topics below. However, the availability of minerals and forests does play an important role in theorizing about long-run growth (as treated by the old conservation literature from Malthus to Jevons, Ciriacy-Wantrup, Scott and Barnett and Morse). As well, open-pit mining and clear-cut logging are often treated as sources of environmental degradation; and the rate of mining and of logging are important elements in greenhouse-gas calculations. Most classroom curricula also include open-access fisheries and their regulation. Indeed much of the second and third topics mentioned below were considered in fishery economics long before environmental economics had been invented: regulation; taxes, subsidies and individual trade rights. From about the Second World War, Canadian economists played important roles in developing concepts in fishery economics.

earth" model were popularized by Kenneth Boulding (1966). Peter Victor wrote an outstanding volume on this in 1972, with application to Canada.

Trade, growth and the environment. In connection with sustainable development, environmentalists like Herman Daly (1973) have expressed fears about influences of trade, globalization and foreign ownership on the environment, growth and sustainability. Their attacks have attracted a vigorous literature, perhaps more theoretical than empirical, in which several Canadian economists have been very prominent.[18]

Measuring growth ("green accounting") Robert Repetto and Herman Daly represent environmentalists who argue that official economic growth data overstates the actual because the statistics do not take into account a country's resource consumption (depletion). Textbooks lay some emphasis on this. Responsively, Statistics Canada has made impressive progress measuring changes in the value of certain resource stocks. Although some Canadian academics have been advisors on these measurement ventures, most write as though they did not exist.

Decision-making. Some economists make theoretical investigations of agreements, contracting, consent and voting, used to arrive at environmental decisions. Their work can be closely related to that in law and economics and in public-choice theory.

Game theory. Some regard the environment as a common-pool or no-property resource, and apply game theory to predicting the outcome of attempts to come to agreement on policy. This work has not progressed as far as that on water use or on fisheries.[19] It would seem that Canadian political scientists and lawyers are ahead of economists in studies of the actual circumstances of environmental decision-making.

---

[18]For example, in a recent paper, B. Copeland, B. Antweiler and S. Taylor (forthcoming) set out a theory of how openness to international goods markets affects pollution concentrations, using trade theory and SO_2 data from the Global Environment Monitoring Project. Combining estimates of scale, composition and technique effects yields the surprising conclusion that freer trade appears to reduce overall pollution.

[19]See Ostrom *et al.* (1994). The authors' very general, and informed, approach to common-pool "resources" has almost nothing to say about polluters or the environment.

Costs and benefits. In Canada, making studies of economic "impact", ranging from changes in local employment to changes in national income are the bread-and-butter of government economists, consultants and some academics. On the demand side, these make use of questionnaire techniques to predict utilization of proposed changes in land or environmental use. On the supply side, they make use of regional input-output techniques.[20] Although in Canada these evaluations are not usually combined into one all-inclusive benefit-cost assessment, each part may be used to support a finding on "feasibility" (more below).

Choice of instruments. Taxes, subsidies, marketable permits, access to nuisance and tort law, contracts, public undertakings, enforcement by damages versus enforcement by injunction, monitoring — these topics in environmental economic fields are outgrowths of similar economic studies in the fields of public finance, public expenditure, industrial organization, and law and economics.

Tort law. A number of economists, now expert in tort law, have investigated the history and modern applicability of common-law remedies for harmful pollution and land use (Dewees, 1995; Posner, 1977, ch. 13). Many provincial health, sanitation and environmental regulations have been drafted and even worded as updates of common-law doctrines.

Regulation. As already mentioned, since the nineteenth century, regulation has been seen as the practical answer to common-property effects on the environment. Pollution regulation takes the form either of control and monitoring of the processes and materials used by a polluter, or control of the amount of emissions themselves. Verification of compliance of the first is much easier than the second, and has long been chosen by local governments, already experienced with quarantine and sanitation controls. It was the low-cost, flexible method chosen to reduce smoke emissions, both industrial and residential. Dewees (1995) has studied equipment requirements by reducing SO_2 emissions from smelters; and Muller has examined pulp mill equipment standards. "Standards" may mean that such equipment regulations have been standardized as between different jurisdictions. Control of

---

[20]Input-output is also used on the demand side, when there is an expected change in the amount or quality of an input.

emissions is more direct, but more costly to enforce, initially.[21] Many economists have contributed theory and empirical research on the results of equipment standards, which are similar to aspects of earlier public-utility and building standard regulations. These are valuable for themselves and for the light they throw on theories such as Stigler's that controlled agencies are vulnerable to being "captured" by the very industry they are set to control.

Taxes and compensation. Some economists who write about taxes are dealing with compensation: the lump-sum bribes, and settlements and charges that are paid when a person is deprived of a use of land or when a polluter is deprived of the use of a process. Others are dealing with fines. In theory, this subject applies to most branches of environmental economics, but in practice it applies mostly to land-use economics. It arises when a wildlife or endangered-species agency (or a voluntary "heritage" group) sets out to control, or acquire, land, marine reserve, seacoast or wetland for habitat conservation. This is an old subject for land economics and for law and economics.[22]

Charges and incentives. In microeconomics, economists are trained to look for pricing, rather than rationing, to control the flow of anything and so minimize the costs associated with the flow. This point of view, extending Pigou's thoughts on using taxes to remove extra social costs, has led to economists' widespread enthusiasm for emission charges, or any kind of quantitative permit fee.[23] Like regulations, fees may vary with the location

---

[21]California, and later all American auto emission regulations imposed on manufacturers are an example of forcing a producer to adopt equipment regulations by setting aggregate emission regulations. For the earlier years of California's regulations of auto emissions, see Dewey (2000, pp. 57-83).

[22]See Schwindt (1992, especially Appendix A-1) for a survey of compensation policies.

[23]Ideally, both pollution charges and quotas vary among seasons and locations; and are flexible as information accrues and circumstances change. For air-pollution charges in Canada, see Baar (1995, pp. 102-103); see also sewage charges and graduated automotive clean-air charges. There is a serious theoretical literature on "prices versus quantities" under uncertainty.

of the emission.[24] Most economists and their textbooks favour these, but there are few actual examples.[25]

Tradable pollution permits. Under the common law applying to water and to land, an owner may have established a reasonable freedom to use his own land, or the right to use the land of another, in a manner that pollutes the environment. Where this was so, the freedom could be bought and sold with the property right. This idea leads on to government-created pollution or emission rights, an influential and practical idea invented by John Dales in 1967, perhaps inspired by western appropriative water rights. The idea has been applied to some air emissions in the United States. In the United States, and even in Canada, there is also a voluntary trade in certificates of reduced pollution.[26] (The similar tradable-quota idea is old stuff in fishery regulation; introduced in New Zealand and Iceland in the 1970s it is today found in 40 Canadian fisheries.) Soon after Dales wrote, the idea of transferable *international* water-pollution permits was recommended in Organisation for Economic Co-operation and Development (OECD) advisory deliberations (see Scott and Bramsen, 1972, pp. 403-404; and Scott, 1976a, pp. 177-218). The OECD did not make much of that idea and proceeded with an agenda of distributional debates about whether polluter or victim country should pay. As a result, although domestic and international tradable air-pollution permit systems were subsequently introduced, tradable *water*-pollution permit systems are still rarely mentioned, even in jurisdictions that have tradable water-diversion permits.

---

[24]For pioneering work by economists on water releases, see chapter by Dorfman in Maass *et al.* (1966, pp. 88-158 and 494- 539); for least-cost removing of organic pollutants from river basins, see various writings by O. Herfindahl and Allen Kneese.

[25]There do exist charges on emissions of industrial pollutants into rivers and estuaries in France, Germany, Holland, Italy and Australia, that vary according to the pollution load. Critics say these are set so as to capture the rent of the right to emit pollutants rather than to discourage pollution.

[26]Tietenberg (1985) is rightly given credit for widespread understanding and acceptance of the mechanics of the idea among U.S. economists.

Economists, Environmental Policies and Federalism   *421*

Counting Canadian Environmental Economists

Environmental economists in Canada can hardly be said to form a group. Those who work with zoologists on fish habitat, those who work on smoky production processes and those who develop statistical indicators of sustainability rarely speak. This is partly because they are divided as between government service, consulting and academia.

We can start with those in provincial government service. They are relatively few in number, perhaps less than 35, coast to coast. Most of their jobs are in evaluation. Although most provincial laws do not explicitly call for economists' studies, they help decision-making about utilization and prices of Crown and private lands for endangered species, wilderness, parks, logging, mining, roads and towns. Not only do they make estimates of likely utilization, impact and cost but also of mitigation and compensation payable.

Turn next to the federal government. I have made no real count, but would guess there are in Ottawa as many economists working on environmental economic questions as in the provinces. They are in five or six departments, notably Environment Canada and Industry Canada. As might be supposed, they are more concerned with the planning of policy or legislation than with application and enforcement, especially when the problems involve international cooperation, trade and productivity. More of their work is published or publishable than I was aware. Anyone would be impressed by Statcan's regular environmental and resource accounts and indicators, and by recent joint reports for the National Climate Change Process on costs and on emissions-permit strategies.

At both levels of government, senior economists from finance departments and treasury boards occasionally lend assistance on complex intergovernmental liaison and legislation issues.

A third category includes the private economic consultants. They are perhaps more relied on by environmental bureaux than by any other branch of government, involved in hearings, assessments and, perhaps especially, lawsuits. Some of them have outstanding capabilities for making survey-based estimates and predictions of willingness to pay, traffic, and so on.

A fourth category includes academics in Canadian economics, agricultural economics, business and public administration faculties.[27] They number about 90, perhaps 5 per cent of the total academic economics establishment.[28] Some belong to the Canadian Economics Association, some to the Canadian Association for Ecological Economics (a political-economy group) and some to the Committee for Resource and Environmental Economics (CREE), more for research-oriented economists. I reckon that of the 90, about 30 do environmental-economics research that shows up in specialized economic journals. [29]

What the Academics Work on

What do Canadian economists write papers about?

One way to find out is by consulting the programs of CREE for the period 1992–2000. I have scored the various subjects by assigning points to each paper according to the number of authors, co-authors and discussants who dealt with it. In the years from 1992 to 2000 the point total for all such papers was 475.[30] I have sorted them into four groupings.

---

[27]There are also energy, fishery, recreational, urban and forestry economists in various faculties, some of whom sometimes work/teach in environmental studies.

[28]About 150 names are on the CREE mailing lists; it includes unknown numbers of non-Canadians, government officials and graduate students. About 65 people come to a CREE meeting. The 5 per cent number comes from comparing 90 with the up-to-2,000 members of Canadian academic departments, estimated by John Helliwell in Howitt (1993).

[29]Browsing through the bibliographies of environmental monographs and textbooks, I found about a dozen Canadian names. The huge bibliography of one European book listed three hundred environmental-economic papers and studies, about 15 of them by Canadians.

[30]At a typical CREE meeting, of those speaking and/or commenting, about 75 per cent were connected with Canadian universities or consultancies, about 20 per cent with U.S. (and overseas) universities and research institutes, less than 5 per cent with Canadian governments, a few with international organizations and none with any environmental organization, Canadian or otherwise.

First, by far the most popular grouping was of papers on more or less traditional land-management topics: fisheries, forests, water resources, mining and energy. Many, but a minority, of these were concerned with modern aspects of resource management, such as sustainable development and ecosystem integrity. (This whole grouping included 30 per cent of all CREE points.)

Second, following land management, came air and water quality and pollution abatement. Most of these papers treated their subjects theoretically (11 per cent of total). This grouping was hard to distinguish from others containing discussions of regulation, law, property rights and enforcement (6 per cent) and another set on tradable permits (5 per cent), (22 per cent altogether).

Third, following pollution, came a group of papers on valuation, specialist and expert reports on existence, option and recreational valuations. Many were by-products of user surveys, often processed by contingent-valuation and travel-cost methods; to these were related a group discussing experimental methods, (20 per cent altogether).

Fourth, well below the valuation grouping, was a set of papers on endangered species and wildlife diversity, along with wilderness and habitat (5 per cent). Related groupings contained papers on sustainable development and growth along with environmental indicators and green accounting (6 per cent), trade, mobility and location, primarily trade theory (5 per cent); and recycling (1 per cent), (adding up to 18 per cent for this group).

These four research groupings account for more than 90 per cent of the activity at CREE meetings. In addition, there were several sessions describing current policies and problems by government economists, and others on federal and international institutions (8 per cent together).[31]

---

[31]The total is 98 per cent, reflecting rounding. Papers were fitted into categories according to their titles, a rough-and-ready procedure. Category percentages may overweigh discussants relative to speakers.

Another, laborious, way to find out what Canadian environmental economists wrote papers about would be to consult their Web sites. Doing this for a few names told me, not surprisingly, that an able economist has the capacity to do many things: teach, supervise, write papers for CREE and for international conferences and journals, act as consultants, run institutes, and so on. To obtain a balanced picture of the professional lives of the whole community of academic environmental economists, however, was beyond my resources.

Anthony Scott

A tentative conclusion is that the single category that engages the largest number of Canadian academic economists is the analysis of the emission of air pollutants. They are, however, perhaps concerned more with contributing to the American and international literature on this global problem than with understanding or improving Canada's problems or policies. (In comparison, members of a group of Canadian "environmental" academics in political science and public administration know more and write much more about Canadian pollution policies.)[32]

At the present time, there seems to be not much contact between Canadian academic economists and their opposite numbers in government. This is illustrated by the literature of the last five years on distributing and trading emissions permits. Some writers have Kyoto greenhouse gas (GHG) quotas in mind, but others are writing quite generally about trading any kind of emission permit. The academics build models and seek a high degree of generality. Looking for various kinds of efficiency under various assumed conditions, they are led to ask about the polluters' permit market when polluters know that there will be a future "adjustment" of the number of permits outstanding (and their price) when further knowledge becomes available. The authors make no attempt to identify their various sets of alternative conditions with any set of conditions actually existing among, say, pulp producers, oil refineries or car owners in Canada, or anywhere else. (At least, they do not do so in their published work.[33]) The team of economists writing *Using Tradeable Emissions Permits 2000* do investigate and explain their ideas about how a stated number of polluters will bid for permits given their uncertainty about how others will respond to the new system. But these economists too do not seem to have come to grips with the uncertainty literature.[34]

---

[32]Consider a very recent political science book on Canadian pollution. In its substantial index of names, it cited only six economists, four of them Canadians. All are referred to as experts on the economy, none as sources or experts on any environmental question.

[33]For a contribution, with a short bibliography, see Kennedy (1999). A similar kind of uncertainty lies behind the "price versus quantity" debate about fishery catch quotas versus taxes on the catch.

[34]In this particular example, the economists in the working group are drawn from a variety of sources, but are mostly from provincial and federal

The Differences and their Explanations

In this section I examine, and offer some explanations for, the difference between the activities and contributions of economists in the United States and abroad and those of Canadian economists.

What are the Differences?

Specialization on theory. Relatively more Canadian academic specialists work on theory than in the United States. Much of this theory tends to be normative — some of it is about minimizing the cost of reaching selected environmental targets; and some of it tracing the effects of selected instruments.

Little Canadian Content. As already mentioned, my impression is that the topics most Canadian economists work on show little knowledge of actual or proposed Canadian policy or issues. They are in tune with the literature, which more than anything reflects the interests of American environmental economists.

American academics *are* interested in United States' policy issues, partly because they get a good exposure to them: indirectly in their graduate schools and directly as consultants and advocates.

---

departments. Their work is tributary to the agenda of the confusing, multi-disciplinary, "national climate change process", working on the "national implementation strategy on climate change" and related "business plans". This "process" draws on 450 experts from industry, academia, NGOs and government, formed into 16 working groups, of which the group producing the emissions permits report is one. The report-producing work of the groups has been co-ordinated by a "national air issues coordinating committee (NAICC)". One can sympathize with the economists trying to design, and explain, and publish a tradable emissions system report, written for individuals drawn from many disciplines. Sympathy aside, their hard work does help to illustrate that there is a gulf between academics and public servants.

Minor Explanations: Theories about why our Economists Write Theory

Publication in international journals. One line of explanation has to do with the influence on young economists' careers of different kinds of research and publication.[35] Their professional success depends in part on the acceptance and publication of their research in journals recognized by their colleagues. This means, primarily, American journals. One correspondent put it to me that young Canadian academics find that American journals simply will not accept a paper about Canadian institutions or environmental problems. So the young economists write "theory" papers, which are more acceptable and interesting to any journal, especially those outside Canada.[36]

Staying mobile. Supplementary to that line of explanation is a view that applies to all in the humanities and social sciences, not just economists of the environment. This is that academics in their first appointments prefer to follow research leads that will keep them mobile, and avoid research topics that will be deemed by prospective employers as being too specific.[37] One way to do this is to work on abstract subjects and methods that are welcomed in all departments in all countries. Those who work on international trade theory are said to be especially welcome in U.S. departments. For some this means simply continuing to work a vein already opened in a Ph.D. thesis in a U.S. graduate school; for others it means a more explicit selection of a portable field.

Impatience with Canadian data and institutions. A third minor line of explanation is that some Canadian environmental economists are impatient

---

[35]See Scott (1967, 1993), in connection with the international migration of social scientists (brain drain) and with the 1990s composition of the membership of the Canadian Economics Association.

[36]"To get an article published in most of today's top rank economic journals, you must provide a mathematical model, even if it adds nothing to your verbal analysis" (Lipsey, 2001, p. 17). The author adds that " several economists" have expressed agreement to this complaint.

[37]See Scott (1993). Other contributors to the symposium tended not to disagree with the explanation.

with what they know of Canadian environmental problems, policies and institutions. This is partly because data and description of Canadian phenomena have not been refined into terms that invite economic analysis. It is easier to join the profession in working over American endangered species and related legislation than it is to bone up on the problems and regimes governing polar bears or migratory birds.

Why are these "minor" explanations? To the extent that the explanations above are correct, they tell us something serious about environmental economics in Canada. These academic economists may be encouraged by their departments to tell their students about resources, the environment and related policy in Canada, but the incentives facing them are mainly for them not to do homework or real research on these matters.

Nevertheless, I call these "minor" explanations because they are actually encountered in most branches of economics in Canada. Getting data and doing research on Canadian topics is difficult, yet it is not as well rewarded as doing theory or research on topics that are welcomed in non-Canadian journals. In all economic fields new theory tends to be developed in unconstrained ways that may be tractable, but are empirically relevant only by accident (Lipsey, 2001, pp. 11 and 19). The question then arises, are there additional forces driving some environmental economists into "internally generated theorizing?" We are looking for what I call the "major" explanation.

Major Explanation: Canadian vs. United States Federalism

As promised, my major theme is that the nature of Canadian federalism puts an imprint on the nature of our environmental *policy* problems. In almost any branch of environmental economics, as the subject is conceived today, the research and theorizing of economists deal with American policy questions. They are questions that at one time were issues for an American government making choices among methods, procedures or policies (e.g., *Methods*: how to value recreation in public land-use decisions. *Procedures:* how to get economic project decisions from the Corps of Engineers. *Policies:* how to deal with endangered species on public lands). Similarly, today's new policy questions for Americans are providing the agenda for the next generation of researchers and theorists.

Anthony Scott

In Canada, the physical environmental problems may be similar to those arising in the United States, but the range of policy choices is different. They seem to be aspects of the same old Canadian confederation trappings: dividing the roles with the provinces, the special position of Quebec, the balance of relations with the United States — all questions that stimulate political scientists but disconcert economists.

United States: federal jurisdiction over environment. As a long-run matter the federal government has picked up, and held on to, responsibilities for expanding the set of environmental functions, imposing participation on the states.[38] True Congress, more than once balking at assuming the regulatory functions of environmental policies, as in the Reagan era of the 1980s and 1990s, has allowed some impatient states to take their own paths. But these have been pauses, not reversals. When Congress musters all its powers, or when the administration addresses itself to all the tasks with which it has been charged, the states must fall in with federal policies and standards, especially if they are to be "funded" for doing so.

The general result is that Washington is the headquarters of environmental policy research. There large statutory agencies undertake the active supervision of air and water quality policy, management of public lands and parks, development of endangered-species policies, and, of course, the conduct of international environmental diplomacy. For economists interested in these matters — as for economists interested in, say, public finance — the federal government is *the* government.[39] They see only one. It

---

[38]These three observed characteristics of U.S. intergovernmental relations in the field of environmental policy, that distinguish it from Canadian intergovernmental relations, are identified by Kathryn Harrison (Fafard and Harrison, 2000, especially pp. 67-76).

[39]For illustration that this has been the case for decades, see Russell (1979). In this conference volume, 31 social scientists, mostly economists, discussed the "new" public-choice theorizing and its applications to energy, environment, education and health problems. Some papers dealt with actual decision-making. In the latter, it is clear that *all* authors and their discussants thought of social choice research as being relevant for the central government. The word "state" hardly appeared. For example, references to the automobile industry/ environmentalist debate over emissions' regulation never mention California, which originated the regulations. References to international fisheries scarcely mentioned the states, which then exercised regulatory jurisdiction.

enables them to treat government as unitary, its policies unique, emanating as it were from a black box. Pondering and proposing environmental policies, they have no more reason to consider the plurality of government than have colleagues specializing in policies for hospitals, museums, highways or naval bases.

Consequently, when economists apply welfare theory, they tend to translate the jargon words social and society as "national", referring to the nation as a whole. When other social scientists analyze the social effects of an environmental policy, they write about the impacts on tribes, states or communities, whereas economists estimate the expected changes diffused throughout the nation and indicated by changes in the national product and its composition. They picture the Washington lawmaker as something like the "planner"[40] at the centre of some expositions of welfare economics, having all necessary reallocating and distributing powers to make progress towards the general (=national) efficiency optimum.

Canada: Shared jurisdiction. In Canada, things are different. Nearly all actual pollution management is carried out at the provincial level. When federal politicians take a deep breath and decide they must act in the matter of, say, pesticides, endangered species, or acid rain, they are usually bracing themselves to induce the provinces to act.

It is true that they can assemble an armoury of powers: spending, POGG, criminal law, commercial shipping fisheries and international-relations. But they have not felt that the mere existence of these powers provides them with a positive justification for taking over all waste emissions or disposal.

Their most widely-accepted function is to negotiate treaties and to see they are carried out.[41] But the latter responsibility is not usually matched by requisite law-making powers. Ottawa is obliged to enter into bargaining and

---

[40]See *Economic Report of the President* for various years, especially 1994, by President Clinton's Council of Economic Advisers, chaired by Joseph Stiglitz.

[41]However, the treaty agreements may merely formalize, or may extend, an agreement already made by a province with a neighbouring U.S. state. These are not unusual. See Alley (1998) and Hodge and West (1998).

coordinating, just as if it were one of the provinces itself.[42] Otherwise, the provinces perceive that the federal politicians could, by choice of standards, implicitly dictate how the burden of complying with international standards was to be distributed.

Some would say Ottawa's strength lies in its coast-to-coast jurisdiction, which enables it to make policies and set standards that apply everywhere, which are then uniform. This is not a unique power, for the provinces can by agreement also achieve uniform laws among themselves. The transactions-cost school would say that the assignment of the function is a matter of whether the political difficulty of federally enacting and enforcing uniform standards is greater than the provinces' bargaining difficulty of agreeing on them and enforcing them (Breton and Scott, 1978, chs. 7 and 8). But as against this approach, the Canadian practical-politics school would say it seems mostly to be a matter of whether federal politicians want to occupy the assignment of powers that already exists, or to escape from it.

Currently, federal politicians are not seeking to exercise wider powers. Instead, "harmonization", "consultation", "all-Canada accord", and so on all indicate their unwillingness to try to supplant the provinces.[43]

Canadian provinces have long exercised powers not only to inspect plants; set safety, sanitary, and construction standards; and make property laws; but also to run the Crown's own lands, minerals, water resources, forests, parks, hunting and wildlife. More so than American states, they have experienced regionwide bureaucracies to do these things. Changes in environmental policy are, to the resource user and polluter, changes in continuing arrangements. The permits, certificates, leases and licences that symbolize provincial powers and ownership are the instruments in which ongoing, routine environmental policy will be embodied.[44]

---

[42]For an informed discussion and description of the workings of federal and provincial governments in a situation — Hamilton Harbour — where Ottawa has many direct responsibilities, see Sproule-Jones (1993, pp. 125-249).

[43]See Harrison (1996), and the essays in Fafard and Harrison (2000), for these regimes.

[44]See chapter by Cohen, Scott and Robinson in Scott, Robinson and Cohen (1995, p. 183), on the jobs of officers requiring them to reconcile, in the field, their departmental, financial and environmental responsibilities.

Economists, Environmental Policies and Federalism   *431*

Consequently, although there are centres of advocacy and of research, there is no national centre having economies of scale in environmental law-making and enlightenment.[45] The economist who would understand and improve the country's environmental policies will not go to Ottawa to find a community of conceptualizers or researchers. The federal government's changing policies are unpredictably responsive to the buck-passing by provinces,[46] to pressures from other nations, and to industrial and environmental lobbyists.[47] Neither is policy-making in the provinces more stimulating. True, there is a long history of introducing and enforcing environmental policies. But if the introduction of any of these was much supported by economic analysis of the alternatives, it was done quietly.[48]

---

[45]Many universities have interdisciplinary environmental or sustainable-development research institutes, recently working on a chosen ecosystem. Canada also has the IISD, the International Institute for Sustainable Development. It is indeed an international centre, giving much attention to environmental problems of the Third World. Canada also has its National Round Table on the Environment and the Economy, which concentrates on making Canadian growth more sustainable. The first of these does some in-house research and publication, but the second relies on consultants to help it explore chosen problems. Two environmental NGOs, Pollution Probe and the Suzuki Institution consistently do some research and writing in-house, often economic in approach. Beyond these, we should notice less-specialized groups like the C.D. Howe Institute, the Institute for Research on Public Policy, the Canadian Chamber of Commerce, the Business Council on National Issues, the Fraser Institute and the Atlantic Institute for Market Studies, and energy, petroleum, wood-product associations, unions, the Sierra Club, Friends of the Earth, the Canadian Wildlife Foundation. All occasionally commission studies with economic content to focus attention on some environmental problem. However, they rarely commission or undertake original research.

[46]The title of Kathryn Harrison's 1996 study.

[47]See Harrison (1996) and the authors in Fafard and Harrison (2000) for Ottawa's repeated cycle of engagement and disengagement, beginning in the 1970s.

[48]Anita Kranjc (2000, pp. 122) and elsewhere says that the details of environmental policies of Ontario (and by implication of Alberta) are driven by emulating U.S. neo-conservatism. See her citations of other studies of provincial policies.

There are good provincial environmental economists, of course, some working on pollution and some on related energy policies, recreation, logging and so on. Probably they work mostly with engineers, biologists, foresters, consultants, and financial colleagues in the provincial treasury, and rarely with each other or federal and international economists.

Is Canada's federal distribution of powers likely to follow that in the United States? Apart from negotiating treaties concerning global pollution, there seems nothing special about the environment that would lead one to predict an early transfer of powers from the provinces to Ottawa. I discussed aspects of this question in Scott (2000).

Here I briefly remind the reader of some frequently made political arguments regarding centralization of powers over the environment. In general, environmentalists favour centralization — to Ottawa — of powers over the environment. Industry is not united on the question, but firms do have several reasons for believing that they can escape from the burden if the provinces have the unnecessary powers. Governments do not necessarily seek powers to impose burdens on polluting industries, preferring to "pass the buck" to the other level of government. However, Ottawa may lose its attempt to not pass the buck, as its international relations' responsibilities will keep it in the centre of the Canadian campaign to live up to the nation's GHG responsibilities. If so, as this assignment of powers accumulates, we may be in for a centralized regime more like that in the United States. If so, Canadian economists may be able to assume that American generalizations about the role of "government" also apply here.

- Environmental NGOs and Green politicians favour centralization of powers. This seems sometimes to be a thoughtless desire to achieve the powerful position of their associated NGOs in Washington, who deal frequently with Congress and with a host of government officials and think-tanks. Such organizations, in Canada, complain that they have grave difficulties selling their arguments (e.g., about endangered species) in ten provinces instead of simply in Ottawa. While it is logically true that if the necessary power were centralized the pro-endangered-species-NGOs could attain their goal by winning only one battle, it is also true that with centralized powers the NGOs could lose the endangered species war by losing only one battle.

- Environmentalists and biologists are said to favour centralized policy-making because it results in uniform environmental conditions. This proposition needs much more analysis than space permits. Legislative centralization does not necessarily lead to uniform policies; uniform policies do not necessarily lead to uniform conditions; and uniform conditions are not environmentally healthy. Also, note the choice of administrative alternatives: politicians with centralized powers over the environment can choose within a wide range of achieving a given environmental condition: at one extreme they can themselves legislate environmental rules, laws and enforcement methods to be applied to each place within their jurisdiction; at the other extreme they can appoint and instruct expert officials to use their discretion in managing these places. All the combinations of these alternatives, and their outcomes and costs, can be achieved by a "centralized" assignment of environmental powers. Note, however, that many of them can also be achieved by a decentralized assignment, by agreements, among smaller jurisdictions.

- Industry is said to favour centralization and uniform regulation if they maintain fair competition among businesses in different provinces, if, that is, they prevent certain provinces from assisting local industries by removing high-cost environmental or pollution rules. Generalization is difficult, however: an industry that believes it can rely on relatively low-cost pollution rules from a certain government will be in favour of giving the necessary powers to a government at that level.

- Industry is said to favour a continued decentralization of environmental powers. It is said that this is because existing provincial enforcement of tenure regulations on Crown lands keeps industry officers in friendly daily contact with provincial administrators, and provincial politicians. For example, compare control over fisheries and over logging. Fishery businesses regulated by mobile federal government officials are visibly less comfortable than their logging colleagues who deal with resident provincial forestry officers. It is also said that local businesses can get more comfortably involved in long-term political alliances with provincial than with national politicians. (However, recent international negotiations show that it is possible for local business persons to work on friendly terms with federal trade, immigration and environmental officials.)

- Provincial and local governments (or some of them) are said to agree with industry in disliking a competitive "race to the bottom" of environmental standards. There is little Canadian research to indicate whether or not there is competition in easing environmental standards, or whether such competition would lead to the relocation of polluting industries. When one reflects that the large-scale polluting industries are oil and gas, pulp and paper, electric power generation and metal smelters, one does not expect much relocation among Canadian provinces.

However, Ottawa may lose its attempt to not pass the buck, as its international relations' responsibilities will keep it in the centre of the Canadian campaign to live up to countrywide GHG responsibilities.

Examples. No wonder that in Canada environmental economists find themselves faced with a jumble of provincial environmental regulations, with no big economic controversy common to them all. Of course, in a federation like Canada, all provincial and local functions, not just the environment, are characterized by a diffuseness of policies. But it does help to explain why Canadian economists, when they study the environment and its challenges, are lured into considering well-defined American policy frameworks.

Hazardous waste sites. It is easy for a Canadian economist to follow his or her U.S. opposite number in assuming that "government" has the choices that now face the U.S. Environmental Protection Agency and its Superfund. But to make this assumption is to duck responsibility for analyzing how Canada's provincial and municipal institutions already deal with abandoned garbage dumps, industrial waste sites, radioactive sites, and seepage from mine tailings-pond seepage.

Taxing emissions.[49] Canadian economists sometimes follow European and American opposite numbers in promoting the efficiency of emissions taxes as against the present rough-and-ready regulations, even though, in Canada, the up-front costs of introducing several taxes in ten provinces would be costly. The responsibility would be that of the provincial finance ministers. They would find themselves collecting different taxes from apparently similar polluters, according to plant location, season, time, weather and so on. Each polluter's assessment would change as these factors

---

[49]This paragraph is about a textbook-type charge per unit of pollutant emitted. There are other "pollution taxes", such as the proposed carbon tax (see Olewiler, 1990).

change. In my opinion, the provinces' present political and fiscal arrangements could not handle the political pressure engendered by using this kind of tax as a corrective.[50] Almost certainly, it would fall back to being regarded as another revenue source, like the tax on alcohol.[51] It is time that some Canadian economist, possibly one learned in the study of taxation, looked into how provincial budgetary procedures might handle charges designed not to raise revenue but to obtain information and to correct waste dumping.

A "national" point of view. Canadian economists thinking in turns of benefit-cost analysis for project selection are likely to follow the American practice of defining benefits and costs as measurable changes in the *national* income (or product): "all final benefits and costs to whomsoever they occur..." as long as they are within the United States. The United States Supreme Court also accepts this principle when, in adjudicating the sharing of a stream between two states, it may award water to the state where it will be used to produce the greater net benefit (from a national point of view).

If this doctrine were widely applied in Canada, it would produce very unfamiliar results. It would mean, when a province is selecting a project, that it ought to choose the one offering greatest national net benefit over one that provides more local income and employment. It would mean, as between upstream and downstream provinces, that they ought to allocate flows to

---

[50]Parliamentary governments, especially provincial ones, are unlikely to take the path-breaking step of delegating tax-setting to administrators, for the change in the amounts to be paid by some polluters could be a politically-sensitive matter. As well, administrators will be unwilling to take responsibility for setting effective deterrent taxes. Of course, any parliament is supreme, and, subject to the written constitution, can legally delegate what it chooses. But it has never chosen to delegate the setting of the rates of other deterrents, such as excises on tobacco and alcohol, or duties on agricultural imports. So it would probably not choose to delegate the setting of an unpopular emissions tax on municipalities, factories or farms. This may also explain why the provinces collect percentage stumpages and similar resource incomes instead of flat-rate royalties.

[51]Provinces, however, do have peak-load prices and tolls on their utilities and highways, and these are analogous to deterrent pollution taxes. Indeed, there are surprisingly few purely regulatory or deterrent taxes at any government level, apart from those on certain imports and on alcohol and tobacco; and these are often regarded simply as revenue sources, with inelastic demands. Public-finance textbook authors, looking for illustrative examples of such taxes, often choose the non-existent pollution tax.

whatever region promises to produce the greater net *final* benefit.[52] I do not believe a *national*-income maximization principle of choice has ever been accepted in Canada. Where local or national governments call for a benefit-cost analysis they want a "multiple account" report revealing perhaps how the alternative versions of a project would affect the national income, but mostly how it would provide local jobs and how it would affect various financial funds and accounts.[53] As for interprovincial projects, Canadian selections usually emerge from intergovernmental bargaining, not from principles of national income maximization.[54] It is time for economists to think hard about what *general* rules ought to be recommended for project selection in Canada by provinces that want to do more than, say, mere local job creation.

Right-sizing versus fragmenting powers over the environment. Canadian economists, thinking about externalities, seem to accept the simplistic idea that control over an ecosystem should not be "fragmented" among small political jurisdictions. In this they echo an older American opinion that, because the typical state[55] had too small an area to make laws and rules for all of a river-basin's interconnected levels and flows, the basin's hydrology and a region's ecology ought both to be internalized within a senior government's borders. Recently a similar view, that at least the

---

[52]Compare parallel accounts of river apportionment in chapters by Barry Barton and Ralph M. Johnson in Saunders (1986, pp. 238 and 253).

[53]I suspect that this is also a reason why, although the making of EIAs is mandatory for nearly all federal undertakings, the making of a benefit-cost assessment is not.

[54]An outstanding example is Krutilla (1967). The World Bank and other agencies has applied cross-border project selection in developing countries. For some theory, see Jones, Pearse and Scott (1980).

[55]This view seems to have been accepted by most water-resource economists. In his 1955 thesis, Otto Eckstein mentions dozens of U.S. federal agencies; scores of river-basin projects; four project purposes; and even one Canadian province. But he rarely mentions states, never as decisionmakers. The same is true of the highly influential Harvard water program of 1955–65, culminating in Maass et al. (1966). For contemporary papers that emphasize state water-resource powers and responsibilities see those collected in Smith and Castle (1964, pp. 341-445).

source and the victims of pollution ought to be within the same jurisdiction, has been stressed (see Paehkle, 2001; and van Kooten and Scott, 1995). Taking these ideals at face value, they hardly apply to many Canadian problem ranges or ecosystems, which typically already are contained within one large province (at least, as the word ecosystem is bandied about in these discussions). For example, the Great Bear forest ecosystem(s) is/are entirely within British Columbia, the Canadian portion of the Great Lakes within Ontario, and even the vast Saskatchewan and Peace River basins each within three.

In any case the economics of the fragmentation complaint is a muddle. Coase's theory of the firm reminds us that just as producers have a choice between integrating and contracting, so the system of government has a choice between handling spillovers within a jurisdiction created among several units at one level of government and handling it by assigning it to a single unit of government at a higher or lower level. We have decades of theorizing about whether to reassign functions to a supranational body, to the nation, to provinces, or to municipalities. All this theorizing tells us to compare the relative difficulty or transactions costs, at each level.[56] For example, to right-size an environmental policy, it can be ceded from provinces with small spans to their larger neighbours, to a joint multi-province body or to the central government or they can re-shape their policies so that citizens may disregard borders and litigate against pollution sources

---

[56]This is the theme of Breton and Scott (1978, chs. 6 and 7). For each province, costs of internalized administration can be balanced against costs of coordination. In general, there will always be problems about the sizes of jurisdictions. Assume that a jurisdiction is persuaded that a river basin or ecosystem should be under an integrated set of land-use controls. If its area is too "small" it will be forced into coordination with its neighbour. If it is too "large" it will be forced into fragmenting its own administration. Both responses have costs.

Anthony Scott

in other provinces.[57] One can invent still other devices for preventing jurisdictional borders from applying suitable policy to a problem.

Note, however, that getting the right area to be governed would not guarantee that a government would exploit this advantage; nor, if it did, that it would make appropriate environmental decisions.[58]

Conclusion on federalism. The purpose of these examples has been to suggest how the differing federal structures of the two countries may explain why economics in Canada has not yet come to grips with the country's environmental policy problems. First, the absence of a central policy-making and policy-analyzing establishment has meant that many Canadian economists are in closer touch with United States and European environmental leaders than with each other. Second, those who do grapple with

---

[57]Water pollution: in the 1960s, the Nordic countries began to give victims of pollution the right to ignore the border and to sue in the source country (see Scott, 1976b). Air pollution: recent informal trading in pollution permits in GHGs allows the benefit of an abatement in one province to be sold to a polluter in another. Doing this may involve class actions. Water jurisdictions: in both Canada and the United States constitutional, treaty or local legislation usually prevents citizens of one jurisdiction from acquiring and importing water from another jurisdiction. In the United States, interstate water compacts may govern the extent of private interstate transactions ("commerce") in water. See Huffaker *et al.* (2001) and related papers in bibliography and Web site.

[58]See Breton and Scott (1978, p. 11); see also van Kooten and Scott (1995). Some aspects of the "fragmentation" of the Saskatchewan River ecosystem among the three prairie provinces was long ago taken care of by agreement among the provinces, with Ottawa as a minor partner. One of the first explicit official recognitions of an ecosystem-wide approach to resource management was that by the International Joint Commission, reporting on the pollution of the Great Lakes. The idea was accepted by the United States and after a few years embodied in the Great Lakes Water Quality Agreement of 1978. In my opinion, the ecosystem approach was needed because there were so many U.S. states with jurisdictions over activities affecting the lakes. In Canada, only the province of Ontario was of importance. If, say, only New York State had been involved in the United States, an ecosystem approach would have required only a state-to-province contract or agreement, with only nominal roles for the national governments. Indeed the fragmentation argument might well have been turned on its head, now asserting that Ontario and New York should each "fragment" their areas to produce smaller matching lakeside regional management units.

Economists, Environmental Policies and Federalism   *439*

analyzing questions about the Canadian environment and its protection have to free themselves from many of the assumptions about policy-making now automatically adopted by United States analysts. There, most environmental issues have drifted into federal-government jurisdiction, and can be safely analyzed as if there were one all-powerful government. Here, the extent to which provincial environmental policies need to be made uniform or just coordinated, and by whom, are still open questions.[59]

Governmental Questions for Economists and Economics Tasks for Governments

What Needs Work?

Canada's future environmental policy-making will be dominated by decisions about reducing the GHGs. Whereas in the past its environmental policies have been fragmented, in the future they will be interdependent. This is because the aim this time is not to get the right balance for each region between change in environmental quality and the cost of doing so, but to find the optimal way of making Canada's contribution to global GHG concentration.

I use the word "optimal" because, as has been seen above, Canadian governments are not agreed on any more specified criterion for project selection or environmental improvement. In particular, neither the provinces nor the federal government have adopted cost-minimization, national-income maximization nor employment maximization.

The study teams in the National Climate Change Process (NCCP) have merely sketched their alternative working suggestions about which industries will be called on to abate their GHG emissions, and, in particular, about how

---

[59]Thanks to Professor Fred Riggs, University of Hawaii, for suggesting to me the importance of the American division of powers (as opposed to the parliamentary system) at the federal level as an explanation of different kinds of policy. Under the heading of openness, this suggestion is also to be found in various political science studies, such as Paehkle (1989); and Fafard and Harrison (2000).

Anthony Scott

emission permits will be distributed initially. The implied invitation to analysts outside the public service to discover the advantages and disadvantages of the alternatives, and make recommendations, has not been followed up. The NCCP has made their data available, and no doubt there is plenty more in the files. Economists can now investigate more fully the regional and inter-industrial implications, and compare their results with published studies of distributing fishery quotas, grazing permits, and U.S. acid-rain permit allocations.

The NCCP suggests that transferable permits be "grandfathered", as is done with fisheries quotas, or auctioned. Should auctioning of permits be considered, there is time to compare the economics of emission-permit auctions with other government tendering and auctioning institutions. How much would it matter that in some regions, or for some pollutants, the number of bidders would be very small? Canadian economists have played a major role in studying the working of existing systems of auctioning natural-resource rights. Other economists have given some attention to the not-very-competitive "sales" by which oil permits, forest-cutting licences and other federal and provincial rights have been allotted. What is needed now is their expert prediction of the results of auctioning individual emission permits in Canada, both regionally and nationally.

Introducing provincial emission permits would involve a double change: not only from command-and-control to a market-like instrument but also from regulating production methods and equipment to regulating the allowable *quantity* of emission. Getting the required quantitative data and setting targets might actually be more difficult and costly than creating a system to allot percentages of these targets to private firms. This is only one of the questions about permits at the provincial level that need economists' examination.

What are the consequences of the non-uniformity of provincial pollution regulations? Is there a role for Ottawa to make sure that policies (not just environmental assessments) are harmonized? Political scientists say the role might be justified by economic considerations, but economists have not said this. Scores of papers, like this one, have mentioned an intergovernmental downward race to the bottom, as governments ease environmental requirements to attract or hold industries. In such a race, the provinces might be urged on by industry, apprehensive of any threat of their competitive position, within Canada, if their rivals in other provinces secure a pollution-regulation advantage. These questions cry for actual case studies and fact-based generalizations.

The economics of interjurisdictional strategy and bargaining is studied by economists as between countries, but hardly between provinces. Yet provincial-level data are available for cross-boundary trade, cross-boundary pollution, and cross-boundary migration, in the presence of differences in pollution regulation. Research using these data would help with certain international-pollution studies, and also have relevance to provincial boundary issues. What would be the result if whole regions (or provinces) were allowed to bid for permits against other regions? What would be the costs if provinces made interprovincial agreements to prevent such bidding, or in other ways prevent a permit drain from their industries to richer ones outside?

Can transaction and administrative costs of alternative regimes be measured? In most discussions of federal versus provincial jurisdiction, and of private litigation versus public regulation versus market-type permits, authors remark that much depends on the associated levels of transactions and administration costs (including those of information and enforcement). Economists give the impression that they know one control instrument is more "efficient" than others in the absence of transactions costs, but they obviously know very little about this when control instruments work imperfectly and also have unknown administration costs. Dewees and a few others have given us a sense of these costs — but more estimates are needed — of instruments used by governments at all levels.

More profoundly, those economists who are interested in public finance and the economics of federalism can use this kind of research to enter the constitutional debate. To what extent could the various powers over the environment be shifted to other levels of government, taking into account the resulting changes in performance, and also the usually theoretical changes in coordination, signalling, administration and mobility costs?

Economists can also contribute to choices about public choice by recognizing that the distribution of GHG permits among people, industries, regions, provinces, and so on, is akin to the distribution of wealth. To a certain extent, tradable permits for GHG emissions can make them the *same* distribution. For example, regions with wealth can buy GHG permits and so enjoy industrial growth. As well, they can buy up and retire permits to emit noxious fumes and local pollutants and so enjoy pollution-free air and water. Low-wealth regions may be in for stagnation. But permits may not be tradable. If so, the initial permit allocation is like an endowment of another kind of wealth, distinct from money. Recognizing this opens the possibility for a "constitutional choice" question of the kind discussed by William

Baumol and by James Buchanan.[60] Under the rules of tradable emissions, the holder of a right in Area A will be predictably unwilling to donate it to an emitter in area B. But if the rules are not yet made, a person might support such a transfer if he knows that all similarly-situated persons will participate in it. The Canadian revenue-equalization system emerged from such a "constitutional" decision. Many economists have helpfully analyzed, criticized and defended this system. They should do the same for the various systems by which GHG and other pollutant emission rights are to be initially distributed.

In this connection, some Canadian economists in the law-and-economics area have considered our expropriation laws and whether to entrench constitutionally the sanctity of property. Yet they have been slow to discuss governmental repossession or narrowing of private leases, etc. on Crown lands. Compensation is asked for, but the question is still open. Analysis is needed of this, and of the sequestering of strictly private lands inhabited by endangered species. This is a modern version of the older "betterment and compensation" land-use question: should private users pay, and should they be paid. In general, government can take either of two routes to improve private care of the Crown lands. It can fortify today's property rights, giving them more exclusivity, transferability and security. Then it can use market instruments. Alternatively, it can continue with rights that have little of these characteristics, attaching to them stipulations and conditions about pollution and land use. Then it must inspect and enforce the conditions. Which is the least costly route? As each kind of land tenure has its own amount of exclusivity, transferability and security, the lesson is to take better care of the environment.

What Governments Can Do to Encourage Research on Canadian Environmental Questions

Most people would agree that Canadian environmental policy as a whole is both unpredictable and unstable. The rules are not as bad as those that macro-analysts once called "stop-go" but they have some of the same hesitancy about them.

---

[60]See Baumol, 1969; Brennan and Buchanan, 1985, pp. 134-149. Amartya Sen similarly referred to an "assurance" principle of joint action.

Part of the reason is economists' own public appearances. Policymakers and the public see that new proposals receive backing from environmentalists and opposition from hired economists. While they may know that from Adam Smith's time economics has been friendly to the idea of public education and other social enterprises, they do not know that it is just as friendly to the idea of public investment in clean water, clean air and biosystem integrity. But economists do not bother to shout all that from the rooftops. They are on the whole allowing much of the field to be occupied by spokesmen who mostly cheer on environmentalists by finding bad guys for them to blame.

Unlike their experience with economists who specialize in health economics or in education and labour-force studies, reporters from the media are unlikely to find many economists they can telephone who will say, "yes I know about that policy proposal". This ignorance is something that government departments and administrators can do something about. They can hold seminars. Of course, there are committees on special questions that do bring economists together, including some outsiders and some from the other level of government. But these are more like business inter-departmental coordinating bodies than seminars or joint working parties. They can circulate their internal studies to a meaningful list of outside economists. They can support untied economic research grants (not the same as offering consulting or modelling jobs). They can offer temporary visitorships to academics and students. They can take a leaf from the book of the Fisheries Research Board of Canada, which long published an interdisciplinary journal that was respected among academics here and abroad. Both levels of government do some of these things for other sciences, but it is rare to find an economist who has seen the inside of an environment or industry department, except as a paid advisor or consultant.

Governments should realize that it is because of their policies that most academic teachers of environmental economics are little more aware of the grand sweep of environmental choices than is any reader of the daily newspaper. It is not enough that they have put some agreements, final decisions and working papers on the Internet. By their policies, they have failed to draw young economists into current concerns, much less encouraged or inspired them to look for research topics. Not surprisingly, many of these economists fall back on their textbooks and their graduate-school course notes for their teaching , and on papers in academic journals to get started on their research, with the results that I have suggested in the sections above.

Both levels of government can make these improvements. The federal government, already having a larger establishment of economists, can move faster and further. The provincial governments have most to gain from even modest steps towards making nearby economists familiar with their environmental problems, policies, available data and studies.

References

Alley, J. (1998), "The B.C.-Washington Environmental Cooperation Council", in Kiy and Wirth (eds.), *Environmental Management on North America's Borders*, 53-71.

Baar, E. (1995), "Economic Instruments and Control of Secondary Air Pollutants in the Lower Fraser Valley", in Scott *et al.* (ed.), *Managing Natural Resources in British Columbia*, 95–131.

Barnett, H.J. and C. Morse (1963), *Scarcity and Growth* (Baltimore: Johns Hopkins).

Barton, B.J., R.T. Franson and A.R. Thompson (1984), *A Contract Model for Pollution Control* (Vancouver: Westwater).

Baumol, W.J. (1969), *Welfare Economics and the Theory of the State*, 2d ed. (Cambridge, MA: Harvard University Press).

Berger, T.R. (1977), *Northern Frontier /Northern Homeland* (Ottawa: Supply and Services Canada).

Boulding, K. (1966), "The Economics of the Coming Spaceship Earth", in H. Jarrett (ed.), *Environmental Quality in a Growing Economy* (Baltimore: Johns Hopkins University Press).

Bregha, F., J. Benidickson, D. Gamble, T. Shillington and E. Weick (1990), *The Integration of Environmental Considerations into Government Policy* (Ottawa: Canadian Environmental Assessment Research Council).

Brennan, G. and J.M. Buchanan (1985), *The Reason of Rules* (New York: Cambridge University Press).

Breton, A. and A. Scott (1978), *The Economic Constitution of Federal States* (Toronto: University of Toronto Press).

Buchanan, J.M. (1975), *The Limits of Liberty: Between Anarchy and Leviathan* (Chicago: University of Chicago Press).

Cain, L.P. (1978), *Sanitation Strategy for a Lakefort Metropolis: The Case of Chicago* (DeKalb: Northern Illinois University Press).

Canada, Department of External Affairs (1964), *The Columbia River Treaty Protocol and Related Documents* (Ottawa: External Affairs and Northern Affairs Departments).

Canada, Tradable Permits Working Group (2000), *Using Tradable Emissions Permits* (Ottawa: Department of Finance; National Climate Change Project).

Carson, R. (1962), *Silent Spring* (London: Penguin).

Ciriacy-Wantrup, S.V. (1952), *Resource Conservation* (Berkeley: University of California Press) (2nd edition, 1963).

Coase, R.H. (1960), "The Problem of Social Cost", *Journal of Law and Economics* 3, 1–44.

Copeland, B., B. Antweiler and S. Taylor (forthcoming), "Pollution and International Markets", working paper (Vancouver: Department of Economics, University of British Columbia).

Dales, J. (1968), *Pollution, Property and Prices* (Toronto: University of Toronto Press).

Daly, H.E., ed. (1973), *Toward a Steady-State Economy* (San Francisco: Freeman).

Davis, R.K. (1968), *The Range of Choice in Water Management* (Baltimore: Johns Hopkins University Press).

Dewees, D.N. (1995), "Sulfur Dioxide Emissions from Smelters: The Historical Inefficiency of Tort Law", WPS No. 44 (Toronto: Faculty of Law).

Dewey, S.H. (2000), *Don't Breath the Air: Air Pollution and U.S. Environmental Policies 1945-70* (College Station: Texas A&M University Press).

Eckstein, O. (1955), *Water-Resource Development: The Economics of Project Evaluation* (Cambridge: Harvard University Press).

Elworthy, S. and J. Holder (1997), *Environmental Protection: Text and Materials* (London: Butterworths).

Fafard, P.C. and K. Harrison, eds. (2000), *Managing the Environmental Union: Intergovernmental Relations and Environmental Policy in Canada* (Montreal and Kingston: McGill-Queen's University Press for School of Policy Studies, Queen's University).

Field, B.C. and N.D. Olewiler (forthcoming), *Environmental Economics,* 2d ed. (Toronto: McGraw-Hill Ryerson).

Galeotti, G., P. Salmon and R. Wintrobe, eds. (2000), *Competition and Structure* (Cambridge: Cambridge University Press).

Harrison, K. (1996), *Passing the Buck: Federalism and Canadian Environment* (Vancouver: UBC Press).

Herfindahl, O.C. and A.V. Kneese (1974), *Economic Theory of Natural Resources* (Columbus: Merrill Publishing).

Hodge, R.A. and P.R. West (1998), "Achieving Progress in the Great Lakes Basin Ecosystem and the Georgia Basin-Puget Sound Bioregion", in Kiy and Wirth (eds.), *Environmental Management on North America's Borders,* 72-107.

Howitt, P., ed. (1993), "CEA Twenty-fifth Anniversary Symposium", *Canadian Journal of Economics* 26(1).

Huffaker, R., A. Michelsen, J. Hamilton and M. Frasier (2001), "The Uneasy Hierarchy of Federal and State Water Laws and Policies" (preliminary draft) at <www.uidaho.edu/~joelh/Projects/MarketBibliography/FederalandState. htm>.

Jones, R., P.H. Pearse and A. Scott (1980), "Conditions for Cooperation on Joint Projects by Independent Jurisdictions", *Canadian Journal of Economics* 13, 231-249.

Kehoe, T. (1997), *Cleaning Up the Great Lakes: From Cooperation to Confrontation* (DeKalb: Northern Illinois University Press).

Kennedy, P.W. (1999), "Learning about Environmental Damage: Implications for Emissions Trading", *Canadian Journal of Economics* 32(5), 1313-1327.

Kiy, R. and J.D. Wirth, eds. (1998), *Environmental Management on North America's Borders* (College Station, TX: Texas A&M University Press).

Kranjc, A. (2000), "Neo-Conservatism and the Decline of Ontario's Environment Ministry", *Canadian Public Policy/Analyse de Politiques* 26(1), 111-128.

Krutilla, J. (1967), *The Columbia River Treaty: The Economics of an International River Development* (Baltimore: Johns Hopkins University Press).

Lipsey, R. (forthcoming 2001), "Successes and Failures in the Transformation of Economics", *Journal of Economic Methodology* (Vancouver: Simon Fraser University).

Maass, A. *et al.* (1966), *Design of Water-Resource Systems* (Cambridge: Harvard University Press).

McKitrick, R. (1997), "Environmental Taxation and Canadian Carbon Emissions Control", *Canadian Public Policy/Analyse de Politiques* 23, 401-434.

McNeil, J.W. (1971), *Environmental Management* (Constitutional study prepared for the Government of Canada) (Ottawa: Information Canada).

Meadows, D.H. *et al.* (the Club of Rome) (1972), *The Limits to Growth* (London: Pan).

Melosi, M. (2000), *The Sanitary City* (Baltimore: Johns Hopkins University Press).

Oates, W. (1972), *Fiscal Federalism* (New York: Harcourt).

Olewiler, N. (1990), "The Case for Pollution Taxes", in G.B. Doern (ed.), *Getting it Green* (Toronto: C.D. Howe Institute), 188-207.

Ostrom, E., R. Gardner and J. Walker (1994), *Rules, Games and Common-Pool Resources* (Ann Arbor, MI: University of Michigan Press).

Paehkle, R.C. (1989), *Environmentalism and the Future of Progressive Politics* (New Haven: Yale University Press).

_____ (2001), "Spatial Proportionality: Right-Sizing Environmental Decision-Making", in E.A. Parson (ed.), *Governing the Environment* (Toronto: University of Toronto Press), forthcoming.

Parson, E.A. (2000), "Environmental Trends and Environmental Governance in Canada", *Canadian Public Policy/Analyse de Politiques* 26(2), S125-S143.

Pigou, A.C. (1947), *Public Finance*, 3d ed. (London: Macmillan, 1962).

Posner, R.A. (1977), *Economic Analysis of Law*, 2d ed. (Boston and Toronto: Little, Brown).

Prest, A.R. and R. Turvey (1967), "Cost-Benefit Analysis: A Survey", *Surveys of Economic Theory*, Vol. III (London: Macmillan), 155–207.

Quirin, G.D. (1962), *Economics of Oil and Gas Development in Northern Canada* (Ottawa: Northern Affairs).

Russell, C.S., ed. (1979), *Collective Decision Making: Applications from Public Choice Theory* (Baltimore, MD: Resources for the Future and Johns Hopkins University Press).

Saunders, J.O., ed. (1986), *Managing Natural Resources in a Federal State* (Toronto: Carswell).

Schumpeter, J.A. (1954), *History of Economic Analysis* (New York: Oxford University Press).

Schwindt, R. (1992), *Report of the Commission of Inquiry into Compensation for the Taking of Resource Interests* (Victoria: the Commission).

Scott, A. (1967), "Recruitment and Migration of Canadian Social Scientists", *Canadian Journal of Economics and Political Science* 33, 495-508.

_____ (1972), "The Economics of the International Transmission of Pollution", in OECD *Problems of Environmental Economics* (Paris: OECD).

_____ (1976a), "Transfrontier Pollution — Are New Institutions Necessary?" in OECD *Economics of Transfrontier Pollution* (Paris: OECD).

_____ (1976b), "Transfrontier Pollution and Institutional Choice", in I. Walter (ed.), *Studies in International Environmental Economics* (New York: Wiley), 303-317.

_____ (1993), "Does Living in Canada make one a Canadian Economist?" in Howitt (ed.), CEA Twenty-fifth Anniversary Symposium, 26-38.

_____ (2000), "Assigning Powers over the Canadian Environment", in Galeotti *et al.* (eds.), *Competition and Structure*, 174-219.

Scott, A. and C.B. Bramsen (1972), "Draft Guiding Principles Concerning Transfrontier Pollution", in OECD, H. Smets (ed.), *Problems in Transfrontier Pollution* (Paris: OECD).

Scott, A., J. Robinson and D. Cohen, eds. (1995), *Managing Natural Resources in British Columbia* (Vancouver: UBC Press).

Sewell, W.R.D. and A.E. Utton, eds. (1986), "U.S.-Canada Transboundary Resource Issues", Special issue of *Natural Resources Journal* 26(2).

Smith, S.C. and E.N. Castle (1964), *Economics and Public Policy in Water Resource* (Development Ames, IA: Iowa State University Press).

Solow, R.M. (1974), "The Economics of Resources or the Resources of Economics", *American Economic Review* 64, 1–21.

Sproule-Jones, M. (1980), *The Real World of Pollution Control* (Vancouver: Westwater).

_____ (1993), *Governments at Work* (Toronto: University of Toronto Press).

Stone, M. and R. Reid (1997), "Opportunity Costs of Spotted Owl Management Options for British Columbia", *Canadian Public Policy* 23(1), 69-82.

Swainson, N. (1979), *Conflict Over the Columbia: The Canadian Background to an Historic Treaty* (Montreal: McGill-Queen's University Press).

Thompson, A.R. (1980), *Environmental Regulation in Canada: An Assessment of the Regulatory Process* (Vancouver: Westwater Research Centre, University of British Columbia).

Tietenberg, T.H. (1985), *Emissions Trading: An Exercise in Reforming Pollution Policy* (Washington DC: Resources for the Future).

van Kooten, C.G. and A. Scott (1995), "Constitutional Crisis, Economics of the Environment, and Resource Development", *Canadian Public Policy/Analyse de Politiques* 21(2), 233-249.

Victor, P. (1972), *Pollution: Economy and Environment* (London: Unwin).

Weiland, P., L.K. Caldwell and R. O'Leary (1997), "The Evolution, Operation and Future of Environmental Policy in the United States", in R. Baker (ed.), *Environmental Law and Policy in the European Union and the United States* (Westport, CT: Praeger).

Willoughby, W.R. (1960), "St. Lawrence Seaway: A Study in Pressure Politics", *Queen's Quarterly* 67 (Spring), 1-10.

World Commission on Environment and Development (Brundtland) (1987), *Our Common Future* (New York: Oxford University Press).

Labour Economics

Cyclical Changes in Short-Run Earnings Mobility in Canada, 1982 to 1996

Charles M. Beach and Ross Finnie

Introduction

This paper uses longitudinal income tax-based data for Canada to examine the cyclical pattern of changes in the earnings distribution and earnings mobility in Canada over the period 1982 to 1996, an interval that includes considerable variation in labour market conditions. Numerous recent studies have noted increasing degrees of inequality and polarization of workers' earnings, especially for men; broad distributional shifts in earnings, especially for women; and changing degrees of earnings mobility for both men and women in Canada over the 1980s and up to the middle 1990s (Picot, 1997; Beach and Slotsve, 1996; Beach and Finnie, 1998). Here we want to focus on the cyclical pattern in these changes.

This research was made possible by the Applied Research Branch of Human Resources Development Canada. The Small Area and Administrative Data Division of Statistics Canada provided access to the LAD data upon which the study is based. The authors also gratefully acknowledge a Social Sciences and Humanities Research Council Research Grant which was critical in earlier stages of the research with the LAD data. Roger Sceviour provided excellent computing assistance.

453

This paper examines basic evidence on how polarization, distributional shifts and measures of the short-run mobility of workers' earnings vary over the business cycle. This can be viewed as updating the C.D. Howe study by Beach and Slotsve (1996), but with much more extensive data and with a data set that has an explicit longitudinal dimension — indeed the LAD file on which this study is based was pioneered by the former Economic Council of Canada of which David Slater was the chair for a number of years. As one may expect, there are evidently major trends on-going in these various aspects of distributional change (Beach and Finnie, 2000). In the present paper, we analyze cyclical patterns in the above distributional features. Alternatively viewed, to what extent are distributional changes in workers' earnings and the related pattern of earnings mobility in Canada concentrated in periods of economic recession, and what effects do strengthening or weakening labour markets have on these different dimensions of distributional change in earnings in Canada?

The study focuses on earnings rather than total income because widening inequality and polarization and declining real incomes over the period have been principally attributes of labour markets, and we wish to abstract from government transfers and other sources of income. By short-run distributional change, we mean year-to-year changes in order to be comparable to conventional studies of annual cross-sectional data (such as the SCF in Canada or CPS in the United States). Much of the discussion also focuses on the mobility of workers' earnings because this is a relatively novel concept on which to have data for Canada and because longitudinal-based mobility measures do a better job at indicating how individual workers' earnings actually change over time than cross-sectional-based estimates.

Cyclical variation in earnings mobility is of interest for several reasons. Mobility and inequality can be viewed as distributional complements. For a given degree of inequality of earnings, more earnings mobility corresponds to securing greater labour market opportunity (Shorrocks, 1978). Cyclical variation in earnings mobility thus shows how changes in labour market opportunity vary over the business cycle. Numerous studies have analyzed cyclical changes in inequality; this is the first to focus on cyclical variation of income or earnings mobility for Canada. This will be useful for better understanding how earnings mobility may be expected to be affected by the current economic slowdown in Canada. Identifying cyclical variation in workers' earnings is also critical to the formal statistical modelling of individuals' earnings changes (e.g., Abowd and Card, 1989) and to the econometric analysis of changes in wage structure and earnings inequality

(Katz and Autor, 1999). For example, to identify possible labour market and distributional effects of a Free Trade Agreement of the Americas in 2005 requires us to understand underlying cyclical effects already present in workers' earnings mobility and their labour market opportunities. Finally, macro aggregates such as consumption and housing expenditures likely depend on workers' expectations of labour markets and income changes, so that earnings mobility measures may provide input to cyclical fluctuation in household expenditure expectations.

Major non-Canadian studies that provide excellent treatment of mobility in terms of underlying basic issues and policy relevance include Atkinson, Bourguignon and Morrison (1992); Duncan, Smeeding and Rodgers (1994); Gottschalk and Moffitt (1994); OECD (1993, 1996); Buchinsky and Hunt (1996); and Burkhauser, Holtz-Eakin and Rhody (1997). The one early Canadian study we are aware of is Kennedy (1989) which uses a Canada Pension Plan administrative file on earnings of middle-aged men over the period 1966–83. Baker and Solon (1999) study earnings dynamics of men over the 1976–92 interval using regression-based variance-decomposition techniques. And several papers by Finnie (1997a, b, c, d) all use the LAD file, but employ a narrow definition of earnings (essentially wage and salary income) and look at earnings quintile shares (rather than median-based population shares).

The main findings of this paper are as follows. First, there have indeed been major cyclical changes in earnings polarization and distributional shifts, and these have been most markedly concentrated in the recessions, particularly the 1990–92 interval, and show relative stasis during the observed periods of expansion. Second, the general distributional pattern observed for men as a whole holds across all age groups, and the general pattern for women as a whole also holds across all age groups (except for entry-age workers), but the strength of these effects differs considerably across age groups. Third, earnings mobility significantly decreases for men during recessions by reducing the probability of moving up the distribution and increasing the probability of moving down about equally, thus markedly decreasing the net probability of moving up. Fourth, for men, the cyclical sensitivity of transition probabilities decreases monotonically with age, so that cross-sectional age-earnings profiles become steeper in recessions and flatter over economic expansions as the earnings of entry-age and younger workers show the greatest cyclical variation.

The paper is organized as follows. The next section describes the main features of the LAD data set used in this study and defines the estimation sample generating the results. The following two sections look at distributional changes from a cross-sectional perspective treating each year as if it were a separate cross-section. This allows one to look at the cyclical fluctuations in the distribution of workers, the polarization of earnings, and the degree of upward or downward shift in the earnings distribution by sex and age group. The fifth section then exploits the longitudinal aspect of the LAD file more fully by examining various measures of earnings mobility, again by sex and age group, and analyzing their cyclical sensitivity. The final section summarizes and concludes.

The LAD Data Set and the Analysis Sample

The master LAD file is a 10 per cent representative sample of all Canadian tax-filers. In order to be as inclusive as possible, we look at total employment income (henceforth "earnings") consisting of all wage and salary income and net self-employment income of all earners (men and women) aged 20 to 64 who were not identified as full-time students in the income year and who received at least $1,000 in earnings (in 1996 constant dollars) as reported on T-1 forms.[1] The intention is to approximate Statistics Canada's concept of "All Earners" while excluding those who have only a limited attachment to the labour market. The resulting sample in 1996 is thus 1.218 million observations or 56 per cent of the full LAD file of 2.167 million observations that year. The biggest exclusions were for those over age 64 (17 per cent in 1996) and under the $1,000 earnings cut-off (20 per cent). The sample sizes vary from 1.033 million observations in 1982 to 1.218 million observations in 1996.

The LAD's coverage (and representativeness) of the adult population is very good since the rate of tax filings is very high in Canada: high-income recipients are required to do so, while low-income individuals have incentives

---

[1]We have also put in place special procedures to deal with individuals who have changed their SINs, who have multiple SINs, and other non-standard cases — see Finnie (1997c) — which comprise of the order of 4 per cent of the file in any given year. Designation of full-time student is based on the tuition and education tax credit responses on T-1 forms.

Charles M. Beach and Ross Finnie

to file in order to recover income tax and other payroll tax deductions made throughout the year, and since 1986 to recover various tax credits. The full set of tax files from which the LAD is constructed are estimated to cover from 91 to 95 per cent of the target adult population (Finnie, 1997d). There has been an increase in the proportion of individuals filing tax forms over time due to the introduction of the federal sales tax credit in 1986, the goods and services tax (GST) credit in 1990, and various other federal and provincial benefits. While this improved coverage means that the LAD has become increasingly representative of the underlying adult population, it also poses potential problems for comparisons of earlier and later years, since the "new" filers are more likely to have low earnings in any given year and hence bias estimates towards slower average growth and stronger net downward mobility. The comparison problem does not, however, appear to be very great and is, in any case, attenuated by the age, student and low-earnings exclusions imposed on the sample (Beach and Finnie, 2001).

The estimation sample is divided into eight separate age/sex population subgroups. Women and men are treated separately because of their different earnings experience since the early 1980s. Each gender is also divided into four age groups: entry workers (age 20–24), younger workers (age 25–34), prime age workers (age 35–54), and older workers (age 55–64). This allows one to see how mobility patterns vary across the life cycle and how these dynamics vary over the business cycle for the different age groups. The 1996 age breakdown is as follows (in thousands of observations):

	Women	Men
Entry (20–24)	49.3 (8.8%)	57.7 (8.7%)
Younger (25–34)	152.6 (27.3%)	174.2 (26.4%)
Prime (35–54)	305.8 (54.8%)	354.1 (53.7%)
Older (55–64)	50.4 (9.0%)	73.8 (11.2%)

The subsamples in 1996 vary from 49,310 to 354,110 observations each. The numbers in earlier years reflect demographic change with larger numbers of younger workers and smaller numbers of prime age workers than in 1996.

In dividing the earnings distribution into lower, middle and upper regions (henceforth "earnings intervals" or EIs), various cut-off levels are used:

- Below 25% of median ("Very low")
- 25-50% of median ("Low")
- 50-100% of median ("Low middle")
- 100-150% of median ("High middle")
- 150-200% of median ("High")
- Above 200% of median ("Very high").

Following the convention in the polarization literature, the cut-offs are expressed in terms of the median earnings level (rather than in terms of quantiles such as earnings quintiles). In order to address the questions of where various individuals lie in the overall distribution of earnings, or how well women and men are doing in the overall earnings distribution, all cut-offs are computed from a common median earnings level for the earnings distribution as a whole each year. Note that the median was virtually the same (in real terms) in 1982 as in 1996 ($25.3 and $25.2 thousand, respectively, in 1996 dollars). So cut-off levels between the earnings intervals were also essentially the same between the two end years. Median earnings also varied remarkably little over the period — from a low of $24.7 thousand in 1984 to a peak of $26 thousand in 1989. This reflects conflicting patterns for men and women as men's (higher) median earnings declined over the period since 1989 while women's (lower) median earnings increased.

Polarization Rates, Distributional Shifts, and the Economic Cycle

This section looks at the basic distributions of male and female workers across earnings intervals, how these have changed over the 1982–96 period, and the evidence for any cyclical variation in these changes.

Table 1 shows the distribution of men and women workers across earnings intervals for the two end years of the sample and for peak (1989)

Charles M. Beach and Ross Finnie

Table 1: Distribution of Workers across Earnings Intervals for Men and Women, Selected Years, 1982–1996 (percentages)

	Very Low	Low	Low Middle	High Middle	High	Very High
All Workers						
1982	11.2	13.4	25.4	22.1	14.8	13.1
1983	12.0	13.9	24.2	21.3	14.8	13.9
1989	11.0	13.5	25.5	22.0	14.2	13.7
1992	12.4	14.0	23.6	21.0	14.0	15.0
1996	12.4	13.9	23.7	20.8	13.5	15.7
Mean	11.77	13.80	24.41	21.29	14.24	14.47
Men						
1982	7.4	9.6	19.8	23.1	20.0	20.1
1983	8.2	10.5	19.1	21.2	19.7	21.3
1989	7.0	9.8	20.2	22.8	19.0	21.3
1992	9.4	11.3	19.5	20.2	17.5	22.1
1996	9.3	11.1	20.1	20.1	16.4	23.0
Mean	8.17	10.52	19.75	21.25	18.41	21.91
Women						
1982	16.7	18.7	33.3	20.6	7.5	3.2
1983	17.2	18.5	31.3	21.4	8.1	3.5
1989	16.2	18.4	32.1	20.8	8.3	4.2
1992	16.0	17.3	28.5	21.9	9.7	6.5
1996	16.0	17.3	27.9	21.6	10.1	7.1
Mean	16.37	17.98	30.38	21.31	8.91	5.03

and trough (1983, 1992) years within the 1982–1996 period.[2,3] Average percentages of workers in each earnings interval over the full sample period

---

[2]In 1996, the five earnings cut-offs dividing the distribution into six earnings groups were $6.3 (thousand), $12.6, $25.2, $37.8 and $50.4.

[3]Standard errors could be calculated for these earnings interval shares as these are multinomially distributed, but the underlying sample sizes are so large they were judged not worth reporting.

appear in the last row of each panel. That men on average have higher earnings than women shows up in men being much more prevalent in the upper two earnings intervals, while women occur more frequently in the lower three intervals.

For men as a whole, the major change was an increasing polarization of workers, characterized by movements from the high and high-middle regions of the distribution (which include many manufacturing and unionized jobs) towards the lower and top ends of the distribution. For women as a whole, the most notable change was the general upward shift of the entire earnings distribution from the lower three regions to the upper three regions of the distribution (due to increases in both wage rates and hours worked).

Cyclical patterns in these shifts are also apparent, particularly for males (who tend to work more in manufacturing and primary-goods sectors than women who are concentrated more in services and public sector jobs which are less cyclically volatile). Between 1989 and 1992, for example, the percentage of men within the lowest two earnings intervals rose from 16.8 to 20.7 per cent. During the preceding 1983–89 expansion, the share had declined from 18.7 to 16.8 per cent. Cyclical changes thus appear to occur most markedly during periods of economic recession and slack labour market performance. For women, however, general downward trends in the bottom three shares and upward trends in the upper three shares appear more predominant. These cyclical patterns are illustrated in Figures 1 and 2.

Now consider the cyclical patterns of earnings polarization and distributional shift in more detail. Polarization of earnings refers to a growing proportion of workers at the two ends of the earnings distribution and a corresponding reduction in the proportion of workers around the middle of the distribution. This has been found by Beach and Slotsve (1996) to characterize the male earnings distribution in Canada based on grouped histograms of cross-sectional SCF data published by Statistics Canada. It would be worthwhile to examine this issue further with the large LAD microdata set. From a cross-sectional perspective, this could be examined by looking at year-to-year changes in

$$(P_{VL} + P_L) + (P_H + P_{VH}) \tag{1}$$

where P_{VL} is the percentage of workers within the very low (VL) earnings interval and the remaining percentages are defined accordingly. (Middle percentages do not enter the formula as the percentages all sum to a 100 per cent and an increase in the lower and upper interval shares implies a

Figure 1: Change in the Earnings Distribution for Men 1989 to 1992

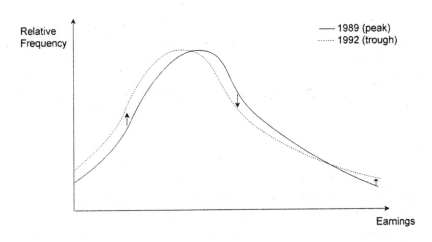

Figure 2: Change in the Earnings Distribution for Women 1989 to 1992

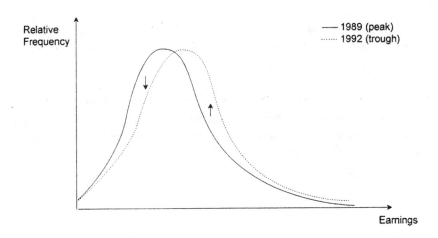

corresponding reduction in the middle interval percentages.) Alternatively, one could also look at the more extreme measure

$$P_{VL} + P_{VH} \qquad (2)$$

concentrating on just the two end interval shares. These are called cross-sectional measures because they do not exploit the panel nature of the data.

Table 2 presents estimates of changes in both these measures of polarization (in the first two rows of each panel). Also presented are the breakdowns of these measures into the portions contributed by the upper and lower ends separately (in the bottom four rows of each panel). Three features are most noticeable from these results. First, a substantial degree of increased polarization is evident in the last column of the table. Among all workers, the interval share of individuals with earnings in the bottom two and top two intervals increased by three percentage points between 1982 and 1996 (a 5.7 per cent increase), while the proportion of workers in just the two extreme intervals rose by 3.8 points (or by 15.6 per cent). The corresponding increases for men were 2.7 and 4.8 percentage points, respectively, and for women 4.4 and 3.2 percentage points. Evidently, the shift is strongest in percentage terms in the two extreme earnings intervals.

Second, the increased polarization for men occurs at both ends of the earnings distribution with increasing shares of workers at both the very low and very high intervals. (Estimates of what fraction of the increased polarization is attributable to increases at one end or the other, however, are not at all robust as they vary greatly with exactly what polarization measure is used.) For women, though, this is not the case as the increased polarization measures really reflect a shift up of the entire distribution such that the increased share in the high and very high intervals (6.5 percentage points) completely swamps the reduced share of workers in the low and very low intervals (-2.1 percentage points). Thus what is going on in the distribution of female earnings is not really well characterized by the term polarization. This will be revisited below.

Third, the most marked changes in the degree of polarization among men's earnings occurred during the two major recessions and particularly over the recession period of 1989–92. In general, earnings polarization increased during recessions (with the biggest increases occurring among low earners) and attenuated during economic expansions (with again the biggest adjustments occurring among low earners) with high earners relatively insulated from such cyclical fluctuations (see Figure 1). But over the full

Table 2: Cross-Sectional Polarization Changes for Men and Women, Selected Years, 1982–1996 (percentage point changes)

	1982–1983	1983–1989	1989–1992	1992–1996	1982–1996
All Workers					
– Beyond 50% of median[1]	2.1	-2.2	3.0	0.1	3.0 (5.7%)
– Change in VL and VH[2]	1.6	-1.2	2.7	0.7	3.8 (15.6%)
– Change in VL and L[3]	1.3	-1.4	1.9	-0.1	1.7
– Change in VL[5]	0.8	-1.0	1.4	0.0	1.2
– Change in VH and H[4]	0.8	-0.8	1.1	0.2	1.3
– Change in VH[6]	0.8	-0.2	1.3	0.7	2.6
Men					
– Beyond 50% of median	2.6	-2.6	3.2	-0.5	2.7 (4.7%)
– Change in VL and VH	2.0	-1.2	3.2	0.8	4.8 (17.5%)
– Change in VL and L	1.7	-1.9	3.9	-0.3	3.4
– Change in VL	0.8	-1.2	2.4	-0.1	1.9
– Change in VH and H	0.9	-0.7	-0.7	-0.2	-0.7
– Change in VH	1.2	0.0	0.8	0.9	2.9
Women					
– Beyond 50% of median	1.2	-0.2	2.4	1.0	4.4 (9.5%)
– Change in VL and VH	0.8	-0.3	2.1	0.6	3.2 (16.1%)
– Change in VL and L	0.3	-1.1	-1.3	0.0	-2.1
– Change in VL	0.5	-1.0	-0.2	0.0	-0.7
– Change in VH and H	0.9	0.9	3.7	1.0	6.5
– Change in VH	0.3	0.7	2.3	0.6	3.9

Notes: [1] $\Delta(P_{VL}+P_L)+\Delta(P_H+P_{VH})$
[2] $\Delta P_{VL}+\Delta P_{VH}$
[3] $\Delta P_{VL}+\Delta P_L$
[4] $\Delta P_{VH}+\Delta P_H$
[5] ΔP_{VL}
[6] ΔP_{VH}
where P_i represents the percentages of workers in earnings interval i.

period 1982–96, the latter attenuation has not recovered all the polarization increases that occurred during the recessions — and this is especially so over the 1990s. As a result, the increases in earnings polarization for men have tended to follow a ratchet pattern over the period covered, notching up significantly during recessions and then easing off relatively little over the ensuing expansion. This does not bode well for when the next recession hits the labour market.

It has been noted above that the earnings distribution for women has generally shifted upward over the sample period, especially over the 1990s. We now look at this more formally. Again from a cross-sectional perspective, this idea could be examined by looking at year-to-year changes in

$$(P_{VH} + P_H + P_{HM}) - (P_{LM} + P_L + P_{VL}) \tag{3}$$

where again P_{VH} is the percentage of workers within the very high (VH) earnings interval and the remaining percentages are defined accordingly. Intuitively, a shift up of a distribution would show up as generally positive changes in the upper set of interval shares and negative changes in the lower set of interval shares. (Recall that the sum of all six shares is always 100 per cent.) So an upward shift will typically be captured by a positive change in the share formula (3), while a downward shift will tend to show up as a negative change. Alternatively, since the biggest changes appear to have occurred in the lower and upper interval shares, one could also look at the more extreme measure of distributional shift

$$(P_{VH} + P_H) - (P_L + P_{VL}) \tag{4}$$

which concentrates on shifts at the two ends of the distribution. Since the polarization measures may be dominated by shifts at only one end of a distribution, it is useful to complement them by further measures of distributional shift per se to see whether a distribution is more appropriately characterized as generally moving up or moving down.

Table 3 presents estimates of changes in both these measures of upward/downward distributional shift. One notices first the virtual absence of distributional shift for all workers (men and women together, first panel). But this hides strong opposite shifts in fact going on within the overall distribution between men and women. The earnings distribution for men shifted down strongly over the 1982–96 period as a whole (right-hand column), while the distribution for women workers shifted even more strongly upward

Table 3: Cross-Sectional Upward/Downward Shift for Men and Women, Selected Years, 1982–1996 (percentage point changes)

	1982– 1983	1983– 1989	1989– 1992	1992– 1996	1982– 1996
All Workers					
– Change in Top Three to Bottom Three EIs[1]	-0.1	0.0	0.1	0.0	0.0
– Change in Top Two to Bottom Two EIs[2]	-0.5	0.6	-0.8	0.3	-0.4
Men					
– Change in Top Three to Bottom Three EIs	-2.0	1.7	-6.5	-0.6	-7.4
– Change in Top Two to Bottom Two EIs	-0.8	1.2	-4.6	0.1	-4.1
Women					
– Change in Top Three to Bottom Three EIs	3.4	0.6	9.7	1.3	15.0
– Change in Top Two to Bottom Two EIs	0.6	2.0	5.0	1.0	8.6

Notes: [1] $\Delta(P_{VH}+P_H+P_{HM}) - \Delta(P_{LM} + P_L + P_{VL})$
[2] $\Delta(P_{VH}+P_H) - \Delta(P_L + P_{VL})$
where P_i represents the percentage of workers in earnings interval i.

(see Figure 2). So the two earnings distributions have strongly converged over the sample period. Also note that the period of most marked distributional shifts occurred over the 1989–92 period of major recession in Canada. Indeed, more than half the shifting occurred over this brief interval — between 58 and 65 per cent of the entire 1982–96 shift for women and 88–112 per cent for men. By contrast, the recessionary period 1982–83 accounted for only 7–23 per cent of the full period shift for women and 20–27 per cent for men. In terms of distributional shift, the early recession and subsequent recovery of the 1990s were a period of quite dramatic and likely historic adjustment.

In an extended version of the current paper (Beach and Finnie, 2001), we also examine whether these cyclical patterns are statistically significant once one nets out underlying trends. This is done by running regressions of earnings interval shares (the proportions in expressions (1) - (4)) as dependent variables on a time trend and the adult male (age 25 and over) unemployment rate (as a proxy for business-cycle effects). The unemployment rate coefficients are referred to as *net* cyclical effects or net responsiveness to unemployment changes. Results in Table 4 show that weak labour markets increase earnings polarization significantly for both men and women with generally much stronger effects for men than for women (see rows one and two). Among men, the action driving the greater polarization of earnings occurs towards the bottom end of the distribution as lower-earnings workers slip down the distribution. Among women, however, the action occurs towards the top end of the distribution as higher-earnings women move up relatively in the distribution. In Table 5, highly significant opposite distributional shifts for men and women stand out clearly. Weak labour markets shift the earnings distribution for men down significantly, but the higher unemployment shifts the women's distribution up significantly in relative terms as women's earnings are relatively less sensitive to weakened labour markets. Both sets of net cyclical effects mirror the gross results already observed in the raw data of Tables 2 and 3.

Patterns across Age Groups

The recent literature (e.g., Beaudry and Green, 2000; or Beach and Finnie, 1998) has found considerable differences in earnings experiences for different age groups in Canada. This is worth exploring further. Table 6 presents earnings interval shares for each of four age groups, entry workers (age 20–24), younger (25–34), prime (35–54), and older workers (55–64). To save clutter, the table focuses on just the 1989–92 recessionary period as well as mean earnings interval shares (P_i's) over the full 1982–96 period.

As can be seen from the latter figures, entry workers are concentrated more towards the lower end of the distribution, and prime age male workers appear predominantly towards the upper end (since the EI cutoffs are based on the overall median earnings level). The general cyclical pattern for men as a whole previously seen in Table 1 (and illustrated in Figure 1) holds

Table 4: Net Cross-Sectional Polarization Responsiveness to Unemployment for Men and Women, 1982–1996

	Men	Women
Beyond 50% of median marginal UR effect	0.687 (4.51)	0.432 (4.75)
Change in VL and VH marginal UR effect	0.611 (4.66)	0.363 (6.14)
Change in VL and L marginal UR effect	0.789 (17.5)	-0.035 (0.43)
Change in VL marginal UR effect	0.496 (16.4)	0.078 (1.37)
Change in VH and H marginal UR effect	-0.102 (0.73)	0.467 (17.8)
Change in VH marginal UR effect	0.115 (0.93)	0.285 (13.4)

Note: See notes to Table 2. Figures in parentheses are absolute values of "t-ratios". Coefficients are marginal effects as defined in the text.

Table 5: Net Cross-Sectional Upward/Downward Responsiveness to Unemployment in Earnings Distributions for Men and Women, 1982–1996

	Men	Women
Change in top three to bottom three EIs	-1.195 (12.6)	1.286 (15.2)
Change in top two to bottom two EIs	-0.892 (6.32)	0.502 (6.37)

Note: See notes to Table 3. Coefficients are marginal effects as defined in the text. Figures in parentheses are absolute values of "t-ratios".

Table 6: Distribution of Workers across Earnings Intervals by Age, 1989 and 1992, and Mean over 1982-1996 (percentages)

Men

	Very Low	Low	Low Middle	High Middle	High	Very High
Entry						
1989	17.9	20.9	36.0	18.8	5.2	1.1
1992	26.6	24.1	31.0	13.6	3.9	0.9
Mean	21.86	22.63	33.19	16.04	5.05	1.25
Younger						
1989	6.4	9.7	22.9	27.8	20.1	13.1
1992	9.0	11.7	22.8	24.9	18.5	13.0
Mean	7.56	10.54	22.28	25.59	19.81	14.23
Prime						
1989	4.3	7.0	14.8	20.7	21.8	31.4
1992	6.1	8.5	15.4	18.9	19.9	31.3
Mean	5.07	7.53	15.07	19.71	20.97	31.64
Older						
1989	8.8	10.6	19.7	21.3	17.5	22.0
1992	11.1	12.5	19.9	18.9	15.6	22.1
Mean	9.51	11.11	19.22	20.72	17.12	22.33

Women

	Very Low	Low	Low Middle	High Middle	High	Very High
Entry						
1989	26.1	24.7	37.0	10.7	1.3	0.2
1992	31.6	25.6	30.8	10.4	1.4	0.2
Mean	28.64	25.33	34.03	10.39	1.45	0.16
Younger						
1989	16.1	17.4	33.0	23.0	7.9	2.7
1992	15.9	17.1	30.3	23.1	9.7	3.8
Mean	16.09	17.13	31.20	23.25	9.15	3.16
Prime						
1989	13.1	16.5	30.6	22.7	10.6	6.5
1992	12.7	15.3	26.9	23.7	11.8	9.5
Mean	13.35	16.39	28.88	22.87	10.99	7.51
Older						
1989	17.9	20.5	31.2	19.5	6.7	4.1
1992	18.0	20.0	28.2	20.4	7.4	6.1
Mean	17.69	19.96	29.71	20.51	7.18	4.91

Charles M. Beach and Ross Finnie

across all age groups, and the general cyclical pattern for women as a whole (in Table 1 and illustrated in Figure 2) also holds across all age groups, except for entry age women whose pattern resembles more that of entry age men. The strength of the cyclical effects, though, differs across age groups, with the strongest shifts generally occurring among entry and younger workers.

Cyclical patterns in polarization rates and distributional shifts by age group are examined in Beach and Finnie (2001). Polarization rates increase in recessions across all age/sex groups. Entry and younger workers of both sex show the strongest sensitivity to unemployment rate changes, while older workers show generally the weakest effects. The cyclical pattern of distributional shifts (both in the raw data and the net unemployment rate effects) across all age groups for each gender mirrors that for the gender as a whole (with the one exception of entry-age women workers). But the strength of the cyclical effects differs across age groups with typically the strongest effects occurring among entry and younger workers.

Cyclical Effects on Earnings Mobility

So far the analysis in this paper has operated as if we simply had a series of large annual cross-sections of data. We now exploit the longitudinal aspect of the LAD file in order to see how workers move about the earnings distribution from one year to the next. This allows us to see better where workers were coming from or went when changes occurred in earnings interval shares and how these earnings dynamics are related to the business cycle. As Beach and Finnie (2000) show, the underlying earnings transition probabilities can be viewed as the basic primitives driving the observed changes in the cross-sectional distribution of workers in the earnings distribution.

Transition Matrices and Earnings Mobility Measures

The principal tool of analysis underlying the dynamic work in this paper is the transition matrix. This provides a general, flexible, data-based approach to the study of earnings mobility (Atkinson *et al.*, 1992). This is a two-dimensional array of earnings intervals (EIs) for an initial year down the left-hand side and of earnings intervals for a subsequent year along the top, and whose elements indicate the percentages of individuals moving from earnings interval i in the initial year to earnings interval j in the subsequent year. These percentages sum to 100 across each row. In order to analyze the cyclical aspects of these dynamics, one-year or short-run transition matrices for the cyclical peak (1988–89) and cyclical trough (1991–92) years are presented in Table 7.[4,5] In the top row of the 1991–92 panel for women, the figures indicate that 83.9 per cent of the women who were in the very high earnings interval in 1991 stayed in that top interval in 1992, while only 3.6 per cent of the top 1991 female earners fell as far as two categories into the high-middle earnings interval. Numbers (in bold) on the principal diagonal running from bottom left to top right are the "staying probabilities" (expressed in percentages). Numbers above this diagonal indicate probabilities of moving down one or more earnings intervals ("moving down probabilities"). Numbers below the principal diagonal represent probabilities of moving up one or more intervals ("moving up probabilities").

The transition matrices thus show that the probability of staying in the same earnings interval is the largest item in each row and that the probabilities decline as one moves further away from the initiating interval. That is, it is much less likely for a worker's earnings to change dramatically from one year to the next than to stay in the same or move to an adjacent interval. Recall, however, that the intervals are fairly wide — either 25 or 50 per cent of the median. This leaves quite a wide range for year-to-year earnings variation (see footnote 2) without workers slipping out of their current earnings intervals.

In all of the transition matrices in Table 7, the probability of staying in the same earnings interval generally rises with the level of earnings. That is, high earners are more likely to continue with their high earnings levels from

---

[4]Again, standard errors could also be calculated for the estimated transition probabilities (Amemiya, 1985, ch. 11), but the underlying sample sizes in this paper are so large they were judged not worth reporting.

[5]We focus on the 1990–92 recession because the data completely cover the period (compared to the early eighties recession where our data only begin in 1982 and hence the transition 1982–83) and because the labour market following the early nineties recession did not really show significant tightening until 1997 (which is beyond the end year of our sample).

Charles M. Beach and Ross Finnie

Table 7: One-Year Transition Matrices for Men and Women, Earners, 1988–89 and 1991–92

Men

1988-89 *(Peak)*

1988/1989	VL	L	LM	HM	H	VH
Very High	0.29	0.43	1.28	2.59	11.64	**83.77**
High	0.55	0.96	3.26	16.21	**64.56**	14.46
High Middle	1.50	2.59	13.72	**63.68**	15.87	2.65
Low Middle	4.91	11.53	**56.65**	22.00	3.74	1.16
Low	16.54	**39.59**	33.82	7.74	1.62	0.69
Very Low	**40.25**	30.61	22.47	5.08	1.11	0.49

1991-92 *(Trough)*

1991/1992	VL	L	LM	HM	H	VH
Very High	0.40	0.62	1.66	2.85	8.97	**85.49**
High	0.85	1.35	4.12	13.25	**65.32**	15.12
High Middle	2.14	3.45	14.23	**62.12**	15.94	2.13
Low Middle	7.06	14.11	**56.54**	18.54	2.83	0.93
Low	19.63	**42.54**	29.85	6.19	1.29	0.49
Very Low	**46.14**	29.58	19.07	3.99	0.84	0.38

Women

1988-89 *(Peak)*

1988/1989	VL	L	LM	HM	H	VH
Very High	0.39	0.49	1.68	4.44	14.17	**78.83**
High	0.52	0.94	4.21	17.80	**66.96**	9.58
High Middle	1.34	2.25	15.76	**70.45**	9.20	1.00
Low Middle	4.64	11.04	**68.38**	14.62	1.09	0.23
Low	17.73	**48.57**	29.99	3.19	0.41	0.11
Very Low	**52.21**	31.19	14.74	1.53	0.27	0.07

1991-92 *(Trough)*

1991/1992	VL	L	LM	HM	H	VH
Very High	0.34	0.54	1.69	3.55	10.00	**83.89**
High	0.62	0.96	4.41	12.85	**67.10**	14.06
High Middle	1.40	2.67	13.26	**71.08**	10.50	1.09
Low Middle	5.60	12.18	**65.61**	14.96	1.35	0.30
Low	20.18	**49.78**	26.23	3.32	0.37	0.11
Very Low	**55.68**	29.38	12.98	1.66	0.22	0.09

one year to the next than are low earners to continue at their low earnings levels. High earners thus have much greater year-to-year stability of earnings than do low earners on average.

Note also that the transition matrices are not symmetric. The elements below the principal diagonal are typically larger than the corresponding elements above, indicating that the probabilities of moving up the earnings distribution are generally greater than the probabilities of moving down. Also, the probability of moving up generally declines as one moves from lower earnings levels to higher ones, while the probability of moving down changes remarkably little over the different regions of the distribution. Thus the net probability of moving up also declines as one moves up the distribution. These patterns are consistent with younger workers being initially concentrated in the lower portion of the distribution and then moving up relatively rapidly early in their careers with individuals' earnings then becoming more stable once they have reached middle age. Note also that the width of the second earnings interval is only 0.25 of the median, while higher interior intervals are twice as wide, so it takes a bigger change in earnings to move out of these intervals, thus reducing mobility across intervals.

A further point of interest is that, except at the top earnings interval, the staying probabilities are higher for women than for men, most markedly so at the bottom end of the distribution. That is, women's earnings are generally less mobile or more stable from one year to the next than men's. This pattern is consistent with women typically having flatter age-earnings profiles than men and with women's earnings being less sensitive to business-cycle unemployment rate variations. The average probability of moving up one or more earnings intervals from 1995 to 1996 was 26.4 per cent for men versus 19.6 per cent for women, and the average probability of moving down was 13.2 per cent for men as compared to 14 per cent for women. Men are thus much more likely to advance their earnings by one or more earnings intervals in a year and are also about as likely to experience year-to-year earnings losses of one or more intervals as women.

The figures in Table 7 also show evidence of cyclical sensitivity. Comparison of the 1991–92 (cyclical trough) transition probabilities with the 1988–89 (cyclical peak) probabilities shows, first, that the staying probabilities (or earnings immobility) towards the lower and upper ends of the distribution increase during recessions — more so for men among lower earnings intervals and for women among the top earnings interval. The probabilities of moving up across earnings intervals — figures below the principal diagonal — generally decline in periods of recession, while the

Charles M. Beach and Ross Finnie

probabilities of slipping down one or more intervals — figures above the principal diagonal — generally rise in recession, though this latter effect is largely restricted to the lower three earnings intervals. That is, over the bottom two earnings intervals it appears that an economic recession is associated with a higher probability of staying (or reduced degree of earnings mobility), a lower probability of moving up, and an enhanced probability of moving down the distribution. The opposite occurs during an economic expansion. This cyclical pattern is also more clear-cut for men's earnings than for women's.

To better see the more salient patterns of dynamic distributional change, however, it is useful to summarize some of the main features of the transition matrices to a smaller and more manageable set of mobility statistics. This is done in Table 8. Here the detailed probabilities of moving up or moving down are summed across each row in the transition matrix. Then the Avg. Prob. of Moving Up is the (simple) average of the six probabilities of moving up across all six earnings intervals in a distribution. Similarly, the Avg. Prob. of Moving Down is the average of the probabilities of moving down across all the earnings intervals. The Avg. Net Prob. of Moving Up is the difference between the former and the latter. Finally, if avg. Pr(S) is the average of the probabilities of staying (expressed as percentages) across all six earnings intervals in a distribution, then

Avg. Mobility = 100 - avg. Pr(S).

Figures on these average probabilities (all expressed as percentages) are presented in Table 8 for the full sample period as well as for the transition between 1987 and 1988 (years of strong economic expansion) and between 1990 and 1991 (years of relatively severe recession). Looking at the average one-year transitions over the full sample period, one sees that average mobility of earnings is substantially higher for men than for women by about seven percentage points. The average probability of moving up is also substantially higher for men than for women — by 7.5 percentage points. The average probability of moving down is only slightly lower for men than for women — by less than one percentage point. But all the average moving down probabilities are less than the average moving up probabilities — indeed about half the size in the case of men and three-quarters the size for women. So the average net probabilities of moving up are also all positive — about 12–13 per cent over the sample period for men and about 4 per cent for women. So the average net probability of moving up is also substantially

Table 8: Average Mobility Measures by Cyclical Phase for Men and Women, 1987–88 and 1990–91

	All Workers	Men	Women
Average Mobility			
1987–88	38.40	42.43	36.08
1990–91	37.80	40.95	35.41
Average across years	37.36	41.25	34.56
Avg. Prob. of Moving Up			
1987–88	23.56	28.24	19.60
1990–91	22.29	24.58	20.48
Average across years	22.95	26.94	19.41
Avg. Prob. of Moving Down			
1987–88	14.83	14.18	16.48
1990–91	15.52	16.36	14.93
Average across years	14.41	14.31	15.14
Avg. Net Prob. of Moving Up			
1987–88	8.73	14.06	3.12
1990–91	6.77	8.22	5.54
Average across years	8.55	12.63	4.27

higher for men than for women — by over eight percentage points — again consistent with lower and flatter age-earnings profiles for women than for men.

There also appears to be a marked cyclical pattern in the net upward probabilities for men being driven by a corresponding cyclical pattern in the average probability of moving up. The probabilities rise in expansionary periods and decline in recessions. The average mobility of earnings declined with the onset of the early 1990s recession — by about 1.5 percentage points for men, but by only about 0.5 of a point for women. So again, the cyclical effect shows up much stronger for men than for women. For men, the average probability of moving up declines by over 3.5 points and the average probability of moving down rises by about two percentage points. Consequently, the average net probability of moving up falls by almost six

Charles M. Beach and Ross Finnie

percentage points. Over the ensuing expansion, these three probabilities moved in the reverse direction. For women, however, the change in earnings mobility between 1987–88 and 1990–91 was weaker, but in the opposite direction from men: a less than one percentage point rise in the probability of moving up, a 1.5 point decline in the probability of moving down, and a resulting 2.5 point increase in the net probability of moving up. The latter probability did not change between 1990–91 and 1995–96, suggesting that the cyclical earnings transition pattern for women is not clearly revealed by the raw data.

Net Cyclical Effects in Earnings Mobility

Just as we earlier looked at how earnings interval shares show significant net cyclical effects after controlling for underlying trends in the data, we now do the same for the summary earnings mobility measures. This will allow a more formal identification of underlying cyclical effects. In this case, the transition probabilities are the dependent variables in a regression analysis (see Beach and Finnie, 2001).

The unemployment responsiveness of the initial-year transition probabilities is illustrated in Figure 3. Periods of high unemployment reduce upward mobility over the lower earnings intervals for both men and women, though more strongly for men than for women, again perhaps because of the relatively greater concentration of males in the more cyclically sensitive manufacturing and primary sectors of the economy, whereas females are concentrated relatively more in the service and public sectors. More generally, weaker labour markets tend to reduce the degree of upward earnings mobility for almost all regions of the earnings distribution for men. But for women, earnings mobility increases over the middle and upper regions of the earnings distribution, again because of the relatively stronger decline in overall median earnings levels in recessions. Thus among men, the biggest (negative) unemployment rate effects occur over the bottom three earnings intervals, while among women they show up (positively) in the high and high-middle regions of the earnings distribution.

Net cyclical effects on the summary mobility measures appear in Table 9. Higher unemployment decreases net earnings mobility significantly for men by reducing the probability of moving up the earnings distribution and increasing the probability of moving down about equally, so that the average net probability of moving up is significantly decreased. For every percentage

Figure 3: Unemployment Responsiveness of Earnings Mobility across Earnings Intervals for Men and Women

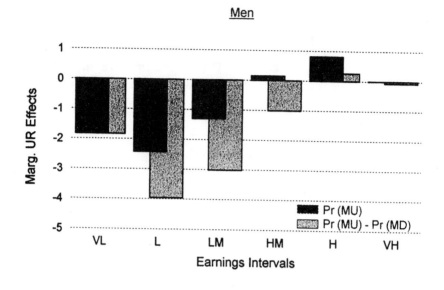

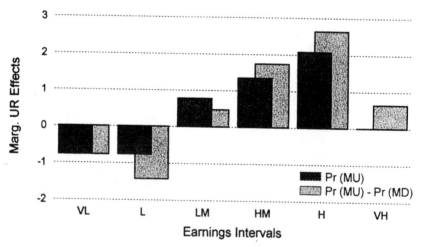

Charles M. Beach and Ross Finnie

Table 9: Net Responsiveness to Unemployment in the Average Summary Mobility Measures for Men and Women, 1982–1996

	Men		Women	
Average Mobility				
Marg. effect	0.096	(0.67)	0.344	(1.34)
Elasticity	0.024		0.34	
Avg. Prob. of Moving Up				
Marg. effect	-0.768	(4.12)	0.447	(2.62)
Elasticity	-0.211		0.102	
Avg. Prob. of Moving Down				
Marg. effect	0.865	(5.07)	-0.103	(0.53)
Elasticity	0.302		-0.072	
Avg. Net Prob. of Moving Up				
Marg. effect	-1.634	(4.99)	0.550	(2.11)
Elasticity	-0.513		0.074	

Note: The unemployment responsiveness coefficients for the average net probability of moving up, Avg Pr (Net), are obtained as the respective coefficients in an OLS time-series regression on Avg Pr (Net) as the dependent variable with the time trend and the change in the (adult male) unemployment rate as independent variables. The "Elasticity" figures for Avg Pr (Net) are obtained as the respective coefficients in an OLS time-series regression on ln (Avg Pr (Net)) as the dependent variable with the time trend and the change in the log of the (adult male) unemployment rate as independent variables. Figures in parentheses are (absolute values of) coefficient "t-ratios".

point increase in the unemployment rate, the average net probability of moving up is estimated to fall by 1.63 percentage points. Expressed differently, if the unemployment rate doubles in a recession (say, from 7 to 14 per cent), the opportunity rate of (annual) advancement in the earnings distribution (i.e., the net probability of moving up) is estimated to be cut in half. Recessions inhibit labour market opportunities while economic expansions promote them. For women, the net cyclical effects are again generally opposite in sign and much weaker, so the unemployment rate effect on the net probability of moving up is positive but only about a third as strong as that of men, reflecting the relative weaker responsiveness of their earnings to the business cycle. Once again, the net cyclical effects largely mirror the gross cyclical patterns observed in the raw data (in Table 8), except perhaps for the stronger net estimated moving down effect among men compared to what was observed in the data.

Earnings Mobility across Age Groups

The analysis in the fourth section revealed quite substantial distributional changes going on for different age groups. It would be useful to follow this up by looking at age-group differences in the underlying earnings mobility as well. As already noted, the underlying transition probabilities can be viewed as the more basic primitives driving the observed changes in the cross-sectional distribution of workers.

When one breaks down populations into separate age groups, the numbers of observations per age group in the samples are obviously reduced, especially among entry (age 20–24) and older (age 55–64) workers. We thus reduce the fineness of the earnings interval breakdown for each age group by collapsing the previous six intervals into three:

$$\left.\begin{array}{l}\text{Very low}\\\text{Low}\end{array}\right\} \rightarrow \text{Low}$$

$$\left.\begin{array}{l}\text{Low middle}\\\text{High middle}\end{array}\right\} \rightarrow \text{Middle}$$

$$\left.\begin{array}{l}\text{High}\\\text{Very high}\end{array}\right\} \rightarrow \text{High}$$

So the earnings cut-offs now are 50 per cent and 150 per cent of the median. The year-to-year transition matrices underlying this section are correspondingly three-by-three.

The resulting average probabilities by age group are presented in Table 10. Here it can be seen that average mobility is highest for younger workers and thereafter declines with age. Again, earnings mobility is higher every-

Table 10: Average Mobility Measures by Cyclical Phase by Age for Men and Women, 1987–88 and 1990–91

Men

	Entry	Younger	Prime	Older
Average Mobility				
1987–88	26.60	26.60	24.73	22.70
1990–91	26.23	24.70	22.93	22.10
Average across years	25.42	25.59	23.76	22.03
Avg. Prob. of Moving Up				
1987–88	16.27	19.57	18.33	11.67
1990–91	12.07	16.23	15.43	9.93
Average across years	14.45	18.45	17.18	11.08
Avg. Prob. of Moving Down				
1987–88	10.33	7.03	6.40	11.03
1990–91	14.17	8.43	7.50	12.20
Average across years	10.98	7.14	6.58	10.95
Avg. Net Prob. of Moving Up				
1987–88	5.93	12.53	11.93	0.64
1990–91	-2.10	7.80	7.93	-2.27
Average across years	3.47	11.32	10.60	0.13

Women

	Entry	Younger	Prime	Older
Average Mobility				
1987–88	24.50	23.13	17.97	17.57
1990–91	22.27	23.20	17.13	16.80
Average across years	22.63	22.80	16.79	16.53
Avg. Prob. of Moving Up				
1987–88	11.20	11.90	10.10	5.30
1990–91	9.23	11.97	10.00	5.43
Average across years	10.05	11.95	9.66	5.26
Avg. Prob. of Moving Down				
1987–88	13.27	11.23	7.90	12.27
1990–91	13.07	11.23	7.13	11.37
Average across years	12.58	10.85	7.13	11.26
Avg. Net Prob. of Moving Up				
1987–88	-2.07	0.67	2.20	-6.97
1990–91	-3.83	0.74	2.87	-5.94
Average across years	-2.53	1.10	2.53	-6.00

where for men than for women. The average probability of moving up is also highest among younger workers and thereafter declines with age for both men and women. The average probability of moving down is highest for entry and older workers and lowest for prime age workers, again for both sexes. The average net probability of moving up for men is highest for younger workers and thereafter declines with age, but for women is highest among prime age workers. The average net probability is everywhere greater for men than for women across all age groups, but the differential is greatest among younger and prime age workers (8.1 – 10.2 points) and lower among entry and older workers (6.0 – 6.1 points). Again, this is consistent with men having generally higher and more concave career earnings trajectories than women.

Net responsiveness of the summary mobility measures by age group is examined in Beach and Finnie (2001). For men, the sensitivity of earnings mobility measures to changes in unemployment decreases monotonically with age. The average probability of moving up is fairly cyclically responsive for all ages attenuating from a marginal unemployment rate effect of -0.82 for entry workers to -0.28 for older workers. When the unemployment rate rises, the probability of moving up falls. The probability of moving down also shows significant cyclical responsiveness declining from 0.62 for entry workers to 0.27 for older workers — it rises along with the unemployment rate. But its strength is generally less than that of the upward mobility. As a result, the net probability of moving up shows significant cyclical variation among all age groups of male workers moderating from -1.44 for entry workers (-0.99 for younger workers and -0.81 for prime age workers) to -0.55 for older workers. Between 50 and 60 per cent of the net upward mobility cyclical effect arises from changes in the probability of moving up across the four age groups of male workers. But perhaps most interestingly, since the shift downward in net upward mobility decreases with age, the earnings advances of entry and young workers will be dampened much more than those of prime age and older workers, thus widening the gap between relatively low earners early in their careers and higher earners later in their careers. The result is that men's *cross-sectional* age-earnings profiles swivel down during recessions and their steepness and concavity are accentuated — as illustrated in Figure 4. In periods of economic expansion, the reverse occurs. For female workers, the net cyclical earnings shifts are far smaller and show no such statistically significant pattern. For example, the unemployment rate effects on the net probability of moving up vary from -0.19 for entry workers to 0.17 for older workers (none of which are

**Figure 4: Cyclical Shift in Men's Life-Cycle Earnings
Cross-Sectional Profile**

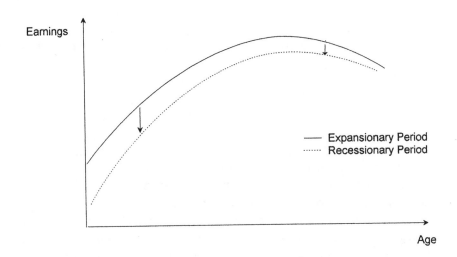

statistically significant). Consequently, women's cross-sectional age-earnings profiles do not show any significant change in shape over the business cycle.

Conclusions and Review

This study has used income tax longitudinal data over the period 1982–96 to look at business-cycle effects on short-run earnings mobility patterns of workers in the Canadian labour market. The approach has involved looking at the proportion of workers in six earnings intervals over time and at dynamic one-year transition matrix summary measures of earnings mobility over time. Four major results have been found.

First, there are major cyclical effects in changes in the degree of earnings polarization and in general upward or downward shifts of the earnings distribution over the 1982–96 period, and these effects are most markedly concentrated in the two recessions over this period, particularly between

1990 and 1992. Weak labour markets increase earnings polarization significantly with generally much stronger effects for men than for women. In terms of general distributional shift, quite opposite cyclical patterns are observed. Weak labour markets shift the earnings distribution for men down significantly, but the higher unemployment shifts the women's earnings distribution up relative to the men's as women's earnings are relatively less sensitive to weakened labour markets.

Second, when these cyclical patterns are observed across age groups, the cyclical effects across all age groups for each gender generally mirror that for the gender as a whole, but the strength of the effects differs across age groups with the strongest effects typically occurring among entry and younger workers. Higher unemployment increases polarization rates across all age/sex groups. Among males, it is the cyclical sensitivity of the earnings of workers at the lower end of the distribution which is driving the results. Among female workers, it is generally the upper end of the earnings distribution where the greatest cyclical sensitivity occurs. Entry and younger workers of both gender show far the greatest sensitivity to unemployment rate changes, while older workers show generally the weakest effects.

Third, year-to-year dynamics of workers' earnings are summarized in terms of measures of earnings mobility, the probability of moving up the distribution across earnings intervals, the probability of moving down the distribution across earnings intervals, and the net probability of moving up across earnings intervals. It is found that higher unemployment decreases net earnings mobility significantly for men by reducing the probability of moving up the earnings distribution and increasing the probability of moving down about equally, so that the average net probability of moving up is significantly decreased. For every percentage point increase in the (adult male) unemployment rate, the average net probability of moving up is estimated to fall by 1.63 percentage points. The unemployment rate effect on the average net probability of moving up for women is only about a third that of men.

Fourth, it is found for men that the cyclical sensitivity of earnings mobility decreases monotonically with age — strongest among entry age workers and weakest for older workers. So the cross-sectional, age-earnings profiles swivel downward and become steeper in recessions and swivel upward and become flatter over economic expansions. For women workers, the net cyclical effects on earnings mobility are far smaller showing no such statistically significant pattern.

Charles M. Beach and Ross Finnie

References

Abowd, J. and D. Card (1989), "On the Covariance Structure of Earnings and Hours Changes", *Econometrica* 57(2), 411-445.

Amemiya, T. (1985), *Advanced Econometrics* (Cambridge, MA: Harvard University Press), ch. 11.

Atkinson, A.B., F. Bourguignon and C. Morrison (1992), *Empirical Studies of Earnings Mobility* (Chur, UK: Harwood Academic Publishers).

Baker, M. and G. Solon (1999), "Earnings Dynamics and Inequality among Canadian Men, 1976-1992: Evidence from Longitudinal Income Tax Records", unpublished paper (Toronto).

Beach, C.M. and G.A. Slotsve (1996), *Are We Becoming Two Societies? Income Polarization and the Middle Class in Canada* (Toronto: C.D. Howe Institute).

Beach, C.M. and R. Finnie (1998), "Earnings Mobility 1982-1994: Women Gaining Ground and Lower Paid Males Slipping", *Canadian Business Economics* 6(4), 3-25.

_____ (2000), "Trends in Short-Run Earnings Mobility in Canada, 1982-1996", unpublished paper (Kingston).

_____ (2001), "Cyclical Changes in Short-Run Earnings Mobility in Canada, 1982-1996", unpublished paper (Kingston).

Beaudry, P. and D. Green (2000), "Cohort Patterns in Canadian Earnings: Assessing the Role of Skill Premia in Inequality Trends", *Canadian Journal of Economics* 33(4), 907-936.

Buchinsky, M. and J. Hunt (1996), "Wage Mobility in the United States", NBER Working Paper No. 5455 (Cambridge, MA: National Bureau of Economic Research).

Burkhauser, R.V., D. Holtz-Eakin and S.E. Rhody (1997), "Labor Earnings Mobility and Inequality in the United States and Germany During the Growth Years of the 1980s", NBER Working Paper No. 5988 (Cambridge, MA: National Bureau of Economic Research).

Duncan, G.J., T.M. Smeeding and W. Rodgers (1994), "W(h)ither the Middle Class? A Dynamic View", in E. Wolff (ed.), *Poverty and Prosperity in the U.S. at the End of the Twentieth Century* (New York: Macmillan), 202-271.

Finnie, R. (1997a), "The Distribution of Earnings in a Dynamic Context in Canada, 1982-92", HRDC Working Paper No. W-97-3Eb (Ottawa: Applied Research Branch, Human Resources Development Canada).

_____ (1997b), "Earnings Patterns by Age and Sex", *Canadian Economic Observer* 10(10), 3.1-3.17.

_____ (1997c), "The Correlation of Individuals' Earnings Over Time in Canada, 1982-92", HRDC Working Paper No. W-97-3Ec (Ottawa: Applied Research Branch, Human Resources Development Canada).

_____ (1997d), "Stasis and Change: Trends in Individual Earnings Levels and Inequality by Age and Sex, 1982-92", *Canadian Business Economics* 6(1), 84-107.

Gottschalk, P. and R. Moffitt (1994), "The Growth of Earnings Instability in the U.S. Labor Market", *Brookings Papers on Economic Activity* 2, 217-272.

Katz, L.F. and D.H. Autor (1999), "Changes in the Wage Structure and Earnings Inequality", in O.C. Ashenfelter and D. Card (eds.), *Handbook of Labor Economics*, Vol. 3 (Amsterdam: North-Holland/Elsevier), 1463-1555.

Kennedy, B. (1989), "Mobility and Instability in Canadian Earnings", *Canadian Journal of Economics* 22(2), 383-394.

OECD (1993), "Earnings Inequality: Changes in the 1980s", *Employment Outlook* (Paris: OECD), 157-184.

_____ (1996), "Earnings Inequality, Low-Paid Employment and Earnings Mobility", *Employment Outlook* (Paris: OECD), 59-108.

Picot, G. (1997), "What Is Happening to Earnings Inequality in Canada in the 1990s?" *Canadian Business Economics* 6(1), 65-83.

Shorrocks, A.F. (1978), "Income Inequality and Income Mobility", *Journal of Economic Theory* 19, 376-393.

Statistics Canada (1995), *Earnings of Men and Women in 1994*, Cat. No. 13-217 (Ottawa: Statistics Canada), 17.

Education and Skills: An Assessment of Recent Canadian Experience

W. Craig Riddell

Introduction

Education, training and skill formation have become prominent public policy issues in Canada and in many other countries. Several factors account for the increased attention being paid to the knowledge, skills and competencies of the population and workforce. Technological change — especially advances in information and computer technologies — and the globalization of production have resulted in growing demand for highly-skilled workers and changes in the nature of skills needed in the workplace. These same forces also appear to have contributed to widening inequality between more- and less-skilled workers in employment, wages and other labour market outcomes. In addition, there is growing concern about future skills shortages, in part due to the fact that the leading cohorts of the well-educated "baby boom" generation are now approaching retirement age and are being replaced by the entry into the labour force of much smaller (though even better-educated) cohorts. Finally, within the economics profession there has been

I thank Patrick Grady, Andrew Sharpe and Thomas Lemieux for comments on an earlier draft of this paper.

a resurgence of interest in the determinants of long-term growth, and "new growth theory" emphasizes the importance of human capital in the creation of new knowledge and in the growth of living standards over time.

These factors explain the increased emphasis on skills and knowledge in economic policy. However, as economic activity becomes more knowledge-based and less dependent on natural resources and physical capital, human capital is also increasingly being viewed as a central component of social policy. Many of our current social programs were shaped during the expansion of the welfare state that took place during the early post-war period. As substantial changes to the economic and social environment have occurred, a major reassessment of these programs has been underway. Governments have begun to move away from "passive" income maintenance programs toward "active" labour market and social policies that facilitate adjustment to change, assist the jobless to find work, and encourage labour force participation. Associated with this shift has been greater emphasis on individual responsibility and on providing those in need of assistance with the opportunity to improve their economic situation — providing a "hand up" rather than a "handout". Investing in the human capital of those with limited marketable skills is a key component of such an approach. As stated by the federal Finance Minister Paul Martin, "Providing security and opportunity for Canadians in the future means investing in their skills, in their knowledge and capacity to learn ... good skills are an essential part of the social safety net of the future."[1]

The increased emphasis being placed on human capital as a component of social policy also reflects the view that education and training may ameliorate pressures for widening inequality in economic and social outcomes. According to this perspective, policies that promote additional investment in education should increase the supply of more skilled workers — thus reducing upward pressure on their wages — and reduce the supply of the less skilled — thus reducing downward pressure on their earnings and employment opportunities. In periods in which the demand for more educated workers is growing rapidly, making higher education more accessible may prevent increases in income inequality that would otherwise occur.

Education is also often regarded as a mechanism for promoting equality of opportunity and social mobility. Productivity and economic growth are

---

[1]Hon. Paul Martin, "Presentation to the House of Commons Standing Committee on Finance", November 2, 1999 <http://www.fin.gc.ca/update99/speeche.html>.

enhanced if the talents of the population are more fully utilized. The efficient allocation of talent requires that those with high ability should be able to pursue productive and rewarding careers whatever their family background. Thus promoting equality of opportunity should be a major objective of economic policy, especially in an environment in which success is increasingly dependent on human resources and knowledge. From the perspective of social policy, equality of opportunity may contribute to social cohesion and a belief in common interests among citizens.

The importance of this emergence of a common emphasis on human capital formation in both economic and social policy has been noted by several observers. For example, Courchene (2001, p. 285) states that we are presented "with a historically unprecedented window of opportunity ... [in which] ... a societal commitment to a human capital future is emerging as the principal avenue by which to promote both economic competitiveness and social cohesion".

The Economic Council of Canada, which David Slater chaired from 1980 to 1985, provided a natural vehicle for periodic study of Canada's education and training systems. Indeed, not only were education and training prominent in numerous Council reports, but the last major study published by the Council was *Education and Training in Canada* (Canada Communication Group, 1992). The purpose of this paper is to survey the current state of knowledge in this area, with particular emphasis on advances and developments during the past decade. In order to keep the paper manageable, my focus will be principally on education and skill formation.

The paper is organized as follows. The first section compares Canadian educational expenditures and educational outcomes with those of other countries. Several educational outcomes are discussed: educational attainment, student achievement, and the literacy and numeracy skills of the adult population. This comparative examination of educational "inputs" and "outcomes" provides a basis for assessing whether Canada obtains good value from its public and private investments in education. The paper then turns to the incidence of educational attainment across the population. What groups or types of individuals are most likely to be well educated, and how has this changed over time? What is the relationship between educational attainment and family background, and has this relationship changed in recent years?

The third section examines evidence on the economic returns to education. The question of how best to interpret the strong positive correlation between education and economic success has long been a subject of debate and controversy. Substantial recent progress has been made on this issue. This literature is briefly reviewed here, and the findings of Canadian studies are discussed. The final section summarizes the main conclusions and discusses their implications for public policy.

Education Expenditures and Outcomes

Education systems vary substantially from country to country. For example, there are important differences across countries in the provision of publicly-funded early childhood and pre-elementary schooling, in the extent to which students are streamed into "academic" and "vocational" programs, in the ways in which school and work experience can be combined, and in the extent to which the system provides a "second chance" for those who drop out at some stage. These and other differences make international comparisons of educational inputs and outcomes difficult. Although considerable progress has been made in improving the comparability of educational data across Organisation for Economic Co-operation and Development (OECD) countries, these institutional differences among education systems should be kept in mind when interpreting comparative statistics.[2]

Investment in Education

Relative to other developed countries, Canada invests a substantial amount on education. Most of this expenditure is publicly financed. Table 1 shows a number of measures of educational expenditure in Canada and other G7 countries, as well as the OECD country average. The top panel reports educational expenditure per student in PPP-adjusted U.S. dollars, an input-based indicator of the quality of education. At both the elementary and secondary and post-secondary levels, Canadian expenditure per student is second highest (after the United States) among the G7 countries and

---

[2]The series of OECD publications *Education at a Glance: OECD Indicators* make a valuable contribution to international comparisons of educational expenditures and outcomes in OECD countries.

W. Craig Riddell

Table 1: Educational Expenditures in G7 Countries, 1995

(a) Expenditure per student from public and private sources, by level of education, in thousands of U.S. dollars converted using PPP exchange rates[1]

	Canada	France	Germany	Italy	Japan	UK	U.S.	OECD average[2]
Elementary & secondary	5,401	5,041	4,690	5,099	4,282	3,810	6,281	4,162
Post-secondary	11,471	6,569	8,897	5,013	8,768	7,225	16,262	8,134
All levels of education[3]	6,396	5,001	6,057	5,157	4,991	4,222	7,905	4,717

(b) Educational expenditure from public and private sources for educational institutions as a percentage of GDP, by level of education, Canada and G7 countries, 1995

	Canada	France	Germany	Italy	Japan	UK	U.S.	OECD average[2]
Elementary & secondary	4.3	4.4	3.8	3.2	3.1	-	3.9	3.7
Post-secondary	2.5	1.1	1.1	0.8	1.0	1.0	2.4	1.3
All levels of education[3]	7.0	6.3	5.8	4.7	4.7	-	6.7	5.6

Notes: 1. Purchasing power parity (PPP) exchange rates are calculated to equalize the purchasing power of different currencies.
2. Unweighted country average.
3. Includes pre-primary (pre-elementary) and undistributed expenditures.
Source: Council of Ministers of Education, Canada and Statistics Canada (2000).

substantially above the OECD average. The gaps between the United States and Canada and other OECD countries are especially large at the post-secondary level. Although not shown in the table, Canadian per student expenditure also ranks among the highest in the OECD at both the elementary/secondary and post-secondary levels (OECD, 2001).

The bottom panel reports expenditure on education as a percentage of gross domestic product (GDP). This measure reflects both expenditure per student and the number of students. It indicates the fraction of total output devoted to the consumption of and investment in education. Even among the G7 countries, large differences are evident in the relative share of national resources devoted to formal education. These differences are much more substantial at the post-secondary than at the elementary and secondary levels. Canada's educational expenditure of 7 per cent of GDP in 1995 is highest in the G7 countries and (although not shown) among the highest in the OECD.[3] In Canada and the United States, the share of GDP devoted to formal post-secondary education is more than double that of all other G7 countries, and substantially higher than the OECD country average.

Canada's relatively high percentage of GDP spent on education reflects both the substantial per-student expenditures on education at all levels, as illustrated in Table 1(a), and Canadian's comparatively high participation rates in education, especially at the post-secondary level, which are described in more detail below.

Canada invests heavily in educating its population. What are the consequences of these substantial expenditures on formal education? The next three sub-sections summarize the available evidence on this question using several measures of educational outcomes. First to be examined is educational attainment, the dimension we know the most about. The discussion then turns to student achievement and the literacy skills of the adult population — two measures of the skills and knowledge imparted by education as well as other activities.

Educational Attainment

Several measures of the educational attainment of the adult population in Canada and other G7 countries are reported in Table 2. The top panel shows the highest level of educational attainment for the population 25–64 years of age. Also shown is the unweighted OECD country average. The bottom panel reports average years of schooling.

By these measures, Canadian educational attainment is high by international standards, reflecting the substantial expenditure on formal education. Eighty per cent of Canada's adult population has completed upper secondary (referred to as "high school" in North America) or post-secondary education, much higher than the OECD average of 64 per cent. Canada's proportion is similar to that of Germany, Japan and the United Kingdom, but

---

[3]The Scandinavian countries and Canada are typically ranked at the top of the OECD in terms of the percentage of GDP devoted to education (OECD, *Education at a Glance*, various issues).

Table 2: Educational Attainment in Canada and G7 Countries

(a) Proportion of the population aged 25–64 years by highest level of educational attainment, 1999

	Canada	France	Germany	Italy	Japan	UK	U.S.	OECD average
Less than upper secondary	20	38	19	57	19	18	13	36
Upper secondary graduate	28	41	53	30	49	57	51	40
Non-university post-secondary	33	10	15	4	13	8	8	11
University graduate	19	11	13	9	18	17	27	14

Source: OECD (2001).

(b) Average completed years of schooling of the population aged 25–64 years, 1995

Canada	France	Germany	Italy	Japan	UK	U.S.	OECD average
13.2	11.2	13.4	10.0	-	12.1	13.5	11.9

Source: OECD (1998).

(c) Ratio of Upper Secondary Graduates to Population at a Typical Age of Graduation, 1996

	Canada	France	Germany	Italy	Japan	UK	U.S.
Both sexes	75	85	86	79	99	-	72
Males	70	85	86	76	96	-	69
Females	81	86	86	82	102	-	76

Source: Council of Ministers of Education, Canada and Statistics Canada (2000).

Education and Skills   491

substantially below the United States where 87 per cent of the adult population have at least a high school diploma.[4] Average completed years of schooling are also among the highest in the OECD, albeit somewhat below Germany and the United States.[5]

Canada stands out in terms of the fraction of the adult population with completed post-secondary education. Canada's proportion (52 per cent) is not only more than double the OECD average of 25 per cent, but is also the highest in the OECD countries and substantially higher than the United States, the country ranked second (where 35 per cent have completed post-secondary education). Canada's extremely high ranking on this dimension arises principally because of the very substantial fraction of the population with non-university post-secondary education — at 33 per cent, triple the OECD average and more than double any other G7 country. At the university level, Canada is above the OECD average (19 per cent versus the OECD average of 14 per cent) and similar to Japan and the United Kingdom, but substantially below the United States where 27 per cent have graduated from university.

Canada's ranking at the top of the OECD in terms of the fraction of the population with completed post-secondary education has lead several analysts to comment that Canada's population is among the most highly educated in the world — even surpassing the United States, the country traditionally regarded as having the most highly educated population. However, it is important to keep in mind that Canadian educational attainment ranks below the United States in two key dimensions: the fraction of the population with completed secondary education and the proportion with a university degree. Thus at the two extremes of the educational attainment distribution — roughly the bottom 20 per cent and top 20 per cent

---

[4]The comparison of Canada and the United States with several European countries is quite sensitive to the definition of "upper secondary education". For example, France and the United Kingdom have both short duration and long duration upper secondary schooling, whereas these are rare in North America. If the short upper secondary programs are excluded, the UK's proportion with upper secondary or higher drops from 82 to 62 per cent and the French figure falls from 62 to 34 per cent. See OECD (2001).

[5]The measurement of years of completed schooling is problematic in countries like Germany where there are extensive apprenticeship programs that combine work and school.

— Canada ranks significantly below the United States. It is in the middle of the distribution where Canadian educational attainment dominates according to these standard measures. In both countries, approximately 60 per cent of the adult population have completed high school or a non-university post-secondary program. However, the composition of this middle group differs substantially between the two countries: in Canada more than half (33 per cent out of 61 per cent) have completed non-university post-secondary education, whereas less than one-sixth (8 per cent out of 65 per cent) of Americans are in this category.

Because of its evident importance in Canada, a closer look at the non-university post-secondary category is warranted. There are two main types of individuals in this group: those with a community college or College d'enseignement général et professionnel (CEGEP) diploma and those with a certificate from a trade school or apprenticeship program. Because high school completion is not necessarily a prerequisite to enter these programs, not all those classified as non-university post-secondary graduates are high school graduates. Furthermore, although many community college programs are two years in length, trade school and some community college programs may be of much shorter duration. For these reasons, one might conjecture that the human capital of some of those in the "non-university post-secondary" group may not be substantially higher than that of the average high school graduate.

The monthly Labour Force Survey, the source of the Canadian data in Table 2, classifies those who report that they completed a community college or CEGEP, apprenticeship or trade school program as having a non-university post-secondary certificate or diploma whether or not they have graduated from high school.[6] To obtain some insight into this potentially diverse non-university post-secondary category, Table 3 reports data from the 1996 Census. The advantage of the Census is that the questionnaire asks about all diplomas, certificates and degrees obtained as well as years of completed schooling. In order to obtain information on individuals' wages —

---

[6]This has been the structure of the educational attainment questions since a major revision to these questions in 1990. Prior to that time, high school completion was required in order to be classified in one of the post-secondary education categories, even in the case of respondents who had completed a trade certificate or community college program.

Table 3: Average Weekly Wages and Years of Schooling by Highest Level of Educational Attainment, Canada, 1996

	All workers			Females			Males		
	%	Average wage	Years of schooling	%	Average wage	Years of schooling	%	Average wage	Years of schooling
No degree	23.4	$582.4	10.1	19.9	$429.3	10.3	26.5	$681.7	9.9
High school graduate	26.2	584.4	12.6	28.0	473.3	12.6	24.7	693.5	12.7
College/trade without high school	9.9	712.5	12.8	8.8	537.6	13.1	10.9	834.6	12.6
College/trade school and high school	23.8	704.1	14.4	26.0	570.4	14.3	21.9	841.7	14.4
All college/trade school	33.7	706.6	13.9	34.7	562.1	14.0	32.8	839.3	13.8
University degree	16.7	941.7	17.5	17.4	786.4	17.4	16.0	1088.3	17.6
All levels of education	100.0	684.9	13.3	100.0	550.3	13.5	100.0	801.6	13.1

Source: Author's calculations from the 1996 Census public use master file (Ottawa: Statistics Canada).

W. Craig Riddell

an additional measure of human capital — the data shown in Table 3 is for those employed in 1995 rather than the adult population.[7]

The data on educational attainment of employed Canadians provides a very similar picture to that of the adult population shown in Table 2. The non-university post-secondary category constitutes 34 per cent of all workers in 1996 versus 33 per cent of the adult population in 1999. This group is a slightly larger proportion of the female workforce (35 per cent) than the male workforce (33 per cent). On average, those with a non-university certificate or diploma have 1.3 additional years of schooling compared to high school graduates. This differential is also a bit larger for females (1.4 years) than males (1.1 years). However, within the non-university post-secondary category there is a substantial gap of 1.6 years of completed schooling between those with a high school diploma (14.4 years) and those without this credential (12.8 years). Indeed, high school graduates have very similar years of schooling to those with a college diploma or trade certificate who did not graduate from high school (12.8 versus 12.6 years). For males, the average high school graduate actually has slightly more years of schooling than his counterpart who completed a trade school or community college program without also completing high school.

This evidence based on years of schooling suggests that the human capital of college/trade school graduates who did not complete high school may be very similar to those whose highest educational attainment is a high school diploma, and substantially lower than those with both a high school degree and a community college diploma or trade school certificate. However, this conclusion does not continue to hold when we use wages rather than years of education as an indicator of human capital. Indeed, for both males and females the average wages of the "college/trade without high school" group are much closer to their college/trade school counterparts who also completed secondary school than they are to those whose highest educational attainment is a high school diploma. This suggests that it is not unreasonable to group together all those with a college diploma or trade certificate, whether or not they also are high school graduates, and despite the substantial differences in their years of schooling.

Relative to other countries, the extent of Canadian non-university post-secondary education may be somewhat overstated because of the Quebec

---

[7]The Census, taken in June 1996, asks about income and weeks worked during the previous year. The wage measure used is the weekly wage for those employed in 1995.

Education and Skills   495

CEGEP system. These institutions provide both "general" and "professional" programs. The former constitute a stage between high school and university, providing the equivalent of the final year of high school and the first year of university in most other Canadian provinces. The professional programs provide the equivalent of the final year of secondary school and a two-year community college program in English Canada.

Graduates of the professional CEGEP programs are similar to graduates of professional/vocational community college programs in English Canada, and are appropriately classified as "non-university post-secondary". Students who pursue the CEGEP general stream and who obtain a university degree will also be appropriately classified in the data as university graduates. However, those who pursue the general stream but who subsequently do not enter or complete university will be measured as "non-university post-secondary graduates" in Quebec but would appear as high school graduates (albeit with some, but incomplete post-secondary education) in English Canada. Some adjustment to the Canadian data to account for this difference may be appropriate.

In summary, according to commonly used measures, Canadian educational attainment is very high by international standards, a finding that is consistent with the country's substantial investment in education. The distribution of the educational attainment of Canadians also has some unique features. At the bottom and top of the educational attainment distribution — specifically, those with less than completed high school and those with a university degree — Canadian educational attainment is similar to that of several other OECD countries and significantly lower than that of the United States. However, in the middle of the distribution — those who have completed secondary school but not university — the proportion of Canadians with a community college diploma or trade school certificate is unusually high and the proportion of high school graduates relatively low. However, this "non-university post-secondary" group is heterogeneous. Canada's provincial education systems have "forgiving" features and provide various routes to a community college diploma or trade school certificate. More than one-quarter of the "non-university post-secondary" group have not graduated from secondary school, and their average years of completed schooling is not much different from those whose highest educational attainment is high school completion. This raises some questions about whether these individuals should be placed in a higher educational attainment category than secondary school graduates. However, these doubts are dispelled to a considerable extent by a comparison of the average earnings

W. Craig Riddell

of this "college/trade without high school" group to high school graduates and the "college/trade with high school" group. In particular, this "market test" suggests that the human capital of the "college/trade without high school" is much closer to that of their "college/trade with high school" counterparts than to secondary school graduates. Accordingly, Canada's high measured educational attainment in the middle of the distribution appears to be real, and not simply due to inappropriate labelling of some of those in the non-university post-secondary category.[8]

Although the overall educational attainment of Canadians is impressive, high school completion has been a weak spot for many years. For example, based on administrative data on the number of graduates relative to the number of 18 year olds, the recent Canadian secondary school graduation rate is near the bottom of the G7 countries and only marginally above that of the United States, the bottom dweller on this dimension (see Table 2(c)). As of the mid-1990s, approximately 25 per cent of 18 years olds had not graduated from high school. This non-completion rate is much higher among males (30 per cent) than females (20 per cent). Some of these individuals graduate after the "normal age" of 18; according to LFS data the high school graduation rate is 81 per cent by age 19–20 and 87 per cent by age 25–29 (Council of Ministers of Education, Canada and Statistics Canada, 2000, p. 91). In addition, as discussed above, a significant number of high school dropouts obtain a college diploma or trade certificate. Nonetheless, Canada's relatively high secondary school non-completion rate is a potential concern.

Measures of educational attainment such as years of completed schooling or highest credential received are frequently used to compare the amount of human capital of the population or workforce over time and across regions and countries. Nonetheless, these are indirect measures of human capital, reflecting principally the inputs of time and other resources into the production of skills, knowledge and competencies. We now turn to measures of the outcomes of human capital formation.

---

[8]For some additional Canadian evidence, see Ferrer and Riddell (2001). Nonetheless, further investigation of the comparability of these categories across countries appears warranted.

Student Achievement

We know a good deal more about student achievement than we did even a decade ago when the Economic Council of Canada carried out its assessment of Canada's education and training systems. Canada did not participate in the early rounds of international mathematics and science tests carried out in the 1960s and 1970s. However, some provinces took part in the Second International Mathematics and Science Studies carried out in the 1980s, and all Canadian jurisdictions participated in the third round — the Third International Mathematics and Science Study or TIMSS — carried out in the mid-1990s. In addition, there was Canadian involvement in some other international studies of student achievement in the 1980s and 1990s, and the decade of the 1990s saw the introduction of the Canadian School Achievement Indicators Program which has now completed two rounds of testing.

Table 4 summarizes some of the key results from TIMSS, the most recent international tests of achievement in mathematics and science.[9] These data have the advantage of providing information on student performance on a common set of tests administered in numerous countries. For the present purposes, one disadvantage is that the set of countries is very diverse, and includes several countries that we do not normally compare ourselves to — both "high achievers" such as Korea, Singapore and Hong Kong and "low achievers" such as Iran, Kuwait and Portugal. The set of countries participating in each test also varies, so the international average needs to be interpreted cautiously.

In order to provide information on student achievement that is comparable to our previous analyses of educational expenditure and attainment, the top panel of Table 4 reports mean scores for the G7 countries that participated in TIMSS (Canada, France, Japan and United States) as well as the international average score.[10] For each test there are unfortunately only two other G7 countries as comparators. In Grade 4 mathematics, Canada is the lowest of the three G7 participants and the only member of this group

---

[9] Canada Communications Group (1992) and Riddell (1995) summarize and assess the results of earlier Canadian student achievement tests.

[10] Results for England and Germany are not reported because these countries did not meet the requirements for a nationally representative sample. The U.S. results for Grade 8 math and science are not shown for the same reason.

W. Craig Riddell

Table 4: Student Achievement in G7 Countries and Canadian Jurisdictions

(a) Student Achievement in Mathematics and Science in Canada and G7 Countries, 1994–95

	Mean value of per cent correct				
	Canada	France	Japan	U.S.	International mean
Grade 4 math	60	-	74[+]	63[+]	59
Grade 8 math	59[+]	61[+]	73[+]	-	55
Grade 4 science	64[+]	-	70[+]	66[+]	59
Grade 8 science	59[+]	54[-]	65[+]	-	56

Notes: + statistically significant above the international mean
- statistically significant below the international mean

(b) Student Achievement in Mathematics and Science in Canadian Jurisdictions, 1994–95

	Mean value of per cent correct						
	Nfld	NB (english)	Que	Ont	Alta	BC	Canadian mean
Grade 4 math	58	58	69[+]	57	65	59	60
Grade 8 math	56	54[-]	68[+]	54[-]	61	63[+]	59
Grade 4 science	62	61	65	62	68[+]	64	64
Grade 8 science	59	57	59	56[-]	65[+]	62	59
Average score	59	58	65	57	65	62	61

Notes: + statistically significant above the international mean
- statistically significant below the international mean

Sources: Robitaille, Taylor and Orpwood (1996, 1997) and Council of Ministers of Education, Canada and Statistics Canada (2000).

that did not score significantly above the international mean. In Grade 8 mathematics, Canada's score is significantly higher than the international mean, but this is mainly due to the reduction in the international average resulting from the addition of several very low scoring countries (e.g., Columbia and South Africa) that did not participate in the Grade 4 tests. Again, Canada is the lowest scoring country among the participating G7 countries.

Canadian performance in science is somewhat better, although still not impressive. At the Grade 4 level, Canadian students' scores were statistically significantly above the international average (64 per cent correct versus 59 per cent) but still significantly lower than those of Japan and the United States, the other two G7 countries that took these tests. At the Grade 8 level, Canadian achievement was above the international average and in the middle of the three G7 participants — above France but below Japan.

Several Canadian jurisdictions over-sampled their student populations in order to provide meaningful results at the provincial level, and these are reported in the bottom panel of Table 4.[11] Substantial provincial variation in student achievement is evident. In mathematics, Quebec student achievement is substantially above the Canadian average and high by international standards, albeit still significantly below the top-ranked countries (Korea, Singapore, Hong Kong and Japan). BC students also perform significantly above the Canadian average in Grade 8 mathematics, and rank well internationally in both Grade 8 math and science. Ontario's student performance is consistently below the national average, and the differences are statistically significant in both Grade 8 mathematics and science. Test scores in New Brunswick (English schools) also consistently fall below the Canadian mean, although only significantly so in the case of Grade 8 mathematics. Finally, Alberta student performance exceeds the Canadian average in all four tests. The Alberta results are particularly impressive in science; at both Grade 4 and Grade 8 they are among the best in the world, exceeded only by Korea and Japan.

In summary, according to the most recent international tests, Canadian student achievement in mathematics is about average among a diverse set of countries. Within the G7, Canada ranks at the bottom of the four participating countries. In science, Canadian student performance is above

---

[11]The results for Canada as a whole are based on a representative sample of schools in all provinces and territories, with the exception of PEI, the only province that did not participate in TIMSS.

average among the full set of countries that took the tests but below average among the G7 participants — above France but below Japan and the United States.

Considerable caution is appropriate in interpreting these summary statistics on student performance in mathematics and science. Many factors in addition to the resources devoted to the school system influence student achievement. For example, relative to other G7 countries, Canada has a high proportion of immigrant children (for whom English or French is often a second language) in its schools. Furthermore, countries may differ in the extent to which they aim to raise average performance or to principally improve achievement among those who would otherwise perform poorly. Nonetheless, these results suggest that Canada does not appear to obtain "good value for money" from the elementary and secondary school system, at least as measured by average student achievement in mathematics and science. Canada ranks at or near the top of the G7 countries in terms of expenditure per student on elementary and secondary schooling but at or near the bottom of the limited number of G7 participants in terms of student performance. More generally, Canada is at the high end internationally in the resources it devotes to elementary and secondary education, but in the middle of the pack in student achievement in math and science.[12]

Although overall national levels of Canadian student performance in mathematics and science are disappointing, some provinces — such as Quebec in mathematics and Alberta in science — are able to obtain high levels of achievement within the existing Canadian social, cultural and fiscal framework. In other provinces, notably Ontario, student achievement in math and science consistently falls below the Canadian average and is relatively low by international standards. The source of these provincial variations is an important subject for research.

---

[12]For example, at the Grade 4 level five countries (Korea, Japan, Netherlands, United States and Australia) had significantly higher science scores and eight countries (Korea, Japan, Singapore, Hong Kong, Netherlands, Czech Republic, Austria and Slovenia) had significantly higher mathematics scores.

Literacy Skills of the Adult Population

Data on student achievement provide some information on the skills of those who will be entering the labour force in the future — i.e., the flow of new entrants. Until recently, however, no nationally representative measures of the skills and knowledge of the existing stock — the adult population — were available. The International Adult Literacy Survey (IALS), which was carried out in over 20 countries during the 1994–98 period, represents a breakthrough in international data collection, providing for the first time measures of the literacy and numeracy skills of the adult population that are comparable across countries and language groups.[13]

The survey provided three measures of literacy: prose, document and quantitative literacy (or numeracy). Details of the tests used to measure these skills are given in OECD and Statistics Canada (1995); the main point is that these measures correspond to information-processing skills needed to perform everyday tasks at home, at work, and in the community. For each respondent, the survey measures prose, document and quantitative literacy on a scale from 0 to 500. These numerical literacy scores are also grouped into five main levels of competency, with level 1 being the lowest and level 5 being the highest. According to Statistics Canada, individuals with only level 1 or level 2 literacy skills have marginal or quite limited capabilities (Crompton, 1996).

Table 5 summarizes some of the key findings from the IALS. In order to maintain comparability with previous sections of this paper, results are reported for Canada and other participating G7 countries (Germany, United Kingdom and United States).[14] The top panel shows the mean score on each of the three literacy scales and the score at the 25th and 75th percentiles of the literacy distribution. The average scores rank Germany at the top (with the exception of the prose scale, on which Canada ranks first and Germany second), followed by Canada, the United States, and the United Kingdom at the bottom. Although the differences in mean scores among these four countries may not appear large, they are non-trivial. For example, on the document scale the mean score in Germany, the top-ranked country, is 285,

---

[13]See OECD and Statistics Canada (1995, 2000) for further details on this survey.

[14]France also participated in IALS, but the French results have not been publicly released.

W. Craig Riddell

Table 5: Literacy Skills in Canada and G7 Countries, 1994–98

(a) Mean scores and scores at the 25th and 75th percentiles of the prose, document and quantitative literacy scales

Literacy scale	Canada			Germany			United Kingdom			United States		
	25th	mean	75th	25th	mean	75th	25th	mean	75th	25th	mean	75th
Prose	243	279	322	245	276	308	233	267	311	237	274	320
Document	243	279	326	256	285	318	230	268	314	230	268	316
Quantitative	247	281	323	265	293	324	231	268	314	237	275	322
Average literacy score	244	280	324	255	285	317	231	268	313	235	272	319

(b) Per cent of adults with low literacy skills[1]

Age group	Literacy scale	Canada	Germany	United Kingdom	United States
16–65	Prose	42	49	52	47
16–65	Document	43	42	50	50
16–65	Quantitative	43	33	51	46
16–65	Document	33	34	44	56
46–55	Document	54	42	53	50
16–65	Document	43	42	50	50

(c) Mean document literacy score and educational attainment

Education	Canada	Germany	United Kingdom	United States
Less than high school	227	276	247	200
High school graduate	288	295	286	266
Post-secondary graduate	318	315	312	303
All adults	279	285	268	268

Notes: 1. Low literacy skills are defined as literacy levels 1 or 2 on document literacy. Literacy is measured on a scale from 1 to 5 with levels 1 and 2 being the lowest levels.

Sources: OECD (1998) and OECD and Statistics Canada (2000).

while that in the United Kingdom, the bottom-ranked country, is 268. An individual with a score of 268 is in the middle of the distribution in the United Kingdom but would be at approximately the 33rd percentile of the distribution in Germany — i.e., about two-thirds of the adult population would have superior document literacy skills.

Compared with many countries participating in the IALS survey, especially continental European countries, Canada, the United Kingdom and the United States display substantial variation in the literacy skills of the adult population (OECD and Statistics Canada, 1995, 2000). This phenomenon is evident in Table 5(a) from a comparison of the lower and upper tails of the literacy distributions for Canada and Germany. At the 25th percentile, the German score exceeds that of Canada on all three literacy scales, with the differential being especially large for document and quantitative literacy. However, at the 75th percentile the Canadian score exceeds that of Germany in both prose and document literacy and is approximately equal to that of Germany in quantitative literacy. In general, individuals in the top 25 per cent of the Canadian literacy distribution have higher literacy skills than their German counterparts, while individuals in the bottom one-quarter of the Canadian literacy distribution have lower skills than their German counterparts.

Panel 5(b) shows the per cent of adults with low literacy skills (level 1 or level 2) by broad age groups.[15] For the adult population as a whole, the ranking is the same as before: Germany has the lowest per cent of adults with low literacy (the exception being the prose scale, on which Canada ranks at the top), followed by Canada, the United States and the United Kingdom. However, important differences in the country rankings are evident among age groups. Among young adults (16–25 years of age), Canadians rank at the top, followed closely by Germans. In the United Kingdom, and especially the United States, the incidence of low literacy skills among young adults is much higher. In contrast, Canada has the highest incidence of low literacy skills among those 46–55 years of age, exceeding even the United Kingdom on this dimension and substantially above Germany.

The bottom panel, 4(c), provides some insight into the relationship between education and literacy in these countries. Among those with less than a completed secondary school education, literacy skills of Canadians are

---

[15]On a scale of 0 to 500, literacy level 1 corresponds to a score from 0 to 225 and level 2 corresponds to a score from 226 to 275.

very poor, substantially below the United Kingdom and Germany but above the United States. However, average literacy scores improve substantially with educational attainment, and this gradient appears to be steepest in Canada. Canadian high school graduates rank second (after Germany) among this group of countries, and post-secondary graduates rank at the top, despite the very large fraction of the Canadian population with completed post-secondary education.

These results suggest that Canadian literacy skills are reasonably good by international standards, especially among younger cohorts and post-secondary graduates.[16] However, the literacy skills of older Canadians and those with less than a high school education are relatively poor. The fact that, on average, young Canadians display high levels of literacy compared to their counterparts in Germany, the United States and the United Kingdom may be due in part to the increased quantity of education received by recent cohorts compared to earlier generations. This possibility is reinforced by the result that Canadian post-secondary graduates achieve literacy scores that are relatively high compared to their counterparts in other countries that participated in the IALS survey.

In all of these countries, a disturbingly large fraction of the population has low levels of prose, document and quantitative literacy. Nonetheless, to the extent that these information-processing skills used in daily activities are an outcome of the education system, this simple examination of the IALS data is more favourable to Canada's education system than was the analysis of tests of student achievement.

Incidence of Education

Educational attainment has risen substantially in the postwar period. Riddell and Sweetman (2000) document the main trends using data from the 1971, 1981 and 1991 Censuses together with recent data from the Labour Force Survey. By breaking down the data into age and birth cohorts, a picture of how schooling levels evolved through time in Canada can be drawn.

---

[16]This conclusion continues to hold if a wider group of countries, including Australia and Sweden, is examined (Riddell and Sweetman, 2000).

The most dramatic changes during the post-war period were increases in basic elementary and secondary schooling. Through time, successive younger age groups exhibit substantial decreases in the proportions of both men and women with only elementary or incomplete secondary education. Much of this increase in educational attainment occurred in the group born between 1940 and 1960 — those now in their 40s and 50s. The significant educational reforms that took place in Canada in the 1960s and 1970s probably facilitated this substantial growth in schooling. Additional factors, including growth in real incomes, declining family size, the shift of employment out of agriculture and into manufacturing and services, and the shift of population out of rural and into urban communities, also contributed to these changes.

Substantial increases have also occurred in post-secondary education, especially for females. The community college system was established in the 1960s and 1970s, and significantly increased post-secondary education opportunities for those who did not attend university. Over time, the proportion of both males and females obtaining a community college (or CEGEP) diploma or certificate has risen from about 30 to 35 per cent. Significant expansion of the university system also took place in the 1960s and 1970s. Following age cohorts through time indicates that male university completion has increased only modestly; for example, the fraction of men with a university degree increased from 19 per cent for those aged 50–59 in 2000 to 20 per cent for those aged 30–39. In contrast, the growth in university attendance and completion among females has been much greater. The proportion of females with a university degree rose from 12 per cent of those aged 50–59 in 2000 to 20 per cent for those aged 30–39.

Apart from the impressive overall growth in educational attainment, the most significant development has been the much more rapid increase in schooling of women compared to men. In the past educational levels of men generally exceeded those of women. However, both high school completion and university undergraduate completion rates are now higher for females (Riddell and Sweetman, 2000). The gender gap in university graduate completion rates has also significantly narrowed.

Educational attainment is similar across language groups (Council of Ministers of Education, Canada and Statistics Canada, 2000). However, schooling levels are significantly lower among the aboriginal population.

Higher education is often regarded as a tool for promoting equality of opportunity and social mobility. Indeed, the case for substantial public financing of post-secondary education is more often based on such equity considerations than on beliefs about the contribution to efficiency and economic growth. However, if post-secondary attendance is much higher among children from high income families, these equity objectives may not be realized and the financing of post-secondary education may be regressive. Early Canadian studies (for example, Mehmet, 1978; Meng and Sentance, 1982) concluded that in Canada, as in many other countries, children from high income families are much more likely to obtain a post-secondary education. However, as documented by Christophides, Cirello and Hoy (2001), differentials in post-secondary attendance by family income have narrowed. Between 1975 and 1993 the proportion of young adults aged 18–24 attending post-secondary education rose from 33 per cent to 54 per cent, reflecting the rise in post-secondary enrollment discussed previously. The increase among families in the poorest quintile of the family income distribution was from 18 per cent to 44 per cent, a rise of more than 140 per cent. Among families in the highest income quintile, the increase was from 53 per cent to 71 per cent, a rise of about 34 per cent. Thus the gap in the likelihood of a child's attendance at a post-secondary educational institution narrowed substantially over this period. In the mid-1970s, a child's likelihood of post-secondary attendance was almost 200 per cent higher (almost triple) among high income families than among low income families. By the early 1990s, the likelihood was about 60 per cent higher.

Bouchard and Zhao (2000) compare university participation rates of 18–21 year olds by family socio-economic status (SES) using data from 1986 and 1994. In the earlier period, university attendance rates were approximately equal in the lowest SES families and the middle SES families — 13.7 per cent and 14.5 per cent respectively. University participation of 18–21 year olds from high SES families was much higher (33 per cent). Between 1986 and 1994 the largest increases in university attendance were by children in middle SES families — from 14.5 per cent to 25.3 per cent. University participation of children from the lowest and highest SES families increased to 18.3 per cent and 40.2 per cent respectively. Thus the gap in university participation of children from the lowest and middle SES families widened, but the differential between the middle and the highest SES families narrowed.

These findings suggest that the long-term trend in Canada has been towards increased participation in post-secondary education among children of lower income families. However, an important concern is whether this favourable development may have been reversed in the 1990s when tuition fees increased substantially and significant revisions to student loan

Education and Skills

programs took place. This question is an important subject for future research, especially using data from the latter part of the 1990s when the steepest increases in tuition occurred.

Education and Labour Market Success

Schooling may have numerous consequences for individuals and society. For many people, there is some consumption value from the educational process. Human beings are curious creatures and enjoy learning and acquiring new knowledge. Even focusing on the investment aspects, education may enable people to more fully enjoy life, appreciate literature and culture, and be more informed and socially-involved citizens. Although these and other potential consequences of schooling are important and should not be ignored, the consequences of education for employability, productivity and earnings are of substantial importance for both economic and social policy.

As many studies have documented, schooling is one of the best predictors of "who gets ahead". Better-educated workers earn higher wages, have greater earnings growth over their lifetimes, experience less unemployment, and work longer. Higher education is also associated with longer life expectancy, better health and reduced participation in crime (Haveman and Wolfe, 1984).

The strong positive correlation between education and earnings is one of the most well established relationships in social science. Table 6 summarizes the results of two recent Canadian studies of this relationship. The top panel, which is based on Vaillancourt and Bourdeau-Primeau (2001), shows estimates of the private after-tax returns to university programs. These estimates take into account such costs as tuition fees and foregone earnings. Rates of return are highest at the Bachelor's level.[17] Females benefit more from higher education than do males, a reflection of the general finding that the gap between male and female earnings is largest at low levels of education and least at high levels of schooling.

---

[17]Note that in this study Bachelor's degrees include law degrees and degrees in medicine, dentistry, optometry and veterinary medicine.

W. Craig Riddell

Table 6: Estimates of the Private Returns to Schooling in Canada, 1995

(a) Estimates of the after-tax returns to university degree programs[1]

Educational attainment	Males	Females
Bachelor's degree[2]	17	20
Master's degree	nc[3]	5
PhD degree	2	10

Notes: 1. Rates of return by level of education are calculated relative to the next lowest level. For example, the return to a Bachelor's degree is relative to completed secondary school, and the return to a Master's degree is relative to a Bachelor's degree.
2. Bachelor's degree includes health (medicine, dentistry, optometry, veterinary) and law degrees.
3. "nc" indicates "not calculated" because the estimated returns were not significantly different from zero.

Source: Vaillancourt and Bourdeau-Primeau (2001).

(b) Estimates of the before-tax returns to years of schooling and credentials received

	Males	Females
(i) Years of schooling (without credential effects)	5.9	8.6
(ii) Years of schooling (with credential effects)	3.3	5.5
High school graduate	5.2	6.1
College diploma/trade certificate school without HS	7.6	8.4
Marginal effect over high school:		
College diploma/trade certificate with high school	6.6	5.9
Bachelor's degree	22.8	25.2
Marginal effect over BA:		
Medicine	34.1	30.0
Master's degree	4.6	7.0
Marginal effect over MA:		
PhD	4.2	0.8

Source: Ferrer and Riddell (2001).

The bottom panel summarizes some of the findings of the study by Ferrer and Riddell (2001) which analyzes the influence on pre-tax earnings of both years of schooling and "sheepskin effects" — increases in earnings associated with the receipt of a diploma, certificate or degree. When "years of schooling" alone is used to control for the influence of education, each additional year of schooling is estimated to be associated with an increase in weekly earnings of females of approximately 9 per cent and of males of approximately 6 per cent, after controlling for other influences on earnings. These OLS estimates of the return to schooling correspond approximately to estimates of the real rate of return on the investment.[18]

Ferrer and Riddell (2001) find that a more general specification in which both years of schooling and credentials received provides a better fit to the data. In this more general specification, the estimated coefficients on the "years of schooling" variable decline but are nonetheless still substantial (3.3 per cent for males and 5.5 per cent for females). The total return to any specific level of education consists of the "years of schooling" effect and the cumulative impact of the estimated "sheepskin effects". The main point to note for the purposes of this paper is that estimated rates of return to schooling are substantial. Particularly large "sheepskin effects" are associated with the completion of a university Bachelor's degree and with degrees in medicine, dentistry, optometry and veterinary medicine.[19]

These Canadian studies obtain OLS estimates of the "return to schooling" that are similar to those obtained in many studies carried out in the United States and other countries: approximately 8–10 per cent rate of return when the analysis is based on annual earnings and 6–9 per cent when

---

[18]Mincer (1974) showed that the estimated coefficient of the "years of schooling" variable in a log earnings equation equals the rate of return on education if the cost of an additional year of schooling equals the opportunity cost of foregone earnings. Because foregone earnings constitute the main cost of additional years of education, the estimated coefficient on the "years of schooling" variable is frequently referred to as the estimated "return to education".

[19]Although this evidence of substantial "sheepskin" or credential effects may reflect signalling or screening in the labour market, it is also consistent with a human capital perspective if the educational program consists of a package of complementary courses (Ferrer and Riddell, 2001). In addition, in fields such as medicine, the large estimated sheepskin effect may reflect professional licensing requirements and restrictions on entry into the profession.

W. Craig Riddell

the analysis is based on weekly earnings.[20] Such estimates compare favourably with rates of return on physical capital investments.

Many social scientists have, however, been reluctant to interpret the positive correlation between education and earnings as evidence that education exerts a causal effect on earnings. According to human capital theory, schooling raises earnings because it enhances workers' skills, thus making employees more productive and more valuable to employers. However, according to the alternative signalling/screening theory, the positive relationship between earnings and schooling may arise because both education and earnings are correlated with unobserved factors such as ability, perseverance and ambition (hereafter generally simply referred to as "ability"). If there are systematic differences between the less- and well-educated that affect both schooling decisions and labour market success, then the correlation between education and earnings may reflect these other factors as well. In that case, standard OLS estimates of the return to schooling are likely to be biased upwards because they do not take into account unobserved "ability".

This "omitted ability bias" issue is of fundamental importance not only for the question of how we should interpret the positive relationship between earnings and schooling, but also for the emphasis that should be placed on education in economic and social policy. To the extent that estimates of the return to schooling are biased upwards because of unobserved factors, the economic case for investing in education is weakened. Those with higher average ability, perseverance or ambition would be more productive and more successful financially even in the absence of additional schooling. The economic case for investing in education must be made on the basis of the true causal effect of schooling on productivity and earnings.[21]

Perhaps less well understood is the point that the social policy case for investing in education is also weakened if the signalling/screening perspective is a more accurate description of reality than the human capital perspective. The reason is that estimated average rates of return to education may substantially over-estimate the economic benefits that a less-educated person

---

[20]Estimates of the impact of schooling on annual earnings exceed those of the impact on weekly or hourly earnings because those with more education also work more weeks per year.

[21]The economic case for investing in education should also incorporate any social returns to education that may not be captured by the individual receiving the education.

would receive if he/she acquired additional schooling. The estimated average rates of return in the population reflect both the causal effect of schooling on productivity and earnings and the average return to the unobserved ability of the well-educated. However, if those with low levels of education are also, on average, those with low ability or ambition, they can only expect to receive from any additional schooling the return associated with the causal effect of schooling on earnings. That is, average rates of return in the population reflect the causal effect of schooling on earnings and the return to unobserved factors. The marginal return — the impact of additional schooling for someone with low levels of education — may be substantially below the average return. In these circumstances, education may not be very effective in improving the employment or earnings prospects of relatively disadvantaged groups. Similarly, investing in additional education may not be an effective way of offsetting pressures for widening income inequality.

Unbiased estimates of the causal effect of education on earnings are thus very important for current debates about economic and social policy. How can such estimates be obtained? The most reliable method would be to conduct an experiment. Individuals randomly assigned to the treatment group would receive a larger "dose" of education than those assigned to the control group. By following the two groups through time we could observe their subsequent earnings and obtain an unbiased estimate of the impact of schooling on labour market success. Random assignment would ensure that, on average, treatment and control groups will be equally represented by "high ability" and "low ability" individuals.

In the absence of such experimental evidence, economists have tried to find "natural experiments" which isolate the influence of education from the possible effects of unobserved ability. A large number of such studies have now been carried out, using data on identical twins or on sources of variation in education such as those implied by compulsory schooling laws or proximity to a college or university. Card (1999, 2000) provides a thorough discussion of the issues in this literature as well as a review of empirical findings. A consistent result is that conventional OLS estimates of the return to schooling tend, if anything, to *under-estimate* rather than over-estimate the causal impact of education on earnings.

Why do OLS estimates generally understate the true return to schooling, when the presence of "omitted ability bias" should cause the OLS estimate to be upward biased? The reason appears to be that there are two additional sources of bias that operate in the opposite direction. First is the presence of measurement error in educational attainment (especially years of completed schooling). Measurement error in an explanatory variable causes the estimated coefficient to be biased toward zero. Second is what is sometimes referred to as "discount rate bias". The returns to schooling are not the same for all individuals in the population; rather there is a distribution of such returns. Consider the case of individuals with high potential returns to education who do not pursue higher education — perhaps because of low family income, limited ability to borrow to finance human capital formation, or a family background in which the importance of education is not emphasized. For these "high potential return" individuals, a policy intervention that results in increased educational attainment would have a substantial payoff. Indeed, the marginal return to the investment may exceed the average return in the population. In these circumstances, the average return from existing investments in education may understate the payoff to incremental investments.

Two recent Canadian studies have pursued this "natural experiment" approach. Lemieux and Card (2001) study the impact of the Veterans Rehabilitation Act — the Canadian "G.I. Bill". In order to ease the return of World War II veterans into the labour market, the federal government provided strong financial incentives for veterans to attend university or other sorts of educational programs. Because many more young men from Ontario than Quebec had served as soldiers, those from Ontario were significantly more likely to be eligible for these benefits. Lemieux and Card estimate that the VRA increased the education of the veteran cohort of Ontario men by 0.2 to 0.4 years. Further, they estimate the rate of return to schooling to be 14 to 16 per cent, substantially higher than the OLS estimate with their data of 7 per cent.

Sweetman (1999) investigates the impact on education and earnings of the education policy change in Newfoundland that raised the number of years of schooling required for high school graduation from 11 to 12. He estimates that this intervention increased educational attainment of affected Newfoundland cohorts by 0.8 to 0.9 years. Estimated rates of return to the additional schooling are substantial: 17 per cent for females (versus an OLS estimate of 14.6 per cent) and 11.8 per cent for males (compared to an OLS estimate of 10.8 per cent).

As with this growing body of research, these Canadian studies conclude that conventional OLS estimates of the return to schooling are likely, if anything, to be biased downwards, as opposed to being inflated by unobserved ability.

Two principal conclusions follow from this body of research. First, rates of return to investments in education are high — and probably higher than has generally been believed on the basis of previous studies of the impact of education on earnings. Second, the payoff to marginal investments in duration may exceed the average return in the population. There is no evidence that investments in higher education are experiencing diminishing returns because they require society to "reach lower into the ability barrel". Policy interventions that result in additional schooling being acquired by individuals from disadvantaged backgrounds or those who face other barriers to acquiring human capital appear likely to yield a substantial return in the form of enhanced employability and earnings, in addition to contributing to equity objectives.

Conclusions

This paper has provided a general review of the recent Canadian experience relating to education and skill formation. Several conclusions follow from the analysis.

Canada invests heavily in education. Relative to other G7 or OECD countries, Canada ranks near the top in terms of expenditure per student or the fraction of GDP devoted to elementary, secondary and post-secondary education.

One consequence of this substantial expenditure is a population that is well educated by international standards. Canada compares favourably with other G7 and OECD countries in terms of most measures of educational attainment. Compared to the United States, Canada has lower educational attainment at both the bottom (less than completed high school) and top (university degree) of the education distribution. Where Canada stands out is in the middle of the distribution — those who have completed high school or a non-university secondary program. The proportion of Canada's population with a non-university post-secondary education is much higher than that of any other OECD country. However, standard measures may overstate Canadian educational attainment in this dimension to some extent because not all those with a college diploma or trade certificate have completed high school and because of the unique features of Quebec's CEGEP system.

W. Craig Riddell

Student achievement in mathematics is about average among the diverse set of countries participating in these tests, and relatively low among the G7 countries that participated. Student achievement in science is somewhat better, although still relatively low compared to the other G7 participants. These results suggest that Canada may not obtain good "value for money" from its relatively high expenditure on the elementary and secondary school system, at least as judged by student achievement in mathematics and science. However, although the average Canadian performance is less than impressive, some jurisdictions — especially Quebec in mathematics and Alberta in science — achieve results that are excellent by international standards.

The literacy skills of the adult population are above average among the G7 countries that participated in the IALS survey. Canada, like the United States and United Kingdom, has a high variance across the population in its literacy skills compared to European countries such as Germany. By international standards, older and less well-educated Canadians have relatively poor literacy skills, whereas younger and well-educated Canadians have relatively good literacy skills compared to their counterparts in other G7 countries.

Important recent advances have taken place in our understanding of the relationship between education and labour market success. Conventional estimates of the return to schooling appear, if anything, to be biased downward — so the causal effect of education on earnings appears to be higher than previously believed. Further, the marginal return to incremental investments in education may exceed the average return from previous investments. There is no evidence that investments in schooling are running into diminishing returns. These results suggest that investments in human capital remain an important potential source of economic growth and equality of opportunity.

References

Bouchard, B. and J. Zhao (2000), "University Education: Recent Trends in Participation, Accessibility and Returns", *Education Quarterly Review* 6(4), 24–32.

Canada Communication Group (1992), *Education and Training in Canada* (Ottawa: Minister of Supply and Services).

Card, D (1999), "The Causal Effect of Education on Earnings", in O. Ashenfelter and D. Card (eds.), *Handbook of Labor Economics*, Vol. 3A (Amsterdam: North Holland).

_____ (2000), "Estimating the Return to Schooling: Progress on Some Persistent Problems", NBER Working Paper No. 7769 (Cambridge, MA: National Bureau of Economic Research).

Christophides, L.N., J. Cirello and M. Hoy (2001), "Family Income and Post-secondary Education in Canada", *Canadian Journal of Higher Education* 31(1), 177–208.

Council of Ministers of Education, Canada and Statistics Canada (2000), *Education Indicators in Canada: Report of the Pan-Canadian Education Indicators Program 1999* (Toronto and Ottawa: Council of Ministers of Education, Canada and Statistics Canada).

Courchene, T.J. (2001), *A State of Minds: Toward a Human Capital Future for Canadians* (Montreal: Institute for Research on Public Policy).

Crompton, S. (1996), "The Marginally Literate Workforce", *Perspectives on Labour and Income* 8 (Summer), 14–21.

Ferrer, A. and W.C. Riddell (2001), "The Role of Credentials in the Canadian Labour Market", Discussion Paper No. 01–16 (Vancouver: Department of Economics, University of British Columbia).

Haveman, R. and B. Wolfe (1984), "Schooling and Economic Well-Being: The Role of Non-Market Effects", *Journal of Human Resources* 19 (Summer), 377–407.

Lemieux, T. and D. Card (2001), "Education, Earnings, and the 'Canadian G.I. Bill' ", *Canadian Journal of Economics* 34 (February).

Mehmet, O. (1978), *Who Benefits From the Ontario University System?* (Toronto: Ontario Economic Council).

Meng, R. and J. Sentance (1982), "Canadian Universities: Who Benefits and Who Pays?" *Canadian Journal of Higher Education* 12(3), 45–58.

Mincer, J. (1974), *Schooling, Experience and Earnings* (New York: Columbia University Press).

Organisation for Economic Co-operation and Development (OECD) (1998), *Human Capital Investment: An International Comparison* (Paris: OECD).

_____ (2001), *Education at a Glance: OECD Indicators 2001* (Paris: OECD).

OECD and Statistics Canada (1995), *Literacy, Economy and Society* (Paris and Ottawa: OECD and Statistics Canada).

_____ (2000), *Literacy in the Information Age* (Paris and Ottawa: OECD and Statistics Canada).

Riddell, W.C. (1995), "Human Capital Formation in Canada: Recent Developments and Policy Responses", in K.G. Banting and C.M. Beach (eds.), *Labour Market Polarization and Social Policy Reform* (Kingston: School of Policy Studies, Queen's University), 125–172.

Riddell, W.C. and A. Sweetman (2000), "Human Capital Formation in a Period of Rapid Change", in W.C. Riddell and F. St-Hilaire (eds.), *Adapting Public Policy to a Labour Market in Transition* (Montreal: Institute for Research on Public Policy), 85–141.

Robitaille, D.F., A.R. Taylor and G. Orpwood (1996), *The TIMSS Canada Report Volume 1: Grade 8* (Vancouver: Department of Curriculum Studies, University of British Columbia).

_____ (1997), *The TIMSS Canada Report Volume 2: Grade 4* (Vancouver: Department of Curriculum Studies, University of British Columbia).

Sweetman, A. (1999), "What If High School Were a Year Longer? Evidence from Newfoundland", WRNET Working Paper No. 00–01 (Vancouver: Western Research Network on Education and Training).

Vaillancourt, F. and S. Bourdeau-Primeau (2001), *The Returns to University Education in Canada, 1990 and 1995* (Toronto: C.D. Howe Institute).

Contributors

Charles M. Beach is Professor of Economics at Queen's University. He was born in Montreal, earned degrees at McGill University (BA) and Princeton University (PhD), and has taught economics at Queen's University since 1972. His principal areas of research are income distribution, empirical labour market analysis and applied econometrics. He has been involved in several data and policy initiatives for Canada. Since 1995, he has been Editor of *Canadian Public Policy/Analyse de Politiques*. In July 2001, he assumed the position of Director of the John Deutsch Institute. (e-mail: beachc@qed.econ. queensu.ca)

Richard Bird is Professor Emeritus of Economics at the University of Toronto and co-director of the International Tax Program of the Rotman School of Management. He is currently Petro-Canada Scholar at the C.D. Howe Institute, Distinguished Visiting Professor at the Andrew Young School of Policy Studies, Georgia State University, and Consultant, World Bank Institute. During 2001–02, he will be visiting professor of law at Harvard University. His principal interest is public finance, particularly in developing and transitional countries, and he has published widely in this area. (e-mail: richard.bird@rotman.utoronto.ca)

Robin Boadway is Sir Edward Peacock Professor of Economic Theory at Queen's University. He was Editor of the *Canadian Journal of Economics* from 1987–93 and President of the Canadian Economics Association in 1996–97. He is currently co-editor of the *Journal of Public Economics* and the *German Economic Review*, and editorial advisor for the *Canadian Tax Journal*. He serves on the Executive of the International Seminar on Public Economics and the Management Board of the International Institute of Public

Finance. He works in the area of public sector economics, with special emphasis on tax-transfer policy, fiscal federalism and cost-benefit analysis. (e-mail: boadwayr@qed.econ.queensu.ca)

Ross Finnie has been a Visting Fellow at Statistics Canada since 1993 and a Research Fellow and Adjunct Professor in the School of Policy Studies at Queen's University since 1997. He did his first degree at Queen's University and the London School of Economics and his Master's and PhD at the University of Wisconsin-Madison. He was an assistant professor at Laval University from 1989 to 1993. From 1993 to 1997, he was associated with the School of Public Administration at Carleton University. His current research activities include various projects related to earnings and income dynamics, the labour market integration of immigrants, the experiences of post-secondary graduates, the role of literacy and numeracy in labour market outcomes, and the brain drain. (e-mail: ref@qsilver.queensu.ca)

Pierre Fortin is Professor of Economics at the Université du Québec à Montréal (UQAM), which he joined in 1988 after teaching at Université Laval and the Université de Montréal. He holds a PhD in economics from the University of California at Berkeley, a MSc in mathematics from Université Laval and a BA in classical humanities from Jesuit College. His research interests include wage and price dynamics, economic fluctuations and growth, adolescent behaviour, taxation, fiscal and monetary policies, social policy and population economics. In 1995, he was selected by the Quebec Association of Business Economists as "the most influential Quebec economist of the last decade". He is past President of the Canadian Economics Association and is a Member of the Board of Directors of the Centre for the Study of Living Standards. (e-mail: pierre.fortin@uqam.ca)

Patrick Grady is an economic consultant with Global Economics Ltd. He is a former senior official in the federal Department of Finance. Dr. Grady has an AB in political science from the University of Illinois and a MA and PhD in economics from the University of Toronto. He has written widely on economic policy, macroeconomics, and public finance, including: *The Economic Consequences of Quebec Sovereignty* (Fraser Institute, 1991); *Dividing the House: Preparing for a Canada without Quebec*, with Alan Freeman (Harper Collins Canada, 1995); and *Seattle and Beyond: The WTO Millennium Round*, with Katie Macmillan (1995). His most recent book is a novel about the Vietnam War entitled *Through the Picture Tube* (Robert D. Reed Publishers, 2000). (e-mail: P_Grady@on.aibn.com)

Morley Gunderson is a member of the Centre for Industrial Relations and the Department of Economics at the University of Toronto. In 1999, he was appointed the first holder of the CIBC Chair in Youth Employment. He received his BA from Queen's University in 1967, an MA from the University of Wisconsin in 1970 and his PhD from Wisconsin in 1971. From 1985 to 1997 he served as Director of the Centre for Industrial Relations at the University of Toronto. He has published extensively on the labour market impacts of trade liberalization and globalization; gender discrimination, including pay equity; youth unemployment; retirement and pension issues; strikes; and workers' compensation. (e-mail: morley@chass.utoronto.ca)

Malcolm Hamilton is a Principal with William M. Mercer Limited. He graduated from Queen's University as the Gold Medallist in Mathematics, and attended McGill as a National Research Council scholar, receiving his MSc in 1975. He became a Fellow of the Canadian Institute of Actuaries and a Fellow of the Society of Actuaries in 1977. Since joining William M. Mercer Limited, he has concentrated on the design, funding and investment of pension plans and retirement savings plans. He advises some of the largest pension plans in Canada, including the Ontario Teachers' Pension Plan, and the pension plans covering employees of Ontario Power Generation Inc., Hydro One Inc., the Bank of Montreal, Abitibi-Consolidated Inc., Manulife and the National Hockey League. (e-mail: malcolm.hamilton@ca.wmmercer.com)

David F. Helliwell is a Strategy and Transformation consultant with Cap Gemini Ernst and Young in Paris, France. He studied geophysics and economics at UBC and Harvard before becoming an exploration geophysicist. More recently he has studied economics at UBC (during which time he undertook the first analysis of the UBC graduate records), and completed his MBA at the Ecole Nationale des Ponts et Chaussées (ENPC), Paris. (e-mail: david.helliwell@cgey.com)

John F. Helliwell studied at the University of British Columbia and Oxford, and taught at Oxford before returning to UBC, which has been his base since 1967. His first econometric modelling, initiated at the Bank of Canada in 1965, was a monthly structural model of the foreign exchange market. This work was much enriched by David Slater's encouraging and wise advice as the paper's discussant at the 1967 Annual Meeting of the Canadian Political Science Association, predecessor to the Canadian Economics Association. Helliwell's subsequent research has been in macro modelling, energy, international and comparative economics, with more recent attention to globalization, democracy, the brain drain, social capital, and empirical studies of well-being. His recent publications include *How Much Do National Borders Matter?* (Brookings Institution, 1998), *Globalization: Myths, Facts and Consequences* (C.D. Howe Benefactors Lecture, 2000), "Canada: Life Beyond the Looking Glass" (*Journal of Economic Perspectives*, 2001), and *The Contribution of Human and Social Capital to Sustained Economic Growth and Well-Being* (editor and contributor, OECD and HRDC, 2001). He was MacKenzie King Visiting Professor of Canadian Studies at Harvard from 1991–94, and Christensen Visiting Fellow of St. Catherine's College, Oxford, January–July 2001. (e-mail: john.helliwell@ubc.ca)

Kathleen Macmillan is a trade consultant and the President of International Trade Policy Consultants, Inc. Her firm advises businesses and governments on countervailing and anti-dumping cases, tariff issues and other trade matters. She serves on Canada's roster of panelists for disputes under both the WTO and the NAFTA. Prior to becoming a consultant, she served a five-year term as Vice Chair of the Canadian International Trade Tribunal. She began her career as an economist with the Economic Council of Canada. After receiving her MA from the University of Alberta, she also worked for two of Canada's leading economic policy think tanks: the Canada West Foundation and the C.D. Howe Institute. (e-mail: itpc@compuserve.com)

Jack M. Mintz is the Arthur Andersen Professor of Taxation, J.L. Rotman School of Management, University of Toronto and President of the C.D. Howe Institute. He has published over 100 books and articles in the field of public finance and fiscal federalism. He is also Editor-in-Chief of *International Tax and Public Finance*, published by Kluwer Academic Publishers and an Associate Editor of *Contemporary Accounting Research*. He served as the Clifford Clark Visiting Economist and Chair, Technical Committee on Business Taxation, during the years 1996 and 1997. He is director of the International Centre for Tax Studies at the University of Toronto and associate member of several policy institutes. He served as Associate Dean (Academic) for the Faculty of Management 1993–95. He also served as a Special Advisor to the Deputy Minister, Tax Policy Branch, Finance Canada in the years 1984–86; and the Director of the John Deutsch Institute, Queen's University, 1987–89. He has consulted widely with the World Bank, the IMF, the OECD, Governments of Canada, Alberta, Ontario and Saskatchewan, Peat Marwick of Washington, Price Waterhouse of Washington, and Coopers and Lybrand of Toronto. (e-mail: jmintz@cdhowe.org)

Edward P. Neufeld is a graduate of the University of Saskatchewan and completed his PhD at the London School of Economics. He worked for the Bank of England, then was for many years Professor of Economics at the University of Toronto, then a senior official of the Department of Finance in Ottawa including Assistant Deputy Minister of Tax Policy and Legislation, and finally Executive Vice President and Chief Economist of the Royal Bank of Canada from which he retired in 1994. He has written extensively on monetary and financial matters including his 645-page volume on *The Financial System of Canada: Its Growth and Development* (Macmillan of Canada, 1972). He has served on various boards of directors of Canadian corporations and research institutes and is a Visiting Senior Research Fellow of the Centre for International Studies, University of Toronto. (e-mail: epneufeld@compuserve.com)

Lars Osberg is McCulloch Professor of Economics at Dalhousie University. He received his PhD in Economics from Yale University in 1975. He taught at the University of Western Ontario from 1974 to 1977 before moving to Dalhousie University. He has published numerous articles in academic journals and seven books, including *Unnecessary Debts*, co-edited with Pierre Fortin. He was President of the Canadian Economics Association in 1999–2000 and a Member of the Board of Directors of the Centre for the Study of Living Standards. (e-mail: osberg@is.dal.ca)

Sylvia Ostry is Distinguished Research Fellow, Centre for International Studies, University of Toronto. She has a doctorate in economics from McGill University and Cambridge University. Dr. Ostry has held a number of positions in the federal government, among them, Chief Statistician, Deputy Minister of Consumer and Corporate Affairs, Chairman of the Economic Council of Canada, Deputy Minister of International Trade, Ambassador for Multilateral Trade Negotiations, and the Prime Minister's Personal Representative for the Economic Summit. From 1979 to 1983 she was Head of the Economics and Statistics Department of the OECD in Paris. Dr. Ostry has written numerous books and articles, most recently, *Who's on First? The Post-Cold War Trading System* (University of Chicago Press, 1997), *Reinforcing the WTO* (Group of Thirty, Washington, 1998), *The Multilateral Trading System in the New Millennium* (Kluwer Law International, The Hague, London, Boston, 2000) and *The World Trade Organization Millennium Round* (Routledge, London, United States and Canada, 2001). (e-mail: sylvia.ostry@utoronto.ca)

James E. Pesando is Professor of Economics at the University of Toronto, where he has taught since 1971. From 1985 to 1996, he was the Director of the Institute for Policy Analysis at the University of Toronto. Professor Pesando has published and consulted extensively in the area of public and private pensions. (e-mail: pesando@chass.utoronto.ca)

W. Craig Riddell is Professor of Economics at the University of British Columbia and an Associate of the Canadian Institute for Advanced Research. His research interests are in labour economics, labour relations and public policy. Current research is focused on unemployment and labour market dynamics, the role of human capital in economic growth, experimental and non-experimental approaches to the evaluation of social programs, unionization and collective bargaining, gender differences in labour market behaviour and outcomes, unemployment insurance and social assistance, and education and training. He is former Head of the Department of Economics at UBC, former Academic Co-Chair of the Canadian Employment Research Forum, and Past-President of the Canadian Economics Association. He currently holds a Royal Bank Faculty Research Professorship at UBC. He is a member of the Board of Directors of the Centre for the Study of Living Standards. (e-mail: riddell@econ.ubc.ca).

William B.P. Robson is Vice-President and Director of Research at the C.D. Howe Institute. He received a BA from the University of Toronto and an MA from the Norman Paterson School of International Affairs at Carleton University. Before joining the C.D. Howe Institute in 1988, he held positions as an economist with Wood Gundy Inc. and the federal Department of Energy, Mines and Resources. He specializes in Canadian fiscal and monetary policy. He has written extensively on government budgets and their economic effects, and on the Bank of Canada and inflation. He is a familiar commentator on economic issues in the media. (e-mail: w_robson@cdhowe.org)

Anthony Scott is Professor Emeritus in the Department of Economics at the University of British Columbia. He received a Bachelor of Commerce in 1946, and a Bachelor of Arts in 1947, both from the University of British Columbia. He received a Master of Arts from Harvard University in 1949, and a Doctorate from the London School of Economics in 1953. In 1953, he joined the Department of Economics at the University of British Columbia where he remained until his retirement in 1989. He attained the rank of full professor in 1961, and from 1967 to 1971, was chair of the department. His research interests have developed in three areas: the economics of federalism, federal-provincial relations, and the problems of regionalism; the economics of natural resources, particularly as it relates to mining, energy and fishery problems; and the organization of international environmental coordination. (e-mail: adscott@interchange.ubc.ca)

Andrew Sharpe is Executive Director of the Centre for the Study of Living Standards (CSLS), a research organization he founded in 1995. He has held a variety of earlier positions, including Head of Research and Editor, *Quarterly Labour Market and Productivity Review* at the Canadian Labour Market and Productivity Centre and Chief, Business Sector Analysis at the Department of Finance. He is past President of the Canadian Association for Business Economics and served as a founding editor of *Canadian Business Economics* from 1992 to 1998. He currently is Editor of the *International Productivity Monitor*. He received a PhD in Economics from McGill University in 1982. (e-mail csls@csls.ca)

Michael Smart is an assistant professor at the University of Toronto, where he has worked since receiving his PhD from Stanford University in 1995. During 2001–02, he is visiting the London School of Economics. His principal area of research is public finance, and his recent work has dealt with issues of fiscal federalism, tax competition among governments, and the politics of tax policy. His work has appeared in a number of academic and policy journals, including *Journal of Public Economics*, *International Economic Review* and *Policy Options*. (e-mail: msmart@chass.utoronto.ca)

Thomas A. Wilson is a Professor of Economics at the University of Toronto. He has served as Director of the Policy and Economic Analysis Program at the Institute for Policy Analysis since 1987. He is also the Area Coordinator for Business Economics at the Faculty of Management. He currently serves as the chair of Statistic Canada's National Accounts Advisory Committee. He did his undergraduate studies in economics at the University of British Columbia and received an MA and PhD in economics from Harvard University. His research interests include fiscal and tax policy, applied macro-economic modelling and industrial organization. He has also co-authored or co-edited fifteen books including recent volumes entitled *Fiscal Policy in Canada* (co-author with P. Dungan), and *Fiscal Targets and Economic Growth* (co-editor with T. Courchene). (e-mail: twilson@chass.utoronto.ca)

Date Due